I0839747

What Good Condition?

What Good Condition?

Reflections on an Australian Aboriginal Treaty 1986–2006

**Aboriginal History
Monograph 13**

Edited by Peter Read,
Gary Meyers and Bob Reece

Aboriginal History Incorporated
Aboriginal History Monograph 13

National Library of Australia Cataloguing-in-Publication entry

What good condition? : reflections on an Australian
Aboriginal treaty 1986-2006

ISBN 1 920942 90 4 (pbk)
ISBN 1 920942 91 2 (online)

1. Aboriginal Australians - Treaties. 2. Aboriginal
Australians - Civil rights. 3. Aboriginal Australians -
Land tenure. 4. Aboriginal Australians - Government
relations. I. Read, Peter, 1945- . II. Meyers, Gary D.
III. Reece, Bob, 1940- . (Series : Aboriginal history
monograph ; no. 13).

323.119915

The Committee of Management and the Editorial Board
Peter Read (Chair), Rob Paton (Secretary/Treasurer), Jennifer Clarke (Public Officer), Richard Baker,
Gordon Briscoe, Ann Curthoys, Mick Dodson, Brian Egloff, Geoff Gray, Niel Gunson, Luise Hercus,
Dave Johnston, Steve Kinnane, Harold Koch, Isabel McBryde, Ann McGrath, Ingereth Macfarlane,
Francis Peters-Little, Deborah Bird Rose, Gary Shipp

Aboriginal History is administered by an Editorial Board which is responsible for all unsigned
material. Views and opinions expressed by the authors of papers are not necessarily shared
by Board members.

Managing Editor: Ingereth Macfarlane
Copy Editor: Gillian Fulcher

Aboriginal History Inc. is a part of the Australian Centre for Indigenous History, Research School
of Social Sciences, The Australian National University and gratefully acknowledges the support
of the History Program, RSSS.

This publication was supported by a generous subsidy from the Aboriginal and Torres Strait
Islander Commission

Contacting Aboriginal History
All correspondence should be addressed to:
Aboriginal History, Box 2837 GPO Canberra, 2601, Australia.
Sales and orders for journals and monographs, and journal subscriptions:
T Boekel, email: sales@aboriginalhistory.org, tel or fax: +61 2 6230 7054
www.aboriginalhistory.org

ANU E Press
All correspondence should be addressed to:
ANU E Press, The Australian National University, Canberra, ACT 0200, Australia.
email: anuepress@anu.edu.au, http://epress.anu.edu.au

Cover: *Batman's treaty with the aborigines at Merri Creek, 6th June 1835*
Artist: John Wesley Burtt, 1839 - 1917 (Collections: State Library of Victoria)

Design and typesetting by might.Graphic Design

Printing in Australia by University Printing Services, ANU

Apart for any fair dealing for the purpose of private study, research, criticism or review, as permitted
under the Copyright Act, no part of this publication may be reproduced by any process whatsoever
without the written permission of the publisher.

This edition © 2006 Aboriginal History Inc. and ANU E Press

Aufidius: The town is ta'en!

First Soldier: 'Twill be deliver'd back
on good condition.

Aufidius: Condition!...
What good condition can a treaty find
I' the part that is at mercy?

Shakespeare, Coriolanus I.10

Contents

What Good Condition?

Peter Read

Aufidius, the enemy of Rome, asks what use a treaty could possibly be to those at the mercy of the Roman oppressor.

Such a sentiment may seem a pessimistic way to begin a monograph on the proposal for a treaty between Aboriginal and non- Aboriginal Australians, a proposal which has been discussed and dissected for nearly thirty years. But such a sentiment broadly reflects the feelings of many of the writers in the volume, particularly the Indigenous writers. It is not so much that everyone has lost hope, but expectations are lower, hopes are diminished. Perhaps a negotiated settlement may come about – but it won't be called a treaty. Perhaps ratified agreements may occur – but they won't be national agreements. Perhaps there may be a practical settlement – but it won't follow the principles of international law.

These papers in raw form were delivered at a conference held at Murdoch University in 2002. Later they were rewritten, expanded and updated to account for changing conditions within Indigenous Australia. Since then the Aboriginal and Torres Strait Islander Commission has been abolished. The Council for Aboriginal Reconciliation has served out its term.

The papers are arranged in three parts. In the first, authors consider the context and legacy of the residue of treaty proposals and negotiations in past decades. In the second they consider the implications of treaty in an Indigenous, national and international context. The third section concerns some reflections on regional aspirations and achievements. These indeed may be the way forward.

For this production I warmly thank the originators of the conference *Treaty Advancing Reconciliation*, my fellow editors Gary Meyers and Bob Reece, and the monograph production team of the journal *Aboriginal History*. I particularly acknowledge the National Centre for Indigenous Studies, and the History Program, Research School of Social Sciences, Australian National University, for their continuing financial support of the journal.

A generous subsidy by the Aboriginal and Torres Strait Islander Commission in its final weeks of corporate life made the production of this monograph possible.

Foreword

Larissa Behrendt

A treaty between Indigenous and non-Indigenous Australians has been a continuing issue both because of the failure of the modern Australian state to recognise and respect the sovereignty of Aboriginal nations and because of the continuing failure to protect the rights of Aboriginal people.

The recognition of prior ownership and sovereignty – and the rights and interests that flow from that – are part of the symbolic importance of an agreement between Aboriginal and non-Aboriginal Australians, the potential for a treaty to protect the rights of Aboriginal people ensures that it has practical and meaningful outcomes for Aboriginal people. Particularly while Aboriginal people experience poorer health, higher levels of unemployment, lower levels of education, poorer housing and higher rates of poverty, the potential for a treaty to provide a fairer playing field for Aboriginal people is an important agenda.

A large part of the socio-economic disadvantage experienced by Aboriginal people can be attributed to past government policies that actively discriminated against Indigenous people and sought to – directly or indirectly – exclude Aboriginal people from full participation in Australian life.

More recently, the momentum for a treaty gathered again at the end of the decade of reconciliation. ATSIC Chairperson Geoff Clark had placed the notion of an agreement between Aboriginal and non-Aboriginal people clearly back on the agenda at Corroboree 2000 and the Council for Reconciliation, in its Final Report, recommended that a treaty process be developed as part of the on-going work of reconciliation.

While the decade of reconciliation seemed to raise awareness of the importance of renegotiating the playing field between Aboriginal people and other Australians, the Howard government have, from the start, clearly rejected the notion of a treaty and the rights framework that underpins it. Of course, it is a compelling rhetorical claim that talk of treaties, rights and constitutional change does not put food on the table or end high levels of violence in the community. It is easy, when placed in that light, to dismiss the focus on the human rights agenda, especially the treaty, as the privilege of the elite. This is especially so when we see articles published every day noting the increase in incarceration rates, the high levels of violence within Indigenous communities and the continuing poor levels of health and access to education.

But we must not lose sight of the necessity for the symptoms that we treat not to be the only things we target. We need to make sure that we are also attacking the causes. And that comes only through systemic and structural changes and through the protection of the rights agenda. Aboriginal leaders such as Jack Patton and William Cooper, Aden Ridgeway and Mick Dodson have always held the position that the recognition and enjoyment of rights are required if any real, meaningful and sustainable progress is to be attained.

What the issue of a treaty does is to provide a focus point on which to continue our discussion about the relationship between Indigenous and non-Indigenous people. It provides a forum for the consideration of legal issues such as rights and reparations. It also provides a platform from which to decide the kind of Australia we would like to be. It allows us to look at the big picture issues and articulate what an Indigenous vision of a reconciled Australia would be. This will include issues as broad ranging as equality rights, native title, economic rights, rights to hunt and fish, rights to education and to work and rights to self-governance and autonomy.

I have always supported the treaty dialogue because I think we have a responsibility as Indigenous people to articulate an answer to the question: "What is it that you want?" Unless we can answer that, we cannot engage in a negotiation with non-Indigenous Australia about the appropriate way forward. There will be no on-going, meaningful dialogue about reconciliation.

But non-Indigenous people have much to gain from a treaty with Aboriginal people too. A treaty can help to change this relationship by giving us the recognition and respect that Aboriginal people deserve. This idea of recognition and respect through a formal process of a treaty is often referred to as nation-building – as a way of making a stronger, more united and more tolerant society.

There is a strong view that has been put forward by Marcia Langton and Fred Chaney that, particularly in relation to native title, Aboriginal communities are engaged in negotiating with non-Aboriginal interests and governments. This, they point out, highlights how agreement making can result in positive outcomes for both parties and this provides insight into the positive benefits that a treaty – or a series of treaties – could have. They are, after all, negotiated agreements. This plethora of agreement making with Aboriginal people also shows that such negotiated processes are not divisive, as critics often claim, but can create opportunities to empower Aboriginal communities and create a win-win stituation.

There are, also, many concerns about a treaty. Questions like what would a treaty look like, who would have the mandate to sign a treaty and what a treaty or treaties would contain are all questions that the treaty debate throws up.

Whether to have a treaty, what it would look like and what it would contain are important debates and it would be a shame if we were to lose momentum now that ATSIC has been abolished. In fact, it is all the more important that such a discussion continue even though there is no political leadership from the federal government about the relationship between Indigenous and non-Indigenous Australians. This book will make a substantial contribution to those dialogues.

Put not your faith in princes (or courts) – agreements made from asymmetrical power bases: the story of a promise made to Western Australia's Aboriginal people

Steven Churches

> The conquest of the earth, which mostly means the taking it away from those who have a different complexion or slightly flatter noses than ourselves, is not a pretty thing when you look into it too much. What redeems it is the idea only. An idea at the back of it; not a sentimental pretence but an idea; and an unselfish belief in the idea – something you can set up, and bow down before, and offer a sacrifice to … [1]

Introduction

My paper is written from recent personal experience, and though there is dissatisfaction in my reflections on that experience, I should not want to detract from the utility of other papers in this volume. The story that I tell is merely cautionary of the perils of agreements reached where the parties involved have widely different power bases. Which is not to say that agreements or treaties will only ever hold between those who are equals in numbers or wealth.

When I contemplate the success (certainly in recent years) of the Treaty of Waitangi in New Zealand, I am confronted with an acceptance which is iconic. Certainly some Pakeha (Europeans) complain about the contemporary working out of the Treaty, but, operating at a level way above such a mentality, is the assurance which New Zealanders feel in having this agreement as the very foundation upon which the nation is built. An attempt was made at a first formal engagement to regularise the relationship of the Maori and the newcomers who were intent on settling among them.

The Indigenous peoples of Australia had no such foundation document recognising the difficulties in the meeting of two different cultures: the early Governors' proclamations of equality of all before the law were well meaning but, of course, unilateral in their expression and application. It would be the law of the newcomers which would be applied equally.

Alone in Australia, the Aboriginal people of the western third were recognised in a foundation document, the Constitution of Western Australia, which came into force in 1890. That document provided in section 70 that 1% of public revenue should be paid to a Board (not under local political control) for the welfare of Indigenous people. The first lesson to be learnt is one of the need for acceptance: as the colonists publicly said from the time they opened their new Parliament in 1890, this provision was forced on them by the Imperial Government as the

---

[1] Conrad 1976: 13.

price for self-government. The '1% clause' was widely hated, and the colonists set out to repeal it at the earliest opportunity.

The story in this paper is that of the fight over the existence of s.70: a sprawling fight over a century between bureaucrats and statesmen in London and politicians in Perth, do-gooders and lawyers, and the matter was finally brought to legal resolution in 2001 in the High Court decision *Yougarla v WA*.[2] The High Court pronounced the section dead, and my decade and longer involvement as counsel for Crow Yougarla, and before him, Snowy Judamia, came to an end.

The well-spring of generosity to Indigenous peoples

The last successful military field campaigns waged by Indigenous peoples against colonising forces in the nineteenth century[3] were the engagements at the Little Big Horn in late June 1876, and at Isandlwana two and a half years later in January 1879: 200 killed by the Sioux at the first, and 800 redcoats dead by Zulu hand at the latter. But the tide was about to change irrevocably with the industrialisation of the means for making war. As Hilaire Belloc wrote (a fair summary of Rhodes's advance into Mashonaland in the 1890s):

> Whatever happens, we have got
> The Maxim Gun, and they have not.[4]

The 1880s saw a burst of official philanthropy in favour of the Indigenous peoples (presumably on the basis that magnanimity to a conquered foe is the best policy).[5] The US Congress enacted the *Dawes Act* in 1887, which provided for the tribal land of the Blackfeet Indians to be taken from them, to be sold in small allotments, but the proceeds of the sales to be held on trust for the tribe. A Blackfeet accountant, Eloise Cobell, looked into the amounts unpaid by the Federal Government into this trust, and discovered that the total was now running in the order of $US10 billion. She is well ahead so far, having her case against former Clinton Cabinet Secretary for the Interior Norton upheld (at least as to preliminary procedural matters) by the Federal Court of Appeals.[6] Along the way, two former Clinton Cabinet members have been cited for contempt for failing to produce the documents required by the Court.[7]

In 1889 the Tasmanian Parliament passed an Act (No. 67 of 1889) authorising a grant of 300 acres of land 'to Fanny Smith, an Aboriginal'. Truganini had died in 1876: Cassandra Pybus in *Community of Thieves*[8] makes a strong case for Fanny Cochrane Smith being the last full blood Tasmanian Aborigine, and Fanny's story is a happy one of a woman who was self-assured, ran a boarding house in Hobart, and raised eleven children with her husband, James Smith. This personal history rises above the fate of the agreement the Tasmanian Aboriginal people

---

[2] (2001) 207 CLR 344.

[3] The exploits of Jandamarra (Pigeon) in the West Kimberley in the 1890s amounted to guerrilla warfare: see Pedersen 1995.

[4] http://www.nationmaster.com/encyclopedia/Maxim-machine-gun

[5] Motive is, of course, more complex than this comment allows, and a sense of genuine philanthropy flavours much of the intention in drafting s.70, to be discussed below.

[6] *Cobell v Norton* (2001) 240 F 3d 1081 (US CA, D of Col Circt). A computer search in June 2004 reveals much procedural skirmishing since 2001, much of it with the appearance of delay by Government.

[7] The Ilois people of the Chagos Archipelago in the Indian Ocean did well in litigation at the same time: the English Court of Appeal held that the British Government had not had prerogative power in the period 1965–1971 to push these people off their islands to make way for the US airbase at Diego Garcia: *R (Bancoult) v Secretary of State for Foreign and Commonwealth Affairs* [2001]. The reflections of the appeal judges on the senior bureaucrats only a generation earlier could provide a script for 'Yes Prime Minister', and indeed the archipelago has already provided the material for one show in the series, 'A Victory for Democracy'. The English High Court failed to deliver a win to the Ilois at the next round, the successful attempt at strike out by the Government: *Chagos Islanders v The Attorney General, Her Majesty's British Indian Ocean Territory Commissioner* [2003] (Ouseley J) (the subject of appeal at time of writing).

[8] Pybus 1991.

entered into with the colonial authorities, to vacate mainland Tasmania in exchange for free life on Flinders Island, which agreement was the subject of a petition to Queen Victoria in 1846, to no great effect.[9]

But would any of this generosity of spirit extend to the Indigenous people of Western Australia?

The reported condition of the Indigenous people of WA in the 1880s and its impact at the highest level

The claims made in the period 1885–1886 by the Rev John Gribble against the settlers in the northern half of WA for what he saw as their monstrous treatment of the Indigenous people are well known, as is his loss of a defamation suit against *The West Australian* newspaper in 1887 after it had referred to him 'as a lying, canting humbug'. What is less well known in WA is that the then Governor, Sir F Napier Broome, had been receiving contemporaneous reports from two senior government officials, operating independently of each other, confirming Gribble's assertions of depravity and de facto slavery. In April 1886, Lt Col EF Angelo, the Government Resident at Roebourne, wrote to Broome referring to a 'disguised but unquestionable system of slavery carried on under the protection of the British flag' in Roebourne. He named two residents who advertised themselves as able to 'put niggers aboard [pearling boats] at half a Crown apiece'. The local Justices of the Peace who sat on the Bench in Petty Sessions had their own pearling interests, and did nothing about this behaviour.[10] Broome sent a Fremantle Magistrate, Fairbairn, to report on what was going on in the north: his report of February 1887 corroborated that of Angelo. Broome suppressed this information, which never found its way to Gribble's defamation trial.[11]

But Broome cannot have been unaffected by what he had read in the years 1886–1887: in the context of the growing push for responsible self-government in WA in the late 1880s, Broome began a correspondence with the British Secretary of State for the Colonies, Sir Henry Holland (later Lord Knutsford), referring particularly to the needs of the Indigenous people under a colonial constitution in WA. Broome first wrote to Holland on the subject on 12 July 1887 after the Legislative Council had resolved for responsible government. The Governor suggested that there be a Board independent of local political control, and that £5000 per annum be expended by the Board for the benefit of the native population. He concluded delphically:

> Legislation affecting the Natives could, of course, be carefully
> considered by the Governor and, when necessary, by Her Majesty's
> Government, under the ordinary constitutional procedure.[12]

A letter from Broome of 28 May 1888 to Lord Knutsford (as Holland had now become) again set out Broome's proposals on the subject: there should be an independent Board seeing to the welfare of the natives, and £5000, or 1% of public revenue when the Colony's revenue exceeded £500,000 (which it was to do after the discovery of gold in 1893) should be payable to that Board to finance its functions.[13] Broome recorded the hostility of the Legislative Council to the plan for an independent Board, an antagonism which the politicians of WA never dropped, although it was concealed when necessary.

---

[9] Reynolds 1995.

[10] Pullan 1984: 130.

[11] The miserable treatment by both colonial and imperial authorities of men like Gribble and Angelo is recorded in Reynolds 1998.

[12] *British Parliamentary Papers: Colonies Australia* (hereafter BPP) vol 31: 358.

[13] BPP vol 31: 380–2, paras 21–4. All documents referred to from this point, including this one, were before the courts in the litigation described later in the chapter.

With this letter was enclosed a draft Bill for a Constitution for WA, which discloses that Broome was alert to the necessity of entrenching a proposal such as he had just floated: since the attitude of the colonists was predictably adverse, the measure would have to be protected against easy repeal by the new colonial Parliament, the establishment of which was the main object of the pressure for responsible government.

The proposed protection of the 1% measure

In the Bill forwarded by Broome, the 1% provision first surfaces as clause 52. The entrenching of the constitutional arrangements for the colonial Parliament was set out in clause 57, and included tabling of any proposed Bill for change in both Houses of the Imperial Parliament for 30 days prior to any Royal Assent. Clause 52 was not made directly the subject of such restraint in this draft, but Broome suggested that alteration of that provision should be in accordance with the tabling procedure in clause 57.[14]

The idea of tabling colonial laws and amendments had first arisen in the period 1823–1828 in relation to NSW and Van Diemen's Land (Tasmania), when both colonies were little more than military despotisms.[15] The first relevant raising of tabling for colonial constitutional amendments occurred in the *Imperial Act* of 1850, the *Australian Colonies Constitutions Act (No 2)*. Section 32 of that Act provided that amendments to the constitution of the legislatures of the colonies would require tabling at Westminster. They would also require the cautionary treatment set out in the *Australian Colonies Constitution Act (No 1)* of 1842, which provided that legislation impacting on the election to or the constitution of a legislature had to make the journey to London for Royal Assent and back to the colony within two years (lest it become politically stale) and that, on its return, it had to be proclaimed publicly to ensure that the citizenry understood the existence of this new law, which had been given life offshore.

Knutsford sent a revised version of the Constitution back to Broome on 31 August 1888, with the 1% provision now being clause 58, and the entrenching provision (clause 61) now merely requiring reservation 'for Her Majesty's pleasure'. The 1% was still not entrenched, and the requirements involved in the overview by the imperial authorities were now more obscure.[16] The Bill for the Constitution now started to move through the existing WA Legislative Council. Broome reported to Knutsford on 1 April 1889 that, acting on Knutsford's instructions of 15 March 1889 (which are no longer available), clause 73 now provided for certain provisions in the Constitution to be reserved if being altered.[17]

On 29 April 1889 Broome was able to send the Bill, in the final form passed by the WA Parliament, to Knutsford. The 1% provision was now clause (and upon assent, section) 70, and the provision requiring reservation of certain matters if they were the subject of colonial legislation, including s.70, was to be s.73. That section merely specified that those sections set out in s.73 would require reservation. Nothing more was said in the Bill for the Constitution on the content of what was required by reservation.

The colonists sent a delegation to London in April 1890 to persuade the Imperial Parliament to the idea of responsible government for WA. Sir TC Campbell was asked by a member of the Select Parliamentary Committee what he thought of the measures in the Bill regarding Aboriginal people, to which he replied:

---

[14] BPP vol 31: 382, para 24, and for the Bill: 393–5.

[15] Noted by the majority in the High Court in *Yougarla* 207 CLR at 357–8 [28], but not raised in argument: fn 48.

[16] BPP vol 31: 400ff.

[17] BPP vol 31: 424.

> I do not think that they are of any use. I think they will relieve the
> Colonial Government from a sense of responsibility … [which]
> is a pity, but at the same time they will prevent the settlers being
> persecuted by what I may call the Exeter Hall factions.[18]

The Constitution was brought to enactment later in 1890 not merely by Royal Assent (following tabling) and subsequent proclamation, which would have been possible under the 1842 and 1850 Acts, but rather the Imperial Parliament passed the *Western Australian Constitution Act 1890*, to which the Bill for the Constitution was appended as a schedule. The important factor in the Imperial covering Act was that in s.2 it provided that, while the provisions of the 1842 and 1850 Acts which were repugnant to the Constitution should be repealed, such of those provisions 'which relate to … the reservation of Bills … shall apply to Bills to be passed by …' the bi-cameral legislature to be set up under the Constitution. As noted above, the provisions of the 1842 Act (ss.31 and 33) and the 1850 Act (s.32) relating to reservation requirements did so by enumerating aspects of the election and composition of the legislature that would attract the supervisory power of the Imperial authorities by way of reservation.

The question that would arise was what, if any, of these reservation requirements applied through the link of s.2 of the covering Act in the event that s.70 was the subject of legislative alteration. There was a fair argument that the matters directly referred to in the 1842 and 1850 Act reservation provisions had in fact evaporated with the 1890 covering Act, and that the only work left for s.2 was to connect the matters set out in s.73 of the new Constitution, including s.70, to the requirements of the 1842 and 1850 Acts.

The first legislative attack on s.70

Broome's correspondence had correctly stated the level of hostility to both an independent Aborigines Protection Board and the provision that 1% of public revenue be paid to it. Premier John Forrest lost no time making his views known. Of the Board he wrote to new Governor Robinson in 1892:

> … its existence is a grave reflection on the honour and integrity of
> the people of the Colony to do what is just and right to the aboriginal
> population, [and the feeling] is unanimous throughout the colony
> and we shall never be satisfied until this unjust stigma [of s.70] is
> removed.[19]

The flavour of debate in the nascent WA Parliament on the subject of the Indigenous people ranged from indignation at the Imperial imposition of the 1% measure, apparently as the price for responsible government, to Alexander Forrest's more robust enquiries: how many Black lives measured up to the life of one Whitesettler? Forrest, whose statue graces the street corner outside the WA Supreme Court, gave an entirely new meaning to the concept 'disperse', as in 'dispersing the natives'. The Anglican Bishop of Perth, the Rt Rev COL Riley wrote to Governor Smith in July 1896 saying:

> The expression 'Dispersing the natives', should be clearly defined so
> that we may understand what it means.[20]

---

[18] BPP vol 32: 119. On this page and the next appear a further five references from Sir TC Campbell regarding the 'baneful influence' of Exeter Hall, which had apparently caused the WA pearling industry to be regulated out of local control. Exeter Hall opened at 372 The Strand, London in 1831, and became a centre for British philanthropy, the Anti-Slavery World Convention being held there in 1840. Its name became associated with British-based opponents of slavery and those who were concerned for the welfare of Indigenous peoples under pressure from colonists throughout the Empire.

[19] Quoted in Reynolds 1998: 175.

[20] BPP vol 34: 517.

The Bishop was in turn attacked in the colonial Parliament for spreading ' ... the kind of yarn served up at Exeter Hall for the delectation of the old women – some of them wearing petticoats, and some wearing breeches'.[21]

In 1894 the first attempt to despatch s.70 was passed in Bill form in the WA Parliament, and sent to London as a reserved Bill. There it languished, although the WA Parliament followed it up with a memorandum to the new Secretary of State for the Colonies, Joseph Chamberlain, in October 1895, asking that assent be attended to.

Chamberlain wrote back in December 1895 to Governor Smith 'that without further directions from the Imperial Parliament I should not be justified in advising Her Majesty to assent to a measure which would sweep away entirely the reservation which it made on behalf of the natives at so recent a date'.[22] By August 1896 Chamberlain was writing to Smith, tacitly conceding that he would organise the assent, but would first have to 'lay the correspondence before the Parliament with a view to ascertaining the general feeling of the House of Commons on the subject'.[23]

And he did just that, the following February of 1897, when the attention of the entire Parliament was riveted by the Committee of investigation into the Jameson Raid of 1896, the occasion on which a party of settlers from the Cape Province had attempted to overturn the Government of the Transvaal Republic by force. There seemed little doubt as to the involvement of the Cape Premier, Cecil Rhodes, but the question of the day was how far Chamberlain had been implicated in planning and foreknowledge. Despite rising concern over 50 missing telegrams between Chamberlain and Rhodes, Chamberlain sat as one of the members of the Parliamentary Committee of Inquiry.

Though Chamberlain was obviously crumbling in the course of 1896 in his support for s.70 (a turnaround in eight months), Premier Forrest claimed the credit for persuading Chamberlain to this point of view. Forrest told the WA Legislative Assembly that while he had been in the United Kingdom earlier in 1897 attending the Queen's Diamond Jubilee, he had talked to Chamberlain, ' ... and I do not think I was with him half-an-hour before he decided that the colony should have complete control over the aborigines ... '.[24] Forrest explained Chamberlain's dilatoriness in attending to assent as the result of opposition from within the Colonial Office.

Needless to say, no one noticed the material tabled by Chamberlain regarding s.70[25] in February 1897 while he was defying the precepts of natural justice and sitting on the Committee investigating his activities relating to the Jameson Raid, let alone that the s.70 material was placed there preparatory to the abolition of the section. However, the bureaucratic understanding of the law at this stage upset the abolition applecart, and in August 1897 Chamberlain wrote to Governor Smith to say that his Department had drawn his attention to the requirement of s.33 of the 1842 Act, that Bills be assented to and returned within two years of passing the home colony's legislature and being despatched for assent. The 1894 Bill was now stale, and Chamberlain was returning it, with an invitation to send a fresh, improved Bill.[26]

The understanding of the Colonial Office is of particular interest, as it was obviously felt there that the 1842 Act requirements regarding tabling applied to s.70, even though the content of

---

[21] WA Hansard vol IX 1896: 1138.

[22] BPP vol 34: 501.

[23] BPP vol 34: 516.

[24] WA Hansard, 11 November 1897: 395.

[25] Forrest, Hansard 11 November 1897: 395, said to the WA Leg Assembly, 'No one took the slightest heed or notice of the blue book on the table of the House of Commons'.

[26] Papers in the possession of the Library Board of WA.

s.70 had nothing to do with the substance of the issues spelt out in ss.31 and 33 of the 1842 Act as requiring reservation if legislated upon. In other words, the effect of s.2 of the 1890 Imperial covering Act (the *Western Australian Constitution Act*) was adequate to carry over the requirements for reservation from the subjects enumerated in the 1842 Act, to the new subject matter of 1% for Indigenous welfare set out in s.70. If s.2 could work that magic for the 1842 Act, could it work also for the 1850 Act?

The second legislative attack

The colonists duly passed a second Bill for the repeal of s.70 in late 1897, Premier Forrest conceding along the way that 'Of course the Bill would be laid on the table there [the House of Commons] for a certain prescribed time'.[27] The Bill was duly dispatched to London and received the desired Royal Assent in early 1898, and was returned to WA as the *Aborigines Act 1897*. The last payment of the 1% was made in 1897.

Shortly after the Act arrived back in WA, a Mr Thomas Bayley MP asked Chamberlain in the House of Commons what had happened to Chamberlain's suggestion of August 1896 that he lay the correspondence regarding s.70 before the Commons to obtain the feeling of the House. Chamberlain gave the smuggest of replies: his timing in the tabling had paid off. He pointed out that the correspondence had been laid before the Parliament in February 1897, ' … and elicited no expression of opinion adverse … ' to the proposal for the abolition of the Board and s.70. The Bill from the colony had now received the Royal Assent, and that was the end of the matter.[28]

There the story might have finished, but in 1905 an interfering busybody, a meddler, in short just the sort of agitator that Wilde may have had in mind in the passage that ended up in Murphy J's judgement in *Neal v The Queen*,[29] named F Lyon Weiss, started asking questions in Perth as to why the other limb of the 1842 Act requirements for reserved Bills, proper proclamation in the Colony, would not also apply to the repeal of s.70. After all, the two year provision had applied, so why not proclamation, and there had been no proper proclamation in the Colony.

The Premier tired of the correspondence from Lyon Weiss, and wrote to London asking for an opinion from the Law Officers of the Crown to settle the argument against the agitator. On 30 October 1905 the Attorney General and the Solicitor General, Finlay and Carson, later to be Lord Chancellor and member of the Law Lords respectively, delivered an opinion that the *Aborigines Act 1897* was not 'legally valid as the assent of Her Majesty has not been signified in accordance with the terms of [the 1842 Act] section 33'.[30]

The third legislative attack

The WA Parliament set to work immediately to rectify this misfortune, and before the year was out, a new Bill for an Aborigines Act was on its way to London to receive the Royal Assent. This was duly given and the Act returned, complete with the repeal of s.70 and a purported backdating of that repeal to 1897, to be proclaimed in Perth in early 1906 as the *Aborigines Act 1905*.

---

27 WA Hansard, 11 November 1897: 400.

28 British Hansard, Commons, March 1898: 1496–7.

29 (1982) 149 CLR 305 at 316–17.

30 Reproduced in O'Connell and Riordan 1971: 53ff.

The mystery: was tabling at Westminster required of a s.70 repealing Bill?

From the records of the Colonial Office we are able to glean what was not a matter of public discussion at the time: dissension as to the function of the 1850 Act requirement for tabling. Some of the lawyers attached to the Colonial Office thought that tabling had been made applicable to all of the small number of matters listed in s.73 of the WA Constitution, including s.70. If s.2 of the Imperial covering Act of 1890 worked to make the reservation requirements of the 1842 Act, which of course did not have s.70 in mind, apply to repeal of s.70, then equally the requirements of the 1850 Act, being tabling, should also apply. However, it is apparent that the senior hands in the Colonial Office in both 1897 and 1905, despite Forrest's attempts to demonise them in November 1897 as an unelected force within government, were determined against any requirement of tabling.

The impulse of philanthropy at the heart of Empire, so strong in mid-century, had run its course, and the Home Government now sought only accommodation with the new self-governing colonial oligarchies. The tabling of correspondence by Chamberlain in February 1897 was not seen by him as being a constitutional requirement, but merely a courtesy to the House of Commons alone: the material was not tabled in the Lords, as required by s.32 of the 1850 Act.

Nonetheless, the appearance of Imperial might and propriety was preserved, aided by the usual lay confusion over the roles of the various components of Westminster style government. In an essay on Anglican Bishop, and later Archbishop Riley, FJ Boyce wrote that in 1897 ' … the imperial parliament accepted the … Bill which provided for the abolition of the Aborigines Protection Board'.[31]

Enter Don McLeod

Don McLeod worked with Aborigines in the Pilbara from the 1930s, becoming the motive force in the Strelley mob. In the period after the Second World War he organised the Aboriginal station workers into strike action to get proper wages, instead of the baccy and flour that had been the standard to that time. For this McLeod was much hated, and indeed it slowly dawned on me in the years after I first met Don in 1991 that he was the most hated white man in WA. The bitterness lingered on from the moneyed interests, but then nobody wrote a poem for them the way that Dorothy Hewett wrote of Don:

> Clancy and Dooley and Don McLeod
> Walked by the wurlies when the wind was loud,
> And their voice was new as the fresh sap running,
> And we keep on fighting and we keep on coming.
> Don McLeod beat at a mulga bush,
> And a lot of queer things came out in a rush.
> Like mongrel dogs with their flattened tail,
> They sneaked him off to the Hedland jail. (Etc)

The combination of moneyed interests and State force were determined to take McLeod down, and in August 1946 he was convicted of the offence of being near a Blacks' camp

---

[31] Alexander 1957: 68.

without the permission of a Protector: he was there to show an Anglican clergyman, the Rev Hugh Hodge (also convicted) the way to the camp. The WA Supreme Court showed its usual finesse in dealing with police matters[32] and the appeal was refused at single judge and Full Court level, before the High Court threw this conviction out 5–0.[33]

McLeod was aware of the Aboriginal complaints at the loss of the 1%, and set about obtaining legal opinions on his chances of overturning the purported repeal of s.70: one from John Toohey when he was a silk, two from Nick Hasluck at different stages of his career, one from Geoffrey Sawer, and another from John Macdonald QC, who had acted for the Banaban Islanders in their fight with the British Government, determined in *Tito v Wadell*.[34] All these opinions were of the view that it was too late or too difficult to claim the invalidity of 1905 legislation and sue for the money outstanding, unpaid since 1897.

The memory of s.70 had not dissipated with the years. As Sandy Toussaint wrote, referring to the complaints from Aborigines noted by Paul Seaman in his Aboriginal Land Enquiry Report of 1984, 'Whether or not [John Forrest's] challenge [to s.70] was successful remains a significant and not entirely forgotten point of contention'.[35]

In 1989 Peter Johnston of the UWA Law School, inspired by a short paper read to an administrative law group in Canberra by Toohey J (by then of the High Court), wrote an article in the *University of Western Australia Law Review* on the story of s.70,[36] which McLeod read, and was further inspired to the struggle to reinstate s.70. He filed proceedings in the WA Supreme Court in 1993, claiming that the *Aborigines Act 1897*, and the same named Act of 1905 were invalid for failure to adhere to required manner and form: most importantly neither Bill for these Acts had been tabled at Westminster. The action also sued for the money outstanding, about $650 million in 1993, but as the litigation proceeded, it became apparent that time limitations would prohibit any direct claim to the money, so the suit was pared down to the manner and form point.

The litigation: *Judamia v WA*

Snowy Judamia was the eldest of five Elders in the Strelley mob, who had worked with McLeod for many years in mining and pastoral ventures, and who now made themselves the plaintiffs against the State of Western Australia. At an estimated age in his late 90s, Snowy Judamia was of particular use to the plaintiffs' cause because he was born (exact date unknown) prior to 1905, and it was thought this might be of relevance to the question of standing, although in the long run this proved not to be so.

The Crown (ie the WA Government) moved to strike out Judamia's claim, not by reference to the constitutional issue of manner and form, but by highlighting the inadequacies of the statutory provisions in WA provided for suing the Crown (which at common law may not be sued, so that statutory provisions will be required to allow a claim as of right against the government), and by attacking the standing of the plaintiffs. It was said that they did not have sufficient interest or identification with the subject matter of the litigation to make their position more tangibly affected than the general interest of any other member of the community.

---

32 See eg *Trobridge v Hardy* (1955) 94 CLR 147 and *Webster v Lampard* (1993) 177 CLR 598.

33 *Hodge v Needle* (1947) 49 WALR 11.

34 *(No 2)* [1977] Ch 106.

35 McGrath 1995: 251–2.

36 Johnston 1989: 318.

Justice Owen heard the application for strike out in March 1994, and returned the answer in January 1995. The action could not proceed in its present form, although Owen J thought the question of standing should be reserved for argument at a trial if there was one.[37]

The plaintiffs appealed to the Full Court which delivered a 3–0 affirmation of the strike out on 1 March 1996.[38] The Court (Malcolm CJ, Rowland and Franklyn JJ) found the *Crown Suits Act 1947* to be inadequate to the task of allowing the now appellants' case to proceed.

The appellants took the matter to the High Court, which overruled the State court judgements and determined ex tempore 6–0 (Toohey J having absented himself after having written the advice for McLeod many years earlier) after a two-day hearing concluding on 9 October 1996, that the matter should be struck back in and go to trial.

Yougarla v WA

Snowy Judamia died before the matter could get to trial, so the next Elder in age, Crow Yougarla, became the leading plaintiff, and the trial extended over three days in May 1998 under the name *Yougarla v WA*. Justice Murray brought down a judgement in quick time, and the decision in July 1998[39] went against the plaintiffs on the crucial procedural points of standing and the working of the *Crown Suits Act*. In addition, the plaintiffs lost the argument over the operation of an amendment made to the *Interpretation Act* in 1994, which purported to make the *Australia Acts 1986* (Cth and UK) work backwards in time, so that the abolition of any reservation requirements in the Australia Acts was said to embrace the position in 1897 and 1905. Where the WA Constitution at that time had plainly required reservation for the repeal of s.70 (the fight being over the content of that reservation requirement), the Parliament now claimed to have armed a Tardis with power to change the constitutional scenery in the remote past. There was no reservation requirement at all.

However, the plaintiffs did receive a morale boosting result on the major constitutional point: Murray J found[40] that the reservation procedure as it existed in 1897 and 1905 required tabling of the Bills to repeal s.70. For this win, senior counsel for Yougarla, David Bennett QC deserves acclamation. It was to the plaintiffs' great disadvantage that Bennett shortly afterwards became Solicitor General of the Commonwealth, and had to leave the case, in which he had been involved from the proceedings in front of Owen J.

The Full Court (Ipp, Anderson and White JJ) had no trouble despatching the appeal, heard in August 1999, and delivered on 11 November 1999.[41] All three judges agreed that Murray J had been wrong to require tabling for the 1905 Act, although only Anderson J went out of his way to find that there had been no requirements associated with any of the reservations at all, ie, that the Colonial Office lawyers had been wrong in 1897, the Law Officers of the calibre of Finlay and Carson had been wrong in 1905, and there had been no need for the 1905 Act.

The decision of the Full Court is of particular relevance to Aboriginal litigation for the future because of the finding 3–0 that the appellants did not have standing, despite the fact that the High Court decision in Bateman's Bay,[42] decided one month after Murray J's trial judgement, raised serious issues as to the broadening of standing in constitutional cases.[43] Bateman's Bay

---

[37] WA S Ct Lib No 950137, 23 January 1995.
[38] WA S Ct Lib No 960114.
[39] (1998) 146 FLR 128.
[40] (1998) 146 FLR 135–141.
[41] (1999) 21 WAR 488.
[42] (1998) 194 CLR 247.
[43] (1998) 194 CLR at 267.

was cited to the Full Court at length, along with an English Court of Appeal decision *R v Secretary of State for Foreign and Commonwealth Affairs ex p World Development Movement* [44] to the same effect, but the only indication of that fact was the appearance in the list of authorities in argument, not cited in the judgements, of Bateman's Bay, while the English case did not even get that acknowledgement.

Justice Anderson's approach in particular seems, in the light of the standing decisions coming out of the High Court and senior English courts since the mid-1990s, to be extraordinarily rigid, or just perverse. His theme was that since the appellants had put on no evidence to prove that they had suffered financial loss as the result of the repeal of s.70 (he noted that there had been ongoing funding for Aboriginal welfare of some sort since 1897), they had no tangible interest in the fate of s.70:

> In my opinion, the appellants have not demonstrated that they
> have any interest in the subject matter other than the concern that
> every right-thinking citizen might have about an alleged episode of
> unconstitutional conduct on the part of government that has passed
> into history. No doubt, the concern of the appellants is more strongly
> felt because they are Aborigines. In my opinion, however, it is clear
> in point of law that that is insufficient to give them standing to bring
> this action. [45]

Certainly, at the special leave application to the High Court in August 2000, Gummow and Kirby JJ behaved like gun-dogs sighting the first startled quail when standing was mentioned. The keen interest displayed all came to nought, as in February 2001 Gummow J presided over a directions hearing at which he severed the case, so that the appellants would have to win their manner and form point before the other Crown defences, including standing, would be surveyed by the Court.

The High Court hearing duly took place in March 2001, and the decision was delivered 7–0 against the appellants on 9 August 2001. [46] Six members of the Court (Gleeson CJ, Gaudron, McHugh, Gummow, Hayne and Callinan JJ) joined in a joint judgement to the effect that the 1842 Act reservation requirements operated in respect of s.70, but by a process of subtle statutory interpretation involving provisos, the wording of s.32 of the 1850 Act did not apply. It followed that the 1905 Act was valid and it worked to backdate the repeal of s.70 to 1897.

Justice Kirby alone fell for the Anderson J line that the subject matters referred to in the 1842 and 1850 Acts reservation requirements did not look at all like s.70, so they did not affect its repeal. That approach leaves unanswered what work was to be done by the references in the 1890 Imperial covering Act back to 1842 and 1850.

There is a mordant irony in a Court which did not exist when s.70 was enacted in 1890, sitting on its fate in 2001, particularly as the needle threaded by the majority six Justices on provisos (not argued by either party to the argument in the manner adopted by the six) may be rebutted by reference to a Privy Council advice in 1973, itself reversing a Barwick CJ High Court decision in *Commissioner of Stamp Duties (NSW) v Atwill*. [47] Atwill had not seemed relevant to the manner in which the two sides' arguments were prepared in writing prior to the hearing, and it was not cited to the Court, which then evolved an argument of its own. I had

---

[44] [1995] 1 WLR 386.

[45] (1999) 21 WAR 510, [81].

[46] (2001) 207 CLR 344.

[47] [1973] AC 558 at 561G to 563D.

not thought to see the day when I would want appeals to the Privy Council from Australia to be reinstated.

The Court had cited to it a case from the Tudor period, *Villers v Beamont*,[48] in which Dyer J (as he then was) held that legislation dealing with the rights of widows to property ought to be construed in their favour, as women had no representation in Parliament. Where there was legislative uncertainty as to meaning, it seemed that the same principle should apply in respect of the then disenfranchised Indigenous people of WA, but the Court did not advert to this point.

It remains only to note that the history employed by the Court (not being material argued) was at best unfortunate: the majority referred to the pre-1850 uses of tabling of colonial legislation,[49] leaving the impression that tabling was an old hat idea before the turn of the nineteenth to the twentieth century, when in fact the NSW Parliament introduced it into the NSW Constitution of 1902. Tabling was the requirement for certain constitutional changes.[50]

In the course of argument, Gummow and Gaudron JJ even tried to introduce the idea of tabling as advantageous to the powerful commercial classes in the colonies, citing the example of WC Wentworth.[51] This shows no realisation of the course of nineteenth century philanthropy, and the pressure exerted by Aboriginal Protection Societies and their like in London: the WA Parliamentary debates of the 1890s are littered with the colonists' fear and loathing of the 'Exeter Hall faction'.[52] But Kirby J bought exactly this 'historical' justification,[53] asserting that the settlers would have been more likely to have had access to the members of the Imperial Parliament than the Aboriginal people of WA. If this were true, slavery would have continued untrammelled throughout the nineteenth century, rather than being the subject of British Parliamentary abolition throughout the first third of that century.

Justice Kirby alone quoted any of the voluminous historical materials cited to the Court. He set out some of the letter of 28 May 1888 from Broome to Knutsford, referred to above,[54] but even though he was quoting from the very page, Kirby J did not notice the plain intention on Broome's part that the 1% be protected against tampering, by the reservation of any amending Bill.[55] In the end Kirby J's historical analysis amounts to no more than hand wringing over the unhappy fate of an historically meritorious idea: the acceptance that settlers had better access to the Imperial Parliament was followed by the vapid conclusion that we can now never know if tabling would have made any difference or not.[56] Needless to say, from the point of statutory interpretation and constitutional review, such speculation is utterly devoid of meaning.

What is singularly lacking in either of the High Court judgements, conspicuously so in the joint effort, is any sense of real moral purpose, which immediately informs the knowledgeable reader that choices are being taken which will need to be dressed in the clothes of strict

---

[48] (1557) 3 Dyer 146; 73 ER 319.

[49] (2001) 207 CLR at 357–358 [28].

[50] See Dixon J in *AG (NSW) v Trethowan* (1932) 44 CLR 394 at 432.

[51] Austlii transcript of 27 March 2001, p20 of 60.

[52] See text and footnote at fn 18, and text at fn 20 above.

[53] (2001) 207 CLR 389 [130].

[54] (2001) 207 CLR 381–382 [105]. See text after fn 14 above.

[55] The concern expressed by Broome to entrench the 1% clause may be found at BPP vol 31: 382, para 24, the reference to alteration in the manner stated in clause 57 of the Bill being to the forerunner of s.73, the section in the 1890 Constitution which would provide for reservation of Bills on some topics to the British Government. Clause 57 of the 1888 Bill specifically referred (vol 31 BPP: 395) to tabling at Westminster, which requirement ceased to exist in express terms in the 1890 Constitution. The High Court avoided the large amount of documentary material that revealed that between 1897 and 1905 very divided views existed in Whitehall between senior government lawyers and functionaries as to whether tabling of the 1897 and 1905 WA Bills for the repeal of s.70 required tabling at Westminster.

[56] (2001) 207 CLR 389 [130].

legalism, creating the illusion that there were no choices at all. Contemplate Murphy J in Neal[57] on the basis of Aboriginal grievance: the quote from the NSW Aboriginal Progress Association in 1938 says it all: ' … there are enough of us remaining to expose the humbug of your claim … '.

Conclusion

The Aboriginal interest in s.70 was always doomed, as it depended from inception on a bargain between the Imperial and colonial authorities, and when the Imperial Government lost the stomach for the fight, there was only the law left for the Aborigines to turn to. However, in the nature of twentieth-century history, they would always be too late in getting to the possible legal remedies.

And when they sought those remedies they were met, particularly on the part of the WA Supreme Court, with a withering blast of reminders that they were out of time to use the *Crown Suits Act* remedies against the Crown, that the Parliament could change constitutional facts backwards in time over a century to deny their rights, and in any case they did not have standing. The system was not theirs to use, leaving the question, of course: if not five Elders from the Pilbara, then who would have standing to sue over an allegedly invalid repeal of a statutory provision in favour of Indigenous people?

I began this paper with Conrad having his character Marlow musing on the idea that might be the redemption for the wresting of the Earth away from the Indigenous peoples. Although *Heart of Darkness* is set in the Congo, I wonder how much of Conrad's reading of Western Australian atrocity stories in *The Times* in the 1890s ('Magistrate flogs two blacks to death' is my personal favourite) affected his poised view of the inevitable horrors of colonisation and expropriation.

And what was that idea (so brutally overthrown by the realisation of Kurtz)? The Court door having been slammed on the Indigenous interest in what was meant to be their recompense for land loss, recapturing that idea seems to me to be important for WA. In *Can these Bones Live?*, Veronica Brady observes that:

> Ultimately, if there is no criteria of right and wrong beyond that of
> human reason, then interest is the key and social power the ultimate
> arbiter as Hobbes argues and as colonial practice illustrates.[58]

Brady then cites others to come to the conclusion that the argument must be 'that every human being, regardless of race, class or gender is essentially valuable'. To me this still seems to be in the realm of human reason, but it is also emotionally affecting, and goes a long way to my subliminal notions of Conrad's 'idea' as having been to do with a sense of proportion in human affairs.

My problem at this juncture is that I cannot see a treaty bringing about that end in Australia at the present. I fear that the First Nations of this land will have to make and stake out the claim for their own dignity, unassisted by State authority, and only when that is achieved may a treaty serve to celebrate what will be obvious to all but the hardest of hearts (and which should have been obvious all along), that we all share this community together as equal participants and members.

---

[57] 149 CLR at 317–319. [58] Brady 1996: 134.

References

Books, articles and official transcripts

Alexander, F (ed) 1957, *Four Bishops and their See*, UWA Press.

Australian Legal Information Institute (Austlii) transcript of 27 March 2001.

Brady,V 1996, *Can these Bones Live?*, Federation Press.

British Hansard, Commons, March 1898.

British Parliamentary Papers: Colonies Australia vols 31, 32, and 34, Irish University Press.

Conrad, J 1976, (first published in 1902), *Heart of Darkness*, Pan Books, London.

Johnston, PW 1989, 'The repeals of section seventy of the Western Australian Constitution Act 1889: Aborigines and Governmental Breach of Trust', *UWA Law Review* 19: 318.

McGrath, A (ed) 1995, *Contested Ground: Australian Aborigines under the British Crown*, Allen & Unwin.

O'Connell, DP and A Riordan 1971, *Opinions on Imperial Constitutional Law*, Law Book Co, Melbourne.

Papers in the possession of the Library Board of WA.

Pedersen, H 1995, *Jandamarra and the Bunuba Resistance*, Magabala Books, Broome.

Pullan, R 1984, *Guilty Secrets: Free Speech in Australia*, Methuen Australia.

Pybus, Cassandra 1991, *Community of Thieves*, Minerva Australia.

Reynolds, H 1995, *Fate of a Free People*, Penguin, Melbourne.

—— 1998, *This Whispering in our Hearts*, Allen & Unwin, St Leonards, NSW.

WA Hansard, vol IX, 1896.

WA Hansard, 11 November 1897.

WA S Ct Lib No 950137, 23 January 1995.

WA S Ct Lib No 960114.

Legislation

Aborigines Act 1897 (Imp).

Aborigines Act 1905 (WA).

Australia Acts 1986 (Cth and UK).

Australian Colonies Constitution Act (No 1) 1842 (Imp).

Australian Colonies Constitutions Act (No 2) 1850 (Imp).

Crown Suits Act 1947 (WA).

Dawes Act (US) 1887.

Interpretation Act 1994 (WA).

Western Australian Constitution Act 1890 (Imp).

Case law

AG (NSW) v Trethowan (1932) 44 CLR 394.

Bateman's Bay Local Aboriginal Land Council v The Aboriginal Community Benefit Fund PTY Ltd (1998) 194 CLR 247.

Chagos Islanders v. The Attorney General, Her Majesty's British Indian Ocean Territory Commissioner [2003] EWHC 2222 (QB) QBD.

Cobell v Norton (2001) 240 F 3d 1081 (USCA, 8th Circt).

Commissioner of Stamp Duties (NSW) v Atwill [1973] AC 558.

Hodge v Needle (1947) 49 WALR 11.

Neal v The Queen (1982) 149 CLR 305 at 316–17.

R (Bancoult) v Secretary of State for Foreign and Commonwealth Affairs [2001] QB 1067.

R v Secretary of State for Foreign and Commonwealth Affairs ex p World Development Movement [1995] 1 WLR 386.

Tito v Wadell (No 2) [1977] Ch 106, 1977 Chancery Reports 156.

Trobridge v Hardy (1955) 94 CLR 147.

Villers v Beamont (1557) 3 Dyer 146; 73 ER 319.

Webster v Lampard (1993) 177 CLR 598.

Yougarla v WA (1998)146 FLR 128.

Yougarla v WA (1999) 21 WAR 488.

Yougarla v WA (2001) 207 CLR 344.

National encounters between Indigenous and settler peoples: some Canadian lessons

Ravi de Costa

Introduction

The most complex projects facing formerly colonial nation-states may be their attempts to create new and lasting arrangements between descendants of Indigenous and settler peoples which meet all their aspirations and needs. Many advocates focus on a constitutional or at least a legislative process by which to reach such arrangements, most commonly called treaties.

In this paper, I examine what some think is the most systematic and comprehensive post-colonial process ever devised: the British Columbia treaty process. I describe the process variously, using the figure of *national encounters*, in order to draw attention to the most misunderstood aspect of treaty-making. Treaties, I argue, are not simply the single encounter of coherent Indigenous and settler communities: the solemn and dignified exchange of recognition between the elders of two very different tribes. In fact, and against most of the representation of treaty-making, they are at least as much processes of these communities encountering themselves in their diversity. We see this diversity in the array of needs and the panoply of institutions that must be satisfied for treaties to work; the past must be served no less than the present and future. Each part of the putative community encounters others as well as encountering the parts of the 'other side' in a process of dizzying complexity.

This suggests a much harder task than many have envisaged. The question of community stability and coherence within liberal-democratic societies like Canada and Australia is increasingly under discussion as social, economic and cultural change now appears a permanent feature of life; Indigenous communities face many similar challenges in addition to the often very basic imperatives to survive as communities in the face of degrading economic and social circumstances as well as pressures to assimilate. Treaties cannot be seen as some magical device for restoring balance throughout these diverse social formations; they are better seen as a framework to enable different parts of a nation to encounter each other in dialogue and negotiation.

Old encounters: the long path to a treaty process in British Columbia

There is a long and complex history of treaty-making in Canada. With few exceptions, this history does not encompass British Columbia.[1] An explanation for this can be found in the

---

[1] The main exceptions are the Douglas treaties reached on Vancouver Island in the 1860s. Other agreements are the source of some historical interest, notably the Barricade treaties reached between authorities and the Carrier peoples around the Prince George area in the early 1900s. The 1908 agreement, Treaty 8, straddled the Alberta-British Columbia border. It was the subject of an adhesion by the McLeod Lake Band in 2000, who have recently entered the treaty process in order to achieve self-government, something not part of the old 'numbered' treaties. The only 'modern' treaty is the Nisga'a Final Agreement (NFA) also concluded in 2000 but reached through a separate process known as the comprehensive claims policy.

differing interpretations made by colonial authorities of the 1763 Royal Proclamation, which reserved all lands west of the Rocky Mountains as the hunting grounds for Indians. Without recounting that entire history, it is important to note that the colony (and Province after 1871) of British Columbia observed neither the intention of the Proclamation nor the facts of Native possession. In effect, British Columbia was considered terra nullius or empty land.

This assumption was frequently challenged by Native peoples.[2] However, early political representations were largely ignored and from 1927–51, land claims activity by Natives was prohibited by amendments to the *Indian Act*.[3] Soon after the prohibition was lifted, the exceptionalism of British Columbia, in not having negotiated the status of Native peoples through treaties, began to come under increased pressure from three related sources: direct action by Native peoples; more favourable jurisprudence; and shifts in federal policy.

From 1951 there was a rapid evolution of organisational structures and political strategy for Native land claims. A range of bodies emerged to make their claims, including the Native Brotherhood of British Columbia, the Union of British Columbia Indian Chiefs, the British Columbia Association of Non-Status Indians, the Alliance of British Columbia Indian Bands and the United Native Nations.[4] Though the styles and goals varied, land was a crucial issue for all. Government intransigence in the face of these developments was soon reflected in a rise in direct action across the Province.

Tennant suggested that 1973 saw the start of 'the contemporary era of BC Indian political protest', the timing influenced by events at Wounded Knee in South Dakota.[5] Activities soon mushroomed: blockades of logging roads and government offices; protest marches; obstruction of railway development; and, particularly the assertion of traditional resource rights.[6] George Manuel, a highly influential British Columbia Native leader called for 'sophisticated civil disobedience', referring to an 'army' of activists who would take up arms in the struggle if necessary.[7]

By the early 1980s, direct action targeted resources industries systematically. Such was their effect through that decade that in 1989, David Mitchell, a member of the provincial Cabinet and Vice-President of the lumber company Westar, described Provincial authority as having in some areas broken down completely: 'it is no longer certain who controls the forests in north-west British Columbia'.[8] This was a crisis in an economy so heavily dependent on the resources sector for jobs and export earnings. Forestry products are especially important: Canada is the world's largest exporter of forest products, a third of which come from British Columbia.[9] This equates to over CAN$15B in export revenue, half of the total value of exports from the Province, and nearly 5% of total exports from the whole of Canada. Though employment levels are declining, over 100,000 people are still directly employed by the sector in a workforce of 1.9m.[10]

Secondly, jurisprudence around aboriginal rights and title started to change rapidly. Initially the province responded to land claims by refusing any acknowledgment and mobilising denials

---

2 For clarity, I use the term Native(s) to refer to all indigenous peoples in the Province; First Nation(s) is restricted to those peoples involved in the treaty process.

3 The Indian Act of Canada.

4 Tennant 1991, McFarlane 1993.

5 Tennant 1991: 174.

6 Tennant 1991: 179–80.

7 McFarlane 1993: 249–50.

8 Glavin 1990.

9 Council of Forest Industries 2000: 11, 21.

10 British Columbia 2001.

such as the 'tense'[11] argument and the 'implicit extinguishment'[12] position. In 1973 the title claim of the Nisga'a, litigated since the 1960s, reached the Supreme Court of Canada in *Calder v Attorney-General of British Columbia*.[13]

The *Calder* decision found that the Nisga'a had held aboriginal title before settlers came, though the judges split over the question of the continuing existence of their title. In their *obiter dicta*, the judges decided that Aboriginal title did not depend upon the 1763 Royal Proclamation, but on proof of occupation since 'time immemorial'; extinguishment by the Crown must be 'clear and plain'.[14] A busy period of litigation ensued which extended the scope of potential aboriginal title while increasingly developing its content. The *de facto* attitude of the Province that its territory was *terra nullius* was becoming increasingly untenable.

The British Columbia Supreme Court deepened the doubts over government authority and tenure, granting injunctions against resource activities in various corners of the territory: on Vancouver Island, in the remote north-east of the Province, in the southern Okanagan Valley and on the North Coast, injunctions allowed for the possibility of continuing title. At McLeod Lake, a protest that involved unsanctioned logging gave rise to a ruling that allowed the band to sell their 'illegal' timber.[15]

A direct consequence of the reforming jurisprudence – and the third source of pressure on provincial exceptionalism – was federal policy reform. After *Calder*, Prime Minister Trudeau directed the Indian Claims Commission (which had hitherto dealt only with grievances under the older treaties) to start hearing non-treaty claims directly and the comprehensive claims policy was begun.[16] Foster calls this the 'third period' of treaty-making in Canada.[17] There have been a range of settlements reached under that process, though it must be pointed that none of these deal with the populous parts of Canada.

Federal policy had been to negotiate only one claim at a time, resulting in a situation where although many British Columbia Native groups had joined up through the 1980s, 'the line had not moved'.[18]As a bilateral set of negotiations between Native communities and Canada, comprehensive claims presented a vexed question over land: more than 90% of Crown land in British Columbia is vested in the Province, and the courts had determined that federal appropriations of Crown land must be done with provincial agreement.

However, by the 1980s, these pressures, as well as the rise of the conservation movement and a declining market for forestry commodities were making the Province's position less sound. Upon the election of the Vander Zalm government in 1986, the Social Credit party took a more pragmatic stance and by 1989 figures like Jack Weisgerber and Eric Denhoff were revealing fresh thinking within the conservative party. In Weisgerber's speech endorsing the treaty process in 1993, he acknowledged this prior 'strategy of denial' at length: 'We maintained that there was no issue there to discuss. If there was, it was in our minds clearly a federal responsibility and shouldn't involve the province, and we tended to avoid it.'[19]

17

---

[11]The view that confederation had annulled aboriginal title.

[12] The view that any provincial assertion through legislation automatically extinguished title. See Tennant 1991: 216–18.

[13] Calder v Attorney-General of British Columbia [1973] SCR 313.

[14] Calder v Attorney-General of British Columbia [1973] SCR 313.

[15] Tennant 1991: 225.

[16] Tennant 1991: 172.

[17] The first being the pre-Confederation treaties made prior to 1867; the second the 'numbered treaties' from Treaty 1 in southern Manitoba in 1871 to Treaty 11 in the Northwest Territories in 1921. See Foster 1999: 358. There have been various adhesions, including the McLeod Lake Band's adhesion to Treaty 8 in the north-east part of British Columbia in 2000.

[18] Tennant 1991: 206–7.

[19] Weisgerber 1993.

Managing the encounter: the process of treaty-making

The British Columbia Treaty Commission Agreement (the Agreement), was reached in 1992 between three 'principals': the governments of Canada and British Columbia, and the First Nations Summit (FNS), a body bringing together the leadership of communities representing some 70% of British Columbia's Native population. It in turn endorsed an earlier report commissioned by the provincial government, the British Columbia Claims Task Force Report (the Report), which is the foundational and substantive text of modern treaty-making in British Columbia.[20] It made 19 recommendations, and most unusually for a report of its type, all were quickly adopted by both the two governments and the FNS.

Under the terms of the Agreement, the British Columbia Treaty Commission (the Commission) was legislated for in 1993. There would be five treaty commissioners: two appointed by the FNS, one by British Columbia and one by Canada; the Chief Commissioner appointed by mutual consent of the principals. The Report had suggested that the parties negotiate any issues of interest to them and described explicitly how tripartite negotiations would proceed between the province, Canada, and individual First Nations: each set of negotiations in the process – each treaty 'table' – would go through 6 stages.[21]

First Nations initiate the process, each Native group indicating their voluntary participation, setting out who they are and the extent of their traditional territory (Stage 1). This is known as a Statement of Intent (SOI). Then the First Nation and the two governments have to demonstrate their 'mandate', their capacity to negotiate and ratify agreements,[22] and the measures for public consultation they intend to put in place (Stage 2). Once the Commission was satisfied each treaty table was declared ready.

Initial discussions could then begin: what would be the table structure – would there be side-tables to deal with wildlife or taxation issues, for example? The main aim is to get an agenda for future negotiations, a 'Framework Agreement' (Stage 3). This needed to be ratified according to the procedures set out at Stage 2. Substantive negotiations could then begin, working towards drafts of chapters that would become the final text of the treaty. A collection of draft chapters is an 'Agreement-In-Principle' (AIP), which again, requires ratification (Stage 4).

Finally, negotiations would arrive at the final text of Agreement. Here a process of constitutional and legal review is undertaken in addition to further discussions at the table (Stage 5). Effectively the conclusion of negotiations, this document naturally requires ratification by all three parties, using the approach they had committed to at the outset. After this, only implementation of the Final Agreement remains (Stage 6). Once complete, the Final Agreement has the status of an Aboriginal Treaty under section 35 of the Constitution. While the structure of the process invites few criticisms, in practice its operations are the source of considerable frustration. It is worth considering briefly the issues of interest-based negotiations and debt.

Funding

One of the key decisions taken by the principals had been to make First Nations' access to funds (for lawyers, anthropologists, oral history studies etc) largely dependent on loans. Negotiation

---

[20] British Columbia 1991.
[21] BCTC 1999c.

[22] First Nations decided that ratifications would be by community referendum. British Columbia and Canada decided that agreements would be ratified by passage through the Legislature and Parliament respectively.

Support Funding, as it is known, is 80% a loan from Canada, and 20% a grant which Canada and British Columbia split 60/40. Throughout the process this system has been managed by the Commission: $255m has been disbursed, $204m as loans.[23] Loans are due seven years after a table reaches an AIP, and 12 years after the first loan if talks break down. Yet many First Nations object to the very principle of loans. Why, they ask, should Native people go into debt so that settler governments can rationalise Native rights into the dominant political system? It is a reasonable criticism, made compelling by the fiscal weakness of most Native communities in the province.

Interest-based negotiations

A second issue concerns the way in which negotiations are conducted. The clear intention of the principals at the outset of the treaty process was that negotiations would adopt an 'interest-based' form of negotiation. A participant in the process explained the rationale:

> Essentially there's two models of negotiation, there's interest-based, and there's the typical competitive labour-union kind of model. And we came into the process saying 'no, we don't want to compete, we don't want to hide our cards and only put the ones out on the table that we think we should'.[24]

So, an 'interest' for Natives might be something like ensuring that zoning or resources decisions were highly sensitive to concerns for traditional burial grounds. This contrasts with the 'position' that Native groups must control the zoning or resource allocation processes themselves. One of the intentions of this alternative model of negotiation was to help create good will and trust among the parties.[25] It often seems not to have arisen. Although relations between individuals on tables are often good, it has been the view of First Nations that the two government's negotiators do not come and negotiate, but calculate their bottom-line away from treaty tables. Such criticism takes on a new force after the 1999 British Columbia Supreme Court ruling in *Luuxhon*,[26] which confirmed the requirement that negotiations, once commenced by government, must be continued in good faith.[27] Accusations of negotiating in 'bad faith' now encourage a legalistic interpretation, and though the definition of 'good faith' is still unclear, this may be the foundation on which First Nations build their criticisms of the British Columbia treaty process in years to come.[28]

Encountering the issues at treaty tables

These problems in the structure of the negotiating process, though not insurmountable, have drained much of the initial euphoria; it was a sense of optimism and trust that had been thought crucial to the timely conclusion of treaties. However, minimal progress on the substantive questions has raised doubts amongst many observers about whether comprehensive agreements may ever be reached: momentum continues to erode, while alternatives are being explored.

As noted above, theoretically nothing is ruled out on treaty tables, though this is far from the reality. I will demonstrate this, and explore some of the associated tensions, by briefly considering several of the issues the parties have been failing to resolve over the last ten years: land 'quantum' and interim measures; compensation; and 'certainty'.

---

[23] BCTC 2003b: 40.

[24] Didluck 2000.

[25] Govier 2000.

[26] Luuxhon et al v HMTQ Canda et and Nisga'a [2000]. BCSC 1332.

[27] BCSC 1332 at paras 71–5.

[28] The Snuneymuxw, for example, appeared awake to the strategic value of the 'bad faith' line in their negotiations during 2000. See Wagg 2000.

Quantum and interim measures

Quantum refers to the package comprising both what the governments envisage as 'treaty settlement lands',[29] as well as cash to fund Native administration and development. Reaching agreement in this area has been a frustrating experience, not least in urban areas where little Crown land is available and very large cash sums are being proposed by First Nations. In some cases, agreements on quantum have been reached at tables which have then not gained community acceptance. The reasons for this may be found deeper, in Native attitudes to their history of subjugation and to particular visions of their future, of entitlements based in ongoing identities. However, there appears to be some evidence that after 10 years of the process, First Nations may reach acceptable packages of land and cash settlements. I discuss recent developments on four treaty tables near the conclusion of this paper.

For the bulk of First Nations who have not reached this part of an agreement there remains great dissatisfaction with the implementation of the interim measures policy. The Report had recognised that treaties would take time, explicitly recommending a process for the protection and sharing of lands and resources before each treaty was concluded. A range of interim measure options was contemplated: 1) notification of potential impacts on issues that may be discussed at treaty tables, particularly unilateral action on lands and resources; 2) consultation over that action; 3) consent for such initiatives; 4) joint management processes requiring consensus; and 5) restrictions or moratoria on land and resource use.[30] The Supreme Court ruling in *Delgamuukw* (dealt with below) clearly confirms the wisdom of this policy, and as McNeil has argued, characterised resource activities as *requiring* Native involvement.[31] Yet First Nations have been extremely dissatisfied with the interim measure policy. Again, the province has been reluctant to contemplate interim arrangements until tables reach stage 4. Chief Treaty Commissioner Miles Richardson pointed out the problem with such policy:

> First Nations are largely saying, and I think quite legitimately that,
> 'it's just not on that we continue sitting negotiating at treaty tables
> accumulating huge amounts of debt when the very assets, the very
> resources that we're talking about are rolling by our offices on logging
> trucks'.[32]

In its 2001 review of the process, *Looking Back, Looking Forward*, the Commission pointed out that, of 60 recently agreed measures, only one was a land protection agreement.[33] The 2002 First Nations Economic Measures Fund of $30m keeps entirely within these parameters. More recently there has been some discussions about 'incrementalism', which would see the constitutional protection of some aspects of an agreement before others, as a way of testing out agreements and building good faith. This could mean 'fast-tracking' some parts of an agreement through stages 4–6, leaving areas of disagreement for future negotiations. As yet, no concrete proposals for this have emerged from the principals.

Compensation

The Task Force Report clearly advocated compensation at recommendation 2, allowing for discussions without 'unilateral restriction'. Moreover, it noted that negotiations may 'include consideration of a financial component to recognise past use of land and resources and First

---

20

[29] That is, land that after treaties will be under the exclusive ownership and jurisdiction of FNs.

[30] British Columbia 1991: Recommendation 16.

[31] McNeil 1998: 13.

[32] Richardson 2000.

[33] BCTC 2001c: 11.

Nation's ongoing interests ... The task force encourages the parties to reach a negotiated solution by bargaining with good will and good faith in the determination of compensation'.[34] First Nations have maintained that compensation is one of the fundamental reasons they are involved in the comprehensive process. The FNS resolved in May 1998 that no Final Agreements would be reached that did not clearly set out the wrongs committed against First Nations and offer compensation for them.[35] Their position is certainly representative of many First Nations on this issue:

> All the time the people have been in our territory, making money,
> building businesses, there's been no compensation for our people, and
> it will not be discussed in the treaty process.[36]

Canada maintains that 'history has been dealt with'[37] through its response to the Royal Commission on Aboriginal Peoples: *Gathering Strength – Canada's Aboriginal Action Plan* provided an official apology (particularly to the victims of the residential schools policy) and $350m as a 'healing fund'.[38] Canada insists that the cash component of treaty settlements is an exchange of 'value for value' – that is, the purchase of legal certainty.[39] British Columbia allows for a 'blend of approaches', recognising that while Natives will probably see cash settlements as compensation, the province sees them as providing the basis of future development.[40] Recent agreements on tables have largely deferred the question of compensation.

Certainty

> There were differences in the meaning of the term 'certainty' used
> by witnesses.[41]

If 'certainty' means extinguishment of Native rights, few Native groups in British Columbia are likely to want it. In Canada, a rich vocabulary has been developed to take overt extinguishment phrases out of the language in which agreements are reached. From 'Cede, release and surrender' – the earliest phrasing – to the language of the 1975 *James Bay & Northern Quebec Agreement*[42] in which the First Nation 'releases' all and then is 'granted-back' some of its rights, this has been a productive field.

In 1998 the Province revised its stance, adopting a certainty policy known as 'modify and release'.[43] This is the approach taken in the Nisga'a Final Agreement (NFA), which is the only example of certainty language available from British Columbia, given the lack of concluded treaties. Two of the commissioners submitted that such a 'modification (of aboriginal title) removes uncertainty'.[44] Osgoode Hall scholar Gordon Christie has pointed out, however, that in 'a process of modification some of the properties of a thing alter, while others remain the same. The same thing exists after the modification ...'.[45] Sections 26–31 of the general provisions of the NFA then invite comment. Here the two governments are 'released from future claims'; they have 'a duty to consult' only under the terms of the NFA itself; they gain one indemnity against all 'acts or omissions' that may have infringed aboriginal title before the agreement comes into effect; and gain another against any infringements or *still existing* rights not protected and set out in the NFA.[46] Such provisions are what governments call non-

21

---

34 British Columbia 1991.

35 FNS 2001.

36 Denise Smith 2000.

37 Denhoff 1999.

38 Canada 1997.

39 Tom Molloy, Chief Negotiator, Federal Treaty Negotiation Office. Quoted in Lewis 1998.

40 Lovick 1998.

41 British Columbia 1997: 'Certainty'.

42 Québec 1998 edn.

43 McInnes 1998.

44 BCTC 1999b: 4.

45 Christie 2000: 28:

46 BCTC 2000b: chapter 2.

extinguishment, even though the denial of potential future rights while so many legal doubts remain seems contrary to this.

Many Natives discuss an altogether different idea of certainty. During the Senate hearings as part of the federal government's ratification of the NFA in early 2000, a Gitxsan elder spoke of their desire for 'a set of living agreements', of partnerships between peoples that were flexible and respectful.[47] No concept in Native-settler relations is more fetishized than certainty – but the British Columbia treaty process lays bare the question: is 'certainty' the recognition of Native rights, or an indemnity against their future assertion? It is clearly the case that some in British Columbia feel that the modification of their rights envisaged by the governments is tantamount to a negation of their inherent status as Native peoples. Certainty appears to be an aspect of the treaty-process that reflects an out-dated conception of what treaties are or can be. The concept implies the end of the encounter rather than its beginning.

Legal encounters

In December of 1997, the Supreme Court of Canada gave its judgment in the case known as *Delgamuuk'w*.[48] While there was no determination on the specific question of the aboriginal title of the Gitxsan-Wetsuweten (a First Nation in northern British Columbia), the ruling had major ramifications for the treaty process which continue to be grappled with. The court encouraged 'negotiated settlements with good faith and give and take on all sides'.[49] The judgment then established a new context for such negotiations, by developing a clearer definition of aboriginal title: neither an inalienable form of fee simple nor mere usufructuary (usage) rights, it is 'somewhere in between these positions'. Aboriginal title is a right in land itself, and can encompass a range of practices 'not all of which need be … integral to the distinctive cultures of aboriginal societies'. The opening provided here is the source of ongoing dispute, though such practices cannot include those which would threaten the aboriginal way of life itself.[50] This elaboration of aboriginal title gives further content to s.35. However, it is certain that title is not immune from infringement by the Federal government. In fact the opposite is true:

> [T]he development of agriculture, forestry, mining, and hydroelectric
> power, the general economic development of the interior of British
> Columbia, protection of the environment or endangered species, the
> building of infrastructure and the settlement of foreign populations
> to support those aims, are the kinds of objectives that are consistent
> with this purpose and, in principle, can justify the infringement of
> aboriginal title.[51]

Persky suggested that the wide scope of the phrase 'general economic development' may be minimised by the requirement to consult and an obligation to pay compensation where infringement occurs.[52] The exhortation of the court for parties to negotiate rather than litigate is notable, although it has many precedents, such as in the widely-cited *Martin* case in the British Columbia Court of Appeal, which provided injunctive relief against logging activity to a First Nation on Vancouver Island in 1985. That judge remarked that the people of British

---

[47] Derrick 2000.

[48] Delgamuuk'w v British Columbia [1977]. 3SCR 1010. For a comprehensive analysis of the judgment see the range of scholarly articles available at http://www.delgamuukw.org

[49] Delgamuuk'w v British Columbia [1977]. 3SCR 1010: at para 186.

[50] Delgamuuk'w v British Columbia [1977] 3SCR 1010: at paras 110–11

[51] Delgamuuk'w v British Columbia [1977] 3SCR 1010: at para 165.

[52] Persky 1998: 20.

Columbia were entitled to think that their leadership would negotiate reasonable outcomes on their behalf without the accumulating costs and enmity of litigation.

Several points may be raised, however: exhortations to negotiate, like those for peace, can often elide questions of power, a fact not lost on First Nations, governments or observers of the treaty process. Moreover, the judgment downplayed a number of issues that have proven consistently beyond the abilities of negotiating teams. These include the range of activities and the character of aboriginal jurisdiction or self-government over title lands; the specifics of good faith consultation; and an appropriate level of compensation for extinguished title.

Indeed, a new wave of litigation is underway.[53] In recent jurisprudence in the Supreme Court of Canada, First Nations gained a recognition they had long sought on treaty tables without success: the right to be *consulted* over resource allocation decisions on lands the legal status of which remains in dispute. In the *Haida* judgment, the court pointed to an infringement of that duty and extended it to the corporation involved, lumber multinational Weyerhauser.[54] Such recognition has been at the centre of Native demands since they realised that Europeans intended to settle in their traditional territories. Indeed, part of the energy created by the treaty process at its inception, was its apparent openness to Native interests over resource allocation decisions in advance of final determinations of title. The interim measures process, as I have pointed out, leaves much to be desired. So, in the absence of widespread confidence in negotiations, litigation is seen by First Nations as one way of extending their recognition within Canadian institutions. Their resources, numbers and politically marginal status, will, I suggest, ensure that this remains the case.

Yet, treaty-making must deal with the fact that Indigenous people in Canada are rights-bearing individuals like all Canadians; jurisprudential interest in treaties is not likely to be confined to constitutional discussions about relations between governments. Comprehensive negotiations are also subject to developments in other democratic processes. A recent judgment in the British Columbia Provincial Court, *R v Kapp et al* [2003], ruled as unconstitutional the 12-year old Pilot Sales Agreement that set up Native-only fisheries. Justice William Kitchen felt that, 'the most troubling aspect of this discrimination is that it is government sponsored. The government should be setting an example for the rest of society, but unfortunately, this has not been our history.'[55] Begun in 1992 as a way to both acknowledge Native rights and provide jobs and revenue for Native communities, this program was certainly part of the calculations of First Nations working on treaties.[56]

The status of the encounter

Fifty-five First Nations are involved in the BC treaty process. Several First Nations sit at joint tables, meaning there are 44 tables. Only two Indigenous groups have joined the process since the *Delgamuukw* judgment of late 1997. Others have deprioritised negotiations, some have formally withdrawn. The bulk of First Nations are entrenched in the first substantive phase of negotiations, working towards an AIP. However, five tables have now reached Stage 5, though one, the Sechelt, have been in litigation against the Province since 2000. Before considering what these agreements have achieved, it is necessary to consider the context of treaty or agreement-making within a democratic setting like contemporary British Columbia.

---

[53] BCTC 2004: 2.

[54] Haida Nation v British Columbia (Minister of Forests) [2004] 3SCR 511.

[55] R v Kapp et al [2003] BCPC 0279, at para 235.

[56] Mickleburgh 2003.

During the passage of the enabling provincial legislation in 1992, one event pointed to future complexity: though there was unanimity on the need for comprehensive negotiations, the then NDP government arranged for a reception to celebrate the passage of the bill and the dawn of a new relationship between the peoples. It was planned in advance of the bill's presentation to the Legislature and clearly it was thought that Legislative approval was a mere formality; the real agreement had really taken place between government and the First Nations Summit. The Leader of the Opposition, Gordon Wilson, found this 'contemptuous' of the role of the Legislature, though this did not stop him and his party from supporting the bill.[57]

As negotiations began to deal with substance on issues like fiscal relations, land quantum and self-government, the merely formal role of the Legislature became untenable and bipartisanship began quickly to dissolve. By the mid-1990s there was a chorus of disapproval about the lack of transparency and accountability in treaty-making. It began within resource industry groups hostile to any transfer of control over resources to Native peoples, but quickly found a political ally in the provincial Liberal party.[58] The ratification of the Nisga'a AIP in 1996 gave this campaign a great deal of momentum and set the ground for the referendum policy. When the Nisga'a Final Agreement came before the Legislature in 1999, the government rejected the myriad amendments proposed by the Liberal opposition. After the longest provincial debate ever on a single bill, the government used its numbers to close debate and force a vote; the Opposition voted against ratification but were defeated. Party unanimity on treaties was gone and a nasty period ensued where treaty-making was smeared as undemocratic.[59]

Negotiations continued through the late 1990s but produced negligible results, with a number of First Nations abandoning or downgrading their negotiations. In May 2001 a provincial election in British Columbia radically changed the political landscape: the NDP was tossed out of office, with the Liberals taking 77 of 79 seats in the Legislature. The new government began implementing their only policy on treaties: a referendum to determine what the Provincial government's 'mandate' at treaty tables would be. Consequently, eight referendum questions were put to provincial voters in 2002.[60] These set out principles on issues such as self-government, recreational access to resources, and the protection of private (non-Indigenous) property, which if approved, would become binding under provincial law on treaty negotiators. Much of this was too vague to be helpful: recreational access to which resources, under what circumstances? Other questions were transparently malicious in their presentation of issues which had not arisen at tables, such as the idea that private fee simple (freehold) land might be expropriated.

The entire referendum demonstrated how close the accumulated history of conflict was beneath the surface of an established process. Boycotts by Native peoples and their supporters, including public ballot burning, raised the temperature around Native issues, but also ensured that majority support for the measures would be overwhelming.[61] None of the eight questions was approved by less than 84% of voters, with many receiving over 90% approval.

The full effect of this referendum is not yet clear, though it may already be producing new approaches to the issue of self-government. The referendum had asked voters whether they thought that Native self-government should be 'municipal'; that is, delegated from the

---

[57] Wilson 1993.

[58] de Costa 2002: 311–22.

[59] McInnes 1999, Willcocks 1999.

[60] See BCTC 2002a.

[61] Inwood 2001, Aboriginal Rights Coalition 2002.

Province, as is the case for local government. This was resoundingly approved, though it flatly contradicts the federal government's 1995 policy of an *inherent* right to self-government.[62] In the year since the referendum, several AIPs have come out of tables around the Province, but no uniform approach to governance is visible: several drafts see the parties consent to a Native government but agree that it will be a separate document, not part of the main treaty and not protected by the Constitution. Moreover, the government will exist only for a fixed (unstated) term and will be subject to review by the parties at that time. Others, such as that reached by the Tsawwassen First Nation include a categorical statement that its self-government will be a section 35 right. The Lheidli T'enneh First Nation's AIP provides for some aspects to be protected with others reviewable. It is far from clear how this will square with the result of the referendum and what the effects on the government's legitimacy will be. Elsewhere in provincial politics, a populist and majoritarian vision of democracy is gathering steam, with a Province-wide Citizen's Assembly on electoral reform well underway.[63]

Indigenous leaders at treaty tables must also satisfy their constituents. Throughout the history of the process, a significant number of substantive agreements made at treaty tables (that is, stage 4 agreements on an AIP) have been rejected by Native communities: this suggests that there may be discontinuities between the leadership negotiating the agreement and the community itself. For example, on 21 June 2003 Snuneymuxw First Nation were scheduled to hold a ratification vote for the AIP initialled at their table in March of that year. Jeff Thomas of the Snuneymuxw Treaty Office described why this did not happen: 'We had quite a number of our membership come forward that were not comfortable with the AIP. They did not understand enough to be comfortable in voting.'[64] The AIP was finally ratified in 2004.

Part of the difficulties faced by Native people in terms of ratification is the realisation that such agreements will increase the power of their own leaderships. During the ratification of the Nisga'a Final Agreement (conducted outside the BC process but in a substantially similar manner), the final vote to ratify the agreement included a ballot on a future Nisga'a constitution that had at the time not been seen by the Nisga'a community.[65] The challenges to be faced by indigenous people in developing the capacity to realise the promise of these agreements and to trust in the new political and governing structures they create, are hardly insignificant.

Notwithstanding this, several AIPs have been reached with four active tables now in Stage 5 of the process. The Sliammon, Tsawwassen, Lheidli T'enneh and Maa-nulth communities have reached substantive agreements on a range of issues, though the headline in each case is a mutual position about the 'quantum' each First Nation will receive. Yet crucial issues remain unaddressed, including governance, compensation and certainty.[66]

The Treaty Commission itself may be seen as a barometer of real progress however. The limits of its authority as delegated by Canada, the province and by First Nations remain a visible marker of the difficulties inherent in making treaties. A recent independent review found it to be less than effective in key areas of helping parties reach timely agreements and in its task of keeping the general public informed and supportive.[67] The burden of managing a process in which so many parts of communities must encounter and negotiate with each other appears to be showing. Its Annual Report for 2003 was plaintively titled 'Where are we?'.[68]

---

[62] Canada 1995.

[63] See http://www.citizenassembly.bc.ca/citizenassembly.html

[64] Thomas 2003.

[65] Rinehart 1998a, 1998b.

[66] BCTC 2003b: 9–13.

[67] Deloitte & Touche 2003: 3–10.

[68] BCTC 2003b.

Conclusion

Robert Williams's history of early treaties in North America finds that, for American Indians, early colonial treaties embodied trust by making personal connections and sharing stories. These highly symbolic 'acts of commitment', such as exchanges of gifts or smoking a common pipe, enabled shared processes of justice to begin.[69] In the words of Annette Beier, this is 'made settled by the fact that the first or early performers' example is followed, their confidence confirmed, general expectation of further conformity strengthened and so a general custom launched'.[70]

Modern treaties look nothing like this. In British Columbia, discussion at treaty tables provides neither Native nor settler communities with models of exemplary behaviour, other than perhaps the commonsense principle that it is good for people to talk to each other. In fact, treaty negotiations are highly technical expressions of future systems of rule; the codification of exemplary behaviour, rather than its performance. It could be no other way. Compared to the early colonial examples, both 'sides' are far less homogenous than they were; connections between the two are now innumerable; and structures of legitimacy and authority radically different. The hope that senior figures might enact a performance (or text) that was wholly representative, widely supported and yet aspirational, appears lost amid the regulation and alienation of modern life.

These national encounters must take account of a bewildering number of constituencies, institutions and demands, including the jurisprudential context; the imperative for transparent and democratic processes; the need for swift and cheap results; and the permanent disaffection of some on both sides. Australians, like those in British Columbia and elsewhere who are working towards some resolution of the unfinished business of colonialism, must accept the complexity of the national encounter that is at stake. In do doing, they must be prepared to work on many fronts and to perhaps forgo perfection.

---

[69] Williams 1997: 125.   [70] Beier as quoted in Williams 1997: 125.

References

Newspaper articles

Glavin, Terry 1990, Westar joins Northwest timber protest, *The Vancouver Sun*, February 23.

Inwood, Damian 2001, War council to battle land-claim referendum, *The Province*, July 20.

McInnes, Craig 1998, British Columbia changes treaty approach, *The Globe and Mail*, May 14.

—— 1999, Nisga'a closure enrages Liberals, *The Vancouver Sun*, April 21.

Mickleburgh, Rod 2003, Natives vow to catch, sell BC salmon despite ruling, *The Globe and Mail*, August 2: A7.

Rinehart, Diane 1998a, Close vote on Nisga'a deal 'disappointment', *The Vancouver Sun*, November 12.

—— 1998b, Nisga'a head to polls, *The Vancouver Sun*, November 6.

Willcocks, Paul 1999, BC government pulls plug on debate of Nisga'a treaty, *The Glob and Mail*, April 22.

Transcripts

Denhoff, Eric 1999, Canada, Gitanyow Main Table Meeting, Vancouver, September 17.

Weisgerber, Jack 1993, British Columbia Legislative Assembly Hansard, May 19.

Wilson, Gordon 2003, British Columbia, *Official Report of Debates of The Legislative Assembly*, May 25: 6482.

Books, articles and reports

Aboriginal Rights Coalition 2002, Should we vote No?, available at http://members.tripod.com/arcbc/index.htm

Alfred, Gerald R 1995, *Heeding the voices of our ancestors: Kahnawake Mohawk politics and the rise of Native Nationalism*, Oxford University Press, New York.

Alfred, Taiaiake 1999, *Peace, power, righteousness: an indigenous manifesto*, Oxford University Press, New York.

Assembly of First Nations 2000, 'The Delgamuuk'w/Gisday'wa National Process: Questions and answers' http://www.delgamuukw.org/news/qa.pdf, viewed 12 November 2001.

Asch, Michael 1992, 'Political self-sufficiency' in John Bird and Diane Engelstad (eds). *Nation to nation: aboriginal sovereignty and the future of Canada*, Anansi, Concord Ont.

Barman, J 1996, *The West beyond the West: a history of British Columbia*, University of Toronto Press, Toronto.

British Columbia 1991, Ministry of Aboriginal Affairs (MAA), The Report of the British Columbia Claims Task Force (June 28), http://www.aaf.gov.bc.ca/pubs/bcctf/toc.htm, viewed 24 September 2001.

—— 1993, *Treaty Commission Act* [RSBC 1996] Chapter 461 http://www.qp.gov.bc.ca/statreg/stat/T/96461_01.htm, viewed 12 November 2001.

—— 1996, 'British Columbia's approach to treaty settlement lands and resources' (June 12) http://www.aaf.gov.bc.ca/aaf/pubs/context.htm, viewed 12 January 2001.

—— 1997, Select Standing Committee on Aboriginal Affairs, *Towards Reconciliation: Nisga'a Agreement-in-Principle and British Columbia Treaty Process First Report* (hereafter Towards Reconciliation) (July), Appendix II, Minority Opinions http://www.legis.gov.bc.ca/CMT/36thParl/CMT01/1997/1report/index.htm, viewed 12 November 2001.

—— 2000a, 'Overview of the Final McLeod Lake Adhesion to Treaty No. 8 and Settlement Agreement http://www.aaf.gov.bc.ca/news-releases/2000/mcleodover.stm, viewed 14 January 2001.

—— 2000b, 'Nisga'a Final Agreement', http://www.aaf.gov.bc.ca/treaty/nisgaa/docs/nisga_agreement.stm, viewed 16 August 2001.

—— 2001, British Columbia Statistics A Guide to the British Columbia Economy & Labour Market (April).

—— 2002a, Elections British Columbia, 'Referendum Final Results', http://www.elections.bc.ca/referendum/finalresults.pdf, viewed 19 March 2003.

http://www.gov.bc.ca/tno/negotiation/instr_for_negotiatiors.Htm, viewed 16 March 2003.

2003, *Official report of Debates of the Legislative Assembly, May 25*

British Columbia Treaty Commission (BCTC) 1996, Update (April) http://www.bctreaty.net/updates/april96release.html, viewed 12 November 2001.

—— 1999a, 'Interim report: Strengthening First Nations for treaty purposes', 7 January.

—— 1999b, 'Speaking Notes for Kathleen Keating, Commissioner and Debra Hanuse, Commissioner, to the Prime Minister's Caucus Task Force on the Four Western Provinces' (Vancouver, May 17), http://www.bctreaty.net/files/task%20force.pdf, viewed 12 November 2001.

—— 1999c, 'Policies', http://www.bctreaty.net/files/policies.html, viewed 12 November 2001.

—— 2000), *Annual Report 2000*, http://www.bctreaty.net/files/annuals.html, viewed 12 November 2001.

—— 2001a, Update (March), http://www.bctreaty.net/updates/march01/mar01interim.html, viewed 12 November 2001.

—— 2001b, *Annual Report 2001*,http://www.bctreaty.net/annuals/2001%20Annual%20Report.pdf, viewed 12 November 2001.

—— 2001c, Looking back: Looking forward, http://www.bctreaty.net/annuals/Review.pdf, viewed 12 November 2001.

—— 2001d, Submission to Select Standing Committee on Aboriginal Affairs, http://www.bctreaty.net/files/Submission%20to%20Select%20Standing%20Committee.pdf viewed 12 November 2001.

—— 2002a, Update (May), http://www.bctreaty.net/files/May%20Update.pdf, viewed 11 March 2003.

—— 2002b, *Annual Report 2002*, http://www.bctreaty.net/files/2002%20Annual.pdf, viewed 11 March 2003.

—— 2003a, Update (January), http://www.bctreaty.net/files/January03Update.pdf, viewed 17 March 2003.

—— 2003b, *Annual Report 2003*, http://www.bctreaty.net/files_2/pdf_documents/2003%20Annual%20Report.pdf, viewed 30 June 2004.

—— , Update (February) http://www.bctreaty.net/files_2/pdf_documents/Feb04.pdf, viewed 30 June 2004.

Canada 1995, *The Government of Canada's Approach to Implementation of the Inherent Right and the Negotiation of Aboriginal Self-Government*, Minister of Public Works and Government Services, Ottawa.

—— 1997, *Gathering Strength – Canada's Aboriginal Action Plan*, DIAND, Ottawa.

Canada, House of Commons Special Committee on Indian Self-Government, and Penner, K 1983, *Indian self-government in Canada report of the Special Committee*, Queen's Printer for Canada, Ottawa.

Canada, Task Force to Review Comprehensive Claims Policy, Coolican, M and Indian and Northern Affairs Canada 1985, *Living treaties, lasting agreements: report of the Task Force to Review Comprehensive Claims Policy*, DIAND, Ottawa.

Canada, Royal Commission on Aboriginal Peoples 1996, *The report of the Royal Commission on Aboriginal Peoples*, Minister of Supply and Services, Ottawa.

Christie, Gordon 2000, 'Delgamuuk'w and modern treaties', http://www.delgamuukw.org/research/moderntreaties.pdf, viewed 12 November 2001.

Cornell, Stephen and Joseph P Kalt nd,…. Reloading the Dice: Improving the Chances for Economic Development on American Indian Reservations (Harvard Project on American Indian Development), http://www.ksg.harvard.edu/hpaied/docs/reloading%20the%20dice.pdf, viewed 29 March 2003.

Council of Forest Industries 2000, *Factbook*, COFI, Vancouver.

Dacks, Gurston 2000, Litigation and Public Policy: Lessons from the Delgamuukw Decision, paper presented to the Joint Annual Meeting of the Canadian Political Science Association and the Société québécoise de science politique, Quebec City, Quebec.

de Costa, Ravi 2002 (unpublished), New relationships, old certainties: Australia's reconciliation and the treaty-process in British Columbia, PhD thesis, Institute for Social Research, Swinburne Institute of Technology, Melbourne.

Deloitte & Touche 2003, British Columbia Treaty Commission: An Independent Effectiveness Review, Vancouver, BC, http://www.gov.bc.ca/tno/down/bc_treaty_commission_review_final_dec_2_03.pdf viewed 30 June 2004.

Derrick, Elmer 2000, Gitxsan Treaty Office, Canada *Proceedings of the Standing Committee on Aboriginal Peoples*, Issue no 4, Bil C–9, An Act to give effect to the Nisga'a Final Agreement 1999–2000, Ottawa, February 23.

Didluck, David (2000), Executive Director Lower Mainland Treaty Advisory Committee, Interview August 14.

First Nations Education Steering Committee and British Columbia Teachers' Federation 1998, *Understanding the British Columbia treaty process: an opportunity for dialogue*, FNESC, Vancouver.

First Nations Summit (FNS) 1996, *Treaty-making: the First Nations Summit perspective*, June.

—— 2001, 'The road to treaty negotiations in British Columbia', http://www.fns.bc.ca/files/t-chronology.html, viewed 12 November 2001.

First Nations Summit, Union of British Columbia Indian Chiefs and Interior Alliance 2000, 'Consensus Statement' (January 29), reproduced in Interior Alliance News (July 2000).

Foster, H 1999, 'Indian administration from the Royal Proclamation of 1763 to constitutionally entrenched rights' in P Havemann (ed) *Indigenous peoples' rights in Australia, Canada & New Zealand*, Oxford University Press, Auckland.

Govier, Trudy 2000, 'Trust, acknowledgment and the ethics of negotiation' in Speaking Truth to Power: A treaty forum, http://www.lcc.gc.ca/en/ress/part/200103/traites.pdf, viewed 12 November 2001.

Hamilton, AC, Canada, and Indian and Northern Affairs Canada 1995, *A new partnership*, Minister of Public Works and Government Services Canada, Ottawa.

Haythornthwaite, Gabriel 2000, 'Tossing the template: British Columbia natives reject Nisga'a-style treaties', *Canadian Dimension* 34(5), September/October: 33–6.

Lewis, Burke 1998, 'Into the billions and beyond', British Columbia Report (February), http://www.axionet.com/bcreport/web/980202f.html, viewed 12 November 2001].

Lovick, Dale 1998, 'Address to First Nations Summit' (Squamish Recreation Center, 29 October 1999), http://www.aaf.gov.bc.ca/news-releases/1999/Summit-Oct.29.stm, viewed 15 January 2001.

McFarlane, Peter 1993, *Brotherhood to nationhood: George Manuel and the making of the modern Indian movement,* Between the Lines, Toronto.

McNeil, Kent 1998, Defining aboriginal title in the 90s: Has the Supreme Court finally got it right?, 12th Annual Roberts Lecture (Robarts Centre for Canadian Studies, York University, Toronto, March 25), http://www.delgamuukw.org/perspectives/defining.pdf, viewed 12 November 2001.

—— 1999, 'The onus of proof of aboriginal title', http://www.delgamuukw.org/research/onus.pdf, viewed 12 November 2001.

Persky, Stan 1998, Delgamuukw: the Supreme Court of Canada decision on aboriginal title, Greystone, Vancouver.

Québec 1998 edn, James Bay and Northern Québec Agreement and Complementary Agreement, Sainte-Foy, Québec.

Smith, Denise (Sliammon Chief), 2000 'Summary of proceedings/treaty panel', Island Coast Summit, http://www.islandcoastsummit.gov.bc.ca (August 9).

Snuneymuxw First Nation, British Columbia and Canada 2003, *Snuneymuxw Treaty Negotiations: Draft Consultation Agreements-in-Principle Summary* (April), http://www.idv8.com/snuneymuxwtreaty/images/sfn_aipsummary.pdf, viewed 22 April 2003.

Switlo, Janice 1996, BC Treaty Process – 'trick or treaty?: giving effect to the 'spirit and intent' of treaties – abandoning treaty rights, Union of BC Indian Chiefs, Vancouver.

Tennant, Paul 1991, *Aboriginal people and politics in British Columbia*, University of British Columbia Press, Vancouver.

Thomas, Jeff 2003, Snuneymuxw Treaty Office, personal communication, July 21.

Tsawwassen First Nation 2000, Presentation of Treaty Negotiation Proposal (July 28, http://www.tsawwassen-fn.org/tre/comp/index.html, viewed 12 November 2001].

Wagg, Dana 2000, 'Treaty process breaking down', *Raven's Eye* (February 14), http://www.ammsa.com/raven/FEB2000.html#anchor3541703, viewed 12 November 2001.

Williams, Robert 1997, *Linking arms together: American Indian treaty visions of law and peace, 1600–1800*, Oxford University Press, New York.

29

Legislation

The Indian Act of Canada 1876

Case law

Calder v Attorney-General of British Columbia [1973]
SCR 313.

Delgamuukw v British Columbia [1997] 3 SCR 1010.

Haida Nation v BC and Weyerhaeuser [2002] BCCA 462.

Haida Nation v British Columbia (Minister of Forests)
[2004] 3SCR 511.

Luuxhon et al v HMTQ Canada et al and Nisga'a Nation
[2000] BCSC 1332.

*Martin et al v The Queen in right of the Province of
British Columbia et al* [1985] 3 Western Weekly
Reports, 583–93.

R v Kapp et al [2003], BCPC 0279

Taku River Tlingit First Nation v Ringstad et al [2002]
BCCA 59.

Additional website

http:citizensassembly.bc.ca/citizensassembly.html

Interviews

Didluck, David, Executive Director Lower Mainland
Treaty Advisory Committee, interview, 14 August
2000.

Krehbiel, Rick, Treaty Analyst, Lheidli T'enneh First
Nation, interview, 26 August 2000.

Richardson, Miles, Chief Treaty Commissioner of
British Columbia, interview, 12 October 2000.

Schulmann, Bernard, Policy Analyst Ts'kw'aylaxw First
Nation, interview 23 August 2000.

Doubts about the treaty: some reflections on the Aboriginal Treaty Committee

Peter Read

The year is 1980: Malcolm Fraser's Coalition government is in power. Perhaps without clearly realising it, Australians are nearing the end of a period of bipartisan political agreement on Indigenous issues and a shared faith in the ability of Indigenous people to rescue themselves from what they have suffered. The Northern Territory Land Rights Act,[1] begun by Whitlam and completed in modified form by Fraser, is the most obvious achievement, but there are others. The Department of Aboriginal Affairs, in the minds of more radical thinkers like Departmental Secretary Tony Ayers and Minister Fred Chaney, is intended within a few years to be subsumed and incorporated into a peak Aboriginal body under Indigenous control. The Aboriginal Development Commission (ADC), established in 1980 with a strong and independent Act putting it beyond the immediate reach of the Minister, is at the peak of its power. Indigenous agencies such as the Aboriginal Legal Service and the Aboriginal Health Service are significant powerbrokers in their own right, and are seen by Indigenous Australians to be achievements wrought through their own initiative and their own capacity. The Northern Territory Central and Northern Land Councils, growing in political power, are significant influences even in Canberra. The Fraser government has established a Senate sub-committee under Senator Missen to examine the idea of a treaty between Black and White Australians, though without ever seeming to be particularly enthusiastic about it all. The National Aboriginal Conference (NAC) favours a formal agreement of some kind and has drawn up 27 somewhat contentious proposals. And the Aboriginal Treaty Committee is one-year-old.

The modern idea for a Treaty, which later became known also as a *Makaratta* (an Arnhem Land term meaning dispute settlement), was proposed by Dr HC Coombs in a radio broadcast in early 1979. The Aboriginal Treaty Committee, a voluntary non-government private body, was established on 29 April 1979 with Coombs as chairperson. Its purposes were the obtaining and spreading of information on the need for a formal Treaty agreement between the Commonwealth government and Aboriginal representatives to negotiate on their behalf. Its achievements included the publication of newspaper advertisements, Stewart Harris's book, *It's Coming Yet,* a number of pamphlets on land rights, media publicity, the organisation and encouragement of numerous academic and public seminars and conferences, and nine issues of *Aboriginal Treaty News.*

In 1980 I was asked to do some public speaking on behalf of the Committee. Towards the end of that year I was invited to become a member. More than a little overawed to be in such company as Nugget Coombs, Judith Wright and Charles Rowley, I accepted without knowing

---

[1] *Aboriginal Land Rights (Northern Territory) Act 1976* (Cth).

much about the proposal. Not much effort, in my recollection, was given to persuading Indigenous Australians of the worth of the proposal – whether out of an assumption that they would naturally agree, or because we thought they would work it out for themselves, was not clear. As this paper shows, though, many Aboriginal people prominent in the early 1980s came to oppose the idea and by 1982 their lack of enthusiasm had become something of a problem for the Committee.

The Treaty Committee's basic document, *We Call for a Treaty*, set the proposal in historical and moral terms:

> We, the undersigned Australians, of European descent, believe that
> experience since 1788 has demonstrated the need for the status and
> rights of Aboriginal Australians and Torres Strait Islanders, to be
> established in a Treaty, Covenant or Convention, freely negotiated
> with the Commonwealth Government by their representatives.
> Australia is the only former British Colony not to recognise
> Aboriginal title to land. From this first wrong, two centuries of
> injustice have followed. It is time to strike away the past and make a
> just settlement together. We believe this will be a signal to the world
> that we indeed are one Australian people at last.[2]

The membership of the Committee ranged between the wise and experienced to (given the magnitude of what we were undertaking) the somewhat uninformed. Of these, however, I was the most naive and probably the youngest member by ten years. My chief memory of our meetings is of the rather splendid lunches we had once a month in Coombs's flat in University House, ANU, in which the various sub-committees (in reality just one or two people) reported on progress since the previous meeting.

My brief was 'the oral programme'. I undertook to make a number of cassette-recorded programmes to be distributed to the national community access network of radio stations and the dozens of Treaty support cells which supported the Canberra Committee. The first programme canvassed the views of Coombs, the social scientist Charles Rowley and the anthropologist Maria Brandl, the second the members of the NAC (especially Lyall Munro, head of the Makaratta task force), and their support staff. The third programme reported the opinions of prominent Aboriginal people not associated with the NAC.

In my interview with him, Coombs's first justification for the proposal was moral: that 'White Australians had a very serious problem' in reconciling the acts of invasion, dispossession and violence with their own moral code. The second was practical: that the grievances of the Indigenous people would not go away unless White Australians removed the causes.

Coombs identified a third reason to pursue a Treaty as the legally weak position of the invaders:

> We've become accustomed to think of our occupancy of the land as
> legal, justified and secure. I think, again, each of those assumptions
> can be brought into doubt … And therefore I think we have to
> consider that the kind of security we feel in the occupation of the

---

[2] Reproduced in Harris 1979: 12. The papers of the Aboriginal Treaty Committee are held in the Library of the Australian Institute for Aboriginal and Torres Strait Islander Studies, Canberra. See also Wright 1985.

> land at the present time may very well be called into question,
> certainly by Aborigines, perhaps by White people here, but also by
> nations overseas … And therefore if we wish to feel secure, and for
> our children and grandchildren to feel secure, then I think we have to
> establish the justification, the legitimacy of our occupation. And that
> means the legitimacy of our relationship with the original inhabitants,
> the Aborigines.

As I listen to the interviews again after twenty years, Coombs emerges as the clearest-headed of the Committee members. He respected, he said, Aboriginal suspicions of the Committee proposals, and acknowledged that some were well-founded. He thought that the process of education and negotiation, even if no Treaty eventuated, would be valuable to everyone. Above all, he understood the wide array of Indigenous proposals and demands, already well-developed, which might conveniently be carried forward in a Treaty; but which might equally be negotiated in other arenas.

Although the elected NAC had in 1979 unanimously called for a Treaty to be negotiated, its members were hampered by their own lack of experience and the means to effectively consult with Indigenous Australia. The Twenty Seven Points developed by its Treaty sub-committee seem now, and seemed then, to be ludicrously naive. They included the recognition by the Australian government of prior and continuing ownership, sovereignty and nationhood, a payment of 5% of the GNP for 195 years (the length of time since the invasion to the time of developing these Twenty Seven Points), land rights based on traditional ownership, an Aboriginal bank, rights to all mineral resources in perpetuity, no tax on businesses, no land tax for 195 years, and all existing Aboriginal houses to be made over to their occupants.

In interviews, though, some cooler thinking emerged. Ossie Cruse of New South Wales wanted land returned not on the basis of demonstrated continuing connection but on a needs basis. Rob Riley stressed the need for practical measures, not moral gestures, especially for the return of land as an economic base. Another NAC member, Peter Yu, did not regard Aboriginal support of Coombs's proposal as guaranteed. The mining industry's invasion of Noonkanbah, he argued, illustrated that no negotiations were worthwhile unless Indigenous governing bodies could enforce their decisions, and were themselves safe from arbitrary abolition.[3]

Completing the second programme on the proposals, and aware of much dissatisfaction about them outside the NAC, I saw my next task as interviewing a number of other prominent Aboriginal spokespeople, unconnected with the NAC, to elicit their opinions. These interviews formed the third radio programme. The speakers were Charles Perkins, then head of the ADC and Deputy Secretary of the Department of Aboriginal Affairs; Neville Bonner, a Liberal Senator; Eric Willmot, head of the Australian Institute for Aboriginal and Torres Strait Islander Studies (AIATSIS); Pat O'Shane, Secretary of the NSW Department of Aboriginal Affairs; Gary Foley, Information and Public Relations Officer of the Aboriginal Health Service; and Marcia Langton, History Research Officer at AIATSIS. While one or two favoured a treaty in principle, all were united in their condemnation of the NAC's negotiations, while Bonner and Foley were also critical of Coombs's committee. Foley, however, was critical of everybody. He referred derisively to 'what passes for Aboriginal leadership', and reserved his fiercest

---

[3] In 1980 the Western Australian government amended crucial sections of the 1972 *Aboriginal Heritage Act* to enable the mining company Amax to proceed with mining exploration on Nooonkanbah station in the Kimberley, despite the protests of the Yungnora people.

invective for the NAC advisers. ('*I wouldn't piss on them if they were on fire*', and in reference to our own committee, '*the sooner we get rid of the bastards the better*'.) Perkins was almost as critical of the NAC's proposals, pointing out that every Aboriginal in Australia would have to turn up with a wheelbarrow to be paid compensation out of the NAC's demanded 5% of the GNP.[4] More polite, though almost equally critical, was Neville Bonner, who, grasping for words, finally described the demand for 5 % of the GNP as 'unrealistic'.

The first shared feature of all the interviews was the belief that governments, even if one were ever to sign a document, could not be trusted to honour it. Bonner was suspicious of the enthusiasm with which non-Aborigines had seized upon the idea of a treaty after it had been suggested by one of their own. He had heard, he said, of so many 'wild, weird and wonderful' promises in the course of his political life, so many grand schemes which had come to nothing. His own Senate motion, recommending that the Parliament acknowledge prior occupation and the need for compensation, was passed unanimously in 1975. It became part of the Preamble to the Act establishing the ADC: but, he asked, so what? In practice it seemed to mean nothing:

> I have some reservations about symbolism. It's all very well to say
> 'Aborigines are entitled to Land Rights'. That's a great statement.
> A profound statement. Aborigines are entitled to land rights. But
> implementing them is the basis of everything. Unless the governments
> of the day, the Commonwealth government, is prepared to say 'We
> don't only believe in Aboriginal land rights but we're going to ensure
> that it's going to be possible for Aborigines to have land rights', then
> it's all superfluous. Symbolism is nothing as far as I'm concerned.
> What's the good of this being symbolic? Finally the Australian
> people have accepted the fact that there needs to be a treaty.
> Well that's all very fine, it looks nice on paper, but implementing
> it and the Aboriginal people being able to benefit from it – that's
> what's important.

Bonner found a perhaps surprising ally in Foley, who argued that there could be no faith in democracy, nor in law, (Black or White) nor in documents:

> I really don't have any faith in any piece of paper which purports
> to protect our rights. The only long term protection for Aboriginal
> people I believe is through their own economic strength and their
> own ability to exercise true self determination over their own affairs,
> and the only way that can be achieved is through land rights. Land
> Rights to me means economic independence which in turn, in the
> type of society in which we live, means the true ability to be able to
> determine your own destiny over people. That's the only thing I'm
> interested in. I'm not interested in pieces of paper which guarantee
> this and are signed by such and such and so forth. All I'm interested
> in is true political, and more importantly, in economic independence
> and that can't be gained through bits of paper.

---

[4] After our interview Perkins rang me to ask if I would excise his most personally critical remarks about certain NAC individuals before the programme went to air. I concurred.

Paul Coe claimed a part in an Aboriginal proposal for a Treaty made during the first Tent Embassy in 1972. But ten years later, in 1982, he felt less enthusiastic. The Embassy proposal for a Treaty was intended to be a way to get rid of the status quo established by the English and their successors, who had never acknowledged Indigenous prior ownership, nor the need for negotiated compensation, nor the right to unchallengeable possession the land. But now, in 1982, he was worried about the implication of symbolic equality if the two sides sat down together. Signing a Treaty without thinking through these implications might achieve no more than signing away an Indigenous birthright:

> I think there are dangers for Aboriginal people if and when we
> negotiate a treaty, if those terms are not suitable and equitable for
> Aboriginal people. Once having been negotiated, the descendants
> of the present generation are stuck with the terms of that treaty, and
> it would be very difficult for any generation of Aboriginal people
> to negotiate out of that position. So if we are to proceed with the
> treaty idea, and there are good logical reasons I think why we should
> continue to canvass it and not dismiss it, we should be very wary as
> to what the content of that treaty will be. For instance, will it lock us
> into a future position that we don't wish to be in?

Those most experienced in the mechanisms of Australian government, the civil servants O'Shane and Perkins, pinpointed the serious potential conflict between the federal government and the states. Careful and precise, O'Shane noted that minimum standards for education, for example, were required of Aboriginal people as Australian citizens, not because they were Aboriginal people. Aboriginal people did not, and do not, form a nation. The states owed considerable responsibility to Aboriginal people, and to sign an agreement only with the Commonwealth government would serve to let them off the hook. The reluctance of Western Australia and Queensland (the key states opposed to land rights in the early 1980s) would not be solved by giving all responsibility to the Commonwealth. Yet the states were notoriously difficult to shift. Court challenges in opposition to the 1970 'Blackburn' judgment[5] would be more effective in forcing them to act:

> I'm of the view that all governments have joint responsibility
> and our task is to ensure that they discharge those responsibilities.
> I'm of the view that if you want to ensure that the Commonwealth
> government has greater power and has a firm basis with which to
> exercise that power then what we need are further changes to the
> Constitution. But before we go that far, there's no doubt at all that
> the Commonwealth has exercised far greater power in relation to
> Aborigines than its constitutional basis would suggest.

Now O'Shane put succinctly a common wariness shared by nearly all the speakers: that progress in Aboriginal affairs was coming, and had come, through hard work, through the incremental. The grassroots efforts, the small scale, had achieved so much without the distraction of large gestures: significant improvements in land tenure, and countering racist repression. Treaties, she reminded listeners, are not legislative documents. A Treaty entered into with the

---

[5] *Milirrpum and Others v Nabalco Pty Ltd and the Commonwealth of Australia* (1971) 17
FLR 141. The suit was lost by the Aboriginal plaintiffs.

Commonwealth would be the soft option. After its signing, Aborigines would still have to fight just as hard for land and for housing, against unemployment and against discrimination. ('*We're powerless, that's our problem.*') Her position was that the confusing and diffusing energies going into the Treaty proposal prevented Aborigines from seeing that. Past tactics had been effective. ('*Otherwise we've all wasted 25 years. It's come through sheer hard work.*')

Foley agreed. Everything that had been gained, to him, had been 'fought tooth and nail', and that was the way it would continue to be. ('*Those who disagree are pissing in the wind, selling us out or don't know what they're talking about. Fight for it, in the streets if necessary.*')

Willmot in part concurred. Yes, incremental methods had achieved a great deal over three decades, but who could be certain that the political, or environmental climate would permit the same sort of gains to be made in future? Would incremental progress be able to continue? ('*I don't think that Australia is going to remain sufficiently stable to allow them. If a treaty is not concluded by the end of the 1990s, forget it. It's in our interest to settle for a covenant.*')

At this point, interestingly, Willmot shifted the viewpoint to the other side. Echoing Coombs's concern that non-Aborigines had a shaky legal and moral right to sovereignty, he asked to what extent it was in non-Aborigines' own interests to pursue the Treaty proposal:

> I don't know if new migrants have to sign it, just the Anglophiles and the Aborigines. [But] the thing that I would say if I were a hypothetical white person, in setting out a treaty that ended hostilities … is that it's the end of hostilities. The war's over. And we don't say who won. Then we say that as a result of the war being over, these are the deals of settlement of the war, whatever they are: that Aborigines get such and such and such and such as of today, and white people get largely what they have except what they've given over in the treaty. Plus the legal right to be Australian, to be part of this place. Now that's the value of it to a white person, it's the opportunity to settle it once and for all.
>
> But it strikes me that there is a cultural problem with Europeans in general about this. Sooner or later someone's going to stand up and say: now we are being pushed into the sea, and we're allowing a one-percent minority in this country to do it.

Perkins, head of the Aboriginal Development Commission, was rather more pragmatic. It didn't matter, he reasoned, whether Aborigines were a sovereign nation or not, the point was that they were an identifiable group with a grievance. The fact that all known Native American treaties in the United States had failed to protect them didn't worry him. ('*So what, it might not happen here? If it's realistic and appropriate it might last, and even if it lasts only 20 years, good things will have been done.*')

'Makaratta', the less confrontational term, was supposedly favoured by Prime Minister Fraser to 'Treaty' because it signified peace after internal conflict without a necessary implication of wrongdoing. But who, asked Bonner, had decided that the conflict was over? Surely it would be better for everyone to work towards the Australian government agreeing to some kind of Treaty at least in principle – which so far it had not. Was there a point to it all? Where were the full implications of the 1967 Referendum, carried so overwhelmingly? What had happened to his own Senate motion? Current events in the Northern Territory (he referred to the declaration by the Northern Territory government of a huge area around Darwin to be 'urban', and therefore not claimable) showed that governments could undermine an Act even as powerful as the Northern Territory Land Rights Act.[6] (*Forgive me for being a pessimist, but the only certainty in politics is the uncertainty.*')

How, then, should whatever was required in a Treaty be sealed so that the non-Aborigines could not escape their responsibilities demanded in it? The preoccupation among the Indigenous leaders with the tactics to continue the achievements of the previous decade began to dominate the interview responses. At one point Langton stressed everyday concerns like a guaranteed supply of clean drinking water to every community. At the other, Coe wanted recognition of continuing sovereignty. Could a once-for-all document guarantee either of these polarities, or both, more effectively than the incremental methods which had produced the Aboriginal Legal and Health Services? Langton was proud of the agencies: it was not, she said, until she visited the United Nations that she realised how much in advance of other Indigenous peoples Aborigines had been in creating them:

> In the last fifteen years Aboriginal people have achieved a great
> deal, and also rethought their conditions in Australia, so that in the
> international arenas we are one of the Indigenous groups who have
> devised workable strategies. We have, for instance, legal services,
> health services, housing co-operatives and other organisations
> which are Aboriginal controlled, which have recognition from the
> Commonwealth government, and which provide essential services in
> default of the state and the local governments. That's a tremendous
> achievement in world terms for Indigenous peoples. Because we have
> achieved so much and broadened our own outlook on how we can
> co-exist with other groups in this country … we may be able to
> devise yet better strategies on the proviso that we don't lock ourselves
> into a bounded situation which the ratification of a treaty would
> bring about.

This returned Langton to Paul Coe's caveat that a grand gesture should not blind the Treaty makers to a changing future. The Treaty proposal was sound so long as it did not lock Aborigines into certain positions which would prevent them, for example, from starting other agencies like the already successful Health Services. Strategically, signing a document would not be sound unless the government were pushed to its utmost limits, narrow though these limits evidently were. Why not, then, she asked, follow Coombs's advice? (*'Let's continue to devise strategies for the extension of rights, and wait for a better international moment to push forward with a real treaty.'*)

> I would prefer that a number of court challenges were run to disprove
> a number of assumptions about Aboriginal citizenship and in land
> outside the Northern Territory. The Blackburn decision went against
> us, and until there is an executive decision by all states in Australia

---

[6] *Aboriginal Land Rights (Northern Territory) Act 1976* (Cth).

> then we won't have any land. We can't rely on the state governments
> to make those executive decisions. Not only in relation to land but
> also in relation to basic human needs like water and housing and food
> …

The other major discussed alternative to the Treaty in 1982 was an Aboriginal Bill of Rights. Again, those who had experience of the unproductive tensions between state and federal spheres of government pinpointed the weakness of a Treaty agreed to by the Commonwealth alone. Paul Coe favoured a Bill by Constitutional Amendment, to override the states in relation to rights. Aboriginal prior ownership could in this way be acknowledged without surrendering any historical rights. His gut reaction, he said, was caution. Aborigines not only wanted land, but freedom to determine their own future, to put an end to the arrest rate, stolen children, the policy of genocide and of assimilation enforced by welfare agencies. (*'Until that's done it's meaningless.'*) A Bill of Rights could guarantee rights to children, education and land as a protective shield against state legislation. The 1967 Referendum was disappointing because Aboriginal collective rights had not benefited from the new Commonwealth mandate for shared control over Aboriginal affairs. Collective rights, therefore, could be achieved by a Bill of Rights without the potential of surrendering any claims of first nationhood which signing a formal Treaty might imply. The United Nations should be asked to ensure that negotiations were equitable. Like Foley, Coe held that the ultimate goal of any negotiation was to provide for economic power and freehold land essential to enforce self-determination. Two per cent of the GNP might achieve that.

Perkins the pragmatist advised negotiators to forget about claiming nationhood, or denying the rights of the Whites to negotiate at all. (*'That just confuses your position.'*) It was much more important that Indigenous negotiators start again in deciding what they were negotiating for. (*'Let's set our conceptual parameters.'*) Compensation? (*'Compensation for whom, and for what, and for when? Surely the Treaty was not just about land, but economic issues, psychological damage, the future. What's the whole thing exactly for?'*)

> It's very difficult, because you have to decide what are your areas
> in which you're seeking some compensation or restoration or
> some consideration. You've got cultural, psychological, social, cash
> compensation, land compensation, and how do you work them
> out? Talk about cash compensation: cash compensation for what,
> to whom? For how long? It boggles the mind for anyone to talk off
> the top of their head for what is adequate compensation. What – for
> murdering the various tribes that have been poisoned, and women
> that have been raped, and kids have died because they can't get
> enough to eat? Who's going to be the judge of cash compensation in
> those terms? Not one blackfeller in Australia, I can assure you, and
> no group of blacks, and not one group of whites. It has to be a well
> researched, well thought out document in order to come up with
> any proposition in terms of cash. Then you look at cultural. How
> can we restore Aboriginal culture where it can possibly be restored or
> even reflected upon with some pride, and how do we place that in a
> Makaratta or in a treaty. What are the mechanics of that? It's beyond
> me as an individual to tell you now what is a suitable amount or what
> are the mechanics of it.

We can now ask – 24 years later – what happened? Neville Bonner's motion of acknowledgment of prior ownership embedded in the Preamble of the Aboriginal Development Corporation Act was swept away when that agency was itself abolished in 1988. An Aboriginal Bill of Rights is scarcely discussed any longer outside legal circles. State rights have proved as intractable as O'Shane predicted: the Federal Hawke government's National Uniform Land Rights Preferred Model was destroyed in part by the fierce campaign against it mounted by the Western Australian Burke government. Most involved in the land rights campaigns of the early 1980s seemed unaware that the immense social problems afflicting communities would not evaporate on the granting of title. Few thought much beyond land rights as an end it itself. While the 'Mabo' High Court decision[7] kept the spotlight on land as the fundamental issue in Aboriginal affairs in the early 1990s, the *Native Title Act 1993* unexpectedly, from the viewpoint of 1982, raised the intense intra-Aboriginal dissent which became one of the chief obstacles to workable land title settlement.

There were alternatives. The less controversial, because little known, Aboriginal Land Fund Corporation, chaired by Charles Rowley in the 1970s, became the bureaucratic parent of the Aboriginal Land Corporation which returns land to Aboriginal communities by purchase. The Corporation still carries out in 2005 its important work without either an enabling Treaty or a Bill of Rights.

Another alternative would have led to Aboriginal financial independence. In 1979 Fraser backed a proposal of the framers of the ADC, first suggested by Coombs some years earlier, of a capital fund, whereby the government would add sufficient funds every year, in addition to recurrent spending, to enable Aborigines to be economically independent by the year 2000. The ADC received $20 million in its first year, 1980, only $1 million in the second, and subsequently, when Fraser's nerve was failing and his government unpopular – nothing. It was calculated in 1983 that it would need $450 million annually to bring the total to the required sum by 2000, and of course that did not happen. The momentum of bipartisan enthusiasm for Aboriginal independence was passing. Probably Hawke, if he ever heard of the proposal, would not have wanted Aborigines to have such independence from the rest of the Australia, nor did Keating. That moment had passed. It's now clear that, Treaty or not, Aborigines will never now achieve that kind of freedom or independence of which Fraser seemed to approve in the early years of his government.

Eric Willmot's memorable prediction that the twenty-first century might not be the place for fourth world endeavours seems to have proved accurate so far. Though no one whom I interviewed at the time perceived it, in 1982 we were just passing the apogee of the most creative decade in Aboriginal affairs of the twentieth century.[8] ATSIC Commissioners enjoyed far fewer powers than the ADC commissioners and much less independence. And ATSIC itself was abolished in 2004 by the same process of which Charles Rowley and Peter Yu had warned.

The current government is less, far less, enthusiastic about a Treaty. Advocates might follow Langton's preference for court challenges by Indigenous people in anticipation of a better national and international political moment. Perkins's caveats will be useful here too: to set the

---

[7] Eddie Mabo and four other Torres Strait Islanders in 1982 tried to establish through the courts their traditional ownership of their land. Ten years later the High Court of Australia held that the Mer people had owned their land prior to annexation by Queensland.

[8] The *Native Title Act 1993* is an obvious exception to the generally downward trend since 1982.

conceptual parameters first, to include other issues besides land, cash and sovereignty. Perhaps, in the end, Uncle Neville Bonner was right: the most useful thing that proponents of a Treaty can do now is to try to persuade the federal government, or the federal opposition, that there are sound reasons why the Commonwealth should begin to show interest in such a course.

References

Books

Harris, Stewart 1979, *It's Coming Yet*, Aboriginal Treaty Committee, Canberra.

Wright, Judith 1985, *We Call for a Treaty*, Collins, Sydney.

Legislation

Aboriginal Land Rights (Northern Territory) Act 1976 (Cth).

Aboriginal Heritage Act 1972 (WA).

Native Title Act 1993 (Cth).

Case law

Miliipum and Others v Nabalco Pty Ltd and the Commonwealth of Australia (1971) 17 FLR 141.

Interviews

The interviews with Neville Bonner, Paul Coe, HC Coombs, Gary Foley, Marcia Langton, Pat O'Shane, Charles Perkins and Eric Willmot are held in the recorded sound archives of the Australian Institute of Aboriginal and Torres Strait Islander Studies, Canberra.

Reflections on the history of Indigenous people's struggle for human rights in Australia – What role could a treaty play?

William Jonas

Let me first make two points about the history of the rights of Indigenous people in this country.

First, Indigenous peoples' struggle for recognition of their human rights remains to a large extent unfulfilled. Consequently, the struggle is not, and has never been, well reflected in Australian law. Second, human rights continue to be poorly and rather patchily implemented in our legal system. A focus on human rights in Australian law would therefore leave us missing at least half the story of the struggle for recognition by Indigenous peoples in this country.

Accordingly, I intend to provide an overview of Indigenous people's struggle for recognition of their human rights, noting some of the significant gains that have been made to date as well as restrictions on the exercise of rights. I will conclude with some observations about where we are currently at, the problems we continue to face and how a treaty could assist us to provide the just settlement that continues to elude Indigenous peoples.

Aborigines and Torres Strait Islanders – the Indigenous peoples of this country – have fought for the recognition of their human rights since the beginning of European settlement. We could look to the efforts of every generation of Indigenous peoples and we would find resistance and the assertion of rights – though earlier generations would not have referred to them as 'rights'.

Over the course of the nineteenth century, Indigenous peoples faced decimation of their populations through warfare, disease and dislocation, and the slow but sure dispossession from their lands as the white man's frontier expanded 'on the sheep's back' as Geoffrey Blainey once put it. Yet there was no negotiation with Indigenous peoples about the taking of their land. There was no compensation. The colonisation process was one based on the belief of racial superiority over Indigenous peoples. This was manifested through the assertion of terra nullius – that Indigenous peoples were so low in the social scale as to not have systems of government, property, law and culture that could be recognised. Instead, this land was deemed to be empty – land belonging to no one.

The injustice of this history, and the illegitimacy of this process, has only just begun to be recognised for what it is in recent years. The foundational myth of peaceful, consensual settlement has created what the Aboriginal Provincial Government refers to as a lack of 'moral legitimacy' of the assertion of sovereignty over Indigenous peoples.

By the end of the nineteenth century there had emerged some key themes in the treatment of Indigenous peoples – first, that our numbers were so reduced that we were seen to be a 'dying race', with policies very much oriented towards facilitating this eventuality by 'smoothing the dying pillow'. This approach was implemented largely through a system of segregation of Aboriginal people to reserves and progressively into the twentieth century through attempts at assimilation through the separation of Indigenous children of mixed descent from their families. This was accompanied by the most extraordinary levels of regulation and control over the lives and movement of Indigenous peoples. And this regulation by governments led to an almost total denial of the citizenship rights of Indigenous peoples.

This is very much the situation as it existed at federation in 1900. The federal Constitution of 1900 contained only two references to Indigenous peoples – both of which excluded Indigenous people. Section 127 provided that in the reckoning of the numbers of the Commonwealth 'aboriginal natives shall not be counted', whereas s. 51(26) – the so-called 'races power' – provided the federal Parliament with the ability to make laws with respect to 'the people of any race, other than the Aboriginal race in any State, for whom it is deemed necessary to make special laws'.

There is a perception that because of these provisions the Constitution in fact operated to exclude Indigenous peoples from citizenship in Australia. This is, however, a fallacy. As John Chesterman and Brian Galligan note in their excellent study of Indigenous citizenship in Australia which is titled *Citizens without rights*:

> The exclusion of Aborigines from citizenship was by no means a
> constitutionally ordained necessity, but rather a deliberate product of
> Commonwealth and State government legislation and administration.
> The exclusionary category of 'aboriginal native' was central to the
> institutional definition and development of Australian citizenship,
> and was created by the legislature, defended to a certain extent
> by the judiciary, and most importantly, developed, nurtured and
> administered by the bureaucracy for over sixty years. Far from being a
> product of a rigid constitution, conceived and endorsed by nineteenth
> century colonial racists, the long exclusion of Aboriginal Australians
> from Australian citizenship was implemented and routinely
> administered by Australian governments and bureaucracy until well
> into the second half of the twentieth century.[1]

In this sense the Constitution cannot be seen as a taker of rights – it is not the Constitution, for example, that excluded many Indigenous people from voting or that imposed strict regulation of employment. That instead was the result of a complex web of state and territory laws, regulations and ordinances.

But the Constitution can also not be seen as a protector of rights. Chief Justice Malcolm has written in this volume about the absence of a Bill of Rights in Australia. Many people also often cite the absence of a power for the Commonwealth to make special laws for Aboriginal peoples as problematic in this regard.

---

[1] Chesterman and Galligan 1998: 84.

And there are many examples in the following fifty years which demonstrate that the federal government would use the express limitation of the races power in s.51(26) as a basis for not extending many basic citizenship entitlements to Indigenous peoples. It was, of course, an erroneous reading of the races power to suggest that it did not provide the federal government with the power to include Aboriginal peoples within programs and service delivery which were provided to the general community – instead it simply excluded the establishment of specialised laws and programs.

It must also be said that as a practical matter it is unlikely that – at least in the first half of the twentieth century – direct powers in the federal government to legislate for Indigenous peoples would have been of much benefit or resulted in a different situation to that which eventuated. This is clear by looking at the way that the Commonwealth administered the Northern Territory from 1911, with a system of control strikingly similar to other States at the time. The lack of protection in the Constitution, however, is something that has been of great significance in the recent past.

The movement for recognition of rights in the fifty or sixty years since federation can generally be summarised as one which focused on trying to achieve recognition of basic citizenship entitlements and the achievement of formal equality with the non-Indigenous population – that is, sameness of treatment.

One of the most important examples of this struggle for equality took place on the 150th anniversary of white settlement – Australia Day 1938. An event known as the Day of Mourning was held in Sydney by the Aborigines Progressive Association. Following this day, the Aborigines Progressive Association presented a '10 point plan' – perhaps the original ten point plan – to Prime Minister Lyons on 13 January 1938[2] which included the following demands:

- Commonwealth control of Aboriginal affairs;
- The establishment of a Commonwealth minister for Aboriginal affairs with cabinet rank – something which, incidentally, Minister Ruddock was the first to have achieved;
- The establishment of a Department of Aboriginal Affairs with Aboriginal representation;
- The aim of the department being to raise Indigenous peoples to 'full citizen status and civil equality with the whites in Australia', including through the provision of educational opportunities and equal entitlement to employment conditions, workers compensation and insurance, social security, the application of the same laws of intestacy and transmission of property as white people, to receive wages in cash, and to be able to purchase and own property;
- The application of the same marriage laws and housing entitlements as whites;
- Land settlement policies similar to the soldier settlers scheme to be introduced and financed; and
- Entitlements to maternity treatment and clinic instruction on baby welfare for Aboriginal mothers, among other things.

By 1948, however, there remained significant limitations on Indigenous peoples' freedoms, such as statutory bars on Aboriginal people voting in the NT, WA and the NT; laws which

---

2 See Patten 1938: 1.

allowed removal to reserves in all states and territories except Tasmania; and the formal regulation of Indigenous employment in all states except NSW, South Australia and Tasmania.

At the same time at the federal level, Indigenous people who were under state control through reservations were not entitled to the range of social security benefits that existed at the time (age, invalid and widows pensions plus maternity allowances). Those who were exempt from the legislation also did not automatically have an entitlement to such benefits – it was then a matter of bureaucratic determination as to whether they were 'sufficiently advanced'. Should they be found to be so advanced, the benefits could then be paid to an institution rather than the individual concerned. New legislation in 1959 simplified the system but continued to deny to 'nomadic or primitive' Aborigines any entitlement to welfare. The last exclusionary provisions relating to welfare entitlements were removed in 1966.

I have exhausted the range of exclusions in some detail to highlight the extent of the control and exclusion that was exercised over Indigenous peoples lives. But I also emphasise how recently this approach was implemented, for we are talking about the living memory of many Indigenous people. The implications of this in terms of distrust of the broader community and the lack of skills to participate in the broader society on an equal footing cannot be forgotten or underestimated.

Most of the issues that have been used as examples – voting rights, social security entitlements etc – were remedied by the mid- to late 1960s, and it is also important to recognise this. We also have to reflect, however, on the entrenched disparity that their enforcement until the 1960s has had on Indigenous peoples. In my view, a significant factor that the broader community is still yet to embrace sufficiently is recognition that mere formal equality of treatment is not sufficient to undo generations of systemic discrimination and exclusion. This is a key issue for the treaty debate and I will talk about it again shortly.

Perhaps the culmination of this period was the 1967 Referendum. On 27 May 1967, 90.77 % of Australians agreed to the Referendum question to delete s.127 of the Constitution and remove the words which excluded Aborigines from the scope of the races power.

There had been a growing movement dating largely from the 1950s to alter the two provisions of the Constitution which excluded Indigenous peoples. The government of the day did not support the alteration of the races power as late as November 1965, when it put forward a bill which would see a referendum solely to repeal s.127. In support of this Prime Minister Menzies stated that the exclusion of Aborigines from s.51(26) – the races powers – was not discriminatory and indeed provided 'protection against discrimination by the Commonwealth Parliament'. It is perverse how this comment has come to be true through the passage of the amendments to the *Native Title Act* 1993, which occurred in 1998.

The 1967 Referendum is often seen as 'citizenship maker', but as I have stated this is not true – those reforms took place in the years before the referendum and in some instances – such as in Queensland – did not take place until the 1970s. In many ways this perception has arisen as Indigenous demands in the era that is seen as 'post-1967' is that they are more vocal and focused more squarely on the recognition of Indigenous rights – that is, on the recognition of the distinct status of Indigenous peoples whether through land rights, or calls for measures to protect and maintain culture.

The Referendum is not such a clear point of delineation – such protest became prominent before this, from the Yirrkala bark petition and fight over mining in Arnhem land from 1963 to the Wave Hill walkoff in 1966 to the Freedom Ride of 1965. These events, right through to the creation of the tent embassy on the lawns of Parliament House on 26 January 1972 all contributed to a greater awareness of the desires of Indigenous peoples that extended beyond the provision of basic citizenship entitlements.

These protests motivated the passage of land rights legislation in the NT and racial discrimination legislation at the federal level by the mid-1970s. They also motivated a broader public movement for improving the treatment of Indigenous peoples – perhaps the most relevant of these movements, from the non-Indigenous side of things, was through the establishment of the Aboriginal Treaty Committee in 1979. This Committee published an ad in the *National Times* on 25 August 1979 titled 'We call for a treaty within Australia, between Australians'. It followed the call for a treaty by the National Aboriginal Congress earlier that year.

In their booklet, *Its coming yet…*, the Aboriginal Treaty Committee stated that: 'We believe there is a deep and wide concern among other Australians that our ownership of this land, as defined in the imported British law, should still be based solely upon force, without any documentary recognition of the rights or the quality and courage of those who were conquered. It is time to right this wrong'.[3]

As Bill Stanner, a member of the Treaty Committee, had stated in 1973:

> if you study carefully the words used in any one of our formal statements of policy towards [Indigenous people] you will not find anywhere two things said simply and clearly. The first is that we injured Aboriginal society and owe just recompense to its living members. The second is that what we will do now for them we will do in recognition of their natural rights as a distinct people, not in expression of our sufferance of them, of our acceptance of them, or of our acceptance of them if they will copy our ways.[4]

This is what the call for a treaty was about then. And I would submit it is what it is *still* about some 29 years after these words were spoken.

Accordingly, the Treaty Committee called for a treaty to be negotiated which covered the following issues:

- The protection of Aboriginal identity, languages, law and culture;
- National land rights legislation;
- Conditions governing mining and exploration of natural resources on Aboriginal land;
- Compensation for loss of traditional lands and for damage to those lands and traditional way of life; and
- Right of Aboriginals to control their own affairs and establish their own associations for this purpose.[5]

---

[3] Harris 1979: 1.
[4] W Stanner as quoted in Harris 1979: 74.
[5] As quoted in Harris 1979: 2.

Concern was also expressed at the lack of priority given to Indigenous issues through minimal expenditure by the federal government – often being at a level of about 0.5 of one per cent of the federal budget.

The call for a treaty also had its antecedents in a call for recognition of the fact of dispossession and the provision of compensation by the first Aboriginal Senator, Neville Bonner, on 19 September 1974. The words that Senator Bonner spoke on that day have great resonance today. He said:

> I do not decry the vast sums of money that have been spent by previous governments … on indigenous affairs. I do not deny that the present government … has instigated superbly beneficial programs to improve my fellow Aborigines' and Torres Strait Islanders' way of life within our broader Australian community. But it is truly to no avail, dignity-wise, when it is but an allocating of money for a disadvantaged people, because it is but a form of charity. We, the indigenous people, for far too long have been the recipients of charity – the charity of the government of the day; charity, with its modern day connotations implying a handout mentality.

> What I am seeking is true and due entitlement for dispossession. Surely no one can deny that the aborigines and Torres Strait Islanders were dispossessed of what was theirs by right of inheritance …

> How do you value human suffering, the loss of human dignity, the loss of culture, the loss of a traditional way of life and the destruction of the Aboriginal society? … You can put no monetary value on enforced disintegration. I am asking for compensation for this loss of land – earth – our entire being … I am asking for compensation for our enforced disintegration.[6]

What Senator Bonner proposed was for a set amount to be set aside from the annual budget to become the true entitlement of the Indigenous peoples 'so that we may recapture our dignity and our pride as human beings'. This motion passed through the Senate six months after it had been proposed. Nothing more came of it.

Similarly, the 'deep and wide concern' of the broader community that had been identified by the Aboriginal Treaty Committee about the history of dispossession of Indigenous peoples did not lead to the irresistible campaign for a treaty that they had hoped for. And discussion of a treaty soon went off the national agenda until the signing of the Barunga statement by Prime Minister Hawke nearly ten years later in 1988.

This statement committed the government to:

- Work for a negotiated treaty with Aboriginal people;
- Provide the necessary support for Aboriginal people to carry out their own consultations and negotiations; and
- To stand ready to negotiate when the Aborigines presented their proposals to the government.[7]

---

[6] As quoted in Harris 1979: 6–8.

[7] The text of the Barunga statement is available at http://www.aiatsis.gov.au/lbry/dig_prgm/treaty/barunga.htm

The end result was that somehow, by the end of the decade, treaty had again gone off the national agenda and been replaced by the seemingly less frightening process of reconciliation in 1991.

In my view, it is no surprise that in the decade of fundamental change that was the nineties, treaty had again emerged at the end of the decade.

As I have noted in my recent *Social Justice Reports*, the period beginning with the reports of the Royal Commission into Aboriginal Deaths in Custody and the reconciliation process, have been a significant period of transformation in Australian history.[8] From deaths in custody to the creation of ATSIC, to *Mabo*,[9] the rejection of terra nullius and recognition of the ongoing connections of Indigenous cultures to land, to the *Native Title Act*,[10] Indigenous Land Fund and Social Justice Package proposals,[11] to the 1997 *Bringing them home* report,[12] the foundational myths of settlement and the reality of the history of Indigenous–non-Indigenous relations have been exposed and recognised once and for all.

We have now reached a point from which there is no turning back. Non-Indigenous Australians have been exposed to a version of history which wasn't taught in school and which has brought into question – in the most confronting way – the fundamental basis of their relationships with Indigenous people. We cannot underestimate the significance or importance of this.

But such recognition does not of itself solve the problems that have emerged throughout this history. In short, this recognition has sent us into a no-man's land. As I stated in my *Social Justice Report 2000*, it has exposed the fundamental contradiction at the heart of Australian society.[13] But what have we done, as a society, about this contradiction?

It is my firm belief that rather than acknowledging this contradiction, rather than acknowledging the harm, as a society we have simply put it into the too-hard basket with justifications about the level of 'uncertainty', the 'divisiveness' and the cost of addressing the issue.

And governments have gone to extraordinary, breathtaking lengths to maintain the status quo and prevent the leakage of any power back to Indigenous peoples.

We have seen the excision of the operation of Aboriginal heritage protection laws to allow development to go ahead at Hindmarsh Island (Hindmarsh Island Bridge Act 1997). In legal challenges to this action the federal government conceded that it believed that it was feasible that it could use the races power in the Constitution to introduce 'Nazi-style' laws, rather than that power being solely for laws which are purely beneficial in nature. Ultimately the Court did not resolve this issue, though it hinted strongly that this may indeed be the case.

We have seen the steadfast refusal of the federal government to comply with its human rights obligations by enforcing compliance of states and territories with such obligations by repealing racially discriminatory mandatory detention laws.

[8] Aboriginal and Torres Strait Islander Social Justice Commissioner 2000: 5–8.

[9] *Mabo and Ors v The State of Queensland (No 1)* (1988) 166 CLR 18; *Mabo and Ors v The State of Queensland (No 2)* (1992) 175 CLR 1.

[10] *Native Title Act 1993* (Cth).

[11] Aboriginal and Torres Strait Islander Social Justice Commissioner 1995, *Social Justice Report 1995*, HREOC, Sydney: chapter 5.

[12] HREOC 1997.

[13] Aboriginal and Torres Strait Islander Social Justice Commissioner 2000: 5.

We have seen the rejection of an holistic response to the stolen generations through the partial implementation of the recommendations of *Bringing them home*, the refusal to make reparation and the failure to engage in symbolic gestures of apology.

We have seen marginal improvements in the ratio of deaths in custody and increasing levels of over-representation, despite the constant commitment of governments to address these issues as matters of urgency.

And we have seen the introduction of racially discriminatory amendments to native title laws which have taken a system of checks and balances and re-oriented it away from providing lasting opportunities for Indigenous peoples.

As I said in my *Native Title Report 2001*, the native title system now aims to restrict rather than maximise the benefits to Indigenous peoples:

> As an embodiment of social relations, the native title system places Indigenous interests at a lower level than non-Indigenous interests, every time. As an embodiment of economic relations, the native title system removes Indigenous people's effective control over their only asset: exclusive rights to land and sea country. As an embodiment of political relations, native title fails to recognise traditional decision-making structures.[14]

And I must say that I do not share any optimism that agreement-making processes under the 1993 *Native Title Act* offer a de facto treaty making process. This is too simplistic and fundamentally ignores the point that the native title system as structured is one that is not based on equality and non-discrimination. It does not facilitate the full and effective participation of Indigenous people. It is not a respectful system.

Only when the native title system does provide real equality of opportunity – ranging from adequate, and equitable, resourcing of native title representatives through to the ability to negotiate over economic and development opportunities, through to processes which facilitate Indigenous governance rather than imposed management structures – can it aim to fulfill this broader role.

But to return to an issue I raised earlier, perhaps the greatest problem that we still face is the response to the ongoing, entrenched disadvantage of Indigenous people. So-called 'practical reconciliation' is a cruel illusion of equality, which in fact amounts to a perpetuation of the marginalisation and disadvantage of the past.

I have explored these issues in great detail in my *Social Justice Report 2000*, but to give a brief example – human rights principles relating to non-discrimination on the basis of race in the provision of economic, social and cultural rights – such as the rights to an adequate standard of living, to a minimum standard of health and education for example – provide that governments must take steps towards the 'progressive realization' of such rights.[15] They must identify that a particular issue is one of great priority and seek to address it with urgency and in such a way that the inequality gap is progressively reduced, *within the shortest possible timeframe.*

---

[14] Aboriginal and Torres Strait Islander Social Justice Commissioner 2001: 2

[15] See Aboriginal and Torres Strait Islander Social Justice Commissioner 2000: 24–5, and 2002: chapter 4.

The level of Indigenous marginalisation and disadvantage, and the enormous gap that exists compared to the non-Indigenous population on all measures of economic and social status indicate that addressing Indigenous marginalisation is unquestionably an issue of such magnitude. Yet where are solid commitments to reducing the gap, within the shortest possible timeframe? What are the targets? Where is the accountability?

Or as a member of the Committee on the Elimination of Racial Discrimination put it, why in a modern industrialised nation does less than 2% of the population continue to suffer such dire economic circumstances?[16]

The answer to each of these questions suggests that current progress is unacceptable. There needs to be a deeper appreciation, and an unqualified acceptance, of the simple fact that Indigenous marginalisation is historically derived and the result of systemic racism in this country. It also requires an unqualified commitment to redressing it and to achieving genuine equality with the rest of society. My *Social Justice Report 2000* provided 14 recommendations towards achieving this goal.[17] It also examines the social cost approach proposed by the Canadian Royal Commission into Aboriginal Peoples and the *Closing the gaps* approach adopted by the New Zealand government to similar issues.[18]

This is an issue that is legitimately the subject of negotiation with and commitments to Indigenous people by Australian governments. And it is a matter of fundamental importance for treaty.

I do not make these comments lightly. Nothing less than strong leadership and commitment by governments, and within our own communities, will resolve the often desperate conditions experienced by our peoples. But I want to draw together the two main themes of this presentation.

There are two types of rights that must be recognised for Indigenous peoples to be able to live equally in Australia. Those that are enjoyed by every Australian, including Aboriginal people, commonly referred to as citizenship rights; and those that are inherent to Indigenous people only.

Australia has had almost a decade to establish a fair and just system to allow the benefits of inherent rights to be enjoyed by Indigenous people. This has not eventuated.

Formal equality on its own is not enough. As a tool of social change it is inadequate and, indeed, entrenches the inequality that already exists. The problem is not that Aboriginal people were given equal rights and treated like everyone else. The problem is that these are the only rights that Aboriginal people were given. This type of formal equality is not enough to restore Aboriginal people to their rightful place as the first peoples of this country. We need to go further with rights. We need to adopt a rights approach that does have the capacity to transform social, economic and political relations in Australia.

I have, in my previous annual reports advocated two types of measures, based on rights, which have this capacity.[19] First, measures known as special measures, aimed at achieving equality, rather than assuming it; and second, the full recognition of Indigenous people's inherent rights, in particular native title.

49

---

[16] Aboriginal and Torres Strait Social Justice Commissioner 2000: 58.

[17] Aboriginal and Torres Strait Social Justice Commissioner 2000: 130–2.

[18] Aboriginal and Torres Strait Social Justice Commissioner 2000: 92.

[19] William Jonas was Aboriginal and Torres Strait Islander Social Justice Commissioner from 1999-2004

A combined approach, utilising these two types of rights, has not been adopted by any Australian government as a way of addressing the disadvantage it is designed to transform. When an opportunity did arise to recognise inherent rights through native title it was immediately encased in a legal armature that gave it no room to deliver real outcomes. Its capacity to provide economic opportunities for Indigenous people, to provide equal respect for Indigenous culture, to provide governance structures for Aboriginal communities has been severely limited through the Native Title Act and the common law. The proposal to implement special measures to overcome the destructive cultural, social and economic impact of dispossession with the full participation and consent of Indigenous people through the *Social Justice Package* was never pursued by any government.

For the third time in 30 years, Indigenous people have begun to look to a treaty as an all-encompassing way of addressing the deep contradictions that exist in our society. It will be difficult. But it will ultimately be easier, and I believe less costly, than the maintenance of the status quo which is clearly unsustainable. Let's get it right this time.

Acknowledgments

The author wishes to acknowledge the assistance of Dr Darren Dick in the preparation of this article

References

Aboriginal and Torres Strait Islander Social Justice Commissioner 2000, *Social Justice Report* 2000, Human Rights and Equal Opportunity Commission, Sydney, available at http://www.humanrights.gov.au/social_justice/sj_reports.html#00

—— 2001, *Native Title Report 2001*, Human Rights and Equal Opportunity Commission, Sydney, available at http:/www.humanrights.gov.au/social_justice/nt_reports.html#2001

—— 2002, *Social Justice Report 2002*, Human Rights and Equal Opportunity Commission, Sydney, available at http://www.humanrights.gov.au/social_justice/sj_reports.html#00

Aboriginal Treaty Committee 1979, 'We call for a treaty within Australia, between Australians' (advertisement), *National Times*, 25 August.

Australian Constitution, The

Barunga statement, 1988, available at http://www.aiatsis.gov.au/lbry/dig_prgm/treaty/barunga.htm

Chesterman, J and B Galligan 1998, *Citizens without rights – Aborigines and Australian citizenship*, Cambridge University Press, Cambridge.

Harris, Stewart 1979, '*Its coming yet … ' An Aboriginal treaty within Australia between Australians*, The Aboriginal Treaty Committee, Canberra.

Human Rights and Equal Opportunity Commission 1997, *Bringing them home*, HREOC, Sydney.

Patten, J (ed) 1938, *The Australian Call – The Voice of the Aborigine*, April, issue 1, 1.

Legislation

Native Title Act 1993 (Cth).

Native Title 1998

The political aspects of creating a treaty

Roderic Pitty

> What is needed is an instrument like the track of a cable railway, which
> allows movement forward but prevents any movement backward,
> when the engine of progress becomes too weak for the climb or
> breaks down. A treaty would be such a track *(Harris 1985: xv)*.

Introduction: two excuses for not having a treaty

The contemporary project of creating a treaty within Australia, yet with international standing, to recognise Indigenous peoples as original owners of this land has grown in significance in the last three decades, since it was raised in a modern political context by Jack Davis, then President of the Western Australian Aboriginal Association. Davis had sent a pamphlet to the Federal Council for the Advancement of Aborigines and Torres Strait Islanders (FCAATSI) which included a new proposal about the need for a treaty to be signed by leaders of European and Aboriginal communities. At that time Jack Horner was the FCAATSI secretary. He wrote to Davis in August 1969, saying his concerns about compensation for the denial of Aboriginal land rights had led to an interesting discussion at the FCAATSI executive meeting the previous month. Then Horner, speaking personally rather than for FCAATSI, suggested that the proposal for a treaty seemed 'rather unreal at present', because there was a political weakness in this otherwise good idea. The idea was necessary since it provided a way to establish 'a legal basis for land ownership' in Australia. The weakness was raised by Horner in a question: 'Where are the Aboriginal leaders to come from?' He wrote that, while 'leaders are coming forward', most were 'hand-picked', so 'it will mean hand-picking your treaty signatories'.[1] Yet who would do the picking, and for whom?

Davis continued to raise his treaty proposal in subsequent years. Horner recalls him doing so in 1972 at the FCAATSI conference in Alice Springs.[2] Around that time, in March 1972, Larrakia people of Darwin sent a petition to then Prime Minister, Billy McMahon, requesting that a treaty process be established. They said the government should appoint 'a Commission to go around to every tribe and work out a treaty to suit each tribe'. McMahon ignored the petition for months, then he replied that no Australian government would negotiate in this way with its subjects. He also said that treaties were not negotiated in Australia in the past because it had been too hard to find the right people to talk with.[3] McMahon used these excuses to avoid talking politically with Aboriginal people, while preparing to use his police to attack the Aboriginal Embassy outside Parliament House.

Those two excuses have been used ever since to keep the idea of a treaty negotiating justice for Indigenous peoples off every government's political agenda. The idea of a treaty is either dismissed as unthinkable in Australia, because cultural diversity is repressed by what James Tully has called the liberal imposition of uniformity, or else the political process of making a treaty is presented as impossible to create, because of too much division.[4] Expressed in terms

---

[1] Horner to Davis, 9 August 1969: 1.

[2] Interview with Jack Horner, 20 January 2005.

[3] Wright 1985: 14–15; Langton 2001: 21. For the political context, see Rowley 1978: 1–19.

[4] Tully 1995: 55, 198.

of repressing diversity while creating division, McMahon's excuses for not having a treaty are not logically consistent, but the politics of obstruction rarely is. The first excuse was reflected in Prime Minister Howard's comment that 'a nation … does not make a treaty with itself', made in response to the massive reconciliation march across Sydney Harbour Bridge in May 2000.[5] This excuse is essentially a nationalist belief, originally expressed in the racist idiom of White Australia, that there is only one nation in Australia, that all Australians should have only the same culture as a result of assimilation. In that view, every Indigenous tribe (or nation) has ceased to exist in any political sense, so no government is obliged to work out what each tribe (or historical group of Aboriginal communities) needs, through a process of genuine negotiation. Government just tries to isolate Indigenous people as individuals, treating them as if they are exactly like other Australians. Yet that means ignoring them as they really are, since politically they are not numerous as individuals, at least in most marginal seats. It also, as Pat Dodson has pointed out, means ignoring the enduring cultural and political reality of Australia, which comprises 'two sovereign people inhabiting one land'.[6]

Behind the pretence that the government cannot negotiate a treaty with only a part of the Australian nation is the real belief that Indigenous peoples politically are not worth negotiating with, since they lack electoral influence. Thus, the first excuse for not creating a treaty is actually about unequal power. The real political claim made by those who dispute the appropriateness of negotiating 'a treaty within Australia, between Australians' (as expressed by the Aboriginal Treaty Committee in the late 1970s),[7] is that no treaty will occur, because Indigenous peoples cannot force governments to act.

Whether that is an enduring reality is doubtful, despite all the steps backward by Howard in the past decade. His old objective is to impose assimilation, by claiming that all Australians must be treated as having just the same rights and responsibilities. Yet, if the policy choice between Nugget Coombs and Paul Hasluck has 'been settled for the time being in favour of Hasluck', as Pat Dodson worries is the case, this is not because of Howard's rhetoric.[8] It is just a result of his power. Howard thinks little differently to McMahon, but the connections between Australia and the outside world have changed in the past generation. Simply asserting that the Australian nation cannot negotiate with itself is no longer enough to stop calls for a treaty. More and more people are aware of international parallels, particularly in New Zealand and Canada, which show that such rhetoric is mischievous. Hence the second excuse for avoiding a treaty – that it's too hard to find the right people to talk with – is politically now more significant than the first. This is one reason behind the replacement of an elected Aboriginal representative body with a consultative committee chosen by government. It allows Howard to make the obstacles to a treaty seem insurmountable. Whereas Horner wondered about Aboriginal leaders gaining authority to speak not just for themselves but 'for whole groups', politicians opposed to a treaty have sought to ensure that there will never be such authority.[9]

While the abolition of the Aboriginal and Torres Strait Islander Commission (ATSIC) indicates the power that government retains over Aboriginal resources, it does not represent any new excuse for not having a treaty. ATSIC became involved in its last years in promoting the idea of a treaty to many Indigenous peoples across Australia, through workshops, a think tank and a national conference.[10] Its demise does not change the political challenges of creating

---

[5] Quoted in Brennan et al 2005: 70.

[6] P Dodson 2005b: 3.

[7] Harris 1979: 12; Rowse 1997: 218.

[8] P Dodson 2005a: 7. Howard's rhetoric asserts assimilation by denying the historical context of the present situation of Aborigines, but it does not focus on the future. See Behrendt 2003a: 3–6.

[9] Horner to Davis, p 1. See also O'Shane 1991: 148–9.

[10] See ATSIC/AIATSIS 2003.

a treaty, although it poses challenges for Aboriginal peoples.[11] Despite reduced access to services for communities, ATSIC's disappearance might even clarify what needs to be done, to gain the political position of authority from which a treaty can be negotiated. When the Larrakia people proposed in 1972 an investigative Commission created by government to formulate suitable treaties to be put to members of each tribe for their consent, they presumed not only authority on the part of the tribes, but a complementary authority and commitment to the process on the part of government. No doubt their experience with elections since then has highlighted the complexities of creating a treaty, particularly in view of 'non-core promises' made by politicians, such as Bob Hawke's 1988 affirmation of a treaty at Barunga.[12] Yet, governments come and go, and social attitudes change. This leads to new opportunities for creating the instrument for real progress towards Indigenous justice. For these to be realised, there must be a growing consensus about what the treaty project seeks to do. The following analysis attempts a summary in broad terms of the key premises, form, purpose, substance and process of a treaty, in order to assess the potential that exists for making a treaty real. The analysis proceeds from the simpler to the more complex issues.

Basic premises: why a treaty is necessary and feasible

There are two key premises on which the need for a treaty is based: 1) an agreement should have been made by the colonisers when they first arrived in other peoples' lands, since they were instructed to do this and this was clearly the proper thing to do according to international law;[13] and 2) despite centuries of opposition to Aboriginal peoples' autonomy, the Australian state has not eliminated a distinct Indigenous political domain. Both points need to be accepted for negotiating a treaty to make sense, but the second premise is arguably much more important than the first. The first premise is just historical, whereas the second is current. They are connected, and the importance of each is reflected in a reference to ATSIC by the New Zealand scholar Paul McHugh,[14] in his magisterial comparative analysis of legal aspects of the re-emergence of Indigenous self-determination in former British colonies, *Aboriginal Societies and the Common Law*.

McHugh says ATSIC's structure did not transcend the 'two fundamental features of Crown sovereignty in Australia'. These, he says, 'were, first, the absence of any formal Aboriginal consent to Crown sovereignty by way of treaty, which related, secondly, to the absence of a history of sustained political relations [with Indigenous peoples] typical of the other jurisdictions', such as New Zealand and North America. He describes the Howard government as having a 'more ruthless approach to Aboriginal relations' than Australian governments since McMahon, but suggests that it has not managed to return to the old denial of the reality of Aboriginal peoples as politically distinct entities within Australia.[15] Thus, an international observer sees the second premise as substantial.

The first premise is beyond dispute. Much has been written about how the English colonisers were told and failed to obtain 'the consent of the natives'. If this tragedy is not yet the key story

---

[11] P Dodson 2005a: 9.

[12] Recorded in *Land Rights News* 1988; see Langton 2001: 23; O'Shane 1991: 153.

[13] For Governor Phillip's instructions 'to live in amity and kindness' with the natives see McHugh 2004:159, and 111 for the relevant British practice of international law.

[14] McHugh 2004.

[15] McHugh 2004: 343, 365, 504. See also Stanner's 1972 statement (quoted in Barwick 1988: 11) about 'two necessary admissions', that settlers 'injured Aboriginal society and owe just recompense to its living members', and that this must be done by recognising their rights not by acts of charity.

of our school texts, it is well known in the Aboriginal oral history of what 'Cook' did not do.[16] Yet, without the second premise, such historical knowledge would lead to regret, not to action and reparation. As Langton and Palmer point out, it is the continued existence of Aboriginal polities that indicates the real potential for a broader and more enduring settlement, which could prevent another government-imposed reversal.[17] The present government is trying hard to eliminate distinctive Aboriginal social and political life by reducing Aborigines to mere dependent and marginalised consumers, but previous governments have failed to attain this ruinous aim, and there is less likelihood now of systemic destruction. A distinct but compressed Aboriginal political arena remains alive, if not well, despite all the pressures of forced 'political assimilation' by liberal democracy and punitive paternalism to which Aboriginal peoples remain subject.[18] Consequently, it is feasible and necessary to seek an agreement, that is, a treaty, to respect the integrity of this autonomous Aboriginal life.

There are two important ways in which the strength of the second premise for a treaty has been demonstrated in recent decades, since the idea of a treaty was raised after the 1967 referendum. First, the High Court's decision in *Mabo v Queensland (No 2)*[19] not only highlighted the historical lack of Indigenous consent but also the continuing need to negotiate that today. This was stressed by Kevin Gilbert in a letter to Prime Minister Keating in 1992. He pointed out that, without a treaty, Australia continues to lack 'a lawful basis of Sovereignty', which can be obtained only through a genuine negotiation 'on Aboriginal terms, with care and respect for the rights and humanity of all in this land, including the land'.[20] Ultimately the disappointment of native title cannot be resolved through the courts, but only by a political settlement. The bureaucratic and judicial obstacles to native title have created much conflict. Yet what has emerged from the disappointment is a clearer sense that Aboriginal polities have retained what Lester-Irabinna Rigney has called an 'inherent jurisdiction', which 'is an original source of authority' not based at all on Australia's colonial constitution.[21] The conservative trend of the High Court since *Mabo* highlights the continuing need for a treaty, that is, an agreement which can prevent hard-won Aboriginal land rights from 'continually being wound back and undermined'.[22] While the resistance to attacks on inherent land rights has failed in the courts and parliament, it has shown that Aboriginal leaders continue to demand negotiations, and are wary of being tricked. This creates a basis for going beyond native title, towards a settlement or a treaty framework that depends on political rather than legal decisions.

Second, the significance of Aboriginal negotiating authority has generally become clearer as a result of comparisons with other countries and international treaty-making. Australia is peculiar historically in not having made and broken domestic treaties. Yet because of this survival of an Aboriginal political domain, the core of which has always been the attempt to recreate dimensions of self-determination, it is not really so different from other settler colonies such as New Zealand and Canada.[23] This similarity has become increasingly evident as a result of two decades of international campaigning by Aborigines and Torres Strait Islanders together with other Indigenous Peoples at the UN. What is distinct about Australia is the extreme reluctance of politicians to create a framework for equal negotiations with Indigenous peoples about their future relationship with the Australian state. It is difficult to change such recalcitrance, but

---

16 Rose 1984, 1991.

17 Langton and Palmer 2003: 43; 2004: 43–9.

18 Stokes 2002: 206–9. For an earlier discussion of the Aboriginal domain see Rowse 1992: 18–43.

19 (1992) 175 CLR.

20 Gilbert 1995: 372, 374.

21 Rigney 2003: 74.

22 Ross 2001: 154.

23 Stokes 2002: 206.

there are political lessons from recent attitudinal changes among politicians in New Zealand and parts of Canada. As well as particular models of contemporary treaty-making and ways to keep governments accountable which have relevance for Australia,[24] the broad lesson is that, eventually, as a result of much agitation and pressure for genuine negotiations, there has been a willingness by some politicians to talk with Indigenous peoples who claim and assert alternative sources of authority, outside the governmental domain. There has also been much reluctance, expressed in New Zealand in attempts by government to limit what can be negotiated through financial pressure, but, despite that, there has been little support for denying Indigenous authority by assimilation.[25] It is no wonder that the current Australian government has tried to keep quiet its responses to international criticism by the UN committee which has been looking at compliance with the *Convention on Eliminating Racial Discrimination*, since this interaction raises clear parallels with developments elsewhere.[26]

Those sceptical about or opposed to creating a treaty in principle either dispute the existence of a distinct Indigenous political domain, or do not believe that creating a treaty will address urgent social problems. The latter objection, raised during the 1980s by Pat O'Shane, now looks less convincing given the worse health of Aborigines compared to Maori in the past generation.[27] A direct link has to be made between demands for a treaty and the urgent social needs of Indigenous people, as stressed by Darryl Cronin and also the National Indigenous Youth Movement of Australia.[28] This would answer the main real objection raised to creating a treaty, which is that it would not improve Indigenous peoples' lives.[29] Yet a treaty/agreement is about establishing a partnership, so the crucial foundation is accepting a partner's independent authority, and essential needs. If the existence of an enduring Indigenous polity is acknowledged, genuine dialogue becomes possible concerning all the complex aspects of creating a treaty and thus meeting these needs through a partnership, not denying them through conflict. This is a political not a judicial matter. In isolation, it has occasionally received an affirmative response even from conservative politicians (for example, statements about the need to accept aspects of continuing customary law to gain the respect of Indigenous youth). Yet the failure of all governments to accept Indigenous self-determination in practice has contributed to the dismal outcome of many official programmes, particularly in health and reducing the incarceration of Indigenous people. So the argument for creating a treaty must contrast the current denial of Aboriginal social justice with an affirmation of the two premises outlined: the colonisers should have made a political agreement with Indigenous peoples, and the continued existence of an Aboriginal polity.

Essential form: coherent and binding clarity

While these historical and contemporary premises mean that creating a treaty is feasible, it does not follow that any conceivable treaty would be an appropriate agreement. Whether a particular treaty that may in future be negotiated is advisable for both parties will depend on the nature and terms characteristic of the specific agreement. During the first phase of widespread discussion about a treaty, in the early 1980s, questions were asked about whether both parties would be interested in creating a treaty. One non-Aboriginal proponent of a treaty, Peter Read, asked directly if Aboriginal peoples would be interested in an agreement that somehow transferred

---

[24] Behrendt 2003b: 22–4; McGlade 2003: 127, 135.

[25] Kawharu 2005: vi; Mutu 2005: 203–4; M Durie 1998a: 132, 190–4, 212; McHugh 1997: 203.

[26] Marr 2005.

[27] Central Australian Aboriginal Congress 2002: 3; see O'Shane 1991: 147, 155.

[28] Cronin 2003: 164; NIYMA 2003: 108–10; Brennan et al 2005:10. For a regional emphasis on this link, see Yu 2001.

[29] O'Shane 1991, noted in McGlade 2003: 130. See the diagram in Behrendt 2003a: 124.

sovereignty (or historical legitimacy) from themselves to the Australian government, whatever they get in return. He commented that, 'it may, indeed, be in the interests of white people to seek a treaty now to legitimise their own place in Australia', but suggested that 'at present it does not seem to be in the black interest', because it is not clear how they will benefit from the deal.[30] This was the essential reason for O'Shane's scepticism about a treaty. The problem was noted by Coombs, one of the leading proponents of a treaty, who acknowledged that Aborigines may 'refuse to negotiate a settlement which confers legitimacy at any price' on Australian institutions which in their experience do not deserve this, until there is fundamental change.[31] The challenge of creating a treaty is to work out a genuine agreement that states clearly what must change for Australian institutions to deserve legitimacy in Aboriginal eyes.

Part of the difficulty in creating a treaty is that a gap often exists in the broad justifications for a treaty as presented by Indigenous peoples and settlers. There is a risk that the different parties to a treaty are 'talking past each other', rather than engaging in productive dialogue. This is a major problem that has characterised Indigenous–settler relations in New Zealand as well as Australia.[32] One summary of this problem by Rowse (following from McHugh) outlines the stereotypical positions as follows:

> Leaders of the settler nation look to their treaty as a contract
> which *rules off the past* and legitimises the nation. Leaders of the
> Indigenous people strongly resist closure of the present and future
> from the past which created them. Leaders of the settler nation find
> it difficult to entertain signing a treaty which acknowledges and
> perpetuates Indigenous sovereignty. Leaders of indigenous people
> may not commit themselves to a strong legal and political notion of
> sovereignty, but they are keen to reserve a moral notion of sovereignty,
> a notion which resists codification and finalisation and which assures
> them a practice of permanent critique (emphasis added).[33]

The contrast may be starker than that, because many Indigenous people would reject as second-class a merely 'moral' notion of sovereignty, as if they cannot qualify for legal and political respect for their own authority. The extensive debate concerning Article 3 of the UN *Draft Declaration on the Rights of Indigenous Peoples* (affirming self-determination without any qualification) shows that such distinctions are unlikely to be helpful for the task of generating agreement about a treaty. Nevertheless, Rowse warns against accepting the above stereotypes as unchanging positions, since that would obscure the potential for overcoming this cultural gap.[34]

What is required to bridge that gap is initially an agreement on the essential form of a treaty, which then makes possible further agreement on the more complex issues concerning the purpose and substance of any treaty. The formal aspect of a treaty should not be ignored, just because the issues of purpose and substance are likely to be more contentious and complex. Indeed, it is precisely because of those larger difficulties that an initial agreement about the form is crucial, since it would provide a way of avoiding the stereotypes of cross-cultural misunderstanding. The broad importance of the form of a treaty can be shown with reference

---

[30] Quoted in Rowse 1997: 221.

[31] Rowse 1997: 222.

[32] Metge and Kinloch 1978.

[33] Rowse 1997: 222–3. For an international commentary, see Coates 1998: 45, 74–6.

[34] Rowse 1997: 223.

to Kevin Gilbert's poem 'A Question to God', in which a child asks why 'grant a weak man eyes', the magnificent gift of sight, when all they are used for is to 'falsely judge' by prejudice, polluting their potential 'by a lack of love'.[35] The form of a treaty must be clear enough to withstand prejudice. While any treaty could be, and probably will be, subjected to much wilful misunderstanding propagated by those opposed to Aboriginal justice, the form of a treaty is vital to its capacity to survive all such political attacks.

The form of a treaty is distinct from its substance or content, that is, the particular rights and responsibilities it affirms, in the sense that many different particular or potential agreements could be made, all of which comprise the same formal structure. Thus the form of a treaty logically needs to be accepted and agreed upon prior to consideration of content and substance. The significance of the crucial formal elements of a treaty is that they mean the agreement has the potential to be enduring, and be relied upon so that any misunderstandings concerning content do not destroy the legitimacy of the agreement as a whole. Thus the form of a treaty is most closely related to its enduring purpose, the objective or broad social aim that it seeks to establish.

There are at least three vital elements of a properly formed treaty: 1) the commitments must be voluntarily accepted and thereafter upheld; 2) the substantive rights must be clearly expressed and comprehensive; and 3) there must be consistency and complementarity in this expression. Each of the elements is important. Without all of them, a treaty could be vulnerable to abuse, or wilful neglect or misinterpretation. However, it is worth remembering that creating a treaty is a political process, which will be subject to much opposition, particularly by people with resources and power who are opposed to Aboriginal justice. The strength of a properly formed treaty is that it could survive such attacks, because a consensus about the treaty's essential form would make it of enduring significance. In this respect, there are lessons for Australia from New Zealand history concerning how the 1840 Treaty of Waitangi has retained a core meaning despite many attempts since then from settlers (including, in 1877, the highest government-appointed judge in the land) to literally nullify it.[36] That treaty was conducted in Maori but the English version contained a fundamental change in meaning, shifting what was a genuine exchange into an apparent act of submission. Yet the original version has survived all attempts at nullification and served as a beacon for attempts to create cross-cultural understanding in New Zealand during the past generation. The significance of that experience for Australia is not that the Treaty of Waitangi has been a solid protection of Maori rights, which many Maori would dispute, but rather that it has provided an enduring focus across the generations for Maori efforts to assert their right to self-determination.

The first crucial aspect of a properly formed treaty is that it is not just a symbolic gesture (such as a token reference in a new preamble to the Australian Constitution, supposedly without any legal consequences). There will of course be much symbolism in a treaty, but it would be misplaced without substantive commitments of a binding nature upon the parties. This key element was highlighted by Coombs and others in the Aboriginal Treaty Committee. They sought a real institutional change in how Australian politicians treat Indigenous peoples, not any tokenism. Thus, 'as Coombs was keen to explain, a treaty would provide *a formal change* in Aboriginal status within the Australian system of government, to the *effect* that any legislation inconsistent with the principles of the treaty could be *challenged*'.[37] A genuine treaty must 'give

---

35 Gilbert 1991: 89.   36 Kawharu 2005: vi.   37 Rowse 1997: 220–1 (emphasis added).

rise to binding obligations' that could not be later renounced by a government at whim.[38] This means any treaty would have to have more enduring force than mere Commonwealth legislation (such as the *Racial Discrimination Act*)[39] which can be disregarded by subsequent legislation (which occurred with the passage of the *Native Title Act*).[40] Otherwise a treaty would become easily discredited in Aboriginal eyes and not achieve any substantial effect.

There are other implications from this aspect of the binding nature of commitments created by treaty. Coombs explored some of these in arguing for an essential international dimension of a treaty, which he said could usefully be seen as an 'act of self-determination' supervised by the UN.[41] This raises issues of process, which will be discussed further later. Here it is worth emphasising the importance of the voluntary nature of the commitments made in a treaty. This issue was raised in the Aboriginal Treaty Committee's newsletter in the early 1980s by H Sculthorpe, an Indigenous Tasmanian, who commented that any acknowledgement of white property rights by Aborigines in a treaty would be 'made under duress and for the lack of a viable alternative'.[42] A broadly similar issue has arisen in New Zealand, concerning Maori responses to government efforts to impose a fiscal cap on compensation for historical breaches of the Treaty of Waitangi by the Crown. The overwhelming Maori response to this government policy has been to point out that any agreements made under such duress can not be considered 'full and final' and might well lead to subsequent Maori claims in the future.[43] This is not necessarily a problem for Maori who traditionally take the past with them into their future, but it does pose a challenge for any government pretending that a treaty will finally resolve the historical legacy of past dispossession. If a government is genuinely interested in negotiating a treaty, it should be concerned to ensure that the agreement is entered into voluntarily by both parties, since otherwise there is unlikely to be any transformation in the status of Indigenous peoples, and the conflict that the treaty was to resolve would be perpetuated into future generations rather than reduced.

The second essential formal element of a treaty is that it contain a very clear expression of the rights and responsibilities that both parties have agreed to respect. This requirement is connected logically with the previous one, since without clarity in the expression of a treaty then the commitments that it is meant to enshrine could be readily avoided. Thus there is a crucial need for honesty in what is being sought and obtained through a treaty. While this point was emphasised by the Chief Justice of Western Australia, David Malcolm (see this volume), it does not follow that lawyers, or the legal form of expression, is something that no treaty can do without. This may sound strange, because international treaties are professionally the creation of lawyers, for whom they often have more significance than for politicians. Yet the most enduring and significant of international treaties, such as international human rights conventions, are not merely the creation of lawyers. Furthermore, any international treaties which have a double-standard embedded in them – or, more accurately, which are often misinterpreted in a hypocritical way by the powerful to force others to change – are at risk of losing their binding nature, because the original bargain is no longer being respected (as is occurring with the Nuclear Non-Proliferation Treaty, with potentially catastrophic consequences). Because the political process of reaching and maintaining a treaty will be subject to misunderstanding and much opposition, it is important that these risks be reduced through clear and concise commitments.

---

[38] Barwick 1988: 9.

[39] *1975* (Cth).

[40] *1993* (Cth).

[41] Coombs 1994: 208, 210, 226–9.

[42] Rowse 1997: 221.

[43] Mutu 2005: 203-4; see also M Durie 1998a: 132.

The third essential aspect of a successfully formed treaty is that all the commitments by the respective parties are consistent and complementary. The coherence of a treaty is a vital element of its form, so that all the parts of the treaty work together and are not contradictory. This requirement means it that is very important that any compromises or concessions judged necessary to achieve a treaty politically are not made at the expense of diminishing the treaty's integrity and dynamic capacity. In other words, the different commitments made by government and by Indigenous peoples in a treaty must be mutually reinforcing, and not oppositional.

This crucial element of coherence is closely related to the previous two aspects of a treaty's form. This can be seen in the Treaty of Waitangi, which contains three basic articles. These guarantee, in the succinct paraphrase of Eddie Durie, a senior Maori judge and head of the Waitangi Tribunal for two decades, 'governorship for the Crown, autonomy for Maori, and citizenship for all'. Durie, a lawyer, stressed the importance of the concise phrasing of the articles and their coherence for the Treaty of Waitangi's endurance as a 'living document', despite a long history of neglect by government of its responsibilities under the Treaty.[44]

There is another, unwritten fourth article affirming respect for Indigenous as well as non-Indigenous religion.[45] This highlights two crucial aspects of the Treaty of Waitangi: first, that each article only makes sense as part of a genuine partnership between settlers and Maori, and secondly, that the treaty is 'authority for the proposition that the law of the country would have its source in two streams'.[46] What the Treaty of Waitangi established was a basis for a bicultural political relationship, albeit one dominated by the pressures and legacies of colonisation. The relationship emerges from 'the reconciliation of two potentially conflicting sets of expectations, not the imposition of the norms of one party upon the other', because the treaty's fundamental principle is to ensure 'a flexible partnership'.[47]

Enduring purpose: renewing self-determination

In order for a treaty to provide a framework for such an enduring partnership, it must be capable of appropriate reinterpretation in terms of common values or a joint purpose, which the parties to the treaty share. Yet, because of the influence of stereotypical perspectives about 'moving on' from the past noted above, such a common purpose will be difficult to create in Australia. It has to be created politically and cannot be presumed to exist, as the rejection by McMahon of the Larrakia petition (and the later failure of Labor governments to conclude any alternative agreement) demonstrate. Whereas a consensus about the premises of a treaty should be achievable without much difficulty, and an understanding of the importance of the essential formal aspects of a treaty might be reached quickly, questions of a common purpose or vision pose direct challenges. This is because state (as well as federal) governments have continued to operate pragmatically, with little vision of a cooperative and inspiring future. Again, the lesson from New Zealand is that the purpose of a treaty is 'about the future more than the past', which means that it is not mainly about ensuring adequate compensation for colonial wrongs (which is impossible), but 'planning a future' together based on creating new living relationships in this land.[48]

This potential purpose of a treaty has at least two crucial elements: 1) enabling a new partnership by sharing power with Indigenous peoples; and 2) valuing Indigenous heritage

---

[44] E Durie 1991: 156, 165.

[45] E Durie 1996: 460.

[46] E Durie 1996: 460–1; see the discussion in D Williams 2005: 375–83.

[47] J Williams 1991: 192; Coombs 1994: 147, noted in Rowse 1997: 223.

[48] M Durie 1998b: 190, 193; see also Jones 2005.

dynamically through cultural renewal. In some respects, much of what the Council for Aboriginal Reconciliation tried to achieve from 1991 to 2000 relates to these points, although critics who thought that the issue of a treaty deserved more explicit attention earlier in the process of public education and community outreach have now been vindicated.[49] Public opinion is notoriously difficult to estimate accurately concerning such a complex political matter, but one fact that appears clear is a large generational difference in the attitudes of non-Indigenous Australians to a treaty. A telephone opinion poll in August 2001 found overall support for a treaty at 52%, but a higher percentage of those aged 25–39 years (59%), and a much higher percentage of those under 25 years (74%), in contrast to about a third (35%) of those aged 55 years and above.[50] Those figures are the result of a general opinion survey, reflecting little exposure to the issues involved in a treaty, with the government trying to dismiss it from the political agenda using the old epithet, 'separatism'.[51] While only broadly indicative, those figures suggest that an orientation to the future is an essential dimension of creating a politically viable treaty.

The first crucial element of a future oriented perspective is the need for power-sharing between government and Indigenous peoples. This is at the heart of the difficult political process of creating a treaty, as Michael Mansell has made clear. Reviewing various statements from two inquiries in the early 1990s about the need to empower Aboriginal people, he says:

> These [inquiries] point out that taking decision making away from Indigenous peoples is a major part of the problem. The logic is that a treaty must look at political self-rule. If there are to be limits of self-rule, those limits should be negotiated, not imposed.[52]

Further, Mansell highlights the paradigm shift that needs to occur in relations between governments and Indigenous peoples by claiming that a treaty worth having would involve a new dimension of equality in Australia. This is because, in his view, a treaty must be a political (not a welfare or social service) compromise, and 'a political settlement recognises that Indigenous peoples are not coming to the negotiating table as defeated people but as sovereigns: emphasising *equality of scale with government*, not with other individuals'.[53] Like Maori intellectuals in New Zealand, Mansell argues that, while issues of 'restitution for the original owners' are crucial to a treaty, any compensation or reparation in a treaty must be seen, not as closing off the past, but as part of 'a focus on the future'.[54] Without a shift to a paradigm of negotiating self-determination equally with governments, Mansell argues that a treaty could not be justifiable.

The difficulty of achieving this paradigm shift and empowerment is partly a result of the influence of the stereotypical perspectives about the past, present and future sources of legitimacy noted above. Sovereignty is presumed by governments (and by even the more radical of judges on the High Court, such as Kirby J) as indivisibly belonging to the Crown. Yet, as Coombs emphasised, since governmental authority in Australia has long been divided federally, it is not conceptually difficult to imagine a negotiated sovereignty with Indigenous peoples deriving from a treaty.[55] It is obviously difficult to get governments to treat with Indigenous peoples on an equal constitutional basis, given how Australian governments negotiate among themselves.[56]

---

49 For a review of the council's outcomes, see Brennan et al 2005: 18–22.

50 Snapshot of a Nation, *Age*, 8 October 2001: 11 (reporting an opinion poll of 9 and 15 August.)

51 Metherell and Peatling 2001.

52 Mansell 2003: 11.

53 Mansell 2003: 15 (emphasis added). See also Ross 2001: 154, 157, and Behrendt 2003a: 54–5.

54 Mansell 2003: 16, 17; compare M Durie 2005 and Jones 2005.

55 Coombs 1994: 150, 206–9; see also J Williams 1991: 195; Renwick 1991: 209–18; Brennan et al 2005:74.

56 See Brennan et al 2005: 31–2, 45–6.

But the metaphor of 'two streams' joining to form a flowing river, used by Durie J in New Zealand and Pat Dodson in Australia, conveys that such power-sharing involves not the threat of separatism but a promise of coexistence and partnership in the future.[57]

Achieving progress in the central agenda of power-sharing is likely to depend on a related shift in attitudes by governments on the issue of Indigenous cultural *revival*. Unfortunately, the way in which native title has been dealt with in Australia, through narrowly-based litigation in the courts, has compounded rather than reduced the obstacles to such a shift. This can be seen most clearly in Justice Kirby's judgement in the *Fejo* case.[58] This involved a claim by Larrakia people for a restoration of traditional title over lands around Darwin which were, in part, granted to a settler in 1882 then resumed by the Crown in 1928 and used first as a quarantine station, then as a leprosarium until 1980. Justice Kirby agreed with the rest of the High Court in ruling that, once 'extinguished', native title over what was then unused Crown land could not be revived, even though he accepted that the Aboriginal custom on which the traditional title would be based 'may still' exist. His reason was that, otherwise, there would be 'a serious element of uncertainty' introduced into Australian land law. Thus the Larrakia people, who petitioned government for a treaty several years before that land became vacant, could not get their traditional land rights recognised after *Mabo* because this potentially challenges too many non-Indigenous interests. This example shows clearly why a treaty that establishes a new political relationship of equality between governments and Indigenous peoples is essential. Without it, Indigenous peoples are at risk of having their cultures defined in the same way as the High Court defined native title, as a 'fragile' thing that one old, exhausted grant to a long gone settler necessarily 'blows away' from existing 'forever'.[59]

There is a world of difference between the findings of the High Court in a particular case and the existence of cultural diversity, as the *Yorta Yorta* case demonstrated most disappointingly.[60] One tragic irony of that case is that a Labor government in Victoria disputed the real process of Indigenous cultural survival and customary renewal two decades after conservative historians and politicians such as Geoffrey Blainey and Jeffrey Kennett had accepted a dynamic view of Indigenous culture (in submissions to the Law Reform Commission's inquiry into Aboriginal customary law).[61] Thus the contested and fraught character of native title litigation has contributed to a conflation of two very different things: the continued renewal of Indigenous custom (which Kirby did not doubt in the Larrakia case), and the ability of governments to negotiate politically with those renewing custom. A treaty is needed to remove that conflation, by recognising that Indigenous self-determination should keep on being renewed. Guidance about that purpose should be sought not from any Australian courts, but rather from the revival of Indigenous culture in art.

Principles of substance: recognising Indigenous rights

A political acknowledgement by government of the survival of dynamic and evolving Indigenous traditions is a crucial foundation for adequately defining the substantive content of a treaty. Issues of content are often discussed under the heading 'unfinished business', particularly as

---

[57] E Durie 1996: 461; P Dodson 1996; Behrendt 2003a: 107–8. Dodson's metaphor, deriving from a traditional meeting of fresh and salt water, is powerful given the massive need to revive river flows.

[58] (1998) 156 ALR 721.

[59] (1998) 156 ALR 721 at 757–60.

[60] (2003) 214 CLR.

[61] Pitty 1999: 49–52; For Yorta Yorta perspectives on the renewal of tradition, see Harvey 2003.

a result of the inconclusive nature of the 1990s reconciliation period.[62] This phrase is meant to convey the difficulty in getting the government to negotiate about the content of a treaty, rather than a difficulty in broadly identifying the main issues that must be negotiated. Mick Dodson has observed that 'identifying what we are talking about so far as unfinished business is concerned is not going to be too difficult because most of the work has already been done', but 'generating national collective political will to implement the agenda is the real difficulty'.[63] This suggests that there are two complementary aspects to defining the content of a treaty: 1) recognition of Indigenous peoples as first peoples with distinct rights; and 2) agreement on how governments must act to respect those rights.[64] Both aspects are equally important and would need to be specified when the content of a treaty is being formulated. Dodson also emphasises the need for the negotiation process to 'have the flexibility to allow for new or more specific issues to be identified for negotiation in the future'.[65] Flexibility is important but it needs to be clearly defined. What is being sought is not any kind of flexibility, but rather only the flexibility that would enable an existing partnership, created by a treaty, to be further developed and extended into new areas. This is very different from the flexibility that many governments are used to, that is expediency. The challenge in identifying the principles of substance to be included in a treaty is that of creating an instrument for flexible progress, not regress, as suggested in Stewart Harris's image of a device for climbing up hills.

There have been several historic attempts by Aboriginal peoples, such as the 1988 Barunga statement, to outline to government the range of core issues that would need to be included in a treaty. Larissa Behrendt has analysed these and summarised the key Indigenous demands thus:

- Recognition of past injustices
- Autonomy and decision-making
- Property rights and compensation
- Protection of cultural practices and customary laws
- Equal protection of rights.[66]

She comments about the Barunga statement that it 'is a combination of claims for special treatment and equal rights, underlined by a strong demand for control of decision-making processes'.[67] Essentially those demands have been repeated in various formulations for twenty years. Behrendt shows that they substantially overlap with what Indigenous people in Australia understand by asserting Indigenous sovereignty. She also emphasises that the demands are interdependent, so that a treaty would not be adequate without including all of them outlined in substance.[68]

Behrendt's analysis demonstrates that there is a strong basis for consensus amongst Indigenous peoples within Australia about the essential, necessary components of a worthwhile treaty. Particularly because of how the promises concerning native title in the early 1990s (such as substantial compensation and an effective social justice package) subsequently evaporated in the hot air of non-Aboriginal recalcitrance, it is unlikely that future aspirants for national

---

[62] See M Dodson 2003: 30–2; P Dodson 2000: 12–19.

[63] M Dodson 2003: 31.

[64] M Dodson 2003: 32.

[65] M Dodson 2003: 39.

[66] Behrendt 2003a: 123; see her discussion in chapter 4. Compare P Dodson 2000: 17–18; see also Brennan et al 2005: 131–4.

[67] Behrendt 2003a: 89.

[68] Behrendt 2003a: 115–6.

Aboriginal leadership would propose a framework for resolving unfinished business with government that is less demanding than the above summary. Indeed, scepticism about any government's capacity to deliver on all of these demands is strong. The historian and poet Tony Birch expresses such scepticism directly:

> I couldn't imagine any Aboriginal person sitting at a table and signing
> a document with a non-Aboriginal government, at the moment,
> and see it as having any realistic basis, *no matter what it says* ...
> I would rather see something happen first before I saw any signing
> of documents (emphasis added). [69]

This comment reflects the lack of trust at a political, rather than a social, level that has resulted from three decades of broken promises. However, it is significant that Birch's reason for critical caution relates not to any doubt about the content of what should be agreed, but rather to whether any government could be trusted with an agreement. Yet ironically, that is a crucial reason for obtaining a treaty, so that promises are no longer broken with the arrogance of power. While Birch comments that 'Maori people have suffered a lot' since the Treaty of Waitangi was signed, which is true, there is a strong Maori consensus about the need in New Zealand to 'affirm the constitutional inviolability of the Treaty'.[70]

There is no such consensus in Australia, and that remains the basic reason for the comparatively much worse position of Indigenous peoples here (in terms of rights and social conditions) than in other settler states. In specific situations, such as the hostility of state governments to native title, there is clearly a large gap between the basic Aboriginal demands for justice and the current policies of those governments. That is a major reason why, for all the difficulty of reaching a national treaty agreement, it is essential. Regional and local initiatives are vital. They can fit within what Mick Dodson has called 'a national treaty framework model, which allows for treaty-making on a national, state-wide or local basis'.[71] Yet it must by now be clear that national leadership is required to initiate a shift towards power-sharing with Indigenous peoples. Otherwise, as Mansell points out, all that will be negotiated is the delivery of services. Further, without a national Indigenous agenda of renewing self-determination, any failure of negotiations would mean 'the government gets what it wants, with or without a treaty'.[72] Indeed, as Behrendt and others insist, it is the 'inherent power imbalance between the parties' that is the major obstacle to successfully negotiating a treaty.[73] This is why negotiations about the substantive principles of a treaty must occur at a national level, with no veto exercised by state governments, although specific agreements could be made regionally or about specific issues while negotiations proceed.[74]

In 2005 the main problem with creating a treaty in Australia seems to be a reverse of the problem that Jack Horner wondered about in 1969. The question that Horner asked was 'where are the Aboriginal leaders to come from?' That may still be asked, and answered by Aboriginal people as they struggle to create a more representative replacement for ATSIC.[75] The question now could be phrased as 'where are the European leaders to come from?' In the public arena of the past decade, only on one occasion has a non-Aboriginal leader (albeit not a

63

---

[69] Quoted (from interview on 23 January 2003) in Behrendt 2003a: 108.

[70] Behrendt 2003a: 108; M Durie 1998a: 213.

[71] M Dodson 2003: 32.

[72] Mansell 2003: 14. See also Cronin 2003: 164.

[73] Behrendt 2003b: 27; Rigney 2003: 86; NIYMA 2003: 113.

[74] Behrendt 2003b: 26, 28.

[75] See the diagram of a possible Sovereign Aboriginal Congress inside the cover of Gilbert 1993.

party political one) ever outlined a response to the common Aboriginal demands summarised above. This was done in August 1996 by Sir William Deane, as Governor-General, in his inaugural Lingiari lecture, 'Some Signposts from Daguragu'. These signposts were marked out to draw some broader lessons from the return of land to the Gurindji after a long struggle. Deane emphasised the need to acknowledge past injustice, linking this to current inequality, and the need for reparations and respect for the developing Indigenous cultures. He called for 'a partnership between the nation as a whole and the Aboriginal and Torres Strait Islander peoples' in which they 'play a major active role'. He also noted that only a demonstrated commitment by government to resolving all 'the terrible problems oppressing' these peoples today could create 'the mutual trust necessary for true consensus about the future'.[76] Deane noted that areas of disagreement would arise about when such a consensus might be reached. Yet, for all the obstacles that might emerge on the road to a treaty, he argued that it was apparent that this road 'is not impassable'.[77] Because of his stature and the extent to which the signposts that he envisioned corresponded significantly with Aboriginal demands, events since then have not changed that judgement.

Creating a process: inclusive and open negotiations

The validity of Deane's judgement will be tested when a number of non-Aboriginal politicians venture to use his signposts and see the future to which they may lead. Then a genuine dialogue might develop between them and Indigenous peoples about creating a future partnership. At present, it is significant that discussion about the process of creating a treaty is essentially occurring mainly amongst Indigenous political actors. Their concern with the key elements of this process suggests that they see clearly why a treaty of settlement is required, and are exploring in depth how the process towards it can be negotiated successfully. Fortunately, there are too many specific proposals to be summarised in a few points. Yet, in the spirit of Kevin Gilbert's memorable ode to Jimmy Barker, the following might become essential elements of an effective treaty process: 1) the negotiations must be properly resourced with a technology transfer; 2) the negotiations should encompass international perspectives; and 3) the timetable for negotiations must be open, dynamic and urgent.[78] Each point deserves further consideration and extensive debate, because this is ultimately the most difficult political aspect of creating a treaty. Even with positive assessments of the previous nine points in the sections above, efforts towards creating a treaty could be obstructed or delayed if the process does not receive enough critical attention. That is impossible here, but it is worth remembering, by analogy, that Maori are still fighting against government recalcitrance for an adequate political process to be created to recognise the constitutional status of the Treaty of Waitangi.[79]

Many issues are raised by the need for a properly resourced process of treaty negotiations. What needs to be avoided is the cheap and nasty native title mediation experience, in which Indigenous claimants have had to respond to a multitude of antagonistic opponents, with governments essentially representing the opponents not committed to mediation at all.[80] The basic conditions for an effective political process are that it is open and inclusive of all peoples who are directly affected by the decisions to be made. This must be demonstrated institutionally, as well as by active measures to overcome the Aboriginal scepticism expressed by Birch. A commitment to an independent and ongoing Treaty Commission, such as proposed

---

[76] Deane 1996: 10–15.

[77] Deane 1996: 10.

[78] See Gilbert 1991: 101 ('Jim B').

[79] See M Durie 2005, Jones 2005, Kelsey 2005, McHugh 2005, Sharp 2005 and D Williams 2005.

[80] See Atkinson 2002.

by Pat Dodson, would constitute such a measure. It would be bicultural and include various Indigenous perspectives.[81] This might be paralleled by roving bodies inquiring into urgent issues, such as health, so that the Treaty Commission is fully informed about social needs. In the spirit of a true partnership, such bodies might put pressure on governments to respond adequately to Indigenous needs even before a treaty is agreed.[82]

It is possible that, even if effective institutions within Australia are created to encourage and facilitate treaty-making, major problems will arise, and conflict within the treaty process will be resolved only through a mutual capacity to seek broader perspectives. Such perspectives are a crucial aspect of building what Deane called the 'mutual trust' that can develop into a consensus of support for a treaty. Although Australia is a diverse country, it cannot be presumed that all of the useful perspectives about a treaty process here are contained within this continent. Indeed, it would be a strange and narrow-minded faith in nationalism to think that, particularly when the High Court has noted (albeit by default, in the *Fejo* case) that other former British colonies are more advanced in facing the challenge of creating an enduring partnership with Indigenous peoples. Consequently, it would be sensible, although initially quite challenging, for a parallel international treaty monitoring commission to be created, comprised particularly of Indigenous people from other lands who are able to devote time and energy to the task of facilitating agreement here. An important proposal in this respect has been made by Mary Graham, advocating the use of properly qualified intermediaries and the inclusion of a crucial international dimension in treaty negotiations.[83] Graham's idea is to apply the 'Oslo Model' (used to redress longstanding conflicts in the Middle East, Guatemala and Sri Lanka) to help both facilitate and supervise a treaty process in Australia. This proposal extends Behrendt's argument that it is inappropriate to make Indigenous peoples negotiate with two levels of government here, by pointing out, as Whitlam once said, that Australia is answerable to 'the rest of the world' for a treaty.[84]

The other essential aspect of the process of creating a treaty is that the timetable for negotiations must be open and dynamic, not constrained by any particular date or by vested interests, as occurred with the Native Title Act, which Coombs considered the result of an inadequate process.[85] If it is going to be successful, the process of creating a treaty must build a dynamic of its own. The ultimate test of that is whether the process can be derailed (to continue with Harris's metaphor) once people are actually in the cable car heading for a better outlook. In that respect there is a real kernel of truth in the provocative suggestion made by Richie Ah Mat to the Treaty Advancing Reconciliation conference, that the conservative forces in Australian politics will have a role in creating a treaty, if it ever eventuates.[86] Their role will not be as initiators, nor even promoters, but it must be as tolerators of difference, and ultimately opponents of sabotage. Whether they can cope with that challenge remains to be seen. However, that implies that the building of a treaty must appear in some sense, and at a crucial time, as an effective adjustment by Australia to international and historical realities that it can no longer ignore. While various suggestions have been made about how a treaty might be

65

---

[81] See P Dodson 2000: 18, and Behrendt 2003b: 27.

[82] See Behrendt 2003b: 28–9, and NIYMA 2003: 111–12.

[83] Graham 2001: 9. For a Maori perspective see Wickliffe 1996.

[84] Behrendt 2003a: 169; Behrendt 2003b: 26. For Whitlam's 1972 policy speech, see Clark 1973: 203. While Whitlam did not use the word 'treaty' he was responding to demands of the Larrakia and others.

[85] Coombs 1994: 209–14.

[86] Ah Mat 2002, cited in Langton et al 2004: 26. See also Langton in Brennan et al 2005.

supported by the existing Australian Constitution (which is a paradox, considering its history), the significance of the international legal constraints upon Australia which followed from the 1967 Referendum (as argued by Kirby J in the *Kartinyeri* case) should not be overlooked, as they may actually be vital.[87]

Conclusion: from premises to process

The creation of a treaty recognising the unique status of Aborigines and Torres Strait Islanders as *first peoples* of Australia has many complex aspects. This analysis has attempted to show that there are more reasons for optimism about the treaty project than might appear to be the case. Whereas in 1969 questions might have been legitimately raised about who could negotiate for the first peoples, now the outstanding obstacle to a treaty is rather, who can face the challenge to negotiate for Australia? The challenge is one of seeking partnership not domination, diversity not uniformity and searching for a common justice rather than an old control. A treaty is possible because old forms of controlling Indigenous peoples in Australian cannot be easily re-instituted, and because there are reasons to believe that Indigenous advocates of a treaty have clarified much of what needs to be done (except, perhaps, where to find a partner). At least, it now appears true that, if the challenge of creating a treaty is accepted in Australia, Indigenous peoples will not be duped by the deceit of power.[88]

---

[87] See Kirby 1998a. See also M Dodson 2003: 34–8; McGlade 2003: 134–5.
[88] See Gilbert 1994: 72.

References

Books, articles and reports

Atkinson, Wayne 2002, 'Mediating the Mindset of Opposition: the Yorta Yorta case', *Indigenous Law Bulletin*, February–March, 5(15): 8–11.

ATSIC/AIATSIS 2003, *Treaty: let's get it right!*, Aboriginal Studies Press, Canberra.

Barwick, Diane 1988, 'Making a Treaty: the North American Experience', *Aboriginal History*, 12(1): 9–26.

Behrendt, Larissa 2003a, *Achieving Social Justice: Indigenous Rights and Australia's Future*, Federation Press, Sydney.

—— 2003b, 'Practical Steps Towards a Treaty: Structures, Challenges and the Need for Flexibility' in ATSIC/AIATSIS 2003, *Treaty: let's get it right!*, Aboriginal Studies Press, Canberra: 18–29.

Brennan, Sean, Larissa Behrendt, Lisa Strelein and George Williams 2005, *Treaty*, Federation Press, Sydney.

Central Australian Aboriginal Congress Inc. 2002, Position Paper: *Treaty and Health*, July.

Clark, Claire (ed) 1973, *Australian Foreign Policy: towards a reassessment*, Cassell, Melbourne.

Coates, Ken S 1998, 'International Perspectives on Relations with Indigenous Peoples' in Ken S Coates et al *Living Relationships – Kokiri Ngatahi: The Treaty of Waitangi in the New Millenium*, Victoria University Press, Wellington: 19–103.

Coombs, HC 1994, *Aboriginal Autonomy*, Cambridge University Press, Melbourne.

Cronin, Darryl 2003, 'Indigenous Disadvantage, Indigenous Governance and the Notion of a Treaty in Australia: An Indigenous Perspective' in ATSIC/AIATSIS 2003, *Treaty: let's get it right!*, Aboriginal Studies Press, Canberra: 151–65.

Deane, Sir William 1996, Some Signposts from Daguragu: the inaugural Lingiari lecture, delivered in Darwin, 22 August.

Dodson, Mick 2003, 'Unfinished Business: A Shadow Across Our Relationships' in ATSIC/AIATSIS 2003, *Treaty: let's get it right!*, Aboriginal Studies Press, Canberra: 30–40.

Dodson, Pat 1996, *Reconciliation at the Crossroads*, address to the National Press Club, May 1996, Australian Government Publishing Service, Canberra.

—— 2000, *Beyond the Mourning Gate: dealing with unfinished business*, 2000 Wentworth lecture, 12 May, Australian Institute of Aboriginal and Torres Strait Islander Studies.

—— 2005a, 'The Death of ATSIC – So What?', *Australian Options*, 40, Autumn: 6–9.

—— 2005b, Speech to Reconciliation Australia's National Convention Workshop, Canberra, 30–31 May, available at http://www. reconciliationaustralia.org/ipload/Speech%20by %20Patrick%20Dodson.doc, viewed 12 June 2005.

Draft Declaration on the Rights of Indigenous Peoples 1993, UN, Geneva, UN Doc E/CN.4/ Sub.2/1993/26, available at http://www.unhchr. ch/huridocda/huridoca.nsf/(Symbol)/E.CN.4.SUB. 2.RES.1994.45En?OpenDocument

Durie, ETJ 1991, 'The Treaty in Maori History' in William Renwick (ed) *Sovereignty and Indigenous Rights: The Treaty of Waitangi in International Contexts*, Victoria University Press, Wellington: 156–69.

—— 1996, 'Will the Settlers Settle? Cultural Conciliation and Law', *Otago Law Review*, 8(4): 449–65.

Durie, Mason 1998a, *Te Mana, Te Kawanatanga: the Politics of Maori Self-Determination*, Oxford University Press, Auckland.

—— 1998b, 'The Treaty was Always About the Future' in Ken S Coates et al, *Living Relationships – Kokiri Ngatahi: The Treaty of Waitangi in the New Millenium*, Victoria University Press, Wellington: 189–93.

—— 2005, 'Tino Rangatiratanga' in Michael Belgrave, Merata Kawharu and David Williams (eds) *Waitangi Revisted: Perspectives on the Treaty of Waitangi*, Oxford University Press, Melbourne: 3–19.

Gilbert, Kevin 1991, *The Blackside: People Are Legends and other poems*, Hyland House, Melbourne.

—— 1993, *Aboriginal Sovereignty, Justice, The Law and Land (includes Draft Treaty)*, 3rd edn, Burrambinga Books, Canberra.

—— 1994, *Black from the Edge*, Hyland House, Melbourne (with photography by Eleanor Williams).

—— 1995 [1992], 'Mabo Case Necessitates a Treaty: an open letter to the Prime Minister' in Irene Moores (ed) *Voices of Aboriginal Australia: Past, Present, Future*, Butterfly Books, Springwood: 371–4.

Graham, Mary 2001, *Application of the Oslo Model for Relations Between States and Indigenous Peoples*, Foundation for Aboriginal and Islander Research Action (FAIRA) Aboriginal Corporation, Brisbane.

Harris, Stewart 1979, *'It's Coming Yet …': An Aboriginal Treaty Within Australia Between Australians*, Aboriginal Treaty Committee, Canberra.

—— 1985, Introduction to Judith Wright, *We Call for a Treaty*, Aboriginal Treaty Committee, Canberra: xi–xv.

Harvey, Kate (ed) 2003, with the Aboriginal Community Elders' Service, *Aboriginal Elders' Voices: Stories of the 'tide of history'*, Victorian Indigenous Elders' life stories and oral histories, Aboriginal Community Elders' Service, Melbourne.

Horner, Jack 1969, letter to Jack Davis, President of the Western Australian Aboriginal Association, 9 August 1969 in Papers of FCAATSI, Series 23 Item 4, AIATSIS Library.

—— 2005, Interview, Canberra, 20 January.

Jones, Shane 2005, 'Cornerstone of the Nation State' in Michael Belgrave, Merata Kawharu and David Williams (eds) *Waitangi Revisted: Perspectives on the Treaty of Waitangi*, Oxford University Press, Melbourne: 20–34.

Kawharu, IH 2005, 'Foreword' in Michael Belgrave, Merata Kawharu and David Williams (eds) *Waitangi Revisted: Perspectives on the Treaty of Waitangi*, Oxford University Press, Melbourne: v–vi.

Kelsey, Jane 2005, 'Maori, Te Tiriti, and Globalisation: The Invisible Hand of the Colonial State' in Michael Belgrave, Merata Kawharu and David Williams (eds) *Waitangi Revisted: Perspectives on the Treaty of Waitangi*, Oxford University Press, Melbourne: 81–102.

Land Rights News 1988, 2(9) July: 'The Barunga Statement' and related articles.

Langton, Marcia 2001, 'Dominion and dishonour: a treaty between our nations?', *Postcolonial Studies*, April 4(1): 13–26.

Langton, Marcia and Palmer, Lisa 2003, 'Negotiating Settlements: Indigenous Peoples, Settler States and the Significance of Treaties and Agreements' in ATSIC/AIATSIS, *Treaty: let's get it right!*, Aboriginal Studies Press, Canberra: 41–52.

—— 2004, 'Treaties, Agreement Making and the Recognition of Indigenous Customary Polities' in M Langton, M Tehan, L Palmer and K Shain (eds) *Honour Among Nations? Treaties and Agreements with Indigenous People*, Melbourne University Press, Melbourne: 34–49.

Langton, Marcia, Maureen Tehan and Lisa Palmer 2004, 'Introduction' in M Langton, M Tehan, L Palmer and K Shain (eds) *Honour Among Nations? Treaties and Agreements with Indigenous People*, Melbourne University Press, Melbourne: 1–26.

Mansell, Michael 2003, 'Citizenship, Assimilation and a Treaty' in ATSIC/AIATSIS 2003, *Treaty: let's get it right!*, Aboriginal Studies Press, Canberra: 5–17.

Marr, David 2005, feature article on the UN Committee on the Elimination of Racial Discrimination and Australia, *Sydney Morning Herald*, 28 March.

McGlade, Hannah 2003, 'Native Title, "Tides of History" and Our Continuing Claims for Justice – Sovereignty, Self Determination and Treaty' in ATSIC/AIATSIS 2003, *Treaty: let's get it right!*, Aboriginal Studies Press, Canberra: 118–36.

McHugh, Paul 1997, 'Crown-Tribe Relations: Contractualism and Coexistence in an Intercultural Context' in G Davis, B Sullivan and A Yeatman (eds) *The New Contractualism?*, Macmillan, Melbourne: 198–216.

—— 2004, *Aboriginal Societies and the Common Law: A History of Sovereignty, Status, and Self-Determination*, Oxford University Press, Oxford.

—— 2005, 'Living With Rights Aboriginally: Constitutionalism and Maori in the 1990s' in Michael Belgrave, Merata Kawharu and David Williams (eds) *Waitangi Revisted: Perspectives on the Treaty of Waitangi*, Oxford University Press, Melbourne: 283–307.

Metge, Joan and Patricia Kinloch, 1978, *Talking Past Each Other: Problems of Cross-Cultural Communication*, Victoria University Press, Wellington.

Metherell, Mark and Stephanie Peatling, 2001, 'Don't use treaty vote to push separatism: Ruddock', *Sydney Morning Herald*, 4 January: 2.

Mutu, Margaret 2005, 'Recovering Fagin's Ill-Gotten Gains: Settling Ngati Kahu's Treaty of Waitangi Claims against the Crown' in Michael Belgrave, Merata Kawharu and David Williams (eds) *Waitangi Revisted: Perspectives on the Treaty of Waitangi*, Oxford University Press, Melbourne: 187–209.

National Indigenous Youth Movement of Australia (NIYMA) 2003, 'A Story of Emergence – NIYMA's Views on a Treaty' in ATSIC/AIATSIS 2003, *Treaty: let's get it right!*, Aboriginal Studies Press, Canberra: 107–17.

O'Shane, Pat 1991, 'A Treaty for Australians?' in William Renwick (ed) *Sovereignty and Indigenous Rights: The Treaty of Waitangi in International Contexts*, Victoria University Press, Wellington,: 147–55.

Pitty, Roderic 1999, 'A Poverty of Evidence: Abusing Law and History in *Yorta Yorta v Victoria* (1998)', *Australian Journal of Legal History*, 5(1): 41–61.

Renwick, William 1991, 'A Variation of a Theme' in William Renwick (ed) *Sovereignty and Indigenous Rights: The Treaty of Waitangi in International Contexts*, Victoria University Press, Wellington: 199–220.

Rigney Lester-Irabinna 2003, 'Indigenous Education, Languages and Treaty: the Redefinition of a New Relationship with Australia' in ATSIC/AIATSIS, *Treaty: let's get it right!*, Aboriginal Studies Press, Canberra: 72–87.

Rose, Deborah Bird 1984, 'The Saga of Captain Cook: Morality in Aboriginal and European Law', *Australian Aboriginal Studies*, 2: 24–39.

—— 1991, *Hidden Histories*, Aboriginal Studies Press, Canberra.

Ross, David 2001, 'Why This Country Needs a Treaty' in Martin Nakata (ed) *Indigenous Peoples, Racism and the United Nations*, Common Ground, Sydney: 153–61.

Rowley, C.D. 1978, *A Matter of Justice*, Australian National University Press, Canberra.

Rowse, Tim 1992, *Remote Possibilities: the Aboriginal Domain and the Administrative Imagination*, North Australia Research Unit, Darwin.

—— 1997, 'Reflections on Contractualism and Coexistence in an Intercultural Context' in G Davis, B Sullivan and A Yeatman (eds) *The New Contractualism?*, Macmillan, Melbourne: 217–23.

Sharp, Andrew 2005, 'The Treaty in the Real Life of the Constitution' in Michael Belgrave, Merata Kawharu and David Williams (eds) *Waitangi Revisted: Perspectives on the Treaty of Waitangi*, Oxford University Press, Melbourne: 308–29.

Snapshot of a Nation 2001, *Age*, 8 October, supplement.

Stokes, Geoffrey 2002, 'Australian Democracy and Indigenous Self-Determination, 1901–2001' in Geoffrey Brennan and Francis Castles (eds) *Australia Reshaped*, Cambridge University Press, Melbourne: 181–219.

Tully, James 1995, *Strange Multiplicity: Constitutionalism in an age of diversity*, Cambridge University Press, Cambridge.

Wickliffe, Caren 1996, 'The Waitangi Tribunal: a Critique – the need for a regional human rights mechanism', *New Zealand Law Librarian*, 2(4): 125–30.

Williams, David V 2005, 'Unique Treaty-Based Relationships Remain Elusive' in Michael Belgrave, Merata Kawharu and David Williams (eds) *Waitangi Revisted: Perspectives on the Treaty of Waitangi*, Oxford University Press, Melbourne: 366–87.

Williams, Joe 1991, 'Not Ceded But Redistributed' in William Renwick (ed) *Sovereignty and Indigenous Rights: The Treaty of Waitangi in International Contexts*, Victoria University Press, Wellington: 190–7.

Wright, Judith 1985, *We Call For A Treaty*, Collins, Sydney.

Yu, Peter 2001, 'Unfinished Business – National Responsibilities and Local Actions' in Sam Garkawe, Loretta Kelly and Warwick Fisher (eds) *Indigenous Human Rights*, Sydney Institute of Criminology Monograph series No 14, Sydney: 248–57.

Legislation

Native Title Act 1993 (Cth).

Racial Discrimination Act 1975 (Cth).

Case law

Fejo and Another on behalf of the Larrakia People v Northern Territory of Australia (1998) 156 ALR 721.

Kartinyeri v Commonwealth (1998) 195 CLR 337.

Mabo v Queensland (No 2) (1992) 175 CLR.

Members of the Yorta Yorta Aboriginal Community v State of Victoria and Others (2003) 214 CLR.

From enforceability to feel-good: notes on the pre-history of the recent treaty debate

Tim Rowse

On 26 April 1979, Dr HC Coombs called together a number of friends and colleagues in Canberra to discuss a new approach to the public debate about Indigenous affairs. Five months earlier, he had circulated a memo in which he observed a faltering in the pace of reform in Aboriginal affairs. What could he and his friends do to sustain and to entrench the reforms initiated in the 1970s? One of those friends, Judith Wright, later recalled that they agreed to form the 'Aboriginal Treaty Committee, whose objectives would include:

- the establishment of exclusive Commonwealth responsibility for all Aboriginal matters (as against the States);

- pressure for a treaty as providing a kind of constitutional basis for the relationship of Aboriginal Australians to the Commonwealth and Australian society generally;

- providing a focus for <u>white</u> political support for the Aboriginal cause.[1]

In reviewing what the Aboriginal Treaty Committee did, I want to underline the first of these objectives – the assertion of Commonwealth power over the States. Below I will suggest why the Aboriginal Treaty Committee conceived of Commonwealth power 'as against the States'. Here I will confine myself to the observation that the question of Australia's federalism can never be far away when issues of justice for Indigenous Australians are being discussed.

Two competing conceptions of social justice

It is a useful simplification of the discussion of Australian Indigenous needs and aspirations in the first few years of the twenty-first century to distinguish two tendencies in the understanding of 'social justice'. On the one hand, we have the strong advocacy of a treaty. This is based on a conception of distinct Indigenous rights, and it has often been associated with a wish to subordinate States and Territories to a Commonwealth that is committed to Indigenous rights. In 2000, for example, Bill Jonas, the Aboriginal and Torres Strait Islander Social Justice Commissioner and a treaty advocate, recommended that the Commonwealth amend the *Commonwealth Grants Commission Act 1973* to require it to enquire, every two years, into State and Territory performance of their responsibilities towards Indigenous Australians.[2] In arguing for this proposal, Dr Jonas noted a House of Representatives Standing Committee comment that, in health service delivery, framework agreements among Australian governments have been mere 'gentleman's agreements that apply in principle only and for which there is no recourse if breached'.[3] The Social Justice Commissioner's human rights approach sought to

---

[1] Wright 1985: 106. Those present were: Coombs, Wright, Stewart Harris, Charles Rowley, WEH Stanner and Dymphna Clark. Wright, 1985: 103, refers to the four men as the 'core members'.

[2] Aboriginal and Torres Strait Islander Social Justice Commissioner 2001: 131–2.

[3] Aboriginal and Torres Strait Islander Social Justice Commissioner 2001: 90.

make the States and Territories accountable to the Commonwealth; the Commonwealth is, in turn, internationally accountable by virtue of its commitment to various global human rights conventions and protocols.

The rival conception of social justice is associated with an ideal of 'cooperative federalism'. Since 1992, COAG – the Council of Australian Governments – has been promoted by all governments as the forum in which to plan a national approach to Indigenous policy. The Council for Aboriginal Reconciliation (CAR) acknowledged COAG's eminence when its final report Reconciliation: Australia's challenge (2000) included the recommendation that:

> [COAG] agree to implement and monitor a national framework whereby all governments and the Aboriginal and Torres Strait Islander Commission (ATSIC) work to overcome Aboriginal and Torres Strait Islander people's disadvantage through setting program performance benchmarks that are measurable (including timelines), are agreed in partnership with Aboriginal and Torres Strait Islander peoples and communities, and are publicly reported.[4]

This recommendation pointed to the common ground that had emerged in the 1990s – what the Howard government has come to call 'practical reconciliation'. This is a powerful notion because it appeals to so many of the ideas held by both Indigenous Australians and their well-wishers about what is necessary to a happy life for Australians. However, because it makes no concessions to the argument that Indigenous Australians have rights that are specifically 'Indigenous rights', this focus on social indicators of 'disadvantage' is – to treaty advocates – necessary **but not sufficient**, and – to treaty opponents – quite sufficient. So the current (2004) climate of debate on Indigenous affairs is characterised both by common ground and by polarity.

In this paper I wish to foreground the polarity that has become characteristic of Australian debate: treaty/Indigenous rights/Commonwealth ascendancy **versus** a 'practical reconciliation' based on cooperative federalism and attaching no significance to 'Indigenous rights'. So pervasively did this polarity structure the discussion of Indigenous Australians' aspirations between the years 2000 and 2004 that it neutralised the long-nurtured doctrine of 'reconciliation'. That term was invoked by both sides of the polarity, so that it became a meaningless, or at least a question-begging, item of cant. No one could be against 'reconciliation', if being for reconciliation embraced such a diversity of views about the rights of Indigenous Australians and about the accountability of governments.

The ultimate purpose of the following historical notes is to remind readers of the ways that discussion about a possible treaty should always be entangled with a view of Commonwealth responsibilities within the federation. However, that our treaty debate cannot or should not avoid issues of federalism was more obvious in the early 1980s than in 2000. As I will show, by 2000, due in part to the characteristic vagueness of the language of 'reconciliation', the discussion had become less about the forms of 'state' and more about the moral and emotional constituents of the 'nation'.

---

[4] CAR 2000a: 105.

First let us go back to the years 1979–83, when the Aboriginal Treaty Committee (ATC) and the National Aboriginal Conference (NAC) stimulated the first phase of the Australian discussion of a treaty with Indigenous peoples. Then I will illustrate the way that 'reconciliation' muddied the waters by shifting the discourse away from questions of government machinery to considerations of national 'healing'.

The Aboriginal Treaty Committee 1979–83

The Aboriginal Treaty Committee's campaign, 1979–83, consisted of four elements: a publications programme, a series of public appearances by such ATC 'stars' as the committee's chair Dr HC Coombs, a university-based research program, and the encouragement of local activities.

The ATC's publications program began with Stewart Harris's book *'It's Coming Yet'... An Aboriginal Treaty*, published in 1979. On 17 January 1980 Don Dunstan launched it, and on 26 March 1980, the ABC's Broadband program was devoted to the book and to the Treaty proposal. A copy was given to every person who had donated $5.00 or more in response to the *National Times* advertisement in August 1979. *'It's Coming Yet'* quickly exhausted the first print run of 5000. On 20 May 1980, twelve months after its first formal meeting, the Committee published its first *Newsletter*, over Coombs's signature. By October 1980, the Committee could send a copy of the second newsletter to some 2000 addresses. In April 1981, the *Newsletter* was replaced by a registered quarterly, printed tabloid size, *Aboriginal Treaty News*. The Committee published nine editions of the *News*, the last in October 1983. By then it had progressed from offset 'scissors and paste' to a professionally typeset page, with photographs and maps in an orderly and pleasing layout. In its final issue the *News* was showing signs of evolving from social movement newspaper to something more rarefied; it carried articles of such length and erudition – Russell Barsh's 'International law and the Miqmaq', Douglas Sanders's 'Indigenous issues in international law' – that the Committee now seemed to be selectively addressing the more academically inclined of its supporters. This was a measure of their success in at least one of their aims: to promote within Australia serious deliberation on the legal instruments available to nation states and Indigenous peoples seeking just settlements.

Universities were essential sites for the Committee's work. There the concept of a treaty could be clarified and made respectable in seminars and conferences. On 4 June 1980 Charles Rowley addressed an ANU convocation luncheon on 'Why a Treaty with the Aborigines?' On 17 July 1980 Gervaise Coles of the legal section of the Department of Foreign Affairs joined Coombs, Robert O'Neill and Ralph Harry in a colloquium on the Treaty at the ANU. The second *Newsletter* foreshadowed similar activities at Mt Lawley CAE, James Cook University and the Universities of Western Australia, New South Wales and Sydney: 'Dr. Coombs has been initiating most of these conferences'.[5] By April 1982 the Committee could claim to have instigated twelve conferences and seminars exploring the justification and means for a treaty over the 36 months since its inception.[6] Coombs saw the Committee's work as a research programme in law and in history, as much as he saw it as a media-based pitch for 'public opinion'. The university-based strand of the Committee's work culminated in a November 1983 conference at the ANU on the application of international law to Indigenous rights in Australia and North America.

---

[5] The Aboriginal Treaty Committee Newsletter 2.

[6] Coombs to Senator Alan Missen 7/4/82, in Commonwealth of Australia (Senate) papers 1983: 568–9.

[7] Aboriginal Treaty Committee 1979.

Although Coombs was not the only Committee member to speak publicly on their work, he seems to have carried most of the burden of public appearances. He had commenced the campaign in 1979 with three well-reported public addresses. On July 8 1980, he joined Roberta Sykes and Tom Kenneally on John Singleton's TV chat show. In June 1980, the *National Times* (8–14 June) carried, in their 'Other Voices' column, one of Coombs's 1979 speeches, his Amnesty address of December 1979. The *National Times*, in which the Committee had displayed its original manifesto as a paid advertisement,[7] seems to have been the Committee's most important vehicle. Coombs found interest as well from the editors of *Social Alternatives*, *The Catholic Leader* and the *Sydney Morning Herald*. Indeed a feature article by the Committee published in the *Herald* won for the ATC a gold citation in the UN Media Peace Prize project. These writings repeated the arguments laid out in Coombs's opening addresses of 1979. The *Herald* article was notable for its concluding appeal to a sense of national occasion.

> In 1988 we celebrate the 200th anniversary of the original British
> settlement. Do we want that anniversary to be a day of mourning and
> of hatred for Aboriginal Australians? What a splendid component
> of that anniversary would be a celebration also of the conclusion
> of a freely negotiated treaty in which Aboriginal rights were
> acknowledged, just compensation awarded and Aboriginal status in
> our society honoured.[8]

While advocating the Treaty, the Committee also helped to publicise any reports or studies that drew attention to the deficient performances of governments and/or to the means to better government. Thus the Committee paid for space in the *Age* on 30 September 1981, inviting those attending the Commonwealth Heads of Government meeting to study the Report of the World Council of Churches Team visit to Australia, June–July 1981; the Reports of the NSW Parliamentary Select Committee on Aborigines, 1980 and 1981; the Reports of the Commonwealth Parliamentary Committee on Aboriginal Health (1979) and Aboriginal Legal Aid (1980); and the Reports of the Commissioner for Community Relations in 1980 and 1981. On 13 August 1981, Coombs wrote to 35 newspapers arguing that the World Council of Churches report on conditions in Aboriginal Australia added to the justification for a treaty.

In the Committee's own organ, *Aboriginal Treaty News*, it could control the representation of the public debate it was stimulating. The first issue featured on its front page a photo of the mayor of the Gold Coast, Keith Hunt, marking Australia Day 1981 by signing the Treaty Supporters' form. Judith Wright contributed an article urging other local support groups to follow the Gold Coast group in organising similar events. From later issues the reader could learn that the Fremantle City Council had formally recognised that its area had once belonged exclusively to Aboriginal people and that Dymphna Clark had persuaded 62 artists to donate work to a Sydney fund-raising exhibition 'Ab Origine', opened by her husband Manning and by Margaret Valadian at the National Trust Centre, Sydney, on 9 January 1981.

Coombs's public speaking engagements continued throughout 1981. In May, he and Rowley took part in a half-day ANZAAS Symposium at the University of Queensland. On 14 June, Coombs was the guest speaker at a joint meeting of the local committees of Pymble and Gordon, and at the end of August he accompanied Judith Wright to Townsville for a conference at James Cook University on 'Prospects for Change'. At the invitation of Senator Susan Ryan, Coombs

---

[7] Aboriginal Treaty Committee 1979.   [8] *Sydney Morning Herald* 27 November 1980.

and Rowley met with the ALP's national policy committee on Aboriginal affairs on 12 October 1981. Coombs continued throughout 1982 to accept engagements on the Committee's behalf. They included visits to Perth and Geelong in March, and a two-day trip in May to Tasmania, where he addressed a university audience and a Tasmanian writers' luncheon. It was a measure of the impact of the Treaty debate that on 30 September 1981 Senator Missen had announced an inquiry by the Standing Committee on Constitutional and Legal Affairs into the feasibility of a formal agreement between the Commonwealth and Aboriginal people. On 22 June 1982, several members of the Committee (Rowley, Wright, Diane Barwick and Stewart Harris) appeared with their legal consultant Peter Bayne before the Standing Committee. Coombs made his appearance on 9 September 1982.

Land rights and the States

Though treaty advocates mentioned the means of 'practical reconciliation' (as they would later be called) – such as housing, community infrastructure, schools and medical services – one issue of 'Indigenous rights' continued, at this time, to overshadow all others: land. By the early 1980s, there had been strong public interest for almost 20 years in the controversies generated by Aboriginal land claims against the Commonwealth and by the Commonwealth's responses: the Yirrkala petition in 1963, the Gurindji walk-off in 1966–67, the Yolngu court action of 1968–71 and then the land rights bills of the Whitlam (1973–75) and Fraser (1975–83) governments that resulted in the *Aboriginal Land Rights (Northern Territory) Act 1976*. In this sequence of challenges and responses the State governments had been all but invisible, as the Commonwealth set what reformers such as Coombs hoped would be an exemplary pattern of recognition of Indigenous rights. However, in the late 1970s, two States asserted the limits of their cooperation with Commonwealth initiatives that affected their own land administration. In their responses to the Commonwealth's attempt to purchase the Archer River pastoral lease for its Aboriginal owners, the Queensland government blocked the sale, declaring land rights to be contrary to State policy. The case went to the High Court and was resolved in the Commonwealth's favour in 1982 (*Koowarta v Bjelke-Petersen*).[9] In Western Australia, one remote group of Aborigines seemed to have achieved security when the Noonkanbah pastoral lease had been transferred to Aboriginal ownership in 1975. However, the Court government sought to oblige the new owners to accept petroleum exploration on their property. The owners' resistance aroused considerable public sympathy in 1979 and 1980. The Federal Minister for Aboriginal Affairs, Fred Chaney, was openly critical of the Western Australian government for insisting that minerals exploration prevail over Indigenous land owners' wishes. However, the Noonkanbah dispute demonstrated to advocates of land rights that the Commonwealth was not willing to challenge 'States rights' over land use.

The Fraser government also looked weak when challenged by Queensland. In 1978 the Commonwealth had attempted to flex its constitutional muscles in a 1978 law providing for self-determination on Queensland's reserves.[10] Before the legislation could come into effect, the Queensland government de-gazetted the reserves and declared them to be shires. The Fraser government declined to counter this move, and nor would it respond to requests from the remaining Queensland reserves (for example, Yarrabah) for help in implementing land rights and self-management. By 1980 the Queensland and Western Australian governments had prevailed politically over the Commonwealth, even though the Commonwealth had the constitutional authority to enforce a national land rights policy. Frank Brennan and James

---

[9] (1982) 153 CLR 168. [10] *Aboriginal and Torres Strait Islanders (Queensland Reserves and Communities Self-Management) Act 1978* (Cth).

Crawford concluded in a 1990 paper that, notwithstanding the 1967 referendum, there remains a 'hidden constitution' in which Commonwealth power remains limited and residual to the land-use powers of the States.[11] To any interested observer, the pre-eminence of 'States rights' over Indigenous rights had become clear by the time Coombs and his colleagues were into their first year of treaty advocacy.

The ATC therefore had frequent opportunity to argue for some abiding national framework of enforceable fairness. On 27 July 1980, the *National Times* carried the Committee's advertisement appealing for a five-year moratorium on prospecting and mining in the Kimberley and in other areas 'predominantly occupied by Aboriginal Australians'. The ATC's second *Newsletter* told supporters that Coombs had also written to the Western Australian Premier, Sir Charles Court, on April 30 1980, 'asking him to accept the Noonkanbah people's proposal for a three year moratorium and to set up an independent Commission to consider the application of the Woodward Commission's principles to Western Australia'. The Committee called upon the Minister for Aboriginal Affairs Chaney to resign over Noonkanbah, and Coombs also wrote to the B'nai B'rith organisation in Washington to suggest that it would be a mistake to award Fraser a medal for his 'humanitarian' services: Fraser's 'record in his own country denies his suitability for it'.[12] Coombs also spoke at a preview of a film on the Noonkanbah dispute *On Sacred Ground*. 'There are going to be a succession of Noonkanbahs unless Land rights laws are passed so that the Federal Government will intervene', he told the audience.[13]

The Queensland government also attracted the Committee's scrutiny. In June 1980 Coombs published a letter in the *Courier Mail* warning delegates to the second World Wilderness Congress in Cairns that the Bjelke-Petersen government, in order to pre-empt Aboriginal land claims, might seek their support for a national park in Cape York. In March and May 1981 the Committee paid for an advertisement in the *National Times* pointing out that the Queensland government was planning to alienate remnant reserves from their residents. The Commonwealth had the authority to acquire the reserves compulsorily and to vest them in these communities, the advertisement pointed out, but would it use that power? On 27 May 1980 Coombs wrote to Fraser of his concerns about Queensland reserves, and in July he got a letter into the *Age* on this issue and made himself available for media interviews.[14]

Most of *Aboriginal Treaty News* nos 3 (November 1981), 4 (February 1982) and 5 (May–August 1982) comprised running State-by-State commentaries on land rights – abuses, laws and policy developments. Some of the commentary was written (anonymously) by Committee members; other material consisted of reprints of news stories, feature articles and editorials from the daily newspapers, with the *Age*, the *Canberra Times* and the *Courier Mail* particularly prominent. *Aboriginal Treaty News* no 6 (September–October 1982) was a special edition to mark the protests against the Queensland government while it hosted the twelfth Commonwealth Games in Brisbane. The next issue, for the summer of 1982–83,[15] coincided with Fraser's third attempt to seek re-election. In the previous election, October 1980, Coombs had addressed questions to four party leaders and then summarised and criticised their responses. In 1983 he asked: 'Would your Government be prepared to over-ride a State or Northern Territory Government to ensure that land and human rights were provided for Aboriginal Australians?' The Labor Party said that it intended to do so, in Queensland, 'promptly after taking office'; the Coalition

---

[11] Brennan and Crawford 1990.

[12] *The Aboriginal Treaty Committee Newsletter* 2.

[13] As quoted in the *Canberra Times* 9 December 1980.

[14] These actions are all reported in *The Aboriginal Treaty Committee Newsletter* 2.

[15] *Aboriginal Treaty News* no 7.

would go no further than to state that the Commonwealth 'has the power to intervene if necessary and appropriate'.[16] The Committee refrained from advising how to vote, but charged the Fraser government with having 'virtually abdicated its responsibilities for Aboriginal rights and land rights', and with having 'given way on practically all issues to State Governments such as Queensland and Western Australia'. Worse was possibly to come. The Federal government now looked like capitulating to the Northern Territory government's proposed amendments to the *Land Rights Act*. Stewart Harris wrote that Aboriginal people could not be expected to negotiate a treaty with the Fraser government. The Committee concluded that 'This election will mean hope or despair for Aborigines everywhere'.[17]

A parallel Indigenous treaty campaign

When Coombs first circulated friends his ideas about a treaty at the end of 1978, he may or may not have been aware that similar ideas were brewing within the National Aboriginal Conference (NAC), the elected advisory body established by the Fraser government in 1977. In April 1979, the same month as Coombs's first informal gathering to discuss his circulated Aboriginal Treaty Committee proposal, the NAC leadership announced that it would seek to negotiate a treaty with the Australian government. Prime Minister Fraser confirmed on 21 August 1979, two days after the Committee had held its first Press conference, that the Minister for Aboriginal Affairs was examining the NAC proposal. From the moment of that announcement, Coombs and the others on the Committee were faced with a delicate political task: how to relate their efforts to the NAC's dealings with the Fraser government?

The Committee's manifesto in the *National Times* (August 1979) included the outline of a possible procedure for the NAC's dialogue with government.[18] Soon after it appeared, Coombs wrote to NAC leaders and other Aborigines asking them to comment on the Committee's initial efforts to establish a national debate on the Treaty. Their response was positive. Coombs 'reported at a Committee meeting on 3 September that they were pleased with the wording of the advertisement and the publicity gained through the Press conference. It was agreed that separate campaigns, with exchange of information and publications, offered the best chance of success.'[19] Coombs was later to give an account of his understanding with the NAC:

> We do not have Aboriginal members because consultation with the
> NAC and other Aboriginal organisations made it clear that they
> would not welcome a joint organisation which could be represented
> as the instrument of 'white stirrers' and that they wished a Treaty
> to be achieved as a result of Aboriginal initiative and effort.
> They made it equally clear, however, that they would welcome
> our support and help.[20]

In the autonomy of the two organisations and in the separateness of their campaigns Coombs found room to comment critically on the Indigenous mobilisation. In one of his first speeches, on 2 October 1979, he had aired his doubts about the NAC's present capacity to conduct a Treaty campaign in accordance with the traditions of Aboriginal culture.[21]

On 12 November 1979, the NAC held a Press Conference on their proposal, announcing that they were forming a sub-committee specially to canvass ideas and to develop a draft.

---

[16] *Aboriginal Treaty News* no 7.

[17] *Aboriginal Treaty News* no 7.

[18] Aboriginal Treaty Committee 1979.

[19] Wright 1985: 121.

[20] Coombs's responses to a seminar (which he was unable to attend) at the University of Western Australia, 27–28 April 1981. Coombs 1981: 117.

[21] Coombs 1979b.

The NAC also announced that the word 'treaty' would be dropped and replaced by a word from the languages of north-east Arnhem Land – *makarrata*. At the time, *makarrata* was glossed as 'the resumption of normal relations after a period of hostilities'. The next day, Minister for Aboriginal Affairs Senator Fred Chaney welcomed the NAC's substitution of *makarrata* for 'treaty'. In the Senate a week later, he explained that the government did not like the term 'treaty' 'because of the implication that one is in some way talking about more than one Australia or more than one nation within Australia'. By discarding 'treaty', the NAC had reassured Chaney that Aborigines and Torres Strait Islanders saw themselves 'as Australians within the Australian nation'. He reported with evident approval the NAC's wish to use 'something like 18 months for the task it has undertaken'.[22]

Judith Wright has recalled that 'We … were worried by the government's suspicious alacrity over the NAC demand'.[23] The Aboriginal Treaty Committee had been conceived in apprehension and distrust of the Fraser government, and it had been forthright in its subsequent criticisms, including calling for Chaney's resignation over Noonkanbah. The Committee was now worried by the NAC's shift from 'treaty' to *makarrata* and by the NAC's short timetable for formulating a treaty. The Aboriginal Treaty Committee could therefore be glad of their policy of keeping some distance from the NAC's campaign. However, this protocol did not oblige them to stay away from Aboriginal people. As Coombs explained to NAC Chair Jim Hagan on 26 May 1980, 'we hoped to invite Aboriginal leaders and others to speak for or against the treaty idea and be tape recorded, so that Aboriginal groups could hear their own people giving different views on the subject'.[24] For the Aboriginal Treaty Committee to consult Indigenous Australians in this way was consistent with its view that the NAC lacked the resources to sponsor a widespread Indigenous debate.

Meanwhile the NAC had begun its consultations with Indigenous Australians, circulating a leaflet and a questionnaire. Over 19 days in February 1980 Hagan's sub-committee held 15 meetings along the eastern seaboard (from Launceston to Thursday Island) and as far inland as Mt Isa and Mildura. Their efforts were welcomed by the Prime Minister who spoke at a dinner for the NAC on 25 March 1980. In April and May, the NAC's *makarrata* sub-committee was back on the road, visiting 15 towns and capital cities in Western Australia, South Australia and the Northern Territory over 23 days.

On 2 July 1981 the NAC released an interim report on these consultations at a meeting to which Coombs was invited. The report began by reminding readers that 'the Prime Minister has stated that he is now ready to talk to Aborigines about an Agreement, but he will only talk with the National Aboriginal Conference (NAC), because we are elected representatives of the Aboriginal people'. There followed a series of quite specific proposed treaty terms, including reserved seats for Indigenous Australians in Commonwealth and State parliaments, a quota on employment of Aboriginal people in government 'irrespective of their established skills', and the return of skeletons and artefacts from museums.[25] Coombs made public his critical response to what was evidently a draft treaty. The NAC should take more time to develop a debate among Indigenous Australians, he urged. Coombs added that the NAC would need far more resources than the Fraser government had so far allowed, if it were to negotiate on equal terms.

---

[22] Commonwealth of Australia Senate Hansard 19 November 1979: 2427 (for both quotations).

[23] Wright 1985: 123.

[24] *The Aboriginal Treaty Committee Newsletter* 2.

[25] The text of this report was published in *The Catholic Leader* 13 July 1980.

Many of the results of the NAC's first consultations seemed to confirm the wisdom of these remarks. Hagan acknowledged in a letter to the Committee that there was division over the term *makarrata*, with many Aboriginal people preferring 'treaty'. The Aboriginal Treaty Committee gave publicity to these misgivings in its second *Newsletter* (October 1980). In many places, neither concept was yet familiar enough for Aboriginal people to form an opinion. Discussions so far had unearthed doubts that any agreement, whatever it was called, could soon be forged with the Australian government. Central Australian Aboriginal Congress was claiming that if the process of consultation were to result in the necessary 'consensus' among Aborigines, then at least five years of effort would be required: the NAC did not yet have a mandate for negotiations. The Tasmanian Aboriginal Centre warned against a premature settlement that would nip in the bud an emerging Indigenous political consciousness. 'Any agreement at this point in time will be seen as a charitable one … Only when we represent such a threat to the stability and power of white Australia that they are forced to negotiate a treaty with us will a Treaty not be viewed as charitable.'[26]

The NAC sub-Committee's early consultations had given them reason to reconsider whether eighteen months would be enough time to prepare a treaty. Coombs attempted to reinforce their doubts in a letter on 22 September 1980 to Hagan answering his question as to 'who, or what body, on the Aboriginal side should be considered representative in negotiations'.[27] Coombs proposed a six step process in which the NAC would first commission and circulate position papers on treaty issues, then call 'a Convention of representatives chosen by recognised Aboriginal organisations, communities and traditional groups' to discuss them. These representatives would then return to their organisations. The NAC would then recall the Convention to consider a first draft of an agreement to be proposed to the Government, and the Convention would remain in existence to respond to the issues arising from the ensuing negotiations. Final approval or rejection would be a decision of this Convention, not of the NAC by itself. Coombs's suggestion accorded the NAC a central but not a singular role in Indigenous representation. Among Aboriginal leaders the timetable of consultations and negotiations was now controversial. In a Townsville forum, on 1 October 1980, the North Queensland Land Council's Mick Miller was in clear disagreement with the NAC's Bill Bird. According to Judith Wright, on the same platform to speak for the Committee, Bird still thought that a document could eventuate within the term of the current government. Miller was among those preparing for the long haul.[28]

Thus the Aboriginal Treaty Committee found itself in the midst of a lively debate among Indigenous people – a debate that it had helped to stir up. While the Committee told supporters that it did not 'want to be seen as influenced by any particular Aboriginal body', it was effectively taking a position in a debate among Indigenous Australians by arguing for more time, by not fully endorsing the term *makarrata* and – most important of all – by highlighting the Fraser government's failure to face down Queensland's and Western Australia's opposition to land rights. The NAC's hopeful assessment of the Fraser government contrasted with the Committee's growing contempt for that Government. The Committee's editorial policy in *Aboriginal Treaty News* was to make such differences visible. For example, Barrie Pittock, one of the signatories of the Committee's first advertisement in the *National Times,* wrote a piece asking 'What is Wrong with a Treaty?'[29] His suspicions were aroused by the Fraser government's keenness to negotiate

79

---

26 *The Aboriginal Treaty Committee Newsletter* 2: 3.

27 As paraphrased by Wright 1985: 155.

28 Wright 1985: 141–2.

29 Pittock 1981.

a *makarrata*. He agreed with Kevin Gilbert's recent assertion that an agreement could be made only between 'two equal sovereign peoples'. A treaty with teeth, detailed and enforceable in the courts, could not be achieved 'next year or the year after – probably not for a decade or more, if ever'. Pittock confessed his uneasiness 'that the Treaty movement originated amongst whites without strong Aboriginal input and seems to have gathered too much superficial support too quickly'. His closing words warned of his conditional continuing support: 'By all means advocate a Treaty, but make sure it has guts!' Coombs took a similar line. On 11 December 1980, he joined Jack Davis in addressing a meeting in Perth on the Treaty. There he argued that 'Aborigines would be at an enormous disadvantage if a Treaty were concluded before all parties were fully informed ... This will take considerable time.'[30]

80

But how much time? Was the Aboriginal Treaty Committee prepared to commit itself to a timetable? This question was taken up on page one of the first issue of the Committee's new *Aboriginal Treaty News* (April 1981). The Committee judged an agreement unobtainable by Australia Day 1983, as some had suggested. Better to look to the bicentennial year 1988. The possible significance of the Bicentennial thus began to figure in the Committee's strategy of persuading non-Aboriginal Australians that their nationhood was morally flawed. The year 1988 seemed, in 1980–81, to be sufficiently far ahead to accommodate the view that 'years' of consultation and negotiation were required. The timing of the treaty or *makarrata* negotiations was not the only issue that had to be resolved. The issue of who the parties to negotiation would be was starting to become more complicated. In February and March 1981, the NAC and the Minister for Aboriginal Affairs exchanged letters about the possible contents of a *makarrata*. In the course of his comments, the Minister made clear the conception of federalism that underlay his friendly disposition towards the *makarrata*. In effect, he proposed a 'States rights' approach. That is, he noted that the NAC should be negotiating with each of the State governments on those parts of the proposed *makarrata* in which the States had an interest. That would certainly have included land.

As I pointed at the beginning of this paper, Coombs and his Committee wanted a treaty that would bind the Commonwealth to a defence of Indigenous interests from the attacks of the States. Though this point was lost in the mutual courtship of the NAC and the Fraser government over the *makarrata*, it was echoed by the 1983 Report of the Senate Standing Committee on Constitutional and Legal Affairs, *Two hundred years later ...* . The Standing Committee did not argue for or against a treaty. It merely asked: if there were a treaty, how would it fit in to the laws and constitution of the Commonwealth? The Standing Committee's preferred option was that the Constitution be altered by the addition of a Section 105B enabling the Commonwealth to negotiate a compact, according to specified principles, with Indigenous Australians. Section 105B would be modelled on the existing s.105A which empowered the Commonwealth to make financial agreements with the States. When tested in the High Court in 1932, s.105A had proved robust; that is, an agreement in accordance with s.105A could not be changed by any law of the Commonwealth or the States. Section 105B would give the Commonwealth solid constitutional ground on which to stand in that it would provide that 'laws passed pursuant to the compact' would be 'binding upon the Commonwealth and the States notwithstanding anything contained in the Commonwealth or State Constitutions or in any Commonwealth or State law'.[31]

---

30 *Aboriginal Treaty News* no 1.   31 Commonwealth of Australia 1983: 74.

Having set out this proposal, the Standing Committee went on to examine alternative ways that a treaty or compact might be entrenched in the Constitution. Could it come within the existing 'races' power, s.51 (xxvi) or under the 'external affairs' power, s.51 (xxix)? After pages of learned discussion of the history of judicial interpretation of those two existing powers, the Standing Committee decided that they would support 'carefully considered legislation for a compact'. However, the Standing Committee then expressed its 'concern at the political vulnerability to which any such compact legislation would be subject, due to the possibility of amendment or repeal by subsequent Parliaments'.[32] It was better, the Standing Committee concluded, to go for a specific head of constitutional authority modelled on the authority that secured inter-governmental financial dealings.

By 1983 the discussion on Indigenous rights had built upon late 1970s agitation over substantive policy issues such as land rights and service provision and had begun to focus on the reform of Australian federalism itself. Yet in this challenge to States rights we can glimpse the political limits of the fight for Indigenous rights, for in the 1980s there was no political vehicle for a campaign of constitutional reform. When the Keating government decided that it would legislate 'native title', the entities with which it had to negotiate the terms of native title in 1993 were primarily the States and Territories, and only secondarily the representatives of Indigenous interests.

2000 – the treaty debate revived

However, the constitution remained symbolically important. So a day commemorating constitutional reform – Saturday 27 May 2000 – was chosen for a gathering known as 'Corroboree 2000', convened by the Council for Aboriginal Reconciliation (CAR) in the Sydney Opera House. Corroboree 2000 was intended as the climactic statement of the case for 'reconciliation', after ten years of discussion, policy advocacy and marketing campaigns by the Council for Aboriginal Reconciliation. What did this word mean?

Geoff Clark had been appointed a member of CAR in December 1999 and became the first elected Chairperson of ATSIC early in 2000. He brought with him to the ATSIC Chair a desire to highlight the concept of 'Indigenous rights' that was not typical of the rhetoric of CAR as it had evolved in the late 1990s. He proposed an interpretation of 'reconciliation' that was undoubtedly contentious. 'True reconciliation means recognising we possess distinct rights.'[33] He called for the inscription, within the Constitution, of the Indigenous right of self-determination.

> There have been no treaties, no formal settlements, no compacts.
> There now needs to be. There is no mention of Australia's first peoples
> in the Constitution. There now needs to be. The few rights we now
> enjoy remain vulnerable in the absence of constitutional protection.

He challenged the Prime Minister with the words: 'A commitment from Government to negotiate a treaty is essential'.[34]

Prime Minister Howard's speech to the 'Corroboree' avoided declaring any particular understanding of 'reconciliation'. Instead he allowed that its meanings were many and personal: ' … each of us brings our own perspective to the process of reconciliation and the one requirement that we should bring to that is the sincerity of the view that we hold on how reconciliation

---

[32] Commonwealth of Australia 1983: 103.   [34] *Sydney Morning Herald* 29 May 2000.

[33] *Sydney Morning Herald* 29 May 2000.   [35] *Sydney Morning Herald* 29 May 2000.

might be achieved'. In specifying his own sincere understanding of 'reconciliation' he would go no further than to endorse 'practical measures to address [Indigenous] disadvantage'.[35] In a later comment, the Minister for Reconciliation, Phillip Ruddock, while rejecting the term 'treaty', foreshadowed that the Howard government would work towards a 'wider framework agreement with Indigenous people'.[36] The Government's line, reiterated over the next few days, was that a treaty would divide the nation, for example, by opening up disputes about land ownership.[37] In saying this, the government proved more ready than Clark had been to say what a treaty might be about.

In the week following the Corroboree and the hugely popular demonstration across the Harbour Bridge, Clark was in the curious position of claiming that there was now a public mandate for a treaty, without suggesting what the treaty's principal headings might be. The government's position was a little more clear than that: the combined effect of Howard's and Ruddock's statements was to entertain a 'framework agreement' – and not a treaty – which would be about not land ownership (for that would re-open the issues of entitlement debated when the Howard government amended the *Native Title Act* in 1998)[38] but measures to address Aboriginal 'disadvantage'.

The purpose of the Corroboree 2000 events was to bring forth an agenda of policies formulated by the Council for Aboriginal Reconciliation, a body composed of Indigenous and non-Indigenous people appointed by the Government and reflecting a variety of political outlooks. CAR's concluding proposals about public policy did not include anything as bold as Clark's call for a treaty and for constitutional expression of distinct Indigenous rights. CAR's 'Roadmap for Reconciliation' briefly described four 'national strategies' for:

— sustaining the reconciliation process

— promoting recognition of Aboriginal and Torres Strait Islander rights

— overcoming disadvantage

— achieving economic independence

The second of these four strategies, about rights, did not go as far as Clark's call for the constitutional recognition of the distinct rights of Indigenous people. On the issue of 'rights', CAR declared that its objective was for 'all Australians [to] enjoy, in daily life, a fundamental equality of rights, opportunities and acceptance of responsibilities'; and it next announced its wish that 'the status and unique identities of Aboriginal and Torres Strait Islander peoples as the first peoples of Australia, achieve recognition, respect and understanding in the wider community'. The 'Roadmap' thus refrained from linking distinct Indigenous identity with distinct Indigenous rights, and nor did it spell out the legally enforceable entitlements that made up those 'rights'. The constitutional reforms envisaged in the 'Roadmap' were also more modest than Clark's call for the entrenching of distinct Indigenous rights. The Roadmap advocated a referendum on a new preamble that would recognise 'the status of the first Australians'; and it wanted another referendum to remove s.25 of the Constitution and to 'introduce a new section making it unlawful to adversely discriminate against any people on the grounds of race'. Section 25 reads:

> **Provisions as to races disqualified from voting.** For the purposes of
> the last section [on the 'constitution of the House of Representatives'],

---

[36] *Sydney Morning Herald* 29 May 2000.   [37] *The Australian* 30 May 2000.   [38] *Native Title Amendment Act 1998* (Cth).

> if by the law of any State all persons of any race are disqualified from
> voting at elections for the more numerous House of the Parliament of
> the State, then, in reckoning the number of the people of the State or
> of the Commonwealth, persons of that race resident in that State shall
> not be counted.

To remove this inactive section of the constitution would be as effectual as the removal of s.127 in 1967. As in the 1967 referendum, the deletion of anachronistic and inactive bits of the Australian Constitution would symbolise a vague and inconsequential (as far as public policy goes) expression of popular goodwill towards the First Australians. CAR's thoughts about the Constitution typified its anodyne condition in 2000.

In her Corroboree 2000 speech CAR chair Evelyn Scott used words which helped to muddy the distinction between Clark's position and CAR's: 'Our struggle for Indigenous rights and equality is bound up inextricably with the rights of all Australians. Our freedom is your freedom.'[39] That is, Scott alluded to 'Indigenous rights' but immediately used words ('bound up inextricably with') which seem calculated to obscure their relationship to the rights of 'all Australians'. Scott soon made it clear, however, that whatever her words in the Opera House meant, she was not in favour of a treaty. She and her deputy chair, Sir Gustav Nossal, told the Press that, unlike Clark, they did not construe the popular support for reconciliation as a mandate for a treaty.[40] She described the treaty call as 'premature' and warned that 'attempts to jump stages … will hurt rather than help take us forward'.[41] Council member Jackie Huggins agreed with the Scott/Nossal reading of the unreadiness of public opinion, though she added that she was herself in favour of a treaty. However, 'a great deal more understanding, awareness and negotiation is required … ' before Australians would accept such a thing.

> Our social research, publicly released earlier this year, has shown
> strong support for reconciliation and for a document. However,
> support was not so strong, for example, for calling such a document
> a treaty.[42]

Gatjil Djerrkura added his voice to this description of the 'treaty' as premature. To push for a treaty now would only alienate many people from reconciliation, he speculated. *The Australian*'s headline for these Indigenous leaders' responses to Clark was 'reconcile now, treaty later'.

In its promotion of 'reconciliation' CAR did not challenge the public to accept a distinct Indigenous right of self-determination. Reconciliation might, in some people's understanding, entail distinct Indigenous rights, but CAR was careful to accommodate a huge variety of attributed meanings to their key term. For example, in the October 1979 issue of CAR's *Walking Together*, Alan Jones and Pat Dodson gave fundamentally opposed reasons for endorsing 'reconciliation'. The vague inclusiveness of 'reconciliation' was essential to its popularity by 2000, just as the unspecific commitments of the 'Yes' vote in the 1967 referendum had enabled that expression of goodwill towards Indigenous Australians to be widely popular. CAR was not willing to sacrifice the popularity of 'reconciliation' by telling the public that 'reconciliation' was ultimately to be encoded in the constitutional recognition of distinct Indigenous rights. Rather, CAR's promotion of distinct Indigenous identity was clearly qualified by a constraining theme of national unity. As Evelyn Scott reportedly said in her speech to Corroboree 2000: 'the

---

[39] *Sydney Morning Herald* 29 May 2000. [41] *Age* 2 June 2000.

[40] *The Australian* 2 June 2000. [42] *The Australian* 2 June 2000.

new spirit of reconciliation will lead the nation to the healing and unity it requires'.[43] Referring to the Harbour Bridge demonstration in her response to Clark, she used the metaphor of 'steps' to express her argument of gradualism. 'Last Sunday about a quarter of a million Australians walked together for reconciliation. As we take further steps together, let's make sure we keep and build on that support … '.[44]

Indigenous leaders who responded in 2000 to Clark's equation of 'reconciliation' with 'treaty' used language that obscured the difference between two conflicting understandings of liberalism. In one version of liberalism, let's call it 'settler colonial liberalism', there is no place for the notion of distinct Indigenous rights. In this conception, a 'fair go' for Indigenous Australians consists of ending discrimination against them, addressing their socio-economic disadvantage by including them in the processes of wealth and income generation, and even, perhaps, giving them title to land, in recognition that their property rights have been flouted in the past. This version of liberalism was once unchallenged in Australia. It has many reforms to its credit, and its linking of the 'fair go' with national unity remains enormously appealing to a great many Australians. However, it has begun to be challenged by what we might call a 'post-colonial liberalism'. Post-colonial liberalism *affirms respect for difference as the new basis for national unity*. It entertains the idea that Indigenous peoples have certain rights that immigrant peoples and their descendants do not. A rewriting of the national narrative, giving prominence to themes of invasion, resistance and conquest, underpins the principle that there remain distinct Indigenous rights.

When Geoff Clark told the Corroboree 2000 audience that 'true reconciliation means recognising we possess distinct rights' he was attempting to shift the discourse of reconciliation from the homogenising themes of 'settler colonial liberalism' to the differentiating themes of 'post-colonial liberalism'. Whereas Evelyn Scott's response implied that the settler colonial liberalism (and the policy possibilities it contains) was a 'step' on the path to what Clark wanted (a step not to be rushed), Clark's assertion of distinct Indigenous rights declared a choice – a fork in the road – to recognise that Indigenous people had their own special claims on the state.

A metaphor of nation

At least, that is how I like to see it: a clear choice between versions of liberalism. I am aware, however, that these are academic terms of little popular appeal. What does seem to appeal is the language of healing. It is through taking up the 'healing' metaphor that some opinion leaders shifted focus from considerations of the design of the 'state' (such as the rules of our federalism) to imagining the spiritual and moral imperatives of 'nation'.

The roots of this language of nation can be seen in some of the arguments advanced in 1979–83 by the Aboriginal Treaty Committee. Though Coombs did not speak or write of 'healing', he had promoted a treaty as a way to remedy a flaw in Australia's nationhood. A treaty, he had suggested, would benefit all Australians, for not only would it give 'security for Aboriginal occupation of these lands', it would also 'bestow legitimacy and some colour of justice to our sovereignty over this continent … ' It would 'bring to an end the long period of hostilities between black and white Australians, enable them to compose their differences and to embark together on a future of peace and friendship'. A treaty would form 'a kind of constitutional basis

---

for the relationship of Aboriginal Australians to Australian society generally'. Our occupation of this continent, he had argued, 'remains tainted and suspect'. Coombs had wanted to persuade non-Indigenous Australians that they badly needed a treaty because, without it, their nationhood was morally flawed and increasingly subject to hostile international scrutiny. The legal fiction of unoccupied land, which had long underpinned Australian law and sovereignty, was no longer supportable.[45]

From 1983 (I choose that date because it was when the Aboriginal Treaty Committee ceased its work) the notion persisted that Australian nationhood is deeply flawed by the 'unfinished business' of black/white relations. The bicentennial celebrations of 1988 created many opportunities to ponder the origins of Australian nationhood and to doubt the appropriateness of celebration. The High Court expressed this same dubiety in 1992 when it ruled that the Crown had always acted unfairly towards Indigenous Australians and that the whole system of land tenure must henceforth acknowledge 'native title'. Acts of redress to Indigenous Australians were framed as rectifying the foundational flaws of the nation.

When CAR presented 'reconciliation' as unifying the nation, the word 'healing' became prominent in reconciliation talk. This rise of the 'healing' metaphor in the language of Australian nationhood was boosted by the emergence into public prominence of the 'Stolen Generations', especially after the publication of *Bringing Them Home* in 1997.[46] In 2000 some leaders and journalists specified that an official Prime Ministerial apology to the Stolen Generations was the key both to reconciliation and to healing. Healing referred to what was needed both by damaged individuals and by the nation that damaged them.

With good reason, many Indigenous Australians have presented themselves as damaged by the state's assault on their family life. Their complaint is not only of material abuse but of an insult to soul and to psyche. Many of them have acquired the terminology of sickness, recovery and healing in order to make sense of their own individual struggles against substance abuse, including alcohol abuse. Grass roots Indigenous mobilisations around substance abuse have drawn heavily on one particular therapeutic ideology: Alcoholics Anonymous. I first noticed the metaphorical extension of 'healing' in November 1994, when I attended in Sydney an international gathering of Indigenous people on the treatment of substance abuse. I could see then that 'healing' was becoming a metaphor for Indigenous empowerment. The recovery of an alcoholic, in AA therapeutic ideology, is the subject of a universalising narrative in which the individual becomes the indispensable agent of his/her recovery; he/she takes power by taking responsibility for him or herself. The AA paradigm of recovery through responsibility has proved adaptable to the Indigenous ideology of self-determination. Personal journeys from sickness and denial to self-responsibility and recovery have become a metaphor of the recovery, en masse, of a people rendered dysfunctional by colonial oppression.

Once that analogy became popular, it was not a big step to make the observation that the colonists also have been sickened by their power and must take responsibility for their own recovery. CAR's 'Australian Declaration Towards Reconciliation' used AA language when it referred to the nation's obligation 'to own the truth, to heal the wounds', and to embark on 'the journey of healing'.[47] These terms occurred frequently in Evelyn Scott's statements. As well, the term 'walk' rivalled the word 'march' to describe what people did on the Sydney Harbour

---

[45] Coombs 1979a.   [46] HREOC 1997.   [47] CAR 2000a: Appendix 1.

Bridge and other places in May 2000. 'Walk' is another AA metaphor for displaying conviction through action: 'You can't talk the talk, if you haven't walked the walk'. In such language Scott and other CAR figures drew on the notions of personhood deployed (with therapeutic effect for many people, I should add) by Alcoholics Anonymous. Scott's press release on 1 June 2000 criticising the treaty advocates' reading of the Sydney Bridge march was headed 'The long walk to reconciliation can't jump stages'.[48] CAR, under Scott, was 'twelve-stepping' the nation.

The notion of national recovery was foreshadowed, as I have pointed out, in Coombs's observations about Australians having to make good the moral defect in their nationhood. By drawing on the language of AA, CAR entrenched and developed that trope so that the 'healing' metaphor, by 2000, had come to signify the spiritual vicissitudes of a self that is concurrently personal, Indigenous and national. I heard this linking of recoveries in the words of a Koori man I met in April 2000 who told me that he and people like him could not commence their recovery from being members of the Stolen Generations until the Prime Minister had offered the nation's apology.

How was it possible that in the weeks leading up to Corroboree 2000 newspapers sympathetic to CAR, such as the *Sydney Morning Herald*, could present 'reconciliation' in terms that highlighted the personal redemption of John Howard through a Prime Ministerial apology? 'Will Howard walk?' became a resonant question.

I suggest that three factors underpinned the emergence of 'healing' as a metaphor of 'reconciliation':

1. The steady growth of an international Indigenous movement against substance abuse, drawing much of its therapeutic ideology from Alcoholics Anonymous, and involving many Indigenous Australians as both healers and healed;

2. The public ascendancy of the Stolen Generations, through the inquiry that produced *Bringing Them Home*,[49] and the assertion, arising from that report, of the mutually healing power of the State's official apology;

3. The conservative political climate since March 1996, which encouraged attention to themes of personal redemption as an alternative to more problematic and difficult themes of institutional change. (Recall that in John Howard's Corroboree 2000 speech, he welcomed any understanding of 'reconciliation' as long as it was 'sincere'.)

It is necessary to recall how 'therapeutic' the language of 'reconciliation' had become if we are to appreciate the value of ATSIC's leadership over the next few years.[50] By insisting on raising the question of the treaty in 2000, Clark provided an alternative to the fog of CAR psychobabble. Just over a week after the Sydney Harbour Bridge march in May 2000, there was a gathering of Indigenous leaders in Melbourne to discuss reconciliation strategy. It is reported to have included Geoff Clark, Marcia Langton, Charles Perkins, Peter Yu, Gary Foley, Michael Mansell, Aden Ridgeway (by phone), Ray Robinson, Pat Dodson, David Ross and Noel Pearson.[51] Evidently, the meeting endorsed Clark's call for a treaty and sketched a strategy for formulating its points of

---

[48] CAR 2000b.

[49] HREOC 1997.

[50] ATSIC was abolished by legislation passed in March 2005.

[51] This list is compiled from two newspaper reports, by Ben Mitchell in *The Australian* 6 June 2000, and by Debra Jopson and Mark Metherell in the *Sydney Morning Herald* 6 June 2000.

negotiation. There was mention of a 'treaty think tank … to examine issues raised from meetings held in Indigenous communities around the country'.[52] By funding a series of conferences on the treaty in 2002, ATSIC provided forums for Indigenous and non-Indigenous people to return to the questions of institutional design that are implicated in any discussion of enforceable claims – rights – and governmental accountability. Some of the results of those discussions in 2002 are to be found in this book.[53]

---

[52] *The Australian* 6 June 2000.   [53] I have made my own observations about three public conferences supported by ATSIC in 2002 in Rowse 2003.

87

References

Newspapers and Newsletters

Age 2 June 2000.

The Aboriginal Treaty Committee Newsletter, 20 May 1980 (signed by HC Coombs).

The Aboriginal Treaty Committee Newsletter 2, October 1980.

Aboriginal Treaty News no 1, nd (most likely April 1981).

Aboriginal Treaty News no 2, August 1981.

Aboriginal Treaty News no 3, November 1981.

Aboriginal Treaty News no 4, February 1982.

Aboriginal Treaty News no 5, May–August 1982.

Aboriginal Treaty News no 6, September–October 1982.

Aboriginal Treaty News no 7, November 1982–February 1983.

Aboriginal Treaty News no 8, March–June 1983.

Aboriginal Treaty News no 9, October 1983.

Canberra Times 9 December 1980, 30 May 2000.

National Times 25 August 1979, 27 July 1980.

Sydney Morning Herald 27 November 1980, 29 May 2000, 6 June 2000.

The Australian 30 May 2000, 2 June 2000, 6 June 2000.

The Catholic Leader 13 July 1980.

Books, articles and reports

Aboriginal and Torres Strait Islander Social Justice Commissioner 2001, Social Justice Report 2000, Sydney, Human Rights and Equal Opportunity Commission.

Aboriginal Treaty Committee 1979, 'We call for a treaty – within Australia, between Australians' (advertisement), National Times, 25 August.

Brennan, Frank and James Crawford 1990, 'Aboriginality, recognition and Australian law: the need for a bipartisan approach', Australian Quarterly 62(2) Winter: 145–69.

Commonwealth of Australia 1983, Two hundred years later … (Report by the Senate Standing Committee on Constitutional and Legal Affairs on the feasibility of a compact, or 'Makarrata', between the Commonwealth and Aboriginal people), Canberra, Australian Government Publishing Service.

Commonwealth of Australia (Senate) 1983, Standing Committee on Constitutional and Legal Affairs (reference: an examination of the feasibility, whether by way of constitutional amendment or other legal means of securing a compact, or Makarrata', between the Commonwealth Government and Aboriginal Australians), Official Hansard Transcript of Evidence.

Coombs, Herbert Cole 1979a, 'Guest of Honour Talk: ABC', CRES Working Paper: HCC/WP13.

—— 1979b, 'The proposal for a treaty between the Commonwealth and Aboriginal Australians' CRES Working Paper: HCC/WP14.

—— 1980, 'Towards an end to 200 years of aggression and injustice', Amnesty address of 1979, reprinted in The National Times, 'Other Voices' column, 8–14 June.

—— 1981, 'Aboriginal treaty symposium – a statement', Anthropology News 18(8) September: 117–9.

Council for Aboriginal Reconciliation (CAR) 2000a, Reconciliation: Australia's Challenge, Final Report of the Council for Aboriginal Reconciliation to the Prime Minister and Commonwealth Parliament (December), Canberra.

—— 2000b, 'The long walk to reconciliation can't jump stages', press release, 1 June, available at www.austli.edu.au/au/other/IndigLRes/car259.html.

Human Rights and Equal Opportunity Commission (HREOC) 1997, Bringing them home: report of the national inquiry into the separation of Aboriginal and Torres Strait Islander children from their families, Human Rights and Equal Opportunity Commission (HREOC), Sydney.

Jopson, D and Mark Metherell 2000, 'Aboriginal leaders meet to push treaty', Sydney Morning Herald, 6 June: 7.

Mitchell, Ben 2000, 'Indigenous leaders persist on treaty', The Australian, 6 June: 2.

Pittock, A Barrie 1981, 'What's wrong with a treaty?', Identity, 4(2): 31.

Rowse Tim 2003, 'Treaty talk', Australian Policy Online, available at http://www.apo.org.au/webboard/items/00216.shtml (posted 11 February 2003).

Wright, Judith 1985, We call for a treaty, Sydney, Collins/Fontana.

Legislation

Aboriginal and Torres Strait Islanders (Queensland Reserves and Communities Self-Management) Act 1978 (Cth).

Aboriginal Land Rights (Northern Territory) Act 1976.

Native Title Amendment Act 1998 (Cth).

Case law

Koowarta v Bjelke-Petersen (1982) 153 CLR 168.

The challenge for Australia: reconciling the Treaty

Sue Stanton

Preface[1]

It is my first duty today to acknowledge the Nyungar people on whose land we gather today. I acknowledge, and wish to express my deep appreciation to all the Aboriginal communities of this region, and also all the people from the various communities represented here today – local, national and international. I pay homage to their Ancestors and to all their living Elders and associated kin. I also extend greetings and good wishes to all non-Aboriginal and non-Indigenous people present here today and to all those who support the ideals of fairness and justice, for all.

My second duty today is to acknowledge all my Ancestors, my Kungarakan Mothers, my kin – all my Kungarakan and Gurindji families of the Northern Territory.

Throughout my talk today I may use terms such as 'black' and 'white' and I would like to insist here that neither is used in derogatory or insulting manner.

Even though I may refer to Torres Strait Islanders and will use the term 'Indigenous Australians' and or Indigenous Peoples of Australia, essentially this paper is in reference to Aboriginal people of mainland Australia. The terms 'European' and 'Anglo Australians' refer essentially to those descendants of white invaders and latter day settlers, including non-Indigenous European and other migrants.

I especially acknowledge Gurindji family, and notably my Grandfathers, Grandmothers who fought the first big land rights battles at Wave Hill, and also, in recognition of all my Gurindji countrymen, those who survived and those who did not, the experiment that was to become known as 'the stolen generations'.

** * **

We can now look at the *Mabo* decision of 1992[2] as a significant milestone. Most of us saw this as an opportunity for Australia to heal itself and to perhaps be better inclined to deal with Aboriginal people in fairer and equitable manner than it had done in the past. The feeling of optimism arose directly as the *Mabo* judgment promised Aboriginal people the legal power to negotiate with governments and industry in order to achieve their long-held desire to attain political and economic autonomy. The decision was celebrated as more than final recognition of Indigenous Australians as Peoples, and it was seen as more than an issue of land ownership and management. It was a celebration of the attainment of some measure of human rights.

---

[1] Introduction to spoken paper.   [2] *Mabo v Queensland (No 2)* (1992) 175 CLR 1.

That's what we thought at the time. *Mabo* provided the opportunity for Aboriginal people to assert their common law rights, meaning that Indigenous land title based on traditional laws and customs was finally recognised by Australian law – but this recognition was not to last for long. Alas we were to be seriously disappointed. Respect for Australian law suffered yet another serious blow for most honest people, both Indigenous and Anglo and other Australians.

It would be wise of Indigenous Peoples of this country to seriously consider any further arrangements and negotiations with Australian government and Australian law, and perhaps time to consider the words supposedly uttered by Native Americans when negotiating treaties with the United States government – no frivolity intended, but those words are 'White man speak with forked tongue!'

We only have to know a little of Australia's colonial history, and to simply observe what is happening and being said in the present, to know that Aboriginal people were, and still are, placed out of sight and out of mind. The racial policies of segregation, the removal of citizenship rights, which should have been automatically granted under common law, the theft of ancient and vast estates, were all solutions, not only for the new nation at Federation, but to suit the present political agenda too. While the past Australian nation visited its own brand of evil on Aboriginal people and, ultimately on itself by laying its very foundations on the twin evils of invasion and genocide, mostly those founding principles continue to this day. Mary Kalantzis said:

> … The truths of invasion and the destruction of Indigenous nations
> during the Colonial period were the silent and most illegal modus
> operandi of the so-called settlers. This ineffectual framework of rights
> was abandoned in the era of Federation. A new way of not having to
> speak about Aborigines, called without irony 'Aboriginal protection',
> emerged around the time of Federation and was to last half way into
> the twentieth century. This evolved into a system so authoritarian as
> to amount in many cases almost to incarceration. Aborigines were put
> into the same category as prisoners and lunatics in a society which
> was, at the time, busily setting up modern institutions to remove
> every manner of social evil and such evils out of sight and therefore
> out of mind.[3]

Indigenous Peoples of Australia need to seriously examine some of these past actions and the words of colonising Founding Fathers and other settlers and make comparison between the rhetoric and ask if the intent of the twin evils is still on the agenda – be careful what you ask for, you just might get it!

Xavier Herbert's memorable statement to his fellow Australian countrymen expressed exactly what the real situation for white and non-Indigenous Australia is, even at this point in the history of the nation. Nothing will change, nothing will mean anything until this restitution is made:

> Until we give back to the black man just a bit of the land that was
> his and give it back without proviso, without strings. To give it back,

90

> without anything but complete generosity of spirit in concession for
> the evil we have done him – until we do that, we shall remain what
> we have always been ... a people without integrity, not a nation, but a
> community of thieves.[4]

Before presenting the challenges for Australia, a few words on the term 'Australia' – a word derived from the Latin 'Terra Australis' – carries in its roots a relationship to early modern European exploration and colonialism. Australia means 'the southern land', south from Europe, and the consequence of 'discovery' and 'settlement' that followed imposed a new word:

> {It} was another Latin concept 'terra nullius'. Terra Australia was a
> land to be taken and colonised, as there was no pre-existing human
> habitation of sufficient significance even to warrant the use of the
> concept 'conquest'. From the point of view of European civilisation,
> Terra Australia was an empty land.[5]

But we all know this was not the truth – well at least we should all know by now that the myth of terra nullius has been exposed.

> There were people here already, a civilisation so subtle, variegated
> and complex that it is almost beyond comprehension from within
> a modern frame of reference – its systems of land tenure, forms of
> farming, kinship structures, cosmologies and languages. As the myth
> of 'terra nullius' has collapsed, so have the heroic claims to discovery
> and settlement. And the myth of English origins is contested by the
> fact that this is not simply an English settler society.[6]

One of the first challenges for Australia is for it to recognise that all the above terms have dispossessed mainland Aboriginal people of their separate identities, and that the current movement named multiculturalism, supposedly initiated and buoyed in the spirit of reconciliation, continues this dispossession as it sets out to strip, indeed rob Indigenous peoples of Australia of their unique cultural identities. Its definition also negates any reason for talk of treaties or other binding agreements, or collaborative dialogue and mutual arrangements.

The challenge of multiculturalism, if Australia is serious about it, is that it should not dictate the agenda. Especially it should not expect different ethnic and cultural groups to wear the mantle of multiculturalism while Anglo Australia remains outside the all-encompassing ethnic umbrella. This umbrella, constructed by the descendants of British invaders and non-Indigenous others, is built on specific criteria dictated by dominant western society and its culture of superiority which in turn is heavily influenced by strict racial codes. Multiculturalism in Australia is not a new or recent phenomenon but has been in operation in its present colonising form even before the introduction of the White Australia policy's official *Immigration Restriction Act 1901* slowed that agenda down for a while. However, that agenda continued for Aboriginal people through the policies of 'protection' and 'assimilation' and continues today in the rhetoric of many non-Indigenous Australians, including government ministers and others in high office who insist on a brand of equality that would see Indigenous peoples of Australia being 'just like us'. The challenge for Australia is to make that 'just like us' equality a reality.

91

---

[4] Herbert, 1978, as quoted in Aboriginal and Torres Strait Islander Social Justice Commissioner 1997: 20 (citing Australia, House of Representatives 1983, *Debates*, vol 134: 3489).

[5] Kalantzis 1998: 5.

[6] Kalantzis 1998: 5.

How will the idea of the Treaty stand up in this multicultural agenda?

Already the idea of recognition as the Indigenous Peoples of Australia is grossly insulted by the portfolio of Aboriginal and Torres Strait Islander Affairs being lumped in with Immigration and Multicultural Affairs. Before further talkfests and numerous other workshops are held, time should be set aside to consider the implications of Aboriginal people being labelled as simply another ethnic or minority group to be dealt with under Australian government classification of 'other'. Instead Australia should meet the challenge and give true and rightful recognition and fully recognise the difference between long-term and ancient rites and customs of this land's original inhabitants as opposed to those of new and recent arrivals, including Anglo invader/settler roots. Maybe the biggest challenge yet, even before the serious talk of the Treaty or treaties, is for the appointment of an Indigenous Minister of Aboriginal and Torres Strait Islander Affairs. As well, Aboriginal and Torres Strait Islander Peoples deserve more than a government-appointed Aboriginal and Torres Strait Islander Social Justice Commissioner to monitor and represent them.

The challenge for Australia post 1967 Referendum, post-*Mabo* and *Wik* and in a true spirit of reconciliation[7]

The lead-up to the 1967 Referendum saw the modern political movement of Aboriginal people and organisations through the establishment of lobby groups especially. However, since that referendum there has been a growing awareness of the state of Indigenous affairs in Australia, and especially noticeable has been the inappropriate policies of the past, and also of the present. Government policies have always been enacted *on behalf of* Aboriginal people, usually without their input and in most cases without consultation with members of the broader Aboriginal community Australia-wide. Self-determination, an issue which rose to prominence during the late 1960s, actively pursued through the following decades and still being spoken about in the new millennium, is still to be realised. The present political and social situation is not good for Indigenous peoples of Australia and the Government, while the rhetoric in regard to reconciliation between black and white Australia remains just that.

The movement away from the demands of self-determination and towards reconciliation are proving as fruitless as previous attempts, and Aboriginal people are becoming more frustrated as their demand for basic rights continues to fall on deaf ears. What difference will a treaty or treaties make?

Recommendation number 339 of the Report of the Royal Commission into Aboriginal Deaths in Custody stated:

> That all political leaders and their parties recognise that reconciliation
> between the Aboriginal and non-Aboriginal communities in Australia
> must be achieved if community division, discord and injustice to
> Aboriginal people are to be avoided. To this end the Committee
> recommended that all political leaders employ their best endeavours

---

[7] Brought by the people of Cape York in North Queensland: the *Wik Peoples v Queensland* (1996) 134 ALR 637; and *The Wik Peoples v State of Queensland & Ors* and *The Thayorre People v The State of Queensland & Ors* (1996) 187 CLR 1. Both matters were heard in the Australian High Court on 23 December. Known as the Wik decision, this holds that native title can co-exist on pastoral leases, but the rights of pastoral leaseholders prevail over any inconsistent rights that the titleholders might have.

> to ensure bipartisan support for the process of reconciliation and that
> the urgency and necessity of the process be acknowledged.[8]

At the same time the Report also noted:

> The racism under which Aboriginal people labour is institutionalised
> and systematic, and resides not just in individuals or in individual
> institutions but in relationships between the various institutions …
> An institution, having significant dealings with Aboriginal people,
> which has rules, practices, habits which systematically discriminate
> against or in some way disadvantage Aboriginal people, is clearly
> engaging in institutional discrimination or racism.[9]

The Royal Commission recognised and acknowledged the continuing effects of past injustice. It noted that at no time had there ever been formal reconciliation between Indigenous and non-Indigenous Australia, and that the desire of Parliament was that reconciliation be achieved by the centenary of Federation in 2001 (it seems more time and effort went into celebrations of white Australia's federation party than the reconciliation agenda).

The challenge for Australia is to recognise that it was unrealistic for reconciliation to have been achieved within the space of ten short years. This is especially true for the Anglo-Australian population, which own the agenda and is burdened with 200-odd years of colonial histories that tell of injustice towards the Indigenous Peoples. They are the same people responsible for the latter-day racist agendas and policies, and are primarily responsible for the current racial intolerance and continued denial of rights. The challenge for Australia is to follow a process of healing, forgiving and understanding, dealing with legacies of gross disadvantage and injustice, and learning to recognise and value Indigenous heritage as part of national identity. It may take some time to achieve.

Even though the reconciliation agenda may have blurred lines, even though 'Aboriginal Reconciliation' has somehow become an agenda for multiculturalism, it is a good thing in many ways. For Indigenous peoples especially recognise that migrants who came to this country, commencing with the first boatload of 'illegal immigrants' in 1788, suffered levels of discrimination and prejudice not too dissimilar to Indigenous peoples. But they also recognise that many issues remain as 'unfinished business' between black and white Australia. And while the reconciliation convention recognised and 'affirmed the special place of Indigenous people in Australian society' and acknowledged that Indigenous people were 'the original owners' of the land, and Government policy was originally designed to address 'Aboriginal Reconciliation' in its broad framework, it has, like all similar policies of the past ('protection', 'assimilation', 'removal') also failed to deliver.

Continuing trends and talk of a treaty – a historical revision

As observed some 169 years ago by Governor Arthur in Tasmania:

> It was a fatal error in the first settlement of Van Diemen's Land, that
> a treaty was not entered into with the natives … had they received
> some compensation on the territory they surrendered, no matter how
> trifling, and had adequate laws been from the very first introduced

---

[8] Royal Commission 1991: 146.   [9] Royal Commission 1991: 146.

> and enforced for their protection, His Majesty's Government
> would have acquired a valuable possession without the injurious
> consequences which have followed our occupation and which must
> forever remain a stain upon the colonisation of Van Diemen's Land.[10]

While brief mentions of treaty negotiation were made in the earlier colonial days, no formal discussions were ever held. Governor Arthur of Tasmania did urge the English House of Commons in the 1840s to consider making treaties with Aboriginal people, but went no further than that. John Batman negotiated the only treaty made with Aboriginal people with the Kulin at Melbourne in 1835, but it was ruled invalid by the Governor of Victoria. His office ruled that treaties carried out by private citizens were not recognised by the Crown.

Treaties were not mentioned again for at least another one hundred years when in 1975 the Senate passed a resolution by Senator Neville Bonner[11] which urged the Australian Government to at least acknowledge prior ownership of the Australian land mass by Aboriginal People. Also at that time Bonner called for the introduction of legislation to compensate Aboriginal people for the dispossession of their lands. From this historical overview it is obvious that the talk of treaties, reconciliation and compensation for land loss is not new, though it is treated as such. Australia has, over time, been presented with the challenge to right the wrongs of the past and allow itself to move to a new negotiating level, but it refuses to. Even 1967, which told of a growing awareness among the wider community that Aboriginal issues were far from resolved and that some form of settlement was urgently required if black and white Australia were to reach an accord of any description, was not heeded.

The challenge for Australia is not just for closure on many of the Indigenous issues and demands, but to give to its non-Indigenous population the right to make closure as a collective population. The challenge for Australia is for it to recognise this is not just about black Australia, but this is about the disestablishment of the current status quo as this situation has a profound impact on the daily lives, and the future lives of its non-Indigenous citizenry too. However, the Government continues to bury its head in the sand – ignoring calls for uniform national land rights legislation and changes to other inconsistent legislation which continue to confuse and disempower – as it finds the task too difficult due to powerful lobby groups such as representatives of miners and pastoralists who pressure Government into abandoning all talk of a treaty or treaties with Aboriginal people.

The Aboriginal Treaty Committee was formed in 1979 in an effort to educate and perhaps persuade non-Indigenous Australians to accept the general idea of a treaty. However The Senate Standing Committee on Constitutional and Legal Affairs in its 1983 document *Two Hundred Years Later* rejected suggestions of a treaty, adopting the old argument that Indigenous nations of Australia, not being sovereign entities, could not enter into treaty negotiations with the Commonwealth. How convenient is this argument? Still this Committee called for a 'compact' which possibly could eventually be inserted into the Australian Constitution by way of referendum. The challenge for Australia is to revive this discussion in 2002 and to hold this referendum.

---

[10] Arthur to Hay, 24 September 1832, CO280/35, PROL, cited in Ryan 1981:174; see also Harris 1994: 105–6.

[11] Neville Bonner AO (1922–1999) the first Aboriginal person to be elected to Federal Parliament.

The current Prime Minister resists any ideas in relation to treaty. He would never consider anything remotely similar to Hawke's suggestion of a 'Makarrata', as it seems he is quite oblivious to the history of dispossession and the racist and unjust policies of past Australian governments. So far he has only offered this patronising rhetoric:

> I hope we have some kind of written understanding. I don't like the idea of a treaty because it implies that we are two nations. We are not, we are one nation. We are all Australians before anything else, one indivisible nation … within the notion of one undivided united Australian community where our first and foremost allegiance is to Australia and nothing else.[12]

Well hello! The challenge for John Howard and his Australia, is to recognise just that. We are all living on the one land mass but in very unequal positions.

Many Indigenous people share strong views in relation to the 'non-reconciliation' movement, and its lack of commitment to the overall treaty dialogue. Many fail to get excited about the entire concept. Noel Pearson, Executive Director, Cape York Land Council, is one of many who holds the view that Aboriginal people don't need to be reconciled to anything. Many Aboriginal leaders and others condemn the notion of reconciliation and have questioned the motives of such a movement as they are uncertain of its direction and wary of its possible hidden agendas.

The challenge for Australia is to prove that this is not the case.

Many ambiguities continue to surround the concept of reconciliation and a great number of Aboriginal people are cautious about the capacity of the reconciliation policy to put in place the effective and long-lasting changes that are required. After all, Aboriginal people have had extensive experience with government policies in the past and have every right to remain sceptical.

Indigenous critics have also noted that in addition to the ambiguity and vague nature of the reconciliation rhetoric, major issues important to them such as sovereignty, treaty, and land rights, are all conspicuously absent from the overall government agenda. The approach to dealing with Indigenous issues also does not provide any suitable mechanism through which the voices of all Indigenous Australians may be heard. The late Kevin Gilbert, who was Chairperson of the Treaty '88 campaign and who fought for the establishment of a treaty which would enshrine the rights of Aboriginal people as well as advance dialogue on issues of Aboriginal sovereignty, eventually became highly critical of the entire process, and refused flatly to accept either the idea of a Council for Aboriginal Reconciliation or the idea of reconciliation at all. Gilbert however strongly supported the notion of a treaty.[13] He stated:

> We have to look at the word 'reconciliation'. What are we to reconcile ourselves to? To a holocaust, to massacre, to the removal of us from our land, from the taking of our land? The reconciliation process can achieve nothing because it does not at the end of the

---

[12] John Howard 1998.   [13] In 1988 Gilbert, who was awarded the Human Rights and Equal Opportunity Commission's Human Rights Award for Literature, returned the award stating that he could not accept such an award while Aboriginal people were still being denied human rights in their own land.

> day promise justice. It does not promise a Treaty and it does not
> promise reparation for the taking away of our lives, our lands and our
> economic and political base. Unless it can return to us these very vital
> things, unless it can return to us an economic, a political and a viable
> base, what have we? A handshake? A symbolic dance? An exchange of
> leaves and feathers or something like that?[14]

The challenge for Australia in relation to both the Treaty and the reconciliation agenda is to recognise the fear and uncertainty felt by Aboriginal people, to alter its own direction, to recognise that government appointments and not representatives elected by Aboriginal peoples themselves cause much of the distrust and reluctance among Aboriginal people to be involved. Then it must radically change that approach.

Members of the Aboriginal Provisional Government (APG) were highly critical of the processes involved in initial reconciliation agendas, and perhaps are still suspicious of the current Treaty dialogue. Like many other Aboriginal individuals, they know only too well that, usually, those appointed to represent the entire Aboriginal population are not only well chosen, but must be politically middle of the road so as to cause the least amount of stirring and resistance. The challenge for Aboriginal people is not to fall into this trap – the old divide and rule trick.

Michael Mansell of the APG observed that there is an 'uncanny similarity between rhetoric surrounding the policy of reconciliation and that attached to the policies of one-time politician Pauline Hanson and her former One Nation Party party. Like the Prime Minister now, Pauline Hanson spoke of a 'united Australia', 'we are one'. Yet, in very contradictory terms, the Prime Minister also speaks of the 'special position' and 'prior ownership', but he does not wish to make 'special considerations', or to give anything back, or to consider a treaty or treaties.

In conclusion I quote from the words of Glenn T Morris of the Colorado chapter of the American Indian Movement (AIM), who stated in 1992:

> If people are genuinely interested in honouring Indians, try getting
> your government to live up to the more than 400 treaties it signed
> with our nations. Try respecting our religious freedom which has
> been repeatedly denied in federal courts. Try stopping the ongoing
> theft of Indian water and other natural resources. Try reversing your
> colonial process that relegates us to the most impoverished, polluted,
> and desperate conditions in this country ... Try understanding that
> the mascot issue is only the tip of a very huge problem of continuing
> racism against American Indians. Then maybe your ['honors'] will
> mean something. Until then, it's just so much superficial, hypocritical
> puffery. People should remember that an honor isn't born when
> it parts the honorer's lips, it is born when it is accepted in the
> honoree's ear.[15]

Sounds all too familiar when put in the Aboriginal context. Be careful what you ask for – a treaty is a treaty after all.

---

[14] Gilbert as quoted in Mudrooroo 1995: 228–9.   [15] As quoted in Churchill 1992: 219. Ward Churchill (Keetoowah Cherokee), member of AIM since 1972, Professor of Ethnic Studies at University of Colorado, Boulder.

Postscript

I write in memory of Gatjil Djerrkura, respected Elder and spokesperson for Wungurri people and many other Aboriginal people in this country. We must heed some of his final words about the paternalistic model of government. These are the usual rhetorical responses, it seems, to every Indigenous issue. Gatjil referred to the dismantling of ATSIC:

> It is no coincidence that Mr Howard announced his attention to abolish ATSIC ... the manner in which it was made and the language in which it was delivered. In the classic imperial fashion, without negotiation, without understanding and with little empathy, the great white leader announced that Aboriginal people had, yet again, been a 'failure' ... The Prime Minister walks early and often, but he has never walked for reconciliation.[16]

---

[16] Djerrkura 2004.

References

Aboriginal and Torres Strait Islander Social Justice Commissioner 1997, Fifth Report 1997: Report to the Federal Attorney-General as per section 46C.(1) of the Human Rights and Equal Opportunity Commission Act 1986, available at http://www.hreoc.gov.au/pdf/social_justice/sj_report 97.pdf

Churchill, Ward 2002, *Acts of Rebellion: The Ward Churchill reader*, Routledge, New York.

Djerrkura, Gatjil 2004, Our paternalistic model of government, speech at the launch of Mark McKenna's *This Country: A Reconciled Republic?*, reproduced in full in *The Canberra Times,* 14 May.

Harris, JW 1994, *One blood*, Albatross, Sydney.

Howard, John 1998, on *60 Minutes* (Beazley and Howard election debate), 13 September, available at http://www.australiapolitics.com/elections/1998/debate/html

Kalantzis, Mary 1998, Reconsidering the Meaning of Our Commonwealth, Women's Constitutional Convention, Canberra, January 29–30.

—— 2001, 'Recognising Diversity', *The Barton Lecture # 3*, ABC Radio National, 25 February.

Mudrooroo 1995, *Us mob*, Angus and Robertson, Melbourne.

Royal Commission into Aboriginal Deaths in Custody 1991, *National Report*, vol 5, AGPS, Canberra.

Ryan, L 1981, *The Aboriginal Tasmanians*, Allen and Unwin, St Leonards.

Senate Standing Committee on Constitutional and Legal Affairs 1983, *Two Hundred Years Later – A Report on the Feasibility of a Compact or 'Makaratta' between the Commonwealth and Aboriginal People*, AGPS, Canberra.

Legislation

Immigration Restriction Act 1901 (Cth).

Case law

Mabo and Ors v The State of Queensland (No 2) (1992) 175 CLR 1.

Wik Peoples v Queensland (1996) 134 ALR 637.

The Wik Peoples v The State of Queensland & Ors; The Thayorre People v The State of Queensland & Ors (1996) 187 CLR 1.

A treaty for whom?
Indigenous jurisdictions and the treaty sideshow

Eddie Mabo Jnr

My own traditional understanding of ownership is based on more than a symbolic gesture that unfortunately many now use like a cartoon ritual of recognition of country and kin that bears no tangible meaning to how Indigenous people recognise one another. We have always operated out of an understanding of our own and other jurisdictions to land and water. This is what makes us Indigenous people.

My first observation is that I realise that, despite my father's legacy, the legal system of this country remains blind to a concept of a sovereignty enjoyed by Aboriginal and Torres Strait Islander groups prior to European invasion. The evidence that my father and others provided to the courts was recognised as a system of laws and customs relating to land and sea ownership; however, this recognition did not constitute the same rights of ownership and control that one might enjoy if we had been recognised as a nation that had rights to own property outright.

The Australian High Court recognised native title as arising from a prior Aboriginal title to land and waters, but its decision stopped well short of recognising our sovereignty. In fact it stopped well short of recognising the kind of land and sea tenure that is consistent with the concepts of property that we know all too well.

We practise our customs and traditions on a clear presumption of total ownership of our lands and waters, not just on the basis of being like animals that simply used our physical environment as a playground to practise our customs and traditions. They obviously got it wrong: they put the cart before the horse. The kind of title to land that I speak of here must be recognised well before we talk of a treaty. Native title is unfinished business, so a treaty should be a means by which Indigenous people can regroup and understand ourselves as Indigenous peoples and communities. We have to self-determine now if we are to enjoy self-determination in the future!

This is why I find the call for a Treaty by ATSIC and its supporters to be problematic. How can we explore a treaty when our communities are themselves not able to govern themselves efficiently, economically, and politically? While I understand that a treaty may deliver an overarching, more comprehensive mandate for Indigenous peoples and communities to begin developing their communities in ways that are productive and sustainable, I feel we should not be putting all our eggs in one basket.

We should be cautious of the idea that a treaty will represent a 'payload'. This is unrealistic and inherently damaging to the aspirational grassroots people who are struggling on a daily basis to secure the basics of living in this world. The Aboriginal lawyer Noel Pearson believes that 'passive welfare' can be blamed for its capacity to undermine self-sufficiency and cultural traditions. We should not travel along the treaty road until we are sure that it will not give us a 'passive treaty'. This kind of treaty is what Indigenous people in New Zealand and Canada are fighting against. When we examine our own history and the passive ways in which colonial governments recognised our inherent rights as Indigenous people, I begin to ask, 'So what has changed?' The authoritarian nature of mission or government administrators sapped individual and community initiatives, but these initiatives were also sapped by the absence of an overarching recognition of Aboriginal people to own land and self governance.

I am of the opinion that the means by which a treaty is currently being explored is flawed if we do not invest in exploring how we can develop our own jurisdictions and have them recognised first. A diverse range of Indigenous jurisdictions will emerge, a united yet diverse range of jurisdictions which cannot be washed away by any tide of history.

It was one thing for ATSIC to make the strongest possible statements and recommendations about developing a treaty, to hold numerous forums and spend yet more money on educating the great unwashed on the colonial history and genocide of Indigenous people. It is quite another matter as to what the Government and the Parliament will commit themselves to at a negotiating table to discuss a treaty of some kind.

Without doubt Australia needs to complete its constitutional obligations to recognise and protect the rights and interests of the original and continuing owners of this land, but whether constitutional protection can be enjoyed to the extent that Aboriginal and Torres Strait Islander people can assert these rights as part of our everyday citizenship and communal rights is questionable. Why?

I for one believe that our sovereign jurisdiction as Indigenous peoples requires legal structures much more sophisticated than those which serve ordinary Australians. We are after all, not ordinary Australians, and have never been. We continue to be extraordinary Australians.

On a political level, if we are to wait for either the Howard or Beazley government to commit to negotiating a treaty, then we will be waiting a very long time. Their political careers are much more precious to them than fixing up the immorally dispossessed Indigenous people. Bearing this in mind, many of you may agree with me when I say that there has never been a more urgent time to evaluate the political strategies that national leadership are using, especially in terms of how these strategies are perceived to deliver achievable outcomes for Aboriginal and Torres Strait Islander people and communities. There has to be continual reminders that there exists a huge gap between people on the ground and those elitists advocating on our behalf in national forums. Grassroots people in the communities, like myself, live from day to day and in many cases without the time to give a single thought to what their elite leaders are thinking about, writing about, and putting up as a national agenda to governments at all levels.

I want to make what I'm saying here clearer. The leadership and structures which Aboriginal and Torres Strait Islander have created have repeatedly disenfranchised those that they meant to represent. Since the 1970s the experience in Aboriginal affairs has been to gradually maximise the participation of Aboriginal peoples into mainstream administrative structures. We have for too long been the moralising political fodder for the Left and a convenient punching bag for the Right. We've won more political elections for political parties than any other social group in this country's colonial history, but have gained nothing but contempt. We will continue to inhabit and shape the racist fears of white Australians for some years to come and no amount of public education and campaigning for a better understanding of the past is going to wash away a deep fear and loathing for Indigenous people. Unfortunately we live in world where political views are not mobilised amongst ourselves at the grassroots, but is driven by questions created about us by government and those they pay to represent us.

How then can talk of developing a treaty born out of a system that has developed around processes that contain the very jurisdictions and rights that we as Indigenous people should enjoy as Indigenous peoples? *How can we talk of treaty when we have yet to throw off the administrative colonial blankets that they have covered us with for so long?*

While the official message from ATSIC emphasised that ATSIC saw this process as inclusive and not restricted to ATSIC Commissioners and the Regional Councillors there appeared to be no detail on how this process of including all Aboriginal and Torres Strait Islander people came about. On one hand their facilitation of a discussion of a treaty was based admirably on the need for recognising Indigenous Australian sovereignty. Yet we continue to see statements calling for governments to heed messages, borne out in statistical reports for the Federal, State and Territory governments and their agencies, to better target policies and programs to close yawning service gaps between Indigenous and non-Indigenous Australians.

Let me explain this further. If we are calling for discussions and a need to explore a treaty, something that may deliver *optimal self-determination*, how is this related to how we talk to governments about how they can better deliver services to our communities? It just doesn't make sense. If ATSIC were calling on governments and territories to fulfil their legal, political and moral obligations to deliver better services for our people to bring us up to the standards of living and outcomes enjoyed by other Australians, are we calling on them to assimilate us? If the basis of these calls to obligation are based on us being the same, and not on the basis of being Indigenous people whose legal rights are based on platforms of prior occupation and ownership of land, then we contradict the central arguments within the calls for a treaty.

This brings me to important questions. If we are calling for a treaty, whom will this treaty be for? Is the political framework that currently exists to represent Aboriginal and Torres Strait Islander interests in the discussion and advocacy of a Treaty adequate? How can we continue to ignore that we are captives of a colonising government and delude ourselves and pretend to take up a position outside the barbed wire fences of government legislation and policy and call for our own release? The mind boggles.

My father Koiki Mabo had a clear understanding of where he stood in terms of questioning the so-called rights of a colonial government to make decisions about his land and his people. This clarity of perspective seems to have been eroded over the years and it certainly is not evident in the current political leadership (both black and white) that Indigenous people are relying on to represent their interests. My fathers' clarity of perspective did not come from working inside the bowels of government. It came from a desire to determine his own destiny. These perspectives exist in Indigenous communities across this nation and they need to be heard and they need to be politically supported.

I was heartened by a call by the former co-chair of Reconciliation Australia, Fred Chaney, for Indigenous groups to act as nations now that native title has delivered a new order. But what exactly is the nature of the new order? Whatever it may be, it is easier said by people who have

101

good intentions but don't understand the realities of being an Indigenous person in a colonial country. Yes, I applaud how groups such as ANTaR are highly supportive of our cause and go to great lengths in organising public awareness events right across this nation. However, it's often forgotten that this is not a new struggle but a struggle that was initiated by Indigenous people and that the emphasis and focus must shift back to our hands for better or worse.

A reconciled Australia will arrive the day when Indigenous people are in charge of defining who white Australians are, not the other way round. If we are an ethnic group, so too are white people, but as we all know, they live in a privileged world where they can pretend not to be an ethnic group. This raises an important question. If white people are an ethnic group, can we begin to audit our contribution to their wealth?

More and more we need to explore how supporters can enhance the way Indigenous people and communities participate in all types of debates, not just debates that are obviously ours to have, but ones that many Australians feel we have no interest in. I feel that multicultural policies past and present have not adequately recognised Indigenous peoples as Indigenous peoples. I work in an urban community where there are 161 identifiable ethnic groups of which Aboriginal and Torres Strait Islander people represent two. I know first-hand the diversity of Aboriginality and Islanderness inside my community but legislation and laws define these groups in ways that do not recognise their connection to lands, connections and rights to customary laws and practices.

How will a treaty have an immediate impact on our youth aged 15–19? Only 46% of our young people are at school.

If a treaty contributes to improving the educational outcomes and provides a schooling system that validates their identities as well as prepares them for a future that they can determine, then count me in. But I've seen no evidence to support this notion.

How will constitutional rights change the way that police treat Indigenous children under colonial laws. How will it stop racism? I may sound overly cynical to some but I say these things from a perspective of a grassroots person who knows that even if we had a treaty tomorrow the fundamental social and cultural changes that impede the majority of Indigenous people from enjoying the most basic of human rights would not change. I have also yet to be enlightened on how a treaty will be addressed given that the majority of Indigenous peoples live in settled areas of this nation.

How will those who advocate a treaty deal with this profound contradiction between support for cultural diversity and the way that a treaty will devolve power to this same diversity in Indigenous communities?

Who has the mandate to negotiate a treaty on behalf of all Indigenous people in this country? Was it ATSIC? I think not. Clearly there are Indigenous groups and communities in this country that have no difficulty in garnering the kind of political and geographical identity required to enter into discussions on a treaty on a regional basis.

My father's legacy was not motivated by a need to empower the local CDEP office or a Department of Aboriginal affairs to better broker deals for Aboriginal and Torres Strait Islander people. Quite the opposite. He was motivated by empowering himself and his people to speak for themselves, to speak what they know, and to do this with an understanding that their right to speak about country and protect their lands and seas, to get employed, to get a good education, to raise a family, was based to a greater extent on their rights as Indigenous people. Not as second-hand white Australians or as part of an ethnic minority. His claim to land and sea was about getting the colonial governments and the laws that guided colonial governments to provide clear and unambiguous recognition that:

1) they were in breach of their own laws relating to recognising the original occupants of this country and seas and

2) this recognition should provide certainty to real ownership of land and seas as it has been understood by Indigenous people since eternity.

To a greater rather than to a lesser extent, my father equated the exchange with the High Court of this nation-state of his knowledge of customs and traditions, laws and rituals as clear and unambiguous evidence of his and his people's rights to own their land outright. *He was never unclear on this.*

Insofar as Indigenous people have concepts of having laws that relate land and water without interference from outside of our societies, my understanding is that this has always been the case. Interference from outside only heightened rather than extinguished this awareness.

But how is the current debate about a treaty allowing this to be acknowledged? It is not. It is for this reason that I oppose the treaty idea and especially the political processes that are driving the treaty sideshow.

Our short-term engagements and objectives with governments cannot be dislocated from the long-term objectives of a treaty, but it seems this is exactly what is happening.

For me there is much to do in developing appropriate Indigenous governance structures at the grassroots in readiness for the complications that will arise when we finally reach a treaty negotiation table. Many of these structures can arise by reclaiming the means by which we choose our leadership structures at a regional and local level. We have never enjoyed the benefits from devising and using of our own system of democracy and representation as colonised people. It's time we gave this serious thought. Only through this will we develop Indigenous jurisdictions that are worthy of negotiating a treaty. The current models are flawed and everyone knows it.

Let me finish by saying that the necessary implication of the decision in the Mabo decision was that *terra nullius* has been abandoned. What was put in its place is the question we are now faced with, another challenge for us to consider. It's time that Indigenous people closed the doors and discussed the matter amongst ourselves. Otherwise we will continue to search for yet more answers to that age-old white colonising question that they know keeps us fighting amongst ourselves: *who are you?*

Before we tell them '*who we are*' (for the millionth time) we have to answer this simple question for ourselves. Then and only then can we talk about a treaty.

103

What is a treaty?

Michael Dodson

A treaty is a settlement or agreement arrived at by *treating* or negotiation. A treaty gives rise to binding obligations between the parties who makes them. It acts to formalise a relationship between the parties to the agreement(s).

In international law the word treaty has been used to cover a variety of international agreements. The *Vienna Convention on the Law of Treaties* of 1969 is the international codification of the practice of treaty making previously regulated by the Customary Rules of International Law. The Convention was concluded in Vienna on 23 May 1969 and entered into force on 27 January 1980.[1] The Convention, to which Australia is a party, defines a treaty as an agreement whereby two or more nation states establish, or seek to establish, a relationship between themselves, imposing binding obligations on themselves and governed by international law. (A short overview of the Convention is at Annex 1.)

The term treaty has been used in the domestic context on occasion to describe arrangements between individuals, for example in conveyancing for the sale and purchase of property. A domestic treaty would by description be bound by domestic law alone and not be subject to international scrutiny.

The word 'treaty' covers a range of ideas and concepts, including, a contract or compact, a covenant, an agreement, a settlement or international arrangements between nation states. In so doing, it acts to regulate a variety of relationships depending on the nature of the relationship.

The treaties of North America between First Nations or First Peoples (sometimes referred to as 'Indians') and the British in the prevailing legal discourse are not considered international treaties in the sense of agreements between independent and sovereign nations. What most of the treaty documents did express is the notion that the Indians constituted separate and sovereign peoples who had their own laws, and were capable as nations and tribes of forming and breaking their own alliances with others, including the colonial powers, and who also had national or tribal territories under their control. Thereby, acknowledging that there is a distinct relationship between the two groups defined by agreement(s).

The legal discourse mentioned above, has arrived at its present place in a journey over several centuries in what Martinez Cobo describes as the process of domesticating relations with Indigenous peoples.

---

[1] 1155 UNTS 331

This process essentially was (and still is!) part and parcel of the colonisation process. The European colonising powers (and their successors) sought to transform the status of Indigenous sovereign nations into state domesticated entities. This was attempted in various ways.

To divest Indigenous peoples of their sovereign attributes the main weapon utilised was to strip them of their jurisdiction over their ancestral lands and refuse to recognise their societal organisation and status as subjects of international law.

Whatever the accepted legal position comes to be will not then, as it is not now, be a position that is shared by Indigenous First Nations who are party to such treaties.

A treaty, therefore, is an agreement between two parties who seek to have their relationship with each other spelt out. It would therefore be a recognised relationship bound by the specific principles agreed to by the parties.

Principles underlying a treaty may include:

- recognition of Aboriginal and Torres Strait Islander peoples as the first peoples of Australia and of the distinct rights which flow from this;
- agreement to the necessary reforms for a more just society; and
- the setting of national standards to inform local or regional treaties and agreements.

The international legal meaning of treaties is a position clearly and unequivocally already adopted by the present Australian government as reason for rejecting calls for a treaty. It is obvious that in light of such entrenched attitudes the term treaty must be viewed in the broadest possible sense and efforts made to build confidence in the process (and its ultimate objective) on all sides. Martinez Cobo rightly noted in his treaty study that one should avoid making oneself a prisoner of existing terminology.[2]

What is required is innovative thinking. To put Martinez another way, a Eurocentric historiography of treaties must be put to rest if we are to progress to new treaty making.

Why do we need a treaty?

Unlike Canada, the United States and New Zealand, Australia has never formally recognised a treaty with Indigenous peoples. Although there were attempts made by people such as Augustus Robinson and Batman, these were never formally recognised nor upheld by the British Colonial powers at the time.

Aboriginal people did have recognised customs and power structures (and still do) that recognised treaties in a variety of forms. This has been clearly noted by Augustus Robinson, who answered an advertisement in the local newspaper to treat with the Tasmanian Aborigines. Clearly, this establishes a link to the type of relationship that existed, at the time of the first contact, between Aboriginal people and the 'settlers'. Thus, drawing attention to the fact that a treaty was seen as a necessary way of defining the relationship between Aborigines and the settlers. And, as such, clearly highlighting that the settlers recognised as early as 1820 that a treaty was of value to the relationship as it was their belief that it would stem the violence and deprivation that Aborigines were suffering from first contact.

---

[2] Martinez Cobo 1987: Add.4.

This is significant in a contemporary setting as it points to the way in which Aboriginal people have been disenfranchised by the tide of history. First, on the basis that their rights have never been formally recognised by the settlers or past government. Second, their rights have been affected by the way in which the relationship has been one sided. History shows that Aboriginal people have been painted in a certain light. Often portrayed as the 'native savages' with no concept of 'civilised' customs. This has been misleading, to both the Aborigines of the past and those of the present. History, in a sense, has been the victimiser (for want of a better term) of Aboriginal people simply by maintaining the construct of Aboriginal people as native savages.

> A treaty acts both to restore the lost and suppressed dignity, while defining the Aborigines in what should be seen as a true sense.
>
> Arguably, a treaty could have recognised and protected Indigenous rights and led to a just Constitutional basis for the Australian Federation.

For example, Aboriginal and Torres Strait Islander peoples were completely overlooked as relevant parties in the formation of the Australian Federation. If a treaty had been in place, and constituted by the principles noted above, the structure of Federation would no doubt have incorporated Aboriginal rights and position in the Federal system. In Australia, it was not until the *Mabo* decision that the government recognised the property rights of Aboriginal and Torres Strait Islanders. The British, with the exception of Australia, recognised these rights in all its other colonies.

The basis of British sovereignty up until the Mabo decision relied on a ruling in 1889 of the Judicial Committee of the Privy Council,[3] which said that Australia was not occupied by conquest or cession but rather it was *practically unoccupied, without settled inhabitants or settled law at the time it was peacefully annexed.* This is essentially the doctrine of *terra nullius*, which the High Court, in the *Mabo* judgment, overturned.

The Mabo decision has not delivered a just settlement of the historical grievances of Aboriginal and Torres Strait Islanders. These claims are not only defined in terms of meeting the physical needs of Indigenous peoples but they also have for Aboriginal and Torres Strait Islanders a moral dimension.

The moral component will never be met by better informed government policies or programs of service delivery which focus on health, housing, education, housing etc. *The so-called practical reconciliation.* To cater for the moral imperatives there has to be a recognition and acceptance by government of two necessary truths:

- Aboriginal and Torres Strait Islander societies have been injured and harmed throughout the colonisation process and just recompense is owed; and

- The status of Aboriginal and Torres Strait Islander peoples as first peoples and the distinctive rights and special status based on prior occupation that flow from that.

Intensive government programs aimed at bringing about equality with other citizens will not, of itself, provide justice for Indigenous Australians. Some still believe this is a form of compensation for past injustices. This approach ignores two important issues, namely the

---

[3] Privy Council in *Cooper v Stuart* (1889) 14 AC 286 at 291; *Mabo v Queensland* (no 2) 175 CLR 1

adequacy of the compensation and the right of peoples to self-determination. This 'welfarist' approach is just as sinister and destructive as the older paternalistic policies of assimilation.

Culture and identity is every inch of our land and every inch of our history.

The time is right to talk about a treaty with the approach of the Centenary of Federation. Even the word, 'federate', derives from the Latin word, *foedere: to make a treaty*.

A recent AC Nielsen Age poll showed that 53% of Australians are ready to embrace the concept of a treaty.

A national treaty here will reflect an Australia that has matured as a nation. It is important to realise that a national treaty does not stop Indigenous communities and other local, regional, state and territory stakeholders from signing treaties with each other at those levels.

Finally, and perhaps above all, a treaty or treaties will deliver the ultimate certainty to the relationship between Aboriginal and Torres Strait Islanders and the rest of the country's population.

What are the benefits of a treaty? (Why would the government agree?)

A *properly negotiated* treaty will deliver

- agreed standards;
- a framework for settling relationships between Indigenous peoples and governments at local, regional, state, territory and federal levels;
- legal recognition including Constitutional recognition that Aboriginal and Torres Strait Islander peoples have inherent rights which must inform all processes of governments in Australia;
- improved services such as health, housing, education and employment in accordance with the legitimate aspirations of Indigenous peoples; and
- certainty.

Australian law and the legal framework for a treaty

There are perhaps four ways in which a treaty could be negotiated in Australia between Indigenous peoples and the Commonwealth Government. These are:

- An agreement under international law in the form of a treaty
- An agreement that is supported by the Constitution
- An agreement that is supported by legislation
- A simple agreement

I discuss below these options for a legislative framework, however I would urge that a single treaty may not suffice.

An agreement under international law in the form of a treaty

The immediate issue implicit in this approach is the continued existence of Aboriginal and Torres Strait Islander sovereignty as this option is a proposition that would have two sovereign parties: the Commonwealth of Australia and the Aboriginal and Torres strait Islander peoples would enter an agreement enforceable under international law.

Apart from the need to be in writing this approach poses some difficulties in the Australian domestic political context. Not only do the parties have to have the capacity to conclude treaties under international law but they must also be sovereign entities possessing international personality or status. The Commonwealth of Australia is obviously regarded internationally as a sovereign entity and possesses international personality. This cannot, as a matter of reality, be said to describe the status of Indigenous Australians.

An agreement that is supported by the Constitution

One option to secure a legal treaty is to include the entire text of the document in the Australian Constitution. Such a proposal could set the basis of relationships between the Commonwealth and Aboriginal and Torres Strait Islander peoples and how they would be conducted for the future.

Such an approach has its advantages, for example in providing certainty, but could prove to be inflexible, difficult to change or to remove problems that may be encountered in operation. Obtaining approval for such a proposal would also be very difficult. A bare statement of principles, perhaps providing a framework for the future relationship, might gain approval from the electors. However, any detailed text would be next to impossible to get into the Constitution given the history of failure of referenda in Australia.

Agreeing on the wording and content appears the most confronting task. These matters would first have to receive support from Indigenous peoples. A bill for a law is then required from the Federal Parliament followed by a majority of people in a majority of states voting in favour.

Another Constitutional option is to insert a special section into the Constitution, which would give a broad enabling power to the Commonwealth Parliament to negotiate a treaty or treaties with representatives of Aboriginal and Torres Strait Islander peoples. This could be based on the present Section 105A as a model. This section of the Constitution provides as follows:

Agreements with respect to State debts (Inserted by No 1.1929, s.2.) 105A.

(1) The Commonwealth may make agreements with the States
with respect to the public debts of the States, including –

    (a) the taking over of such debts by the Commonwealth;

    (b) the management of such debts;

    (c) the payment of interest and the provision and management
of sinking funds in respect of such debts;

    (d) the consolidation, renewal, conversion, and redemption of such debts;

    (e) the indemnification of the Commonwealth by the States in
respect of debts taken over by the Commonwealth; and

    (f) the borrowing of money by the States or by the Commonwealth,
or by the Commonwealth for the States.

(2) The Parliament may make laws for validating any such agreement
made before the commencement of this section.

> (3) The Parliament may make laws for the carrying out by
>   the parties thereto of any such agreement.
>
> (4) Any such agreement may be varied or rescinded by the parties thereto.
>
> (5) Every such agreement and any such variation thereof shall be binding upon
>   the Commonwealth and the States parties thereto notwithstanding anything
>   contained in this Constitution or the Constitution of the several States
>   or in any law of the Parliament of the Commonwealth or of any State.
>
> (6) The powers conferred by this section shall not be construed as being limited in
>   any way by the provisions of section one hundred and five of this Constitution.

110

If such a proposal received support from the electors at a referendum it would give the Commonwealth Parliament plenary powers to enter such treaties. It potentially gives great security to Aboriginal and Torres Strait Islander peoples and would not require the support (although desirable) of the States. It would also avoid the need for the Commonwealth to have to rely on some other (uncertain) enabling power presently existing in the Constitution, like Section 51. (xxvii).

The High Court of Australia has said, referring to sub-section 5 of Section 105A, that:

> … the effect of this provision is to make any agreement of the
> required description obligatory upon the Commonwealth and
> the States, to place its operation and efficacy beyond the control
> of any law of any of the seven Parliaments, and to prevent any
> Constitutional principle or provision operating to defeat or diminish
> or condition the obligatory force of the Agreement.

A new Section 105B could be perhaps inserted which would enable the Commonwealth to have the power to make the treaties as presently spelt out in the first paragraph of 105A. This paragraph would then be followed by a non-inclusive list of those things that might form the content and substance of the treaties, in very broad terms.

The terms of the treaties could set other requirements, for example, forms of dispute resolution and the power to vary the treaty provision by the parties. The new 105B would also require an automatic validation of the treaty or treaties entered into before the new section took effect. This would allow existing agreements, if so desired, to be brought under the new section. There could also be a power for the parliaments to pass laws enabling them to carry into effect the terms of the treaty or treaties; this would mean the Commonwealth could authorise the States, in certain agreed circumstances to exercise the Commonwealth power.

A possible 105B:

> (1) The Commonwealth may make a treaty or treaties with persons or bodies
>   recognised as representatives of Aboriginal and Torres Strait Islander peoples of
>   Australia with respect to the status and rights of those people within Australia
>   including but not limited by the following:
>   (a) restoration to Aboriginal and Torres Strait Islander peoples or to some of
>   them of their lands which were owned and occupied by them prior to 1770;

(b) compensation for the loss of any land incapable of being restored to the Aboriginal and Torres Strait Islander peoples or some of them;

(c) matters of health, education, employment and welfare;

(d) matters of political status, representation and organization, including self-government;

(e) matters of inherent sovereignty and the sharing of sovereignty;

(f) matters of language, culture, heritage and intellectual and cultural property;

(g) the law, including Aboriginal and Torres Strait Islander law and custom, relating to the exercise of judicial power by the Commonwealth of Australia or any State or any Territory within Australia;

(h) Any other matter identified by Aboriginal and Torres Strait Islander peoples in relation to their status as first peoples and nations.

(2) The Parliament shall have the power to make laws for the validating of any such treaty or treaties made before the commencement of this section. Such laws shall not be altered, amended, rescinded or repealed by the Parliament without the free and informed consent of the Aboriginal and Torres Strait islanders party to the treaty or treaties as well as a two-thirds majority vote of the members of both houses of the Parliament entitled to vote.

(3) Any treaty or treaties made may be varied or rescinded by the parties thereto and as such shall supersede any prior treaty or treaties for the purposes of this section.

(4) Subject to sub-section (2), the Parliament shall have the power to make laws for the implementation by the parties of such treaty or treaties.

(5) Any laws passed under clauses 2 and 4 shall be binding upon the Commonwealth, the States and Territories within Australia, notwithstanding anything contained in this Constitution or the Constitutions of the several states or the self governing laws of any territory or any law of the Commonwealth, or of any State or territory.

(6) Any variation or alteration or rescinding of this section shall occur in the following manner

(a) notwithstanding section 128 a bill for a law for a referendum shall not be introduced into the Parliament without the Parliament having obtained two-thirds majority support of the Aboriginal and Torres Strait Islander peoples;

(b) the terms of the treaty or treaties permits such alteration, amendment or rescinding, and if so, are complied with.

Sub-section (5) would give full force of the Constitution to laws passed to effect the treaty or treaties.

This approach removes the complexity of trying to incorporate the text of a treaty into the Constitution.

An agreement that is supported by legislation

Any legislation passed by the Commonwealth parliament must fall within a scope of power given to the parliament by the Australian Constitution. There are two potential 'heads' of power. Section 51 (xxvii) (the 'races power') and Section 51 (xxix) (the 'external affairs power')

The 'races power'

The Commonwealth Parliament has passed laws like the *ATSIC Act*, the *NT land rights Act* and the *Native Title Act* using the power given to it under the Constitution via Section 51 (xxvii):

> 51. The Parliament shall, subject to this Constitution, have power
> to make laws for the peace, order, and good government of the
> Commonwealth with respect to:
> (xxvi) the people of any race for whom it is deemed necessary
> to make special laws:

Prior to the referendum in 1967 the Commonwealth Parliament had no power under the Constitution to make laws for the Aboriginal and Torres Strait Islander 'races'. The power since then has sometimes been used in a discriminatory fashion. For example the Hindmarsh Island[4] and Native Title Act amendment legislation.[5] It should be noted the Council for Aboriginal Reconciliation in its final report to the Federal parliament has recommended a new section be inserted into the Constitution making it unlawful to *adversely discriminate against people on the grounds of race.*[6]

There appears to be no doubt that the Commonwealth Parliament has the power under this section of the Constitution to make *special laws*, without predetermining the content of what they might contain, to give effect to a treaty or treaties.

There is an obvious political limitation in the use of this power most recently exemplified by the amendments by the present government to the *Native Title Act*. The vulnerability arises from the capacity of later parliaments (depending on which political party or parties has a temporary majority) to substantially repeal or amend such legislation. This potential political exposure represents a substantial impediment to the use of the existing Constitutional power under this 'head' to implement a treaty or treaties.

The 'external affairs power'

The Commonwealth Parliament has power under the Constitution to make laws with respect to external affairs under Section 51 (xxix), which reads as follows:

> The Parliament shall, subject to this Constitution, have power
> to make laws for the peace, order, and good government of the
> Commonwealth with respect to:
> (xxix) External Affairs.

This section gives the Parliament the power to enact legislation governing and regulating all Australia's relations with other countries.

---

[4] Hindmarsh Island Bridge Royal Commission (1996) AILR 46; (1996) ALIR 315.

[5] *Native Title Amendment Act 1998* (Cth).

[6] Final report of the Council for Aboriginal Reconciliation, 2000: recommendation 3.

This is a very broad power and generally the conduct of external affairs does not require legislative action as these matters are usually accomplished by executive action. A law is required however if that executive action requires an appropriation of money and/or a need to put into domestic or internal effect arrangements made as a result of the conduct of external affairs. For example the accession by Australia to the *Convention For the Elimination of all Forms of Racial Discrimination* was an executive decision and internally given effect to by the enactment of the *Race Discrimination Act 1975*.

It is arguable that this power enables the Commonwealth Parliament to make laws on an indefinite array of subjects provided each met the description of an external affair. A treaty or treaties with the Indigenous peoples of Australia could fall within such a description. For example, the poor socio-economic circumstances of Aboriginal and Torres Strait Islanders are of concern to many countries with strong links to Australia. If the reason (in part) is to allay these concerns and improve international relations with these countries then it could arguably be described as an external affair (given domestic effect to by the treaty or treaties). What requires demonstration is that the subject matter of any legislation is a matter for international concern.

Reference of powers by states

The Commonwealth Parliament can enact laws by reference to matters referred to it by state parliaments. The most recent example, perhaps, concerning Indigenous issues, was the Framlingham and Lake Tyers Act of the Victorian Parliament.[7]

Section 51. (xxxvii) of the Constitution provides:

> 51. The Parliament shall, subject to this Constitution, have power
> to make laws for the peace, order, and good government of the
> Commonwealth with respect to:
> Matters referred by the Parliament or Parliaments of any State or
> States, but so that the law shall extend only to States by whose
> Parliaments the matter is referred, or which afterwards adopt the law:

The fourth way in which a treaty could be negotiated in Australia between Indigenous peoples and the Commonwealth is by simple agreement.

A simple agreement

A treaty or treaties could be negotiated in the form of a simple agreement, placed in the realm of the statutory and common law of contract.

The contract or agreement could create legally enforceable rights and obligations. This is essentially the way in which the United States of America dealt with Native American tribes between 1788 and 1842 (242 treaties made during that time). The power to make treaties in the United States comes from Article I section 8 of the American Constitution, which empowers the United States Congress:

> to regulate Commerce with foreign Nations, and among several
> States, and with the Indian Tribes;

---

[7] Aboriginal Land (Lake Condah and Framlingham Forest) Act 1987, 27/1, 9/2

In 1871 the United States Congress passed the *Indian Appropriation Act* it provided that:

> No Indian nation or tribe within the territory of the United States
> shall be acknowledged or recognised as an independent nation, tribe
> or power with whom the United States may contract a treaty …

The whole approach of the United States up until then (from 1778) was to acquire Indian lands by purchase through 'treaties'. The status of these agreements never amounted to instruments governed by international law – they were more in the nature of contracts for the sale of land. This of course, in almost every case, was not the way they came to be regarded by the various Native American nations. Essentially, at least from the point of view of the Congress, they were domestic agreements governed by domestic law.

In the *Marshall* cases[8] the concept of domestic dependent nations was denominated by the Chief Justice. This placed the relationship between the United States and the Indian nations as one that resembled that of ward to guardian. Subsequently confirmed by the Indian Appropriation Ac of 1871.

Canada's Royal Proclamation of 1763[9] guaranteed the protection of the Indians under the British crown. The Proclamation acknowledged Indian interests in land the crown having exclusive rights to purchase which it proceeded to do so by way of treaties. Sixty-seven such treaties were concluded between 1725 and 1919, they were formal written agreements to which both parties attached great significance at the time. Legally these treaties, like those in the United States have come to be regarded as domestic arrangements without international character.

Section 35 of the Canadian Constitution provides that:

> The existing Aboriginal and treaty rights of the Aboriginal
> peoples of Canada are hereby recognised and affirmed.

This section was inserted into the Canadian Constitution in 1982, well after the original treaty making era, and not only does it afford protection for those pre-existing treaty rights for Indigenous Canadians it has also ushered in a new era of treaty making. This new treaty making in Canada has met with varying success and, in some instances the failure or complete breakdown in negotiations (compare the Nishga agreement in1996[10] and the breakdown of negotiations with the Dene Nation in the late 1980's).[11] If there is one important lesson to be learned from the recent Canadian experience for Australian context if we are to progress to our first era of treaty making it is the following. Great attention and diligence must be attached to the importance and potential utility of establishing sound; equitable 'ground rules' for the negotiations required drafting and concluding treaties.

In 1840 the British government entered the Treaty of Waitangi with the Maoris of the North Island of New Zealand, the South Island by assertion of British right of discovery. The Waitangi treaty purported to do three things (contested by the Maori):

- Maori acceptance of British sovereignty;

- British crown's protection of Maori possessions; and

- the Crown having the exclusive right to purchase Maori land.

---

[8] Especially 6 /6 Cherokee Nation v. State of Georgia (1831)

[9] Generally known as the Royal Proclamation of 1763 (7 October 1763)

[10] Nishga Framework Agreement, signed 12 February 1996

[11] See http://www.denenation.com/

In 1975 the *Treaty of Waitangi Act* was passed to:

> Observance and confirmation, of the principles of the Treaty of
> Waitangi by establishing a tribunal to make recommendations on
> claims relating to the practical application of the treaty …

How is sovereignty to be understood?

Sovereignty means an indivisible and exclusive power and capacity for self-government along with international recognition of that power. In international law any challenge to the basis of sovereignty (or assertion of it) is to be answered, if possible, by reference to the Inter-Temporal law. That, briefly, means that any questions about the legitimacy of the assertion of sovereignty has to be interpreted by reference to the law in force during that period. For Australia, this is the time of colonisation.

The 'discovery' and 'settlement' of Australia occurred in stages. Captain James Cook was instructed in 1768 to discover what was then known as New Holland. He landed at Botany Bay on 29 April 1770 and by 22 August 1770 had purported to take possession of the entire Australian East Coast on behalf of the British King.

The First Fleet arrived on 26 January 1778 and Governor Phillip raised the British flag on 7 February 1778. The colonisation of the continent had begun. Captain Fremantle took formal possession of Western Australia on 2 May 1829. The first British 'settlers' arrived in 1829 and 1830.

What then were the international rules of acquisition of new territories by European colonising powers in 1770 and immediately thereafter?

There are basically five ways in which new territories can be acquired in international law:

1 Cession

2 Occupation

3 Prescription

4 Accretion

5 Conquest

In the case of Australia occupation or settlement of land that was said to be *terra nullius* is of relevance here. Although the High Court rejected the notion of *terra nullius* in its *Mabo* decision in 1992, settlement is the prevailing view as the source of Australian sovereignty.

Between the sixteenth and nineteenth centuries there were basically three main propositions put forward on the existence or otherwise of the sovereignty of Indigenous peoples.

1 recognition that Indigenous entities had complete sovereignty over their territories

2 Indigenous entities had a restricted or conditional sovereignty over their territories and,

3 total rejection of such sovereignty.

Imperial European powers generally acquired their possession by cession or conquest. In Africa for example, the predominant mode of acquisition became cession and hundreds of treaties were concluded between Europeans and African Nations. Where African Nations were not prepared to settle treaties military force was used. One example is the West African Kingdom of Asante. The British fought three wars and it was not until 1900 that their superior military might overwhelmed the Kingdom. Similar modes of colonisation occurred in Asia.

In New Zealand cession was the mode of acquisition used by the British in the terms of the *Treaty of Waitangi Act*. Article 1 reads:

> The chiefs of the Confederation of the United Tribes of New Zealand,
> and the separate and independent chiefs who have not become
> members of the Confederation cede to Her Majesty the Queen of
> England, absolutely and without reservation, all the rights and powers
> of sovereignty which the said Confederation of individual chiefs
> respectively exercise or possess or may be supposed to exercise or
> possess over their territories as the sole sovereigns thereof.

It should be noted that since European colonising powers began the practice of treaty making with Indigenous peoples there have been substantial differences in the construction of the provisions of these treaties between the parties, particularly as to those relating to the object and purpose of the treaty concerned.

For example, the Maori and Pakeha constructions of the Waitangi Treaty differ on crucial matters including alleged 'transfers' of governance/sovereignty powers and 'land title' to non-Maori settlers, as well as to the actual purpose of the treaty itself. In fact, the version written in the Maori language bears little resemblance to the one written in the English language.

In North America cession was the preferred mode and in most cases in Central and South America conquest was resorted to. (The Mapuche Parlamentos in Chile are one of a number of exceptions in point).

Territories designated *terra nullius* during the colonisation period were a rarity. Wherever there were people with some form of socio-political organisation the European colonists generally acquired territories by conquest or cession.

When Captain Cook departed England to 'discover' Australian his instructions said:

> You are also with the *consent of the natives* to take possession of
> convenient situations in the country in the name of the King of
> Great Britain or if you find the country uninhabited take possession
> for His Majesty by setting proper marks and inscriptions as first
> discoverers and possessors ... [12]

Cook ignored the natives, cut an inscription in a tree, raised the British flag, violated international law of the time and disregarded the instructions of his superiors.

Cook seems to have regarded Australia as *terra nullius* and the claim was based on an assertion that Aborigines lacked political organisation with settled law. This assertion relies on the erroneous view that there was (or had to be in European terms) one single Aboriginal nation

---

[12] Captain Cook – the first voyage (2), available at http://www.library.ucla.edu/libraries/special/scweb/cookcheck3.htm

which is a nonsense there were over 500 nations with established law and political systems, (the lower Murray tribes were joined in a confederacy!) which was all that was required in international law at the time.

Australia was the exception to British behaviour elsewhere at the time, particularly Africa.

What then was the situation in Australia when the convict colony was established in Sydney Cove? Were the people living in a territory politically organised so as to qualify, in European terms, as territorially sovereign?

It is now beyond argument that although Aboriginal societies did not have centrally organised governments in the European sense at the time, nevertheless there is clear and surviving evidence that in most Indigenous societies in this country there was a clearly demarcated line of authority. Religious leaders exercised (and still do) authority which extends into secular areas. There were, and are, no hard rules demarcating the religious from the secular in Aboriginal societies, where the law is paramount and used to maintain order. There can be no doubt that Aboriginal societies had the means of regulating themselves long before the arrival of Europeans who refused to see these structures.

These types of systems mentioned above have been referred to as segmentary lineage systems and were recognised by the British in Africa during the colonising era. (It was also a system well recognised in South America.) The British did not settle Iboland (later Biafra and now part of Nigeria) by occupation despite the fact the Ibos had no kings or princes. There are numerous other African examples where peoples without centralised systems did not lose their lands because they were 'ownerless'. The practice in Australia or settlement theory is indefensible.

Conquest also cannot fix the defect. A frontier war raged for over a century. Aboriginal people did not 'peacefully' give up the land: they were killed or forcibly removed from the land by British forces or European colonists. There has been no peace treaty therefore; technically a state of war still exists.

Prescription is likewise no answer. Prescription is the consolidation of possession by the continued, constant and sufficiently long practice of government whereby they could argue convincingly they had the continuous and peaceful display of government. This defence is only open to challenge from another nation state, say if the Netherlands challenged Australian sovereignty over Tasmania because Abel Tasman had 'discovered' it. Australia could, in international law, probably defeat such a challenge.

Peaceful and unchallenged are the operative words here. Aborigines and Torres Strait Islanders have never conceded defeat and have challenged the legality of the Australian foundational sovereignty on numerous occasions in the courts of the colonisers, *Mabo* and *Coe*[13] two examples. There is also increasing use by Indigenous Australians of international fora to voice protest and objection and to challenge.

The High Court's decision in *Mabo* although rejecting *terra nullius* and recognising native title did not (and said it could not) challenge the foundations of present Australian sovereignty. As the court said it was a question *not justiciable in municipal courts*. How can the court have accepted the validity of Aboriginal and Torres Strait Islander rights to land but not

---

[13] *Paul Coe v the Commonwealth (1979) 53 ALJR 403*

uphold rights of governance? Why the inconsistent allegiance by the court to the 'occupation' 'settlement' fallacy?

Whatever the High Court has left us with post-*Mabo* as to what is now the foundations of the sovereignty of the Australian nation state is a mystery. The sovereign pillars of the nation state are arguably at the very least, a little shaky legally.

It is important to remember that in modern times sovereignty is rarely vested exclusively in one person or one entity. The feature of modern nation states is a sharing or co-existence of sovereign entities. In Australia since federation it has been divisible between the Commonwealth and the states and territories and local government. The Torres Strait Regional Authority already has a c-existing sovereign responsibility over certain matters.

Internationally there are numerous examples. Nearby Vanuatu was until recently a shared trust territory between the British and the French, the Innuit of Greenland share sovereignty with the Kingdom of Denmark and proposals for shared sovereignty between Israel and the Palestinians is mooted.

The adoption of international treaties requires a level of relinquishment of national sovereignty under the terms of the respective treaties and international law. Australia has been in the business of adopting international treaties for a very long time.

Scope of content

Matters mentioned in the section above dealing with a broad Constitutional enabling power might form the basis for the content of treaties. What the content of these treaties might be is largely an issue for the negotiating parties, what they can agree on and what their imaginations will allow.

Some of the content might include:

- the prohibition of racial discrimination;
- recognition of the rights of equality;
- recognition of the principle of non-discrimination;

(The ideal situation would be to have these three principles embedded in the Australian Constitution)

- access to education and training;
- employment;
- the recognition of distinct Indigenous identities;
- the protection of laws, cultures, and languages;
- the effective implementation of relevant recommendations from a variety of reports;
- law and justice issues;
- resolution for the stolen generations;
- control, ownership and management of land, waters and resources;
- benefits from resource development;
- economic and social development;

- reparation, and compensation;
- self-determination;
- self-government; and
- constitutional recognition.

This is by no way intended to be an exhaustive list. The negotiation process must have the flexibility to allow for new or more specific issues to be identified for negotiation in the future.

The identification of the content of treaties might be achieved through agreed processes under a Constitutional mandate as mentioned above, which would allow the parties to reach agreement on principles which would underpin the negotiations.

Acknowledgments

The author acknowledges the work of the Aboriginal Treaty Committee in the original formulation of the concept of the constitutional entrenchment of a treaty.

References

Canada 1763, Royal Proclamation of 1763 (7 October).

Canada 1996, Nishga Framework Agreement, 12 February.

Canada re Dene Nation, 1990, http://www.denenation.com

Captain Cook – The first voyage (2), http://www.library.ucla.edu/libraries/special/scweb/cokcheck3.htm

Reconciliation. Australia's Challenge, Final report of the Council for Aboriginal Reconciliation to the Prime Minister and the Commonwealth Parliament, Council for Aboriginal Reconciliation 2000...

Hindmarsh Island Bridge Royal Commission (1996) AILR 46; (1996) AILR 315.

Martinez Cobo, JR, 1987, *Study of the Problem of Discrimination against Indigenous Populations*, UN Doc. E/CN. 4/Sub.2/1986/7/Add.4.

Vienna Convention on the Law of Treaties 1969, 23 May, 1155 UNTS 331.

Legislation

Aboriginal Land (Lake Condah and Framlingham Forest) Act 1987.

Indian Appropriation Act 1871 (US).

Native Title Act 1993 (Cth).

Native Title Amendment Act 1998 (Cth).

Race Discrimination Act 1975 (Cth).

Treaty of Waitangi Act 1975 (NZ).

Case law

Cherokee Nation v State of Georgia (1831) (US).

Cooper v Stuart (1889) (Privy Council)14 AC 286.

Mabo and Ors v The State of Queensland (No 2) (1992) 175 CLR 1.

Paul Coe v The Commonwealth (1979) 53 ALJR 403.

ANNEX 1

The Vienna Convention on the Law of Treaties

The Convention was concluded in Vienna on 23 May 1969 and entered into force on 27 January 1980. The international statement is important because it may provide some assistance and guidance in the formulation of rules as to how a treaty or treaties might be negotiated within the Australian domestic context if that be the path that is eventually adopted.

The Vienna Convention is structured as follows:

The preambular paragraphs deal with the fundamental role of treaties in the history of international relations, and recognise the importance of treaties as a source of international law and as a means of developing peaceful co-operation among nations. They note that the principles of free consent and of good faith and the *pacta sunt servanda* rule are universally recognised, and affirm that disputes concerning treaties, like other international disputes, should be settled by peaceful means and in conformity with the principles of justice and international law. The paragraphs also recall the Charter of the United Nations, particularly such as the principles of the equal rights and self-determination of peoples, of the sovereign equality and independence of all States, of non-interference in the domestic affairs of States, of the prohibition of the threat or use of force and of universal respect for, and observance of, human rights and fundamental freedoms for all. And finally, the preamble affirms that the rules of customary international law continue to govern questions not regulated by the provisions of the Convention.

In PART I, the INTRODUCTION, a treaty is defined as:

> an international agreement concluded between States in written form and governed by international law, whether embodied in a single instrument or in two or more related instruments and whatever its particular designation;

PART II deals with the conclusion and entry into force of treaties and pronounces that:

> Every State possesses capacity to conclude treaties.

The Part also deals with the authorisation of acts, the adoption of the text, the authentication of the text, the means of expressing consent to be bound by a treaty and the entry into force of a treaty.

Part III deals with the observance, application and interpretation of treaties. It entrenches the principle of *pacta sunt servanda*:

> Every treaty in force is binding upon the parties to it and must be performed by them in good faith.

Very importantly this part makes it absolutely clear that a State cannot invoke the provisions of its own domestic Constitutional and legal arrangements as justification for its failure to perform a treaty.

Section 3 of this part deals with the interpretation of treaties:

> A treaty shall be interpreted in good faith in accordance with the
> ordinary meaning to be given to the terms of the treaty in their context
> and in the light of its object and purpose.

Part IV of the convention deals with the amendment and modification of treaties, the
general rule being that a treaty may be amended by agreement between the parties if it
is provided for and complies with the Convention and international law. The amendment
rules vary slightly so far as multilateral treaties are concerned.

Part V of the Convention relates to Invalidity, Termination and Suspension of the
Operation of Treaties. The main provision to note is Article 42.2, which says:

> 2. The termination of a treaty, its denunciation or the withdrawal of
> a party, may take place only as a result of the application of the
> provisions of the treaty or of the present Convention. The same rule
> applies to suspension of the operation of a treaty.

However, it is also to be noted that Obligations imposed by international law still apply
independently of a treaty.

The part also variously provides for the invalidating of treaties through fraud,
corruption and coercion to mention the ones of key importance. It is also noteworthy in
this context that the Convention entrenches the principle of *jus cogens*, namely:

> A treaty is void if, at the time of its conclusion, it conflicts with a
> peremptory norm of general international law.
>
> If a new peremptory norm of general international law emerges, any
> existing treaty, which is in conflict with that norm, becomes void and
> terminates.

Article 66 of this Part deals with the Procedures for judicial settlement, arbitration and
conciliation. Under these provisions an application can be made to the International
Court of Justice by a State and the procedure is set out in Annex 1 of the Convention.

Finally part VI of the Treaty is entitled 'miscellaneous provisions' and deals primarily
with Cases of State succession, State responsibility and outbreak of hostilities. The last
two Parts (Part VII and Viii) deal with administrative and procedural matters such as
depository notification, communication and ratification.

Treaty: advancing reconciliation?

The Hon David Malcolm AC

Introduction

Just before the end of his term as Governor-General, Sir William Deane, in an address to the University of New South Wales said:

> [in] the forefront of those challenges [that still lie ahead for Australians] are the challenge to heal the divisions in our society including the unacceptable gap between the haves and the have-nots; the challenge to protect and preserve our environment for future, as well as present, Australians; the challenge to overcome entrenched Aboriginal disadvantage and to achieve true and lasting Aboriginal reconciliation.

He continued:

> In that regard, my abiding regret as my term as Governor-General expires is that we Australians failed to achieve more before the life of the Council for Aboriginal Reconciliation ran out at the end of last year.

> In the search for Aboriginal reconciliation, our Universities have an absolutely critical direct and indirect role to play. The direct role includes the obvious one of encouraging and effectively teaching those Indigenous Australians who are fortunate enough to come within their reach. I say 'fortunate enough' because of the immense gap which continues to exist in many areas of our nation between the educational standards, including literacy and numeracy, of the average Indigenous student leaving school and the average non-Indigenous one. While the position varies in different areas and while there is room for informed disagreement about some details, a number of plain facts are beyond intelligent dispute. For me the most basic of them is that in many remote Indigenous communities, there is, for practical purposes, no chance that an Indigenous student will reach matriculation standard. Indeed, in some of those communities, the standard of the average Aboriginal student at the conclusion of formal education is Year Three (3) primary school. Obviously, in the context of the past treatment of our Indigenous peoples, our Universities have an immense responsibility to ensure that, consistently with the

> maintenance of academic standards, every legitimate encouragement and assistance is extended to the Indigenous students who succeed in entering their doors.[1]

It is an honour to have been invited by Murdoch University to be a Keynote Speaker at this national Conference on racism, land and reconciliation. In the year 2000, when we celebrated the Centenary of our Federation, I was honoured to join the delegation from Western Australia which attended the Corroboree 2000 Reconciliation Conference in Sydney, and later to participate as a leader in the Australians for Reconciliation 'Beyond the Bridge' Walk here in Western Australia in 2001 which culminated with speeches and entertainment in the Supreme Court Gardens. Since 1993, the Judges of the Supreme Court have been pursuing the reconciliation agenda through various Aboriginal cross-cultural awareness programmes and through reaching out in an endeavour to communicate with Aboriginal communities throughout the State when on circuit or otherwise. I have been privileged to have been involved in informal discussions with various Aboriginal leaders and others on the ways and means of bringing together the various disparate groups of Aboriginal people in the Perth metropolitan area in an attempt to develop a united approach, both to reconcile the various factional groups among the Nyungah and others in the area among themselves, as well as to reconcile relationships between the metropolitan Aboriginal peoples, on the one hand, and the remainder of the community on the other.

This paper explores first, the idea or concept of a treaty or series of treaties between Indigenous and non-Indigenous Australians as a step towards reconciling these cultures within the framework of the Australian nation, and second, questions regarding the use of a treaty within the constitutional framework of Australia.

The idea of a treaty and its implementation in Australia

The idea of a treaty between the Indigenous and non-Indigenous peoples of Australia is not new. In 1837 the first Attorney General of New South Wales, Saxe Bannister, made a submission for a treaty to the Select Committee of the House of Commons on Aborigines.[2] The retired Governor Arthur of Tasmania also urged this Committee to consider treaties. In 1835 a treaty negotiated by John Batman with the Kulin people was declared invalid by the Governor of Victoria as it was made by a private citizen.[3] In 1975 the Senate passed a resolution put by Senator Bonner urging the Australian Government to acknowledge the prior ownership of Australia by Indigenous peoples and to introduce legislation to compensate them for dispossession of their land.

In 1979 the Aboriginal Treaty Committee, under the chairmanship of Dr HC Coombs, was established with the 'aim of influencing and mobilising non-Aboriginal opinion in favour of the treaty and of granting land rights and compensation'.[4] This was disbanded in 1983. The Committee's newspaper, *Aboriginal Treaty News*, March–June 1983 edition reported that the Committee was disbanded because its work in influencing non-Aboriginal attitudes had been significant, political parties now gave greater weight to Aboriginal issues, and the Committee had mobilised greater support for independent Aboriginal initiatives.

The idea of a treaty was rejected in 1983 by the Senate Standing Committee on Constitutional and Legal Affairs. The Committee considered that the Indigenous peoples were not a sovereign

---

entity and therefore could not enter into a treaty with the Commonwealth, although they supported a compact which could be inserted into the Constitution by referendum.[5] In the lead-up to the bicentennial celebrations in 1998, the issue of a negotiated treaty was raised again by the then Prime Minister Bob Hawke.[6] A statement of Indigenous aspirations was presented to Mr Hawke at the Barunga Festival in June 1988. The Barunga statement called on the Commonwealth Government to negotiate a treaty recognising Indigenous peoples' prior ownership, continued occupation, sovereignty and rights in a range of areas.[7]

The Prime Minister responded by calling for a treaty to be negotiated between the Indigenous people of Australia and the Government.[8] The concept of an instrument or document of reconciliation was put forward as a formal step in the reconciliation process in a discussion paper released by the Australian Government through the then Minister for Aboriginal Affairs, the Hon Mr Robert Tickner, in February 1991.[9] Mr Tickner said the discussion paper proposed a strategy 'for achieving reconciliation and social justice for Aboriginal and Torres Strait Islander people'. The discussion paper stated:

> [T]he Government's position is that the document which could be called an instrument of reconciliation would be a valuable outcome of the process of reconciliation and such a document should desirably be achieved by the centenary of Federation, 1 January 2001.
>
> However, the process of reconciliation may be as important as the final outcome and the initial focus would be on the process rather than on the document. The best possible outcome is one reflecting a consensus arrived at through extensive community discussion.[10]

While support for an instrument of reconciliation was not unanimous, there was continued support for reconciliation, leading to the establishment of the Council for Aboriginal Reconciliation in September 1991.[11] The Council was given a statutory requirement to seek community views about whether any document or documents of reconciliation would benefit the Australian community.[12]

Since the publication of that discussion paper, the centenary of Federation as the desired date indicated by the former Government for the completion of such a document has passed. The process of reconciliation must be kept alive by the discussion of the issues that are relevant to any proposed document of reconciliation. With the year of the centenary of Federation over and the mandate of the Council for Aboriginal Reconciliation expired, reconciliation has been seen by some as a people's movement.[13] It has been suggested that the difficulty with this approach is that such support often wanes when it comes to specifics such as the recognition of distinct rights, return of lands, self-government and compensation.[14] There has been a call for greater political leadership, as it is the government that has the resources, authority and power to achieve reconciliation.[15]

The present Government has rejected the proposal for a treaty with Indigenous people and has coined the phrase 'practical reconciliation' to describe its policy focus.[16] This involves an emphasis on dealing with social problems and the provision of the resources by the government

---

[6] CAR 2000.

[7] See Indigenous Law Resources 1994.

[8] CAR 2000.

[9] Cockayne 2001: 590.

[10] Tickner 1991.

[11] CAR 2002.

[12] Cockayne 2001: 590.

[13] Cockayne 2001: 577.

[14] Strelein 2000: 260.

[15] Strelein 2000: 260.

[16] Oxfam 2000.

to deliver basic services to Indigenous communities. The argument against this policy has been that it will assimilate Indigenous Australians into mainstream society.[17] It is also argued that the implementation of the policy will remove the decisions as to how and when the services are provided away from the Indigenous people.

Although a fundamental part of the 'unfinished business' agenda, the claims made by the Indigenous people of Australia are not limited to the equal distribution of resources and the enjoyment of fundamental services.[18] The collective enjoyment of distinct cultural rights and collective rights is also claimed and emphasis is placed on a contention that the divide that exists in relation to the equal enjoyment of fundamental citizenship rights reflects the much deeper issue of the identity of Indigenous peoples.[19] In this context, Mr Geoff Clark has argued:

> … let me put it this way, if all of the endemic social and economic
> problems were fixed in our communities tomorrow we would still
> need to address our fundamental human rights. The achievement of
> full 'practical' reconciliation, as the Government describes, would be
> just one step along the road to true reconciliation.[20]

One of the difficulties in commenting on a topic dealing with Indigenous people is the inadequacy of the English language and European culture to speak accurately or authoritatively about the culture and experience of Australian Indigenous peoples. This is true wherever a colonial power has encountered an Indigenous people, because as was said about the Navajo Indians in 1946:

> … each different way of life makes its own assumptions about the ends
> and purposes of human existence, about ways by which knowledge
> may be obtained, about the organization of the pigeon-holes in which
> each sense datum is filed, about what human beings have a right
> to expect from each other and the gods, about [what] constitutes
> fulfilment and frustration. Some of these assumptions are made
> explicit in the lore of the folk; others are tacit premises which the
> observer must infer by finding consistent trends in word and deed.[21]

In my view, the same principles apply to the clash of cultures which commenced a little over 200 years ago when white people first settled in the Great South Land that came to be called Australia. It continues to this day. It is still the principal issue in Indigenous–non-Indigenous relationships, notwithstanding the significant changes in perception that have occurred over the past three decades.

At the time of European colonisation in 1788 the Aboriginal population was estimated to be between approximately 300,000 and 1,500,000 persons. The 2001 Census statistics indicate that the Indigenous population of 410,003 people represents 2.2% of the Australia population.[22] There were perhaps 500 tribes in 1788, and as many dialects and languages, whose people lived in scattered groups throughout the Australian continent. In their *World of the First Australians*[23] Professor and Doctor Berndt undertook a comprehensive survey of traditional Aboriginal culture. It is clear from their work that the complexity of the Aboriginal society was

---

[17] Australians for Native Title and Reconciliation 2002.

[18] Strelein 2000: 261.

[19] Strelein 2000: 261.

[20] Clark 2000.

[21] Kluckholm cited by Supreme Court of Alberta 1991: 9–10.

[22] Australian Bureau of Statistics 2002

[23] Berndt and Berndt 1999 *[1964]*.

not recognised by Europeans at the time of first colonisation in 1788. Many Australians still have difficulty accepting it now.

The Aboriginal system of law prior to British colonisation was reviewed in the 1971 case of *Miliipum v Nabalco Pty Ltd*.[24] *Miliipum* involved a claim by a group of Aboriginal people in the Northern Territory, citing the authority of the common law, to a proprietary interest in certain land. They were unsuccessful. Justice Blackburn said of the Aboriginal system of law in the Northern Territory at the time of colonisation that:

> … it shows a subtle and elaborate system highly adapted to the country in which the people led their lives, which provided a stable order of society and was remarkably free from the vagaries of personal whim or influence. If ever a system could be called 'a Government of laws' and not of men it is that shown in the evidence before me.[25]

The need for a process of reconciliation between Aboriginal and non-Aboriginal persons has been recognised for many years. The first real step in this reconciliation process was the so-called 'Aboriginal Referendum' of 1967 in which the then Federal Coalition Government and the Labor Opposition joined to give a unanimous commitment to constitutional change to effectively give Aboriginal people full citizenship. The Australian people responded to that clear and powerful message – and a record 92% of the Australian population supported the referendum proposing the change.

Since that time there has been an evolution of thought on the part of non-Aboriginal people that has been reflected in the actions of successive Commonwealth governments irrespective of party composition. The process of reconciliation has never been far from the political agenda. Each new report which detailed Indigenous disadvantage, each new programme which failed to achieve its objectives, each new incident which highlighted the divisions between Indigenous and non-Indigenous people and the mounting signs of Indigenous anger and frustration with the pace and direction of reform, has served to remind us that the process of reconciliation had to take place.

In developing a formal document of reconciliation, there are many issues to be taken into consideration including: what form it might take; how it could be developed; what rights might flow from it; who might negotiate it, and in particular, who might be party to it. Other issues for community consideration may be whether such a document or documents should be legally binding, and whether such a document should reflect or go beyond the developments in international law relevant to Indigenous people.

In addition to a national document of reconciliation the nation needs documents of recognition and agreement between Indigenous communities and various sectors of the wider community, for example, at local government level and between Indigenous communities and industry representatives such as mining and pastoral organisations. Already there are some positive examples of such agreements and documents that show it can be done when people from all sides are committed to making it happen.

On 17 July 2001, Nyungah Elders and Alan Carpenter, Minister for Education, signed an historic agreement at Swanbourne, one of the Western suburbs of Perth.[26] The Agreement

---

[24] (1971) 17 FLR 141.   [25] 17 FLR 141 at 267.   [26] Nyungah Circle of Elders 2001.

marked the culmination of nearly three years of negotiations between 18 Nyungah Elders and the Education Department. The Agreement relates to an important Aboriginal Site in the area of Lake Claremont (formerly known as Butler's Swamp) and the relocation of the Swanbourne Primary School at the old Swanbourne Homegrounds land, where Swanbourne High School had been located. The Site is of great significance to Nyungah people, being home to Nyungah people for generations and various Nyungah Elders, alive today, during the 1930s and 1940s. In recognition of the importance of the Site and the use of part of the land for educational purposes, the Agreement provides for the implementation of a pilot programme relating to the teaching of Nyungah history to children.

As of 29 May 2002, there were 41 determinations of native title across Australia. In addition, 48 Indigenous land use agreements have been registered and about 2,700 agreements have been made between developers and native title parties relating to future development activities.[27] Of course, no document of itself will solve the many problems which lie in the path of reconciliation. However, I believe that without a document that expresses some clear commitment to reconciliation the nation and our national identity will remain incomplete. At a 1997 Workshop held by the Australians for Aboriginal Reconciliation in association with the Supreme Court of Western Australia and the Law Society of Western Australia, Patrick Dodson said that without a formal document of reconciliation, '[t]he wounds of our nation's past will remain unhealed and will continue to fester and poison the body politic'.[28]

Negotiated agreements between parties at local and regional levels are one of the effective responses of the High Court *Mabo* judgment. Such agreements can avoid the complexities and, no doubt, the cost and length of time that occupy the courts and the court battles that take place. The achievement of negotiated agreements is a better way of resolving the complex and difficult issues involved. While the local agreements entered into by some of our cities, local government authorities and Aboriginal people are, in most cases symbolic in nature, they have recognised both the groups' continuing rights and interests and acknowledged the ongoing contribution that both groups make to the life and development of the relevant city or local government area.

The question of a national document of reconciliation throws up many challenges to us as a nation and raises the question of what it is we want to achieve. The use of the word 'treaty' to describe such a document has created quite a deal of controversy in Australia.[29] The central issue the treaty proposal seeks to address is the question of the ongoing relationship between Indigenous and non-Indigenous Australians.[30] The term 'treaty' immediately suggests a particular type of legal relationship, based on agreement between two sovereign entities, which many people find disturbing.[31] At best the use of the term is seen by some as a misnomer for what has been described as:

> ... an umbrella document providing direction and perspective to all
> areas of policy, including land rights, self-management, customary
> laws and recognition of Aboriginal culture and religion ... a national
> declaration of shared principles and common commitments.[32]

---

[27] Ruddock 2002.   [29] Fraser 2000.   [31] Cockayne 2001: 590.

[28] P Dodson 1997.   [30] Cockayne 2001: 590.   [32] Hawke 1988: 7.

At worst, it is seen by others as a deliberate 'recipe for separatism' and used to suggest that within Australia there are the seeds of a separate nation state,[33] or 'about nothing more than compensation and power'.[34]

One of the central concepts of Indigenous difference is that of sovereignty. The justification for there being no treaties in place between the British Crown and Australia's Indigenous peoples is that there was no sovereign in Australia.[35] It remains arguable, however, that under both international and British law of the time, Indigenous Australians possessed the characteristics of sovereignty: ownership of a defined territory, a distinct, permanent population, the capacity for international relations and identifiable forms of government.[36]

This does not mean that Indigenous sovereignty continues to exist and Australian courts have consistently ruled that the process of colonisation was effected by non-justiciable 'acts of state', rendering the question of the continuing existence of Indigenous sovereignty unanswerable.[37] This non-justiciability of Indigenous sovereignty creates a space for a negotiated, political settlement that is fundamental to the larger achievement of reconciliation.[38] It has also been argued that the possibility of original Indigenous sovereignty has important contemporary ramifications. A United Nations Special Rapporteur suggests that without consent of the Indigenous people, any deprivation of original Indigenous sovereignty is unlawful.[39] If this is correct, a negotiated settlement will provide a forum for the seeking and giving of Indigenous consent to exist within the sovereignty of the Commonwealth of Australia. It has also been suggested that in 1788 the Indigenous people may have exercised an overall 'de facto authority' over the lands they respectively inhabited. By invoking this authority and acting through leaders, their descendants could negotiate a series of agreements with the Commonwealth.[40]

The argument that Aboriginal sovereignty persists is based on the theory that sovereign rights, self-determination rights or self-government do not emerge from the state but are inherent in Indigenous peoples' authority and collective identity.[41] However, to be enforceable within the colonial structure in the absence of international recognition, these rights depend upon judicial acknowledgement by the state.[42] In Australia we have a history of implicit recognition of the status of Indigenous peoples as self-governing with a unique relationship to the state through land rights legislation and statutory authorities dedicated to self-management, but the extent of this recognition is a reflection of the relationship between Indigenous peoples and the colonising state.[43]

Although treaties have proved to be an effective legal form for documenting the outcome of negotiations, they are not a cure-all.[44] Resources must be made available for Indigenous groups to negotiate and prepare amongst themselves common negotiating positions so that they can determine the role of the treaty in the context of their own laws.[45] The plurality of Indigenous voices must be accommodated with room made for Indigenous dispute resolution techniques. Once a common position is reached, then Indigenous groups could enter into negotiations with the relevant parties.[46] Also, terms such as 'self-determination' and 'self-government' create in some people's minds the possibility of separate states and governments. As evidenced by the Canadian experience, it is not the case that coming to terms with the problems of the Indigenous people necessarily divides or fragments a nation.[47]

129

---

[33] Cockayne 2001: 591.

[34] Strelein 2000: 264

[35] Cockayne 2001: 591.

[36] Cockayne 2001: 592.

[37] Cockayne 2001: 592.

[38] Cockayne 2001: 592.

[39] United Nations 1999. See also Cockayne 1002: 592.

[40] Lane 1999: 122.

[41] Lane 1999: 122.

[42] Lane 1999: 122.

[43] Strelein 2000: 262.

[44] Cockayne 2001: 593.

[45] Cockayne 2001: 593–4.

[46] Cockayne 2001: 593–4.

[47] Strelein 2000: 260.

The term 'agreement' has slightly different connotations than the use of 'treaty'. In his 2000 Vincent Lingiari Memorial Lecture, former Prime Minister Malcolm Fraser noted that when the word 'treaty' was used in Australia, the immediate reaction of politicians, journalists, commentators and editors indicated that they were disturbed by the use of the word.[48] Mr Fraser argued that, perhaps, in Australia we should simply use the term 'agreement'.[49] The other side of the argument is that we should be honest about what is being sought without concern for those who may be nervous about popular support.[50] The law and mechanisms for the making of agreements are already available given the number of agreements that are already in place throughout Australia. The first agreements made under the provisions of the *Aboriginal Land Rights Act* in the Northern Territory were signed more than 20 years ago in 1979.[51] Since then there have been agreements signed between Australian Indigenous people and resource extraction companies, railway, pipeline and other major infrastructure project companies, local and state governments, farming and grazing bodies and universities. Some are registered under the terms of the *Native Title Act*;[52] others are simple contractual agreements.[53]

Non-Indigenous Australians may not realise that the majority of us are in charge of our own lives in ways that many Indigenous Australians are not.[54] Life expectancy and health are a good indication of this point. Important factors in the improvement of the life expectancy of the Maori people of New Zealand include Maori control of health services and health service provision in a wide context of language and development education designed to close the training gap between Maoris and non-Maoris.[55] This is what 'self-determination' should be seen as meaning to Indigenous people – being able to take charge of one's own life. Self-government does not have to mean the establishment of a separate sovereignty and dividing the country. For example, it can apply to running schools and local community health centres.

The Canadian experience demonstrates the success of local level agreements between Indigenous and non-Indigenous peoples.[56] However, there are some issues such as constitutional recognition that must, and can only be addressed at a national level. The diversity of the Indigenous peoples of Australia necessitates that national, regional and localised responses will be needed to reconcile the sovereignty of the Crown with Indigenous peoples' rights and status. The need for differentiated outcomes has been recognised in the native title process. State framework agreements are being negotiated that reflect the engagement between Indigenous peoples and governments. A national treaty could create a framework that would allow negotiations based on the recognition of rights, negotiated opinions and limitations.[57] It would allow Indigenous peoples to address issues as a collective, self-governing and sovereign interest, rather than as a corporate interest.[58]

The importance of treaties between States and Indigenous peoples has been recognised by the United Nations, which in 1989 appointed a Special Rapporteur on treaties, agreements and other constructive arrangements between States and Indigenous peoples.[59] While there is no simple or uniform answer to the question of rights for Indigenous people in Australia, there is a wealth of experience from other countries such as the US, Canada and New Zealand.

Of the nations that previously relied upon the common law to protect human rights, Australia stands out as the only one that continues to put faith in this method of protection.

---

[48] Fraser 2000.

[49] Fraser 2000.

[50] Strelein 2001: 260.

[51] Langton 2002.

[52] *Native Title Act 1993* (Cth).

[53] Langton 2002.

[54] CAR 2002.

[55] CAR 2002.

[56] Strelein 2000: 26.

[57] Strelein 2000: 26.

[58] Strelein 2000: 26.

[59] Oxfam 2000.

The US, Canada, South Africa, India, Pakistan, and New Zealand have all adopted a Bill of Rights, whether in statutory form or constitutionally entrenched. Even more importantly, in recognition of its accession to the European Convention on Human Rights, the United Kingdom enacted a Bill of Rights in 1998 as part of its domestic law.

The omission of a Bill of Rights from the Australian Constitution is one of the elements which marks it as different from the United States Constitution, from which a number of other provisions were derived. The omission was not by accident. The inclusion of a Bill of Rights was proposed and debated at the Conventions, which preceded and informed the drafting of the Australian Constitution. Its inclusion was defeated, somewhat ironically, on the basis that a 'due process' provision would undermine some of the racially discriminatory colonial laws in place at that time, including those that were concerned with immigration and others which were to the detriment of racial minorities. It appears that the founders were careful to ensure that the provisions of these laws would not be open to challenge on the basis of individual rights or constitutionally entrenched provisions such as a provision for due process.

The centenary of Federation stimulated public debate on the subject of the need for fundamental reforms to the Australian system of government. The various popular Constitutional Conventions organised by the non-partisan Constitutional Centenary Foundation, commemorating the constitutional conventions of the 1890s, commencing with the Sydney Convention of 1891, each tended to identify support for the inclusion of recognition of fundamental human rights in the Constitution, as well as a preamble recognising the prior occupation and special position in Australia of its Indigenous peoples. Similar sentiments came out of the various Schools Constitutional Conventions organised under the auspices of the Constitutional Centenary Foundation. In the end, however, the political and constitutional debate in the period leading up to the centenary was dominated by the republic issue and debate about the preamble. These issues also dominated the official Constitutional Convention sponsored by the Commonwealth, culminating in our latest Constitutional Referendum in 1999. That, of course, dealt with the question of whether we should become a republic and the proposals relating to the Preamble to the Constitution. The Bill of Rights debate seems to have disappeared in the wake of these other issues. Although the constitutional change required to implement a republic could have been an opportune time for incorporating a Bill of Rights, the fact that the republic issue has faded, at least for the time being, does not mean that the crucial issue of protection of human rights should also be put aside.

Central to any process of a treaty or an agreement between Indigenous peoples and the State must be the achievement of reconciliation between the different Indigenous groups so that they can join together in an instrument of reconciliation as a national level united group for the purposes of negotiation. An acceptable process of reconciliation must be found for Indigenous groups with the objective of respecting differences, but joining together as one. Many Indigenous groups have been fighting one another over the disappointments of the last decade or have found their resources consumed by administrative needs.[60] Tensions exist in many parts of Australia between those Indigenous people who can demonstrate that their ancestors lived in the area and those who have arrived in the area more recently. Much of this conflict has clear historical origins in European settlement and is a by-product of the dispossession and forced relocation of Indigenous peoples.[61] There may be little prospect of success in carrying out

---

[60] Hagen 2001.   [61] Hagen 2001.

negotiations when different groups of Indigenous people are speaking with different voices and seeking different things.[62] Conflicting perspectives amongst the Indigenous people must be heard and dealt with so that leaders can emerge who have the support of all Indigenous people and are willing and able to take on the challenges of pulling together communities.

Conclusion

Australia's lack of progress in reconciliation weakens our capacity to offer credible criticism of the human rights record of other countries. The aspirations of the Aboriginal peoples do need to be recognised. The Aboriginal people themselves likewise need to recognise the current position and aspirations of others, including pastoralists and miners. There is a role for governments here to reconcile the aspirations and interests of all parties. In his first Ministerial Statement to the Northern Territory Parliament, Minister John Ah Kit MLA said:

> Aboriginal people in the territory must escape from the cargo cult
> mentality of the government doing everything for them; of relying
> on the empty rhetoric of playing the victim. Aboriginal organisations
> must bite the bullet and develop new, innovative strategies to
> overcome the cancerous ideologies of despair.
>
> The other side of that coin is that the government – in partnership
> with the Aboriginal people – must allow the development of forms
> of governance that allow Aboriginal people the power to control their
> lives and communities.[63]

The opportunity for reconciliation will be lost by the adoption of hard-line adversarial positions by any of the parties with a vested interest in the outcome. We should learn from the experience in Canada, New Zealand and the United States where successful accommodations have been reached. The processes adopted in those countries can be adapted for adoption here. Experience has shown that a process of consultation, mediation and reconciliation of land claims based upon mutual respect is essential and as important as the ultimate outcome.

It is often argued that making special provision for Indigenous people, as by providing an Aboriginal legal service or funding such a service, infringes the principle of equality before the law and is discriminatory. Experience in the United States and Canada suggests that the principle of equality before the law is consistent with special treatment of Indigenous peoples, for whom there is a specific constitutional responsibility. The Canadian Parliament, in the exercise of its power with respect to Indians can validly enact special laws based upon a 'legitimate legislative purpose in the light … of long and uninterrupted history' or on 'Indian customs and values' provided that they do not exclude Indians from the enjoyment of basic rights and freedoms.[64] In the United States, federal legislation dealing specifically with Indians is consistent with the guarantee of equal protection before the law if there is a rational basis 'for the legislative classification in the light of its legitimate purpose'. As in Canada, the United States courts have been strongly influenced by the special federal responsibility for Indians under the Constitution.[65]

---

[62] Local and Regional Agreements 1997.

[63] Ah Kit 2002.

[64] Attorney-General of Canada v Canard (1975) 52 DLR 3d 548: 575; and see Slattery 1987.

[65] Morton v Mancari 417 US 535 at 555, 1974.

[66] Supreme Court of Alberta 1991.

What needs to be recognised is that treating unequals equally can infringe the principle of equality before the law as much as by treating equals unequally. In this respect I note that the *Report of the Task Force on the Criminal Justice System and its Impact on the Indian and Metis People of Alberta,*[66] published in April 1991 under the Chairmanship of the Hon Mr Justice Robert Cawsey of the Supreme Court of Alberta, commences with a quotation from *The Sacred Tree,* namely:

> The final lesson ... is the lesson of balance, for wisdom teaches how all things fit together. And balance, when applied to the interconnectness of all human beings, becomes justice. With its aid, the traveller can see all things as they really are. Without it, there can be no peace or security in the affairs of the world.

133

References

Books, articles and reports

Ah Kit, J 2002, Ministerial Statement, Northern Territory Parliament, 7 March 2002, http://www.nt.gov.au/ocm/speeches/20020305_ahkit_aboriginal.shtml, 8 March 2002.

Australian Bureau of Statistics 2002, *2015.0 Census of Population and Housing: Selected Social and Housing Characteristics, Australia*, AGPS, Canberra, available at http://www.abs.gov.au/ausstats/abs@nsf, viewed 17 June 2002.

Australian Institute of Aboriginal and Torres Strait Islander Studies, available at http://www.aiatsis.gov.au/lbry/dig_prgm/treaty/atc.htm

Australians for Native Title and Reconciliation 2002, *Why 'practical reconciliation' is bad policy*, available at http://www.antar.org.au/prac_rec.html, viewed 23 June 2002.

Berndt, Ronald M and Catherine H 1999, *The World of the First Australians [1964]*, 5th edn, Aboriginal Studies Press, Canberra.

Clark, G 2000, A long journey into daylight for all Australians, *Sydney Morning Herald*, 8 May, http://old.smh.com.au/news/specials/local/corroboree/corro21.html, viewed 23 June 2002.

Cockayne, J 2001, 'More Than Sorry: Constructing a Legal Architecture for Practical Reconciliation', *Sydney Law Review* 23(4): 577.

Council for Aboriginal Reconciliation (CAR) 2000, *Documents of Reconciliation*, Corroboree 2000 Sydney, available at http://www.austlii.edu.au/au/orgs/car/docrec/policy/brief/terran.htm, viewed 18 June 2002.

Deane, Sir William 2001, On the Occasion of the Conferral of the Degree of Doctor of Laws Honoris Causa and the Delivery of the Occasional Address – University of New South Wales, Sydney, available at http://www.gg.gov.au/textonly/speeches/2001/010518.html, viewed 18 June 2002.

Dodson, P 1997, Reconciliation and the Law Learning Together Workshop, Australians For Aboriginal Reconciliation in association with the Supreme Court of Western Australia and the Law Society of Western Australia, 21 February.

Fraser M 2000, The 5th Vincent Lingiari Memorial Lecture, 24 August, available at http://www.austlii.edu.au/au/orgs/car/media/240800Lingiari.htm, viewed 18 June 2002.

Hagen, R 2001, *2001 – Time for a Treaty? Some reflections*, August 2001, http://www.netspace.net.au/~rodhagen/2001-the%20state%20of%20play.html, viewed 22 June 2002.

Hawke, R 1988, 'A Time for Reconciliation', in K Baker (ed) *A Treaty With the Aborigines?*, Institute of Public Affairs, Canberra.

Indigenous Law Resources, Reconciliation and Social Justices Library 2002, *Walking Together The First Steps*, available at http://www.austlii.edu.au/au/other/IndigLRes/car/1994/1/140.html, viewed 20 June 2002.

Lane, PH 1999, 'Nationhood and Sovereignty in Australia,' *The Australian Law Journal*, 73(2).

Langton, M, 'A Treaty Between Our Nations?' Inaugural Professorial Lecture, University of Melbourne, available at http://www.Indigenous.unimelb.edu.au/lecture3.html, viewed 18 June 2002.

Local and Regional Agreements, available at http://www.austlii.edu.au/au/other/IndigLRes/car/1997/3/book4?pages/041rao2.htm, viewed 22 June 2002.

Nyungah Circle of Elders, Joint Press Release, 17 June 2001, available at http://www.nyungah.org.au/statements/swanbourne.html, viewed 22 June 2002.

Oxfam, Community Aid Abroad 2000, 'Reconciliation – Where to from here? The Case for a Treaty, *Polliewatch*, no 42, available at http://www.caa.org.au/campaigns/polliewatch/reconciliation.html, viewed 23 June 2002.

Ruddock, P 2002, 'Native title works, but land alone won't fix Indigenous problems', *Age*, 14 June.

Slattery, B 1987, 'Understanding Aboriginal Rights', Canadian Bar Review 66(4).

Strelein, L 2000, 'Dealing with 'Unfinished Business': A Treaty for Australia', *Public Law Review* 11(4).

Supreme Court of Alberta 1991, *Justice on Trial (Cawsey Report): Report of the Task Force on the Criminal Justice System and its Impact on the Indian and Metis People of Alberta*, vol 1, Main Report, March.

Tickner R 1991, Aboriginal Reconciliation A Discussion Paper, available at http://www.churchandnation.pcnsw.org.au/C%20&%20N%201991.pdf

United Nations 1999, *Study on Treaties, Agreements and Other Constructive Agreements Between States and Indigenous Populations: Final Report*, United Nations, Geneva.

Legislation

Native Title Act 1993 (Cth).

Case Law

Attorney-General of Canada v Canard (1975) 52 DLR 3d 548 at 575.

Morton v Mancari 417 US 535 (1974).

Miliipum v Nabalco Pty Ltd (1971) 17 FLR 141.

International Human Rights: bases for Indigenous rights

Garth Nettheim

Introduction

This paper discusses two aspects in which International Human Rights Law may be relevant to the discussion of a treaty between Indigenous and non-Indigenous Australia. First, international human rights norms may provide a basis for the *concept of a treaty* between a State and the Indigenous peoples within the boundaries of that State. Second, these norms, particularly those codified in various human rights treaties and other instruments can provide a basis for the *content* of any such instrument.

1. The concept of a treaty

Defining 'Treaty'

Until fairly recent times, the word 'treaty' was used for any sort of agreement or compact. Even today, the term 'private treaty' is used if one buys a house other than at auction. But dictionaries now use the term in the more limited sense of 'a formal agreement between two or more independent states' and 'the formal document embodying such an international agreement'.[1] The 1969 *Vienna Convention on the Law of Treaties* defines the term, for the purpose of the Convention, as 'an international agreement concluded between States in written form and governed by international law, whether embodied in a single instrument or in two or more related instruments and whatever its particular designation'.[2]

Defining 'State'

If we proceed with this modern, limited definition of what is a 'treaty', what, then, is a 'State'? Can we say that Aboriginal and Torres Strait Islander peoples constituted States, such that the term 'treaty' would have been appropriate at the beginning of contact with Britain? Even if they did constitute States at that time, can we say that they still have the essential characteristics of States today, such that any agreement now between them and Australia would merit the term 'treaty'?

Again, modern International Law offers a widely accepted definition of the term 'State'. The *Restatement of the Law (Third). The Foreign Relations Law of the United States*[3] follows the *Montevideo Convention on the Rights and Duties of States*[4] and defines a State as having the following characteristics:

---

[1] *The Macquarie Dictionary* 1997: 2253. An additional definition as encompassing 'any agreement or compact' is regarded as obsolete by *The Oxford English Dictionary* 1970: 309.

[2] *Vienna Convention*, Article 2, para 1(a).

[3] *Restatement* 1987: para 201.

[4] *Montevideo Convention* December 1933: Article I.

> Under International law, a state is an entity that has a defined
> territory and permanent population, under the control of its own
> government, and that engages in, or has the capacity to engage in,
> formal relations with other such entities.

An additional element is recognition by other States. This State-centred concept of International Law was largely developed by European nations which had their own conceptions of the sort of characteristics – particularly the sort of governmental structures – that would merit recognition.

Treaties with Indigenous peoples

By and large, European nations acknowledged the political authority and the sovereignty of non-European peoples in those territories where they wished to establish permanent settlements. They did so by negotiating formal treaties with them. This was British imperial policy and practice in North America and the Pacific and elsewhere. Consider the Admiralty's secret instructions in 1768 to Lt James Cook for his first great voyage into the Pacific in the event that he should discover the Great South Land:

> You are also *with the consent of the natives* to take possession of
> convenient situations in the country in the name of the King of Great
> Britain, or, if you find the country uninhabited take possession for
> His Majesty the King by setting up proper marks and inscriptions as
> first discoverers and possessors.[5]

When Cook made landfall on the eastern coast of what is now called Australia in 1770, he did encounter natives, but did not gain their consent before he proclaimed British sovereignty at Possession Island. His reasons were various and, apparently, involved some degree of erroneous speculation that the land was literally uninhabited (*terra nullius*), apart from small groups living on the coastal fringes.[6]

But at least the Government's policy had been clearly stated. It was subsequently followed more faithfully when Britain asserted sovereignty over New Zealand on the basis of the Treaty of Waitangi. The policy had been followed previously in the settlement of North America, and was followed by the US Government as it expanded across the continent. The policy was followed in Canada which still negotiates treaties with First Nations today.

The US Congress expressly forbade the negotiation of any more treaties in 1871:

> hereafter no Indian nation or tribe within the territory of the United
> States shall be acknowledged or recognised as an independent nation,
> tribe or power with whom the United States may contract by treaty:
> *Provided, further,* That nothing herein contained shall be construed
> to invalidate or impair the obligation of any treaty heretofore lawfully
> made and ratified with any such Indian nation or tribe.[7]

However, Professor Charles F Wilkinson points out that much of what had previously been achieved by treaties continued to be achieved through a variety of other government acts which he designates 'treaty substitutes'.[8]

---

[5] Cited in Bennett and Castles 1979: 253–4 (emphasis added).

[6] Reynolds 1987: 31–3, 51, 53, 54.

[7] *Indian Appropriations Act of 1871* (USA).

[8] Wilkinson 1987: 8, 63–8, 101–3.

Indigenous peoples in International law

Professor S James Anaya has argued persuasively that what are now termed Indigenous peoples were regarded as subjects of International Law until well into the nineteenth century when the settler States proceeded to deny any such status and to 'domesticate' them.[9] Arguably, they are still subjects of International law today.[10]

Defining 'Indigenous peoples'

At this stage, it is appropriate to consider an accepted International Law definition of the term 'Indigenous peoples'. The Indigenous peoples of the world have long and bitter experience of being subjected to definitions imposed on them by settler States, and they have resisted moves to include a definition in the UN *Draft Declaration on the Rights of Indigenous Peoples*. Their argument was that it was for Indigenous peoples themselves to identify themselves. But Martinez Cobo, in his *Study of the Problem of Discrimination against Indigenous Populations* for the UN Sub-Commission on Prevention of Discrimination and Protection of Minorities, offered a working description which has been cited on many occasions:

> Indigenous communities, peoples and nations are those which, having a historical continuity with pre-invasion and pre-colonial societies that developed on their territories, consider themselves distinct from other sectors of the societies now prevailing in those territories, or parts of them. They form at present non-dominant sectors of society and are determined to preserve, develop and transmit to future generations their ancestral territories, and their ethnic identity, as the basis of their continued existence as peoples, in accordance with their own cultural patterns, social institutions and legal systems …
>
> On an individual basis, an indigenous person is one who belongs to those indigenous populations through self-identification as indigenous (group consciousness) and is recognized and accepted by those populations as one of its members (accepted by the group).[11]

The Treaty study

Miguel Alfonso Martinez, as a UN Special Rapporteur, conducted a *Study on treaties, agreements and other constructive arrangements between States and indigenous populations*. He produced for the Sub-Commission on Prevention of Discrimination and Protection of Minorities a preliminary report and three progress reports before presenting his final report, published in 1999.[12] Several extracts from his final report are worth noting in this context:

> 104 … the main finding that emerges … relates to the widespread recognition of 'overseas peoples' – including indigenous peoples in the current sense of the term – as sovereign entities by European powers and their successors, at least during the era of the Law of Nations.
>
> 105. Consequently, the *problematique* of indigenous treaties and other juridical instruments today affecting the lives of these peoples, hinges on what the Special Rapporteur has termed *a process of retrogression*, by which they have been deprived of (or saw greatly reduced) three of

---

[9] Anaya 1996.   [10] The American Society of International Law 1984.   [12] Alphonso Martinez 1999.
[11] Martinez Cobo 1986: para 379.

the four essential attributes on which their original status as sovereign nations was grounded, namely their territory, their recognized capacity to enter into international agreements, and their specific forms of government … Not to mention the substantial reduction of their respective populations in many countries around the world, due to a number of factors including, assimilationist policies.

…

110. In establishing formal legal relationships with peoples overseas, the European parties were clearly aware that they were negotiating and entering into contractual relations with sovereign nations, with all the international legal implications of that term during the period under consideration.

111. This remains true independently of the predominance, nowadays, of more restricted State-promoted notions of indigenous 'self-government', 'autonomy', 'nationhood' and 'partnership' – if only because the 'legitimization' of their colonization and trade interests made it imperative for European powers to recognize indigenous nations as sovereign entities.

112. In the course of history, the newcomers then nevertheless attempted to divest indigenous peoples … of their sovereign attributes, especially jurisdiction over their lands, recognition of their forms of social organization, and their status as subjects of international law.

…

123. Closer scrutiny of the provisions of treaties concluded between indigenous peoples and States also reveals that in most cases the subject of such treaties is common in international law, whatever the historical period considered: thus such treaties deal with questions of war/peace, trade provisions, protection of the subjects/citizens of each signatory party, and so forth.

The Special Rapporteur expanded on these comments in Part III of his final report:

186 … something must be said about the juridical instruments that emerged after the initial contacts in the various periods. Their intrinsic nature, form and content make it clear that the indigenous and non-indigenous parties mutually bestowed on each other (in either an explicit or implicit manner) the condition of sovereign entities in accordance with the non-indigenous international law of the time.

187. It must be stressed that certain States had a very powerful motivation for making these treaties or other international instruments of a contractual nature requiring the consent of participants. Furthermore, this motivation (in the direct interest of the non-indigenous party) was quite clear: to legitimize (via the acquiescence of the autocthonous sovereign of the territories in question) any 'right' (real or intended) with which they could counter opposing claims advanced by other colonial powers vying for control of those lands.

188. However, to acquire such 'rights' via derivative title (since they clearly lacked original title, or because the legality of their presence in those areas was being questioned), required that they seek the agreement of the legitimate holder of the original title, i.e., the indigenous nation in question. The latter would have to do this by the formal cession of their lands (or their sale, or a concession of acquisitive possession or any other type of valid transfer).

189. In accordance with European legal tradition and formalities, this transfer should appear in a document that could be presented as proof before the colonizing power's equals in the 'concert of civilized nations'. The ideal instrument for this, according to the international law of the epoch, was the treaty. Furthermore, the only entities with the juridical capacity to make treaties were (like today), precisely, international subjects possessing sovereignty – their own or delegated by other sovereigns – through the exercise of it.

190. In a second phase of the colonization project and until it peaked – during its 'classical' manifestation or a variation thereof, and especially as of the second third of the nineteenth century – there was a visible increase in the use of military force to acquire vast tracts of 'new' territories. This shift was very much in line with the enormous power already being wielded by the traditional European imperial powers and by others who emerged later to begin their own expansionism.

191. The newcomers' descendants increased their military and economic capacity. That of the indigenous peoples remained (in the best of cases) the same or (most frequently) decreased rapidly, which resulted in both cases in a growing vulnerability of these peoples to the machinations of the non-indigenous, with whom they had possibly made treaties/agreements, but who now wished to ignore their sovereignty and impose a 'new order' on their ancestral homes.

192. Thus began the process that the Special Rapporteur has preferred to call (without any claim to originality) the 'domestication' of the 'indigenous question', that is to say, the process by which the entire *problematique* was removed from the sphere of international law and placed squarely under the exclusive competence of the internal jurisdiction of the non-indigenous States. In particular, although not exclusively, this applied to everything related to juridical documents already agreed to (or negotiated later) by the original colonizer States and/or their successors and indigenous peoples.[13]

Alfonso Martinez also considered agreements which were not designated as treaties, and other 'constructive arrangements' which achieved similar ends, as well as situations where no such measures had been adopted, such as Australia. In his Part IV Conclusions he wrote:

---

[13] Alphonso Martinez 1999.

262. He also has reasons to conclude that there is a widespread desire on the indigenous side to establish (or re-establish) a solid, new, and different kind of relationship, quite unlike the almost constantly adversarial, often acrimonious relationship it has had until now with the non-indigenous sector of society in the countries where they coexist. In the view of the indigenous peoples, this can only be achieved either by the full implementation of the existing mutually agreed-upon legal documents governing that relationship (and a common construction of their provisions), or by new instruments negotiated with their full participation. This perception is shared by the appropriate government officials in a number of countries, including Canada, New Zealand and Guatemala.

263. Finally, the Special Rapporteur is strongly convinced that the process of negotiation and seeking consent inherent in treaty-making (in the broadest sense) is the most suitable way not only of securing an effective indigenous contribution to any effort towards the eventual recognition or restitution of their rights and freedoms, but also of establishing much needed practical mechanisms to facilitate the realization and implementation of their ancestral rights and those enshrined in national and international texts. It is thus the most appropriate way to approach conflict resolution of indigenous issues at all levels with indigenous free and educated consent.[14]

The Special Rapporteur went on to recommend new mechanisms within States to ensure compliance with treaties and agreements, with possible back-up from an international body.

Human Rights law

The references by Miguel Alfonso Martinez to human rights take us beyond classical International Law references to 'States', 'sovereignty' and 'treaties' to modern human rights standards. Of course the *Charter of the United Nations* gives primacy to the place of States, to the 'sovereign equality of all its Members',[15] and affirms that nothing in the Charter 'shall authorise the United Nations to intervene in matters which are essentially within the domestic jurisdiction of any state' (subject to possible enforcement measures under Chapter VII of the Charter).[16]

But Article 1 includes among the purposes of the UN, along with the maintenance of international peace and security,[17] that of 'develop[ing] friendly relations among nations based on respect for the principle of *equal rights and self-determination of peoples*',[18] and it refers to 'promoting and encouraging respect for human rights and for fundamental freedoms for all without distinction as to race, sex, language, or religion'.[19] So peace and security among States is seen as integrally connected with the rights of people, *and of peoples.*

These concepts have been defined and developed in the evolution of International Human Rights Law, particularly the half dozen core treaties, and some influential Declarations. The *International Covenant on Civil and Political Rights* is perhaps the most significant for present

---

[14] Alphonso Martinez 1999.
[15] 1945: Article 2(1).
[16] 1945: Article 2(7).
[17] 1945: Article 1(1).
[18] 1945: Article 1(2) (emphasis added).
[19] 1945: Article 1(3).

purposes in relation to the notion of a treaty or agreement between a State and Indigenous peoples within that State.

Article 1

1. All peoples have the right of self-determination. By virtue of that right they freely determine their political status and freely pursue their economic, social and cultural development.[20]

Self-determination

The concept of 'self-determination of peoples' has been developed most clearly in relation to the peoples of colonial possessions of European powers across the seas. This took the form of the 'decolonisation' process that witnessed the break-up of empires, and the accession to independence and Statehood of most of the former, distant components of those empires. What has been more problematic has been the possible application of the principle of self-determination to minorities within the boundaries of States and to Indigenous peoples.[21]

Of course, self-determination refers to a process. The particular outcome of that process need not be secession to independent Statehood. In 1970 the General Assembly adopted Res 2625 (xxv), *Declaration on Principles of International Law Concerning Friendly Relations and Co-operation among States in Accordance with the Charter of the United Nations.*[22] It states that other modes of implementing the right of self-determination of peoples may be 'free association' with an independent state or 'any other political status freely determined by a people'.

Sarah Pritchard writes that,

> ... self-determination is a technique or method, a continuum of rights, a plethora of possible solutions, rather than an absolute right to full external self-determination in the form of complete independence. It encompasses a range of alternatives to independent statehood, including associated statehood, internationalised territories, federal schemes, autonomy, ethnic, linguistic and religious minority rights to ensure the continued integrity of a people, guarantees of non-discrimination and integration. The basic requirement is a procedure – a freely made choice and the possibility to reconsider arrangements after a suitable interval.[23]

Paragraph 7 of the Friendly Relations Declaration addressed the critical question of the relationship between the right of self-determination, on the one hand, and the principles of territorial integrity and national unity, on the other. The territorial integrity of an existing State is given the preferred position, but this is conditional: such territorial integrity is inviolable only in respect of those States 'conducting themselves in compliance with the principle of equal rights and self-determination of peoples ... and thus possessed of a government representing the whole people belonging to the territory without distinction as to race, creed, or colour'. So a discriminatory denial of human rights to a people, or a failure to allow them adequate representation in government or adequate participation in decisions affecting them, may forfeit the right of a State to deny to such a people a right of self-determination which might *include*

---

[20] The identical language appears in Article 1(1) of the *International Covenant on Economic, Social and Cultural Rights* 1966.

[21] See, generally, Steiner and Alston 2000: chapter 15.

[22] The Declaration is known, for short, as the UN Friendly Relations Declaration.

[23] Pritchard 1998: chapter 6, part B: para [66].

the option of secession. However there are no mechanisms available under International Law to make such a right a reality, other than in the limited range of situations that may precipitate Security Council action under Chapter VII of the Charter.

Indigenous peoples? Or Indigenous populations?

Because of sensitivities of States to the issue of who constitutes a 'people' such as to be entitled to self-determination, the Martinez Cobo study employed the term 'Indigenous Populations', and the same term was used when the UN's Sub-Commission on Prevention of Discrimination and Protection of Minorities was authorised to establish its Working Group on Indigenous Populations. When the International Labour Organization revised its 1957 Convention No 107, which also employed the term 'populations', Indigenous representatives urged it to use the term 'peoples' instead. It eventually did so, in its 1989 *Convention Concerning Indigenous and Tribal Peoples in Independent Countries,* but subject to the express qualification in Article 1 (3) of the ILO Convention No. 169 that the use of the term 'shall not be construed as having any implications as regards the rights which may attach to the term under international law'.

The UN Draft Declaration on the Rights of Indigenous Peoples

The UN Working Group on Indigenous Populations, in consultation with (among others) representatives of Indigenous peoples from around the world, eventually completed the drafting of the *Draft Declaration on the Rights of Indigenous Peoples* in 1993. It was referred to the parent Sub-Commission on Prevention of Discrimination and Protection of Minorities. The Sub-Commission referred it straight up the line to the Commission on Human Rights which, unlike the Sub-Commission and its Working Group, is made up from representatives of governments. That body established its own open-ended Working Group to meet in separate sessions to deliberate on the language of the Draft Declaration. Progress has been slow, and a major sticking point has been the provisions in the Draft Declaration relating to the political rights of Indigenous peoples.

Article 3 of the Draft Declaration simply replicates the language of Article 1(1) of the two Covenants:

> 3. Indigenous peoples have the right of self-determination. By virtue of
> that right they freely determine their political status and freely pursue
> their economic, social and cultural development.

Other provisions of the Draft Declaration deal with aspects of self-determination, notably Article 31 which reads:

> Indigenous peoples, as a specific form of exercising their right to
> self-determination, have the right to autonomy or self-government
> in matters relating to their internal and local affairs, including
> culture, religion, education, information, media, health, housing,
> employment, social welfare, economic activities, land and resources
> management, environment and entry by nonmembers, as well as ways
> and means for financing these autonomous functions.

Other provisions refer to determination of membership (citizenship) and the right to maintain laws, structures, institutions etc. Some provisions deal with rights of public participation.[24]

---

[24] Nettheim et al 2002: chapter 2.

The Draft Declaration is 'soft law', and even if accepted by the Commission on Human Rights and, ultimately, by the General Assembly, will remain 'soft law', with no binding force in International Law. But its provisions relating to the political rights of Indigenous peoples find counterparts in an increasing number of other elements of International Law.

The broader issues of self-determination as to the political status of an Indigenous people would appropriately be settled by an agreement or agreements between the people and the State. Whether such an agreement is called a treaty or something else is a matter of choice.

Treaty proposals in Australia

When the National Aboriginal Conference, in 1979, floated the idea of a latter-day treaty, Prime Minister Fraser objected to the word. Discussion proceeded instead about a '*Makarrata*' (a Yolgnu word). In 1987 Prime Minister Hawke revived the idea of a treaty to settle outstanding issues, but the idea did not proceed beyond 1988. At that time, Mr Howard, as Opposition leader, again opposed the notion of anything called a 'treaty'.

In 1983 the Senate Standing Committee on Constitutional and Legal Affairs produced a valuable report called 'Two Hundred Years Later – A Report on the Feasibility of a Compact or 'Makarrata' between the Commonwealth and Aboriginal People'. The Committee's conclusion was that such a compact was feasible, and it also reported on how such a document might be given Constitutional status. The issue was revisited in the 1988 Final Report of the Constitutional Commission. The Commission made no recommendation, pending the actual negotiation of an agreement.

What support is there from Aborigines and Torres Strait Islanders for an Australian agreement?

In 1994–95 national bodies consulted and prepared reports for the Commonwealth Government on the then-mooted 'social justice package'. The Aboriginal and Torres Strait Islander Commission (ATSIC) found continuing Indigenous support for the concept of a negotiated overall settlement 'underpinned by regional agreements'. It proposed initial development of a framework agreement for the negotiation process. The Council for Aboriginal Reconciliation (CAR) also gave some support to the idea.

The idea of a treaty went off the agenda after the election of the Coalition Government in early 1996, and was revived largely at the time of the 'Corroboree 2000' event in Sydney in May 2000. That was the occasion on which the Council for Aboriginal Reconciliation formally presented the documents on which it had been working. The *Australian declaration towards reconciliation* is largely aspirational.[25] It was accompanied by a document entitled *Roadmap for Reconciliation* which comprised four National Strategies to Advance Reconciliation:

> The National Strategy to Sustain the Reconciliation Process;
>
> The National Strategy to Promote Recognition of Aboriginal and
> Torres Strait Islander Rights;
>
> The National Strategy to Overcome Disadvantage; and
>
> The National Strategy for Economic Independence.[26]

---

[25] CAR 2000a.   [26] CAR 2000b.

In December 2000 the Council for Aboriginal Reconciliation presented its Final Report, *RECONCILIATION. Australia's challenge*, to political leaders gathered in Parliament House, Canberra. In chapter 10, the Council made six recommendations, two of which are relevant to the current discussion:

> 5. Each government and parliament:
>
> > • recognise that this island and its waters were settled as colonies without treaty or consent and that to advance reconciliation it would be most desirable if there were agreements or treaties; and
> >
> > • negotiate a process through which this might be achieved that protects the political, legal, cultural and economic position of Aborigines and Torres Strait Islander peoples.
>
> 6. That the Commonwealth Parliament enact legislation (for which the Council has provided a draft in this report) to put in place a process which will unite all Australians by way of an agreement, or treaty, through which unresolved issues of reconciliation can be resolved.

ATSIC consulted with Indigenous people around Australia after Corroboree 2000 to ascertain whether there was support for pursuing the idea. It established a National Treaty Support Group and a National Treaty Secretariat.[27]

Summary

1. At the time of European takeover of distant lands in the Americas and the Pacific, the assumption was that the consent of the existing inhabitants was required. The British employed the term 'treaty' for this purpose. The underlying proposition was that there was a consensual agreement between juridical equals.

2. The English word 'treaty' has come to be confined only recently to connote a formal agreement between two or more sovereign States.

3. The term 'State' has also been formally defined only in recent times. Many at least of the Indigenous peoples concerned would have qualified as 'States', even within this restricted definition, at the time of colonisation. Hence, the word 'treaty', even in its modern sense, would have been appropriate.

4. When (under such treaties, or without treaty) a European nation established 'sovereignty' over the territories of prior inhabitants, those peoples became subordinated to the colonial power in terms of the State-centred system of international relations and international law. It was in the interest of the Imperial powers to 'domesticate' the status of the Indigenous peoples.

5. But US law has long acknowledged that Native Americans retain a residual 'sovereignty', even if subject to Congress, and there remain, on Indian country, systems of tribal governments and tribal courts. Canada recognises the inherent right of First Nations to self-government, and continues to negotiate treaties with them. Other States (e.g., New Zealand, Denmark, Norway) also acknowledge Indigenous political rights.

---

[27] www.treatynow.org See also ATSIC and AIATSIS 2003. For a recent study and update on the treaty debate, see Brennan et al 2005.

6. The nineteenth-century push to 'domesticate' the status of Indigenous peoples has been countered in recent decades by a restoration of their status as subjects of International law. This is evidenced in a growing number of 'treaties, agreements and other constructive arrangements between States and indigenous populations', as reported by Special Rapporteur Miguel Alfonso Martinez.

7. The restoration of the status of Indigenous peoples as subjects of International law is evidenced also in a number of multilateral instruments. Some relate solely to Indigenous peoples (eg, the UN *Draft Declaration on the Rights of Indigenous Peoples, ILO Convention No. 169*). Others are of general application but make specific reference to Indigenous peoples (eg, *Convention on the Rights of the Child*, and a number of instruments relating to such matters as the environment, trade and finance, and multilateral lending institutions). Human rights treaties of general application have, through their respective expert monitoring committees, acquired a developing 'jurisprudence' which applies their standards to the specific situations of Indigenous peoples. And the UN itself has developed special mechanisms in relation to Indigenous peoples, notably the Working Group on Indigenous Populations. In 2002 in New York, there was held the inaugural meeting of a new mechanism – the Permanent Forum on Indigenous Issues, comprising eight experts nominated by States and eight representatives of Indigenous peoples from the various regions.

If, in the latter part of the nineteenth century, the status of Indigenous peoples had been 'domesticated', they have once again resumed their earlier status as subjects of International Law. The concept of 'treaty', to govern the fundamentals of their relationship with the State, seems as appropriate today as it was in previous times.

2. The content of a treaty[28]

We have a relatively clear picture of the matters that are important to Aboriginal and Torres Strait Islander peoples today as 'unfinished business', thanks to a number of public inquiries, public debates, and Indigenous reports and statements.

Public inquiries and public debates

We have known since the 1960s that Aboriginal and Torres Strait Islander peoples have been seriously over-represented in the criminal justice and juvenile justice systems.[29] One initial response was the establishment of the Aboriginal Legal Services (ALSs).[30] The ALSs have been important, and continue to be important. But over-representation continues, as evidenced in the 1991 *National Report* of the Royal Commission into Aboriginal Deaths in Custody.[31] The Royal Commission offered 339 recommendations, almost all of which were accepted by governments, at least in principle – but subsequent analyses show that implementation has been limited, and the statistics of over-representation remain.[32]

We have also known since the 1960s that land rights is of central importance to Indigenous Australians. And responses through legislation and court decisions have been reasonably substantial. There are particular problems in working out the proper approach to native title

145

---

[28] The following discussion draws partly from Nettheim 2001, and LIAC 2001. It is also partly incorporated in McRae et al 2003.

[29] Eggleston 1976 (based on her Ph D thesis commenced in 1965), followed by other studies by other scholars, plus public inquiries.

[30] It was also a response to cultural and other problems that Indigenous Australians experienced in getting assistance from 'mainstream' sources, as were the establishment of other Indigenous service-delivery bodies in such areas as health, child-care, housing etc.

[31] Royal Commission into Aboriginal Deaths in Custody 1991.

[32] Collings and Jacobsen 1999. A recent update confirms that the problem continues: Steering Committee for the Review of Government Service Provision 2005.

cases, and to meeting the aspirations of people whose country is no longer available for return. And there are serious problems with the 1998 amendments to the *Native Title Act 1993* (Cth).[33]

We have also learned something of the importance of cultural matters, particularly in relation to sites, though some scepticism seems still to surround these matters – witness the saga of the Hindmarsh Island Bridge. There is less awareness about the idea for a continuing role for Indigenous laws, and of the need to adjust Australian laws to accommodate Indigenous law.

There is wide recognition of the historical fact that many Indigenous Australians were removed as children from their families, and that such removal has caused pain and suffering for many of them, and for the families from which they were removed.[34] But there is considerable division as to how – and whether – the nation should respond.

There is little comprehension about claims for self-determination or self-government, that is, the claims of people to be allowed to decide matters of importance to them, and their claims to be full participants in decisions by other levels of government that affect them.

There is perhaps least comprehension about the notion that there are constitutional matters that need to be addressed in the gaining of belated consent to the non-Indigenous takeover of Australia.

The 'Social Justice package'

The Keating Government proposed a three-stage response to the Mabo decision. Stage 1 was the *Native Title Act 1993* (Cth). Stage 2 involved the establishment of the Land Fund and the Indigenous Land Corporation. Stage 3 was a proposal to address the non-land needs and aspirations of Indigenous Australians. For the purposes of Stage 3, the Government asked ATSIC and the Council for Aboriginal Reconciliation to consult widely so as to identify those needs and aspirations and to recommend how they might be addressed. Both bodies produced reports during 1995, and so did the Aboriginal and Torres Strait Islander Social Justice Commissioner in the Human Rights and Equal Opportunity Commission (HREOC).[35]

ATSIC drafted Principles for Indigenous Social Justice which were designed 'to guide all future relationships between the Commonwealth and indigenous peoples'. They would require Commonwealth acceptance of the fundamental rights of Aboriginal and Torres Strait Islander peoples to:

a. recognition of indigenous peoples as the original owners of this land, and of the particular rights that are associated with that status;

b. the enjoyment of, and protection for, the unique, rich and diverse indigenous cultures;

c. self-determination to decide within the broad context of Australian society the priorities and the directions of their own lives, and to freely determine their own affairs;

d. social justice and full equality of treatment, free from racism; and

e. exercise and enjoy the full benefits and protection of international covenants.[36]

---

[33] The Aboriginal and Torres Strait Islander Social Justice Commissioner has continued his scrutiny of these issues in his *Native Title Report 2000*, and in subsequent Native Title Reports.

[34] HREOC 1997

[35] See ATSIC 1995; CAR1995; Aboriginal and Torres Strait Islander Social Justice Commissioner 1995; and Jull 1996.

[36] ATSIC 1995: 10.

The Council for Aboriginal Reconciliation also stressed the issue of socio-economic disadvantage, and referred to such matters as 'citizenship rights'. It distinguished these individual equality rights from 'Indigenous rights' – the collective and distinctive rights of Indigenous peoples to land and waters, culture, and so on.[37]

These categorisations of Indigenous rights are reflected at the international level in the *Draft Declaration on the Rights of Indigenous Peoples*,[38] currently under consideration in the United Nations' Commission on Human Rights. These claims/rights in respect of non-discrimination, territory, political rights and culture find support not only in the Draft Declaration but in a number of international treaties and other instruments, most of which have been ratified by Australia.[39] The Council for Aboriginal Reconciliation's four National Strategies also largely match these formulations.[40]

Focus 2000

In September 1999 ATSIC convened a meeting of some 60 Indigenous leaders to discuss future developments. The meeting produced a list of items of 'unfinished business' as a Statement on Indigenous Rights[41] which the leaders seek to have embodied in an agreement with governments. The list of matters is as follows:

- Equality
- Distinct characteristics and identity
- Self-determination
- Law
- Culture
- Spiritual and religious traditions
- Language
- Participation and partnerships
- Economic and social development
- Special measures
- Education and training
- Land and resources
- Self-government
- Constitutional recognition
- Treaties and agreements
- Ongoing processes

If this is accepted as the list of 'unfinished business', it represents also the specific issues that need to be resolved in achieving reconciliation, and specific items which people may seek to address through negotiation of a 'treaty'. I group them as Citizenship or Equality Rights, on the one hand, and Indigenous Rights, on the other; and I group the Indigenous Rights under the headings of territorial rights, cultural rights and political rights. In addition I make references to selected International human rights standards relevant to these issues. The references are intended to be illustrative only: space does not permit an exhaustive analysis.

---

[37] CAR 1995: 22, 26–7.

[38] 1993, UN Doc E/CN.4/Sub.2/1993/26. In the latter part of 2005 the Commission on Human Rights was replaced by a new Human Rights Council which, in mid-2006, accepted the Draft Declaration as embodied in the 'Chairman's Text'. It now awaits consideration by the General Assembly.

[39] See Nettheim 2001b; and Pritchard and Heindow-Dolman 1998: 3.

[40] CAR 2000b.

[41] Reproduced in P Dodson 1999: 270–3.

Equality/citizenship rights

Equality

The need here is not only to overcome overt racial discrimination. Such discrimination clearly continues. But it no longer has an express legislative basis. And Australia has fairly sophisticated anti-discrimination legislation and machinery at Commonwealth and State/Territory levels which, with some fine tuning, should be able to deal with the more blatant cases.[42]

At the level of International law, both the *International Covenant on Civil and Political Rights* (ICCPR)[43] Article 2(1) and the *International Covenant on Economic, Social and Cultural Rights*[44] (ICESCR) Article 2(2) stress that the respective rights are to be enjoyed without discrimination on the basis of race, and other grounds. The *International Convention on the Elimination of All Forms of Racial Discrimination* (ICERD)[45] deals specifically, and in more detail, with discrimination on the basis of race, and provides the basis, through Constitution s.51 (xxix), 'external affairs', for the validity of the *Racial Discrimination Act 1975* (Cth).

The need is also for what have been referred to as 'citizenship rights' – the rights of Indigenous Australians to comparable levels of services as are available to other Australians, and the progressive reduction of the marked disparities in the socio-economic indicators in such matters as health, housing, education and employment. Such disparities are matters of concern in terms of Australia being a party to the *International Covenant on Economic, Social and Cultural Rights*. They are the focus for the Council for Aboriginal Reconciliation's *National Strategy to Overcome Disadvantage*.[46] They receive detailed consideration in chapter 4 of the Aboriginal and Torres Strait Islander Social Justice Commissioner's *Social Justice Report 2000*.[47]

Special measures

But would special programmes to overcome such disadvantages themselves offend the ideal of equality? This notion, 'the myth of equality', was one of the reasons suggested by Brennan and Crawford for the lack of progress in attending to the aspirations of Indigenous Australians.[48] It remains politically potent in the One Nation party's attack on the 'special privileges' accorded to Indigenous Australians.[49]

But, as Brennan and Crawford observe, the jurisprudence of comparable countries such as the USA and Canada, and of Australia itself, accepts that 'special measures' to overcome disadvantage do not offend principles of equality. The *International Convention on the Elimination of all Forms of Racial Discrimination* expressly permits 'special measures' to overcome disadvantage[50] and even requires State parties to adopt such measures.[51] The Convention is implemented in Australian law by the *Racial Discrimination Act 1975*, section 8(1) of which permits such 'special measures' as exceptions to the prohibition of discrimination.

On a broader view, the sort of measures under discussion do not constitute discrimination in the first place, so as to require authorisation as an exception. Differentiation as such does not constitute discrimination, and the goal of equality is less concerned with formal equality of treatment than with substantive equality of outcomes.[52]

---

42 For an important assessment of the Commonwealth legislation, see Race Discrimination Commissioner 1995.

43 1966, 999 UNTS 171.

44 1966, 99 UNTS 3.

45 1966, 660 UNTS 195.

46 CAR 2000d.

47 Aboriginal and Torres Strait Islander Social Justice Commissioner 2000.

48 Brennan and Crawford 1990: 64–6.

49 Laura Tingle, 1996, quoted from Pauline Hanson's maiden speech in Federal Parliament, and set out facts in response.

50 1966, 660 UNTS 195: Article 1(4).

51 1966, 660 UNTS 195: Article 2(2).

52 Race Discrimination Commissioner 1995, chapter 9; McRae et al 2003: 448–50. For other discussion of these issues, see Aboriginal and Torres Strait Islander Social Justice Commissioner 2001: chapter 1.

Education and training

Education and training are obviously an essential component of the equality agenda. Statistics continue to indicate that Indigenous Australians have markedly lower levels of education and training than the level of attainment for Australians generally. Education and training are also important to many of the other items on the list of 'unfinished business'.

These matters are dealt with in some detail in ICESCR Article 6 (2) and, especially, Articles 13 and 14. Such rights are to be exercised without discrimination of any kind as to race, etc. (Article 2(2)).

Economic and social development

This agenda item also links to the matter of overcoming disadvantage. The Council for Aboriginal Reconciliation's *Roadmap for Reconciliation* has a distinct National Strategy for Economic Independence which is directed to achieving, for Aboriginal and Torres Strait Islander peoples and communities, 'the same levels of economic independence as the wider community'. The Strategy lists essential actions as including access to jobs and resources, effective business practices and skills development. Article 6 and other Articles in ICESCR are relevant to these goals.

Participation and partnerships

This item links to both goals of overcoming disadvantage and economic empowerment by proposing partnerships with business and other private sector bodies.

The idea of partnership also links into the role of governments, particularly in relation to the delivery of services to Indigenous peoples and communities. So does the term 'participation'. I have referred to areas where such participation and partnership have been important, namely the establishment and funding of Aboriginal Legal Services, Aboriginal Medical Services, and so on.

Participation also has a wider reference to the notion that Indigenous peoples should be effective participants when governments and public authorities make decisions on matters that particularly affect Aborigines and Torres Strait Islanders.[53] This notion of public participation takes us into the area of Indigenous political rights, discussed below.

Indigenous rights

The Council for Aboriginal Reconciliation's *Roadmap for Reconciliation* has a distinct National Strategy to Promote Recognition of Aboriginal and Torres Strait Islander Rights which addresses a number of the distinctive Indigenous rights in relation to territorial, cultural and political rights.

Territorial rights

Land and resources

The question of land rights and native title has been at the forefront of the demands of Aboriginal and Torres Strait Islander peoples on the Australian legal and political systems. There has been widespread acceptance of the case for recognising the continuing relationship of Indigenous peoples with land and waters where this can be achieved without displacing post-colonisation titles or public uses of land – and without unduly impeding 'resource development' activities,

---

53 Aboriginal and Torres Strait Islander Social Justice Commissioner 2000: chapter 4.

such as mining. There is also widespread acceptance of the fact that 'country' is central to Aboriginal cultures.

These matters find support in International human rights law through ICERD, Article 5, according to which States parties undertake to guarantee the right of everyone, without distinction as to race (etc), to equality before the law, 'notably in the enjoyment of the following rights', including:

> (d)(v) The right to own property alone as well as in association
> with others;
>
> (vi) The right to inherit.[54]

They also find support in other instruments such as ILO Convention No. 169, Articles 13–15.

Cultural rights

Distinct characteristics and identity

Aboriginal peoples and Torres Strait Islanders have histories and cultures which are distinct from those of other Australians. Of course, many people of Indigenous descent live as part of the broader society and may have little or no knowledge of their Indigenous heritages. But for those who retain connections to their heritage, their claim is more wide-ranging than the claims of immigrant ethnic groups to multiculturalism. It is a claim to recognition of their distinct characteristics and identity as the First Peoples of Australia. It commences with territorial rights, which are central to culture, but goes beyond territory, particularly when territory cannot be regained. These aspirations receive some recognition in ILO Convention No. 169, Articles 2 and 5, and elsewhere.

Culture

Culture has many dimensions, some of which are indicated by separate items on the list of 'unfinished business'. It includes art and ceremony, it includes knowledge of the properties of plants, and a range of other matters which receive inadequate protection under Australian law.[55]

Article 27 of the ICCPR has proved to be significant for Indigenous peoples, even though its primary focus is minorities:

> In those States in which ethnic, religious or linguistic minorities exist,
> persons belonging to such minorities shall not be denied the right,
> in community with the other members of their group, to enjoy their
> own culture, to profess and practise their own religion, or to use their
> own language.[56]

This provision is relevant to the following two items, as well. A number of other instruments are also relevant.

---

[54] See *Mabo v Queensland (Mabo (No. 1))* (1988) 166 CLR 186. See also CERD general recommendation XXIII(51) (18 August 1997) paras 3–5, set out in (1998) *Australian Indigenous Law Reporter* 142.

[55] An analysis of the shortcomings of Australian law to protect Indigenous intellectual and cultural property can be found in a report prepared by Indigenous lawyer, Terri Janke, for AIATSIS and ATSIC: Janke 1998. For a shorter account, see Janke 1999.

[56] 1966, 999 UNTS 171.

Spiritual and religious traditions

These matters are very important to Indigenous Australians. They receive some support from the protection provided for sites and objects by Commonwealth and State/Territory laws. But there have been weaknesses in those laws,[57] and 1998 draft Commonwealth legislation was seen by many – including the Senate – as further weakening protection at national level.[58] The *Hindmarsh Island Bridge Act 1997* (Cth) placed the area in question outside the protection of the 1984 Commonwealth Act,[59] and its validity was upheld by a High Court majority.[60]

ICESCR Article 5 provides for equality before the law in the enjoyment of (among other rights) 'd)(vii) The right to freedom of thought, conscience and religion'. ICCPR Article 18 makes more detailed provision concerning these rights.

Language

This item on the list of 'unfinished business' is largely self-explanatory. Aboriginal people are no longer forbidden to speak their languages, though many have lost their languages, and many languages have themselves been lost. Problems still arise. For example, until quite recently in Northern Territory courts, interpreters were available for a number of languages, but not for Aboriginal languages.

ICCPR Article 14 (3)(f) requires the free use of an interpreter for defendants in criminal proceedings. More broadly, Article 27 provides that minorities shall not be denied the right to use their own language.

Law

Some legislation has recognised Indigenous law in particular matters, such as recognition of traditional marriages, or hunting and fishing rights. Some courts have been able to provide recognition of some aspects of Indigenous laws. Considerable work was done by the Australian Law Reform Commission on the overall situation in its 1986 report,[61] but most of the recommendations have not been implemented.[62]

ILO Convention No. 169, Article 8, provides:

1. In applying national laws and regulations to the peoples concerned, due regard shall be had to their customs or customary laws.

2. These peoples shall have the right to retain their own customs and institutions, where these are not incompatible with fundamental rights defined by the national legal system and with internationally recognized human rights. Procedures shall be established, whenever necessary, to resolve conflicts which may arise in the application of this principle.

3. The application of paragraphs 1 and 2 of this Article shall not prevent members of these peoples from exercising the rights granted to all citizens and from assuming the corresponding duties.

---

[57] Evatt 1996, 1998.

[58] Aboriginal and Torres Strait Islander Social Justice Commissioner 2001: 135–48.

[59] *Aboriginal and Torres Strait Islander Heritage Protection Act 1954.*

[60] *Kartinyeri v Commonwealth* (1998) 195 CLR 337.

[61] Australian Law Reform Commission 1986.

[62] McRae et al 1997: chapter 2.

Political rights

Self-government

The starting point, of course, is that the various Aboriginal and Torres Strait Islander peoples governed themselves prior to colonisation. It is possible to express this self-government in terms of an original 'sovereignty'. Indeed, US law acknowledges the continuing sovereignty of Indian nations, though subject to the ultimate sovereignty of Congress, and Indian nations have their own tribal governments and tribal courts.[63] In Canada, the term 'sovereignty' has largely been avoided in relation to First Nations peoples, but there is increasing recognition of their 'inherent right to self-government'. The issue has been discussed in Australia over recent decades, and it is possible to identify some instances of effective self-government on particular matters. But it would be fair to say that the notion is unfamiliar to most Australians.[64]

Self-determination

This concept derives from several references in the *Charter of the United Nations* and the express language of Article 1 of both Covenants – the *International Covenant on Civil and Political Rights* and the *International Covenant on Economic, Social and Cultural Rights*, as discussed above. Australia has, in the past, supported the use of similar language in the debates on the UN Draft Declaration on the Rights of Indigenous Peoples, but has more recently spoken against use of the term.[65]

Effectively, the concept of self-determination is one that asserts the right of 'a people' to decide its political status. Indigenous Australians argue that, in the absence of an initial treaty or treaties, they have never been able to exercise this right, but that the right still exists. The point relates to the earlier discussion about entry to the Australian polity, and to the debate about a modern treaty.[66]

Constitutional recognition

Various proposals for constitutional change in relation to Indigenous Australians have been put forward over the years.[67] The Council for Aboriginal Reconciliation's National Strategy to Promote Recognition of Aboriginal and Torres Strait Islander Rights contains three proposals relating to the Australian Constitution: first, a new preamble which recognises the status of the first Australians; second, a repeal of s.25, which refers to the possibility that persons of any race might be denied the vote under State law; and third, a general prohibition of discrimination on the basis of race. These proposals were incorporated in Recommendation 3 in the Council's Final Report.[68]

It is not easy to locate a provision in an International instrument which expressly requires constitutional recognition of Indigenous rights. But ICCPR, Article 2, for example, requires States parties to make effective provision for the protection of the enumerated rights, without discrimination, through legislative measures where appropriate, and to provide for enforceable remedies for breach. Australia did implement its principal obligations under ICERD through enactment of the *Racial Discrimination Act 1975* (Cth). But, as an ordinary statute of the Commonwealth Parliament, it can be displaced or repealed (in whole or in part) by a subsequent Commonwealth Act to the extent of any inconsistency.[69]

---

[63] Brennan 1999: 623.

[64] See, generally, McRae et al 2003: chapter 3; Nettheim 1993; Webber 1999; Pritchard 1999: 609–10.

[65] Dodson and Pritchard 1998.

[66] For a number of Indigenous statements on this issue, see Fletcher 1994; and Aboriginal and Torres Strait Islander Social Justice Commissioner 2000: 27–33.

[67] Nettheim 1999; and McRae et al 2003: 173–7.

[68] CAR 2000c: 105.

[69] *Kartinyeri v Commonwealth* (1998) 195 CLR 337.

Treaties and agreements

Recommendation 5 in the Council's Final Report[70] proposed negotiation of a process to achieve 'agreements or treaties' to protect 'the political, legal, cultural and economic position of Aboriginal and Torres Strait Islander peoples'.

It is important to distinguish such a proposal from most of the other items on the list of 'unfinished business', which deal with particular issues that are said to require resolution. The proposal for a treaty of agreement is simply one possible means for expressing resolution of such issues. However this general proposition should be qualified in relation to the fundamental question of entry by Indigenous Australians into the Australian polity. A treaty (again, under that or some other name) seems to be the appropriate instrument to formalise such a high level 'reconciliation'.

The Commonwealth Government indicated in 2002 that is not interested in pursuing this proposal, or in proceeding with the draft legislation which the Council referred to in Recommendation 6, and attached to its Final Report.[71]

Ongoing processes

The Council's Recommendation 6 contemplated a process for negotiating how unresolved issues might be identified and resolved. The Commonwealth Government has supported the ongoing process of reconciliation in a less specific sense by committing some funds to the new foundation, Reconciliation Australia. And there is a general commitment to 'practical Reconciliation', which seems to refer to the Citizenship Rights aspects of the Indigenous agenda, ie, overcoming disadvantage. Otherwise, the list of 'unfinished business' remains to be addressed.

And some of the matters have been referred to monitoring committees under the several human rights treaties to which Australia is a party. During 2000, for example, matters concerning Indigenous Australians were considered, in the context of consideration of Australia's periodic reports, by the expert committees under ICCPR, ICESCR, ICERD and the *Convention against Torture and Other Cruel, Inhuman or Degrading Treatment or Punishment*.[72]

Conclusion

There was no treaty basis for the establishment of the several British colonies in Australia, nor was there Indigenous consent to subsequent constitutional developments in Australia. A negotiated settlement of this fundamental issue would seem to deserve incorporation in a 'treaty', whether under that or some other name.

A number of other items of 'unfinished business' have also been nominated for settlement by negotiation between Indigenous peoples and Australia. The outcomes of such negotiations could also be incorporated in a treaty or treaties. But some may be adequately incorporated in constitutional amendments, or in legislation, or in other measures. Indeed it would be unfortunate for negotiated settlements on some issues to need to wait for settlement of all issues.

153

---

70 CAR 2000c: 106.   71 Commonwealth of Australia 2002: 646–50;   72 UN 1984, [1989] ATS 21.
                      McRae et al 2003: 646–50.

In summary, my general proposition is that there are strong bases in International Law generally, and International Human Rights Law in particular, to support the case for a 'treaty' between Indigenous peoples and Australia. There are also clear bases in International Human Rights Law to support Indigenous peoples in their search for resolution of the outstanding issues, the 'unfinished business', that they have identified.

Acknowledgments

Some of the argument of this paper was later presented in McCrae et al, 2003.

154

References

Books, articles and reports

Anaya, JS 1996, *Indigenous Peoples in International Law*, Oxford University Press, New York.

Aboriginal and Torres Strait Islander Commission (ATSIC) 1995, *Recognition, Rights and Reform*, AGPS, Canberra.

Aboriginal and Torres Strait Islander Social Justice Commissioner 1995, *Indigenous Social Justice: Strategies and Recommendations*, HREOC, Sydney.

—— 2000, *Social Justice Report 2000*, HREOC, Sydney.

—— 2001, *Native Title Report 2000*, HREOC, Sydney.

ATSIC Treaty Project, available at www.treatynow.org

ATSIC and AIATSIS 2003, *Treaty – Let's Get It Right!*, Aboriginal Studies Press, Canberra.

Australian Law Reform Commission 1986, *The Recognition of Aboriginal Customary Laws,* Report No. 31, AGPS, Canberra.

Bennett, JM and AC Castles 1979, *A Source Book of Australian Legal History*, Law Book Co, Sydney.

Brennan, F 1999, 'The Prospects for National Reconciliation following the post-Wik Standoff of Government and Indigenous leaders', *UNSWLJ* 22: 618–24.

Brennan, F and J Crawford, 1990, 'Aboriginality, Recognition, and Australian Law: Where to from Here', 1(1), *Public Law Review* 1(1): 53–79.

Brennan, S, L Behrendt, L Strelein and G Williams 2005, *Treaty*, The Federation Press, Sydney.

Collings, N and R Jacobsen 1999, 'Reconciliation with Australia's Young Indigenous people', *UNSWLJ* 22: 647–54.

Commonwealth of Australia 2002, *Commonwealth Government response to the Council for Aboriginal Reconciliation final report – Reconciliation: Australia's challenge*, AGPS, Canberra.

Council for Aboriginal Reconciliation (CAR) 1995, *Going forward: social justice for the First Australians*, CAR, Canberra.

—— 2000a, *Australian declaration towards reconciliation*, AGPS, Canberra, reproduced in Appendix 1, CAR 2000c.

—— 2000b, *Roadmap for reconciliation*, CAR, Canberra.

—— 2000c, *RECONCILIATION. Australia's challenge*, CAR, Canberra.

—— 2000d, *National strategy for overcoming disadvantage*, CAR, Canberra.

Dodson M and Sarah Pritchard 1998, 'Recent Developments in Indigenous Policy: The Abandonment of Self-Determination', *Indigenous Law Bulletin* 4(15): 4–8.

Dodson, P 1999, 'Lingiari – Until The Chains Are Broken', 4th Vincent Lingiari Memorial Lecture,1999, reproduced in M Grattan (ed) 2000, *Reconciliation: Essays on Australian Reconciliation*, Bookman Press, Melbourne: 264–74.

Eggleston, E 1976, *Fear, Favour or Affection*, ANU Press, Canberra.

Evatt, E 1996, *Review of the Aboriginal and Torres Strait Islander Heritage Protection Act 1984*, AGPS, Canberra.

—— 1998, 'Overview of State and Territory heritage legislation', *Indigenous Law Bulletin* 4(16): 4–8.

Fletcher, C (ed) 1994, *Aboriginal self-determination in Australia,* Aboriginal Studies Press, AIATSIS, Canberra.

Human Rights and Equal Opportunity Commission 1997, *Bringing them home*, HREOC, Sydney.

Janke, T 1998, *Our culture: our future. Report on Australian Indigenous cultural and intellectual property right*, Michael Frankel & Co, Sydney.

— 1999, 'Respecting Indigenous cultural and intellectual property rights', *UNSWLJ* 22: 631–9.

Jull, P 1996, 'An Aboriginal policy for the Millennium: the three social justice reports', *Australian Indigenous Law Reporter* 1(1): 1–13.

LIAC (Legal Information Access Centre) 2001, *Hot topics: reconciliation*, State Library of NSW, Sydney.

Martinez, M Alfonso 1999, *The Treaty Study (Final report, 1999)*: E/CN.4/Sub.2/1999/20.

Martinez Cobo, J 1986, *Study of the problem of discrimination against Indigenous populations, Volume 4: conclusions, proposals and recommendations*, UN Doc. E/CN.4/Sub.2/1986/Add.4.

McRae, H, G Nettheim and L Beacroft 1997, *Indigenous legal issues: commentary and materials*, 2nd edn, Law Book Co, Sydney.

McRae, H, G Nettheim, L Beacroft and L McNamara, 2003, *Indigenous legal issues: commentary and materials*, 3rd edn, Law Book Co, Sydney.

Nettheim, G 1993, '"The Consent of the natives": Mabo and Indigenous political rights', *The Sydney Law Review* 15: 223, reprinted in *Essays on the Mabo decision*, Law Book Co, Sydney.

— 1999a, 'Indigenous Australians and the Constitution', in *Reform – A Journal of National and International Law Reform* 74, Australian Law Reform Commission.

— 1999b, 'Reconciliation and the Constitution', *UNSWLJ* 22: 625–30.

— 2001a, 'Making a difference: reconciling our differences', *Newc LR* 5(1): 3–37.

— 2001b, 'Reconciliation: challenges for Australian law', *Australian Journal of Human Rights* 7(1): 47.

Nettheim, G, GD Meyers and D Craig 2002, *Indigenous peoples and governance structures*, Aboriginal Studies Press, AIATSIS, Canberra.

Pritchard, S 1998, 'The Right of Indigenous Peoples to Self-Determination', in *The Laws of Australia*, Title 1, Aborigines and Torres Strait Islanders, 1.7 International Law, chapter 6, part B, para [66].

— 1999, 'Forging new relationships: some observations on the processes of reaching agreement on a document/documents of reconciliation', 22 *UNSWLJ* 22: 609–17.

Pritchard S and C Heindow-Dolman, 1998, 'Indigenous peoples and international law: a critical overview,' *Australian Indigenous Law Reporter* 3: 473–509.

Race Discrimination Commissioner 1995, *Racial Discrimination Act 1975: a review*, AGPS, Canberra.

Reynolds, H 1987, *The Law of the Land*, Penguin, Ringwood.

Royal Commission into Aboriginal Deaths in Custody 1991, *National Report*, AGPS, Canberra.

Senate Standing Committee on Constitutional and Legal Affairs 1983, 'Two Hundred Years Later – A Report on the Feasibility of a Compact or 'Makaratta' between the Commonwealth and Aboriginal People', AGPS, Canberra.

— 1988, Final Report, AGPS, Canberra.

Steering Committee for the Review of Government Service Provision 2005, Overcoming Indigenous disadvantage: key indicators 2005, Productivity Commission, Melbourne.

Steiner, HJ and P Alston 2000, *International human rights in context: law, politics, morals*, 2nd edn, Oxford University Press, New York.

The American Society of International Law 1984, 'Are Indigenous Populations Entitled to International Juridical Personality?' in *Proceedings, Seventy-Ninth Annual Meeting*: 189–208.

The Laws of Australia 1998, Law Book Co, Sydney.

The Macquarie Dictionary, 3rd edn, 1997, The Macquarie Library Pty Ltd, Macquarie University, NSW.

The Oxford English Dictionary 1970, vol XI, Clarendon Press, Oxford.

Tingle, Laura 1996, 'Behind the Lines: The Speech that Split a Nation', *Age*, 15 November, reproduced in H McRae, G Nettheim and L Beacroft 1997, *Indigenous legal issues: commentary and materials*, 2nd edn, Law Book Co, Sydney; 20–3.

Webber, J 1999, 'Native Title as self-government', *UNSWLJ* 22: 600–3.

Wilkinson, C 1987, *American Indians, time and the law*, Yale University Press, New Haven.

International Covenants and Conventions

Charter of the United Nations 1945, UN, San Francisco.

Convention on the Rights of the Child UN 1989, New York, [1991] ATS 4 28 ILM 1448.

Convention against Torture and Other Cruel, Inhuman or Degrading Treatment or Punishment UN 1984, [1989] ATS 21.

Declaration on Principles of International Law Concerning Friendly Relations and Co-operation among States in Accordance with the Charter of the United Nations 1970, G.A. Res. 2625, Oct 24 1970, UNGAOR, 25th Session, Supp 28, at 121, UN Doc. A/8028 (1971).

Draft Declaration on the Rights of Indigenous Peoples 1993, UN, Geneva, UN Doc E/CN.4/ Sub.2/1993/26.

ILO Convention Concerning Indigenous and Tribal Peoples in Independent Countries (No. 169) 1989, 328 UNTS 247.

International Convention on the Elimination of All Forms of Racial Discrimination (ICERD) 1966, 660 UNTS 195.

International Covenant on Civil and Political Rights (ICCPR) 1966, New York, 999 UNTS 171.

International Covenant on Economic, Social and Cultural Rights (ICESCR) 1966, New York, 993 UNTS 3.

Montevideo Convention on the Rights and Duties of States, December 1933, 49 Stat.3097, 3100, 165 LNTS 19, 25, League of Nations, Geneva.

UN Committee on the Elimination of Racial Discrimination general recommendation XXIII(51) (18 August 1997), as set out in [1998] *Australian Indigenous Law Reporter* 142.

Vienna Convention on the Law of Treaties 1969, 23 May 1969, 1155 UNTS 331.

Legislation

Aboriginal and Torres Strait Islander Heritage Protection Act 1954 (Cth).

Indian Appropriations Act of 1871 (USA) 16 Stat. 544, 566 (1871).

Hindmarsh Island Bridge Act 1997 (Cth).

Native Title Act 1993 (Cth).

Racial Discrimination Act 1975 (Cth).

Restatement of the Law (Third). The Foreign Relations Law of the United States 1988, American Law Institute, St Paul.

Case law

Kartinyeri v Commonwealth (1998) 195 CLR 337.

Mabo v Queensland (Mabo (No. 1) (1988) 166 CLR 186.

Mabo v Queensland (Mabo (No. 2) (1992) 175 CLR 1.

Consent, common law and native title

Stephen W Robson

Native title refers to the recognition at common law of the rights of Aboriginal and Torres Strait Islander peoples to their traditional lands and waters.[1] Australia's basis for this recognition occurred with the High Court's 1992 decision in *Mabo v Queensland (No 2)*.[2] Ten years later, sitting down and reaching agreement with traditional owners is now advocated as a preferable way of developing business in regional Australia.[3] At another level though, the differences between negotiation rights and consent have become blurred and misunderstood.

In reviewing how this came about I'll begin by locating this issue in a broader context. The foundation of common law is associated with the two centuries following the Norman Conquest of England in 1066 when law and government administration separated.[4] Australia embraced common law as a concomitant of the British colonisation process, an aspect affirmed in the *Mabo* decision.[5]

The law of consent has a long presence in common law. Applied to breach of contract disputes, its earliest usage is identified around 1250. The word derives from two roots, 'con' meaning together and part of the verb 'sentire' meaning to feel, think or judge. In brief, it refers to a concurrence of wills. More precise definitions are required though in order to differentiate it from other relevant notions, e.g. submission, acquiescence, duress, deception and permission. It should also be noted that its meaning can vary, depending upon its legal context.[6]

At common law consent was embraced as a protection against the King's use of arbitrary and unilateral power. This is expressed in the statement that the Crown 'cannot take away, abridge, or alter any liberties or privileges granted by him or his predecessors, without the consent of the individuals holding them'.[7] In particular, a grant cannot be superseded by a subsequent inconsistent grant made by another person.[8]

Making the analogy with native title, these statements provide authority for limiting the Crown's power to extinguish or impair it without the consent of the titleholder. Hence in this context, consent is about titleholders exercising their free will over what happens to their title. If the Crown exercises a unilateral power to extinguish a title it is overriding the will of the titleholder. While a right to negotiate provides some opportunity to ameliorate the

---

[1] Bartlett 2000: 3, 23.

[2] (1992) 107 ALR 1.

[3] Huggins and Chaney 2002: 11.

[4] Plucknett 1956: 3–5, 21.

[5] 107 ALR 1: 2 (Brennan J), 3 (Deane & Gaudron JJ), 142 (Toohey J).

[6] Young 1986: 89, 12–13, 7.

[7] Chitty 1937 *[1820]*: 125.

[8] See authorities cited in *Western Australia v Commonwealth* (1995) 128 ALR 1 at 25; also Bartlett 2000: 28.

circumstances, it is not consent's essential feature. Consent does not revolve around participation in decision-making. Rather consent centres on the right of titleholders to control what happens on their land.

The *Mabo* decision

So why is it that this authority has thus far not been accepted as integral to Australia's native title doctrine? One reason derives from the nature of the *Mabo* decision. Here the Meriam People sought recognition of their traditional connections to the Murray Islands. In their final formulation before the court the plaintiffs stated that their title was qualified by being subject to the capacity of the Queensland government to 'extinguish it' by 'clear and plain legislation'. In their submission they argued that the power to extinguish their title had not been exercised.[9] Arguing against recognition of title, the Queensland Government argued that 'no right or interest in any land in the territory could … be possessed by any other person unless granted by the Crown'.[10] Thus the limits on the Crown's power to extinguish native title did not become a main focus.

A second, and more important, reason is that in *Mabo* the majority of the court accepted that the Crown held a power to extinguish native title unilaterally. Justice Brennan expressed this clearly in his summary of general rules concerning executive extinguishment of native title. Here he states that:

> [where] the Crown has validly alienated land by granting an interest
> that is wholly or partially inconsistent with a continuing right to
> enjoy native title, native title is extinguished to the extent of the
> inconsistency. Thus native title has been extinguished by grants of
> estates of freehold or of leases but not necessarily by the grant of lesser
> interests (eg authorities to prospect for minerals).[11]

Furthermore,

> [where] the Crown has validly and effectively appropriated land to
> itself and the appropriation is wholly or partially inconsistent with a
> continuing right to enjoy native title, native title is extinguished to
> the extent of the inconsistency.[12]

A short statement provided by Mason CJ and McHugh J confirms that they also shared Justice Brennan's view.[13] Justices Deane and Gaudron also held that the executive could extinguish native title by inconsistent Crown grant. However, they did consider that this would be 'wrongful' and could create a valid claim for compensatory damages.[14] They did not, however, explore the basis for this 'wrongful act' and whether or not they consider consent to be a factor.

Hence five judges recognising native title at common law (Mason CJ and Brennan, McHugh, Deane and Gaudron JJ) upheld the Crown's power to unilaterally deny or extinguish it by inconsistent grant.[15] This stance then is incompatible with one where extinguishment could only occur with the consent of the titleholders. However, in their judgments none considered

---

9 (1992) 107 ALR 1: 138 (Toohey J).

10 (1992) 107 ALR 1: 16.

11 (1992) 107 ALR 1: 51 para 4.

12 (1992) 107 ALR 1: 51 para 5.

13 (1992) 107 ALR 1: 7.

14 (1992) 107 ALR 1: 4. See also McNeil 1996: 203.

15 McNeil 1996: 197. A somewhat different analysis concerning the judgment of Deane and Gaudron JJ is provided elsewhere. See Bartlett 2000: 29; also Aboriginal and Social Justice Commissioner 1994: 85–97.

those native title cases supporting the latter interpretation. Nor did they examine common law precedent more broadly regarding the Crown's power to extinguish pre-existing customary land rights. Examining this matter Canadian legal scholar Kent McNeil concludes that the 'rule that native title can be extinguished by inconsistent grant is not supported by the common law, and in fact contradicts fundamental common law principles'.[16]

In *Mabo*, Toohey J was alone in referring to cases where the consent of the titleholders was upheld.[17] He cites the cases of *Worcester v Georgia* where Marshall CJ found that the Crown had 'exclusive right of purchase', but this was not based upon a 'denial of the right of the purchaser to sell'.[18] Similarly, in *R v Symonds* Chapman J said that:

> Whatever may be the opinion of jurists as to the strength or
> weakness of the Native title ... it cannot be too solemnly asserted
> that it is entitled to be respected, that it cannot be extinguished
> (at least in times of peace) otherwise than by the free consent
> of the Native occupiers.[19]

Justice Toohey also referred to those cases providing support for the Crown exercising the power of extinguishment unilaterally. Examining the three rationales advanced to support this, he finds them wanting.[20] However, he too did not fully investigate the applicability of consent, instead finding that extinguishment in the case had not occurred.[21]

Political response

A third reason for the marginalisation of consent lies with the subsequent political response. The government did not establish a process, or processes, to complete the work begun by the High Court. Is the power to extinguish native title exercisable only with the consent of the titleholders? Or is this power exercisable unilaterally without account of the traditional titleholders' interests?[22] These questions, posed by Toohey J in *Mabo*, were not addressed. Instead, the Keating government presumed the latter to prevail.[23]

Furthermore, investigations were not made regarding other significant issues arising from *Mabo*. What limits exist on Crown power to extinguish legal rights to land?[24] If, as the High Court recognised, native title survived the 'change of sovereignty',[25] then wouldn't subsequently issued titles be invalid to the extent of their inconsistency with native title? Instead, the government presumed that where inconsistencies arose it would be native title that was extinguished.[26]

Fourthly, the way in which the Government treated the right to negotiate provisions blurred the understanding of consent. The Government's June 1993 Discussion Paper devotes a chapter to negotiation and consent.[27] Its authors establish non-discrimination as a 'benchmark'. This principle seeks to ensure that when the rights of native titleholders are directly compared to those of other titleholders these are not deficient. The authors also acknowledge the possibility that '[i]n recognition of the special attachment of Aboriginal and Torres Strait Islander people to their land there could be additional rights of consent ... '[28] However, the authors argue that, rather than being adopted as a principle, consent should be applied in a more restricted fashion. Their justification relies on Australian experiences as providing legislative precedence for 'qualified consent'.[29]

159

---

[16] McNeil 1996: 197.

[17] (1992) 107 ALR 1: 151–3.

[18] (1832) 31 US 515, 544.

[19] (1847) NZPCC 387, 390.

[20] (1992) 107 ALR 1: 151–2.

[21] (1992) 107 ALR 1: 153–61.

[22] (1992) 107 ALR 1: 150.

[23] *Native Title Act 1993* (Cth): Preamble.

[24] McNeil 1996: 216.

[25] (1992) 107 ALR 1: 2.

[26] Australian Government Solicitor 1998: C2.

[27] Ministerial Committee on Mabo 1993: 60–4.

[28] Ministerial Committee on Mabo 1993: 63.

[29] Ministerial Committee on Mabo 1993: 61–4.

The approach in the 1993 Discussion Paper is unfortunate on three grounds. One is that the authors do not discuss the precedents in common law for the application of consent to the recognition of native title. Another is that in their discussion of examples they do not consider that the context had changed with *Mabo*. Furthermore, it is questionable whether one of the examples can really be described as 'qualified consent'. The use of consent in the *Aboriginal Land Rights (Northern Territory) Act 1976* (Cth) is different from a right to negotiate, since the land councils hold a power to refuse exploration licences.[30] Thus this should be more aptly described as an example of unqualified consent. Having transformed consent into a right to negotiate, this approach provided the basis for the *Native Title Act 1993* (Cth).

The Act[31] also links the right to negotiate provisions with special measures as understood in Article 1(4) of the *International Convention on the Elimination of All Forms of Racial Discrimination*. In December 1993 during the parliamentary debate over the legislation, Foreign Minister Gareth Evans justified this link on the grounds that these are rights 'not enjoyed by non-Aboriginal titleholders'.[32]

However, the Convention indicates that:

> [special measures are] taken for the sole purpose of securing adequate
> advancement of certain racial or ethnic groups or individuals
> requiring such protection as may be necessary in order to ensure such
> groups or individuals equal enjoyment or exercise of human rights
> and fundamental freedoms.[33]

The Convention also cautions to avoid the consequence that such measures 'lead to the maintenance of separate rights for different racial groups and that they shall not be continued after the objectives for which they were taken have been achieved'.[34] This does not sit easily with Australia's approach since it refers to circumstances where the measures are temporary, and special is understood as something additional to existing rights.

Yet if consent is a right arising out of common law, like recognition, it is neither temporary nor special in the sense of a measure to overcome discrimination. Nor does its essential feature arise from comparisons with other titles, as suggested by the non-discrimination principle. Rather, it is a principle in its own right and essential to respecting the recognition of native title. Furthermore, Evans was incorrect. A right of consent for a titleholder when the Crown seeks to extinguish title is a right enjoyed in the community more broadly, and Aboriginal and Torres Strait Islander peoples should not be denied this equality.[35]

The subsequent political debate over the Howard Government's Native Title Amendment Bill further obscured the origins and understanding of these rights. One reason was that the Government portrayed the debate over the right-to-negotiate provisions as one between

---

[30] s.42.

[31] *Native Title Act 1993* (Cth): Preamble.

[32] Australia, Senate, 21 December 1993.

[33] See the *Racial Discrimination Act 1975* (Cth): Schedule reprint of the *International Convention on the Elimination of all Forms of Racial Discrimination*.

[34] See the *Racial Discrimination Act 1975* (Cth): Schedule reprint of the *International Convention on the Elimination of all Forms of Racial Discrimination*.

[35] McNeil 1996: 216–19.

supporters of substantive equality and those, like itself, who were inclined to apply formal equality.[36] Those opposed to the changes largely accepted this terrain.[37] As a result, the genesis of the right-to-negotiate provisions originating in consent did not become a focus for discussion.

Another reason for the lack of serious discussion of the genesis of the right-to negotiate provisions arising from consent arose from the political portrayal of 'special'. The Prime Minister campaigned to reject those rights that provide an 'advantage … to one section of the Australian community over others'.[38] The result is that some now incorrectly associate a 'special measure' with some sort of unfair free kick. Its specific source as a measure adopted by the Keating Government to partially compensate Indigenous people in the face of sweeping extinguishment of native title has largely been forgotten.

Conclusion

The marginalisation of consent, then, has been reinforced by not one, but several, factors. The issue though is more than just an academic concern. A right to consent is also a value held by peoples and articulated when resisting arbitrary and unjust dispossession of their lands. During the debates over native title legislation several gatherings brought together people from many different Aboriginal and Torres Strait Islander communities. Meetings around the Peace Plan[39] and in Eva Valley[40] in 1993 both clearly expressed the desire that extinguishment of native title should not occur without the consent of titleholders. In the debate over the Howard Government's Native Title Amendment Bill the National Indigenous Working Group made plain that it did not consent to the changes.[41] During this time these voices were not heard. Caution and inclination to protect customary rights did not prevail and measures to unilaterally extinguish native title were adopted. On the basis of what has been described above a grave injustice has been committed.

What possibilities are there, then, that this matter will be rectified and consent will form a more general basis to relations with Aboriginal and Torres Strait Islander peoples? Modification of the native title principles is one possibility. The absence of full and thorough consideration of consent in the *Mabo* case could invite a re-examination from either the court or parliament. Another possibility is that consent will be embraced through the push for a treaty/agreement. A virtue of this form over legislative solutions is that consent is embedded within its very framework. The core idea is that Australia's first peoples should have their distinct status and freedom respected through their consent to Australia's constitutional framework.

Acknowledgments

Thanks to Professor GD Meyers and Dr Ian Barns.

---

[36] Australia, House of Representatives 1998: 173.

[37] For a detailed analysis of the amended right to negotiate provisions, see Meyers and Raine 2001.

[38] Australia, House of Representatives 1998: 6042.

[39] See Tickner 2001: 112–33; Brennan 1995: 45–6.

[40] Eva Valley Statement 1993.

[41] See Australia, Senate 1998. The statement from the National Indigenous Working Group was 'read into the Hansard' by ALP Senator Nick Bolkus, Greens (WA) Senator Dee Margetts and Australian Democrat Senator John Woodley.

References

Aboriginal and Social Justice Commissioner 1994, *Native Title Report—January–June 1994*, AGPS, Canberra.

Australia, House of Representatives 1998, *Weekly Hansard*, no 10: 6042, 3 July.

Australia, Senate 1993, *Weekly Hansard*, no 15: 5476, 21 December.

—— 1998, *Weekly Hansard*, no 10: 5179–82, 7 July.

Australian Government Solicitor 1998, *Native title: legislation with commentary by the Australian Government Solicitor*, 2nd edn, Australian Government Solicitor, Canberra.

Bartlett, RH 2000, *Native title in Australia*, Butterworths, Chatswood NSW.

Brennan, Frank 1995, *One land, one nation: Mabo: Towards 2001*, University of Queensland Press, St Lucia, Queensland.

Chitty, J 1937 *[1820]*, *A Treatise on the law of prerogatives of the Crown*, 19th edn, Sweet & Maxwell, London.

Commonwealth of Australia 1998, Native Title Amendment Bill 1997: Explanatory Memorandum. House of Representatives, Canberra.

Eva Valley Statement 1993, as reprinted in M Goot and T Rowse 1994 (eds) *Make a better offer: the politics of Mabo*, Pluto Press Australia, NSW: 233.

Huggins, Jackie and Fred Chaney 2002, 'Building blocks, not roadblocks required', *The Australian* 30 May: 11.

McNeil, Kent 1996, 'Racial discrimination and unilateral extinguishment of native title', *Australian Indigenous Law Reporter* 1(2): 181–220.

Meyers, GD and S Raine 2001, 'Australian Aboriginal land rights in transition (Part II): The legislative response to the High Court's native title decisions in Mabo v. Queensland and Wik v Queensland', *Tulsa Journal of Comparative & International Law* 9(1): 95–167, available at http://www.lexis.com/research/retrieve?, viewed 8 May 2002.

Ministerial Committee on Mabo 1993, *Mabo: The High Court Decision on Native Title,* Discussion Paper, AGPS, Canberra.

Plucknett, TFT 1956, *A Concise history of the common law,* 5th edn, Butterworth & Co, London.

Tickner, Robert 2001, *Taking a stand*, Allen & Unwin, NSW.

Young, PW 1986, *The law of consent*, The Law Book Co Ltd, Sydney.

Legislation

Aboriginal Land Rights (Northern Territory) Act 1976 (Cth).

Native Title Act 1993 (Cth).

Racial Discrimination Act 1975 (Cth).

Case law

Mabo and Ors v The State of Queensland (No 2) (1992) 107 ALR 1.

R v Symonds (1847) NZPCC.

Western Australia v Commonwealth (1995) 128 ALR.

Worcester v Georgia (1832) 31 US 515, 544.

'Treaty': what's in a name?

The Hon Justice Michael Barker

Introduction

In the lead-up to the Bicentennial celebrations of the British settlement of Eastern Australia, the conclusion of a treaty between Indigenous Australians and other Australians was given active and serious consideration. The proposal was given life by the National Aboriginal Conference of 1979 that called for a treaty to harmonise relations between Aboriginal and other Australians.[1]

Among those arguing in the affirmative in the debate 20 years ago were a number of prominent non-Aboriginal Australians, including the late Dr HC (Nugget) Coombs a former Governor of the Reserve Bank of Australia, who constituted the Aboriginal Treaty Committee. These people represented a significant section of the broader Australian community who believed a rapprochement between Indigenous and other Australians was long overdue and should be concluded before the Bicentenary. It was contended then that a national treaty could settle wide-ranging historical, political, economic, social and 'land rights' grievances while charting a new course for the future.[2] At the time, the call was for a *'Makarrata'*, or 'compact', to be recognised as part of Australia's constitutional arrangements and enshrining the right of Australia's Indigenous peoples to self-determination through such measures as a national land rights scheme, a say in natural resource development on Indigenous lands, compensation for the historic expropriation of Indigenous lands and governmental rights over Indigenous affairs.[3] As in most things, we today have much to learn from history. In particular, discussion of the prospects of making a treaty in the first part of the twenty-first century can benefit from the 1980s Treaty debate. The lessons learned then remain relevant. Indeed, much of the rhetoric and the detail remain similar. This paper considers the history of the treaty debate, the potential need and constitutional arrangements for a modern treaty, and its potential relationship to native title rights.

The Treaty debate: history and constitutional considerations

The National Aboriginal Conference, which promoted the treaty proposal, believed that there should be a two-stage negotiation process: first the negotiation of a national 'Agreement in Principle' preferably entrenched in the Constitution, and secondly, the negotiation of more detailed regional agreements.[4]

---

[1] Keon-Cohen and Morse, 1984, provide a reasonably contemporary account of the genesis of the Treaty proposal.

[2] Keon-Cohen and Morse 1984: 87.

[3] See eg, Harris 1979, Keon-Cohen 1981.

[4] NAC Submission 1983.

Twenty years ago, the treaty debate occurred in the pre-Mabo/native title era, though the Australian community was then familiar with the availability of statutory Aboriginal land rights in the Northern Territory and growing acceptance of the idea in the Australian States.

Following its election in 1983, the Commonwealth (Hawke) Government raised the possibility of a national land rights scheme to overcome the lethargy of state governments in introducing regional schemes, although it lost much of its political enthusiasm for the idea when the Western Australian (Burke) Labor Government in 1984, in the face of opposition from the powerful resource industry lobby, backed down from its commitment to introduce a State scheme. The Commonwealth suggested nothing could be achieved in the areas of education, health, housing and land rights without the involvement of the States and Territories.

The Senate Legal and Constitutional Affairs Committee report 'Two Hundred Years Later …', which dealt with the feasibility of a *Makarrata*, perceived there were a number of basic problems in negotiating a treaty, not the least of which were the selection of negotiators to represent the Indigenous interests and the lack of resources available to negotiate with the Commonwealth Government on anything approaching equal terms.

The 1980s Treaty debate recognised that many Indigenous groups might not qualify for land grants under a 'traditional owner' formula like that employed in the *Aboriginal Land Rights (Northern Territory) Act 1976* (Cth) and would need to be given direct land grants or the financial means to acquire land to meet Indigenous needs. The *Aboriginal Land Fund Act 1974* (Cth) was enacted in recognition of this and set up the Aboriginal Land Fund Commission, a forerunner of the Indigenous Land Corporation that operates today, to ensure Aboriginal people had access to funds to acquire land.

This approach was anticipated by the *Aboriginal Land Rights Act 1983* of New South Wales which enshrined a proposal that a sum equivalent to 7.5% of annual State land tax receipts be paid to the New South Wales Aboriginal Land Council for a period of 15 years to be applied at least in part towards the acquisition of land by land councils. These ideas reflected the Aboriginal Treaty Committee's proposal, taken up by the National Aboriginal Conference in 1982, that there should be a payment of 5% of the Gross National Product (GNP) per annum for a period of 195 years to Aboriginal peoples.[5] Similarly in the early 1980s, various attempts were made or proposed in a number of Australian States to grant land directly to Aborigines by means other than the use of a 'Traditional Owner' formula.[6] In the early 1980s it was considered that a Treaty might be given constitutional recognition and the force of law in a number of ways. Constitutional entrenchment of principles concerning Indigenous peoples was considered the best way to guarantee recognition of the place of Indigenous peoples in Australian society and the best means of providing a platform for the negotiation of substantive rights and interests. Canada's experience suggested constitutional amendment and regional agreements enshrined in legislation were appropriate and achievable to reflect an historic compact.[7]

In Australia, the Constitution may be amended in accordance with the rules laid down in s.128, that is, by a majority of Australian electors and a majority of Australian States agreeing to the amendment. Constitutional experience suggested then, as it does now, that securing an amendment to the Constitution to incorporate a treaty would be an extremely difficult, if not

---

[5] NAC Newsletter 1982: 3, cll 1 and 4.   [6] Barker 1984.   [7] See eg, Keon-Cohen and Morse 1984, and Hanks 1984: 48.

an impossible, task.[8] However, the fact that Australians voted to amend the Constitution in 1967 to recognise the right of Aborigines to vote and for the Commonwealth Parliament to make laws under s.51(26) for 'the people of any race for whom it is deemed necessary to make special laws', may provide heart to those who would otherwise think the task an impossible dream!

Whether or not constitutional entrenchment of the substance of a treaty is achievable, it is a different, and significant, question whether the Commonwealth Parliament has the necessary power to pass a national law to effect a treaty between Indigenous and non-Indigenous Australia. If it has, the Parliament could do what s.128 makes improbable. In the 1980s, s.51(26) of the Constitution was thought by many to provide the necessary power to the Parliament to make the statute that would recognise the Treaty. The so-called 'race power' was at that time, as now, largely untested.

The 1980s was a period of constitutional power-testing. In the Tasmanian Dam case, *Commonwealth v Tasmania*,[9] the High Court of Australia not only recognised the wide scope of the Parliament's power to make laws implementing international treaties and covenants to which Australia was a party pursuant to the 'external affairs' power in s.51 (29), but some judges also suggested the Parliament's so-called 'race power' was not limited by subject matter.

The Senate Legal and Constitutional Committee report 'Two Hundred Years Later...' expressed the view in the light of the Tasmanian Dam case that, even on 'the narrowest view of s.51(36) which emerges from these judgements, it would appear that if the Parliament deems that the necessity exists and passes special laws for the benefit of the Aboriginal race, such laws will be valid'.[10] The Committee noted that the scope of the power would enable laws to be made in respect of such matters as the protection of Aboriginal sacred sites, language and culture and also to give effect to Aboriginal law. Academic opinion concurred.[11] There is no substantive reason to doubt this opinion today.

It would also have been possible then, as now, to contemplate a 'co-ooperative federalism' solution to implementation of a treaty. The Commonwealth and each State and Territory could agree, as they have done in relation to a number of common interest matters in recent years, including corporations law, to make laws in substantially the same form in their respective jurisdictions by way of implementation of a treaty.

Such an agreement could be encapsulated in an inter-governmental agreement in which the financial obligations required to implement the Treaty are set out and apportioned between the Commonwealth, on the one hand, and States and Territories, on the other. Undoubtedly the Commonwealth's power to influence a positive treaty outcome through financial incentives would be critical to the successful deployment of such a strategy. But even money may prove insufficient an incentive to move all State and Territory governments to dance to the Commonwealth's tune.

While each State and Territory Parliament could constitutionally act to bring about the terms of the treaty in its region of influence, unilateral action by some States and Territories would be unlikely to achieve anything but a regional satisfaction of the legal and moral underpinnings of the calls for treaty.

---

[8] See history and discussion of s.128 Constitution in Thomson 1983.

[9] (1983) 158 CLR 1.

[10] 'Two Hundred Years Later': 92.

[11] See eg, Lindell 1984: 248, and Hanks 1984: 28–37.

Thus, not unlike Reconciliation today, the means of implementation of a Treaty in the 1980s was at the least a difficult practical, legal and constitutional problem. The answers to the questions 'What is it?', and 'How do you bring it about as a matter of Australia law?', were not easy then, and they are no easier to resolve now.

The Treaty debate in the post-Mabo era and the recognition of native title

The treaty issue has been put on the national agenda again in this new century by the Aboriginal and Torres Strait Islander Commission (ATSIC). At Corroboree 2000, Mr Geoff Clark, Chair of ATSIC, stated:

> There (have) been no treaties, no formal agreements and no compact.
> There now needs to be.
> There is no mention of the first peoples in the Constitution.
> There now needs to be.[12]

In some ways little has happened since the 1980s push for a treaty: the demands that ignited the treaty debate now drive the reconciliation debate, for there truly is much 'unfinished business' in relation to Aboriginal dealings in Australia. The music may have changed a little but the words are much the same.

What has happened since the 1980s, however – perhaps because of the moral forces then unleashed – is that native title has arrived on the Australian legal scene. In June 1992, in *Mabo v Queensland (No 2)*,[13] the High Court of Australia held that the common law of Australia recognised and would enforce rights and interests enjoyed by Indigenous persons under native title. In 1993, the *Native Title Act (1993)* (Cth) was passed by the Commonwealth Parliament to regulate the recognition and enjoyment of native title as defined in s.223 of that Act. In the light of these legal and statutory developments it is reasonable to ask whether the *Native Title Act* has delivered substantively so that no more need be done on the treaty front.

Although seen by some as a giant macropod bounding across the Indigenous Australian landscape and sweeping up and returning to Indigenous peoples their ancient lands, the question remains whether native title does or can achieve what a treaty once promised and reconciliation now demands.

There can be little doubt that native title has fundamentally changed Australian legal theory and practice. In a more symbolic sense it has also changed the way Australians of all ethnic backgrounds see themselves and treat each other. Native title is founded on the notion of equality of people and peoples, a fundamental human right. It has confronted a nation not used to resolving competition amongst its citizens for scarce resources and their own cultural identities on the basis of racial equality.

While the notion that all persons are equal and that there is no place for discrimination in our society, or in our legal rules, may still be causing consternation in some quarters, by and large and increasingly governments and good citizens, especially good corporate citizens, are 'getting on with the job' in recognising native title and finding practical and legally enforceable outcomes that benefit Indigenous people.

---

12 Clark 2000.   13 (1992) 175 CLR 1.

Indeed, the *Native Title Act* is designed to achieve native title outcomes that go a significant way towards realising the expectations that talk of treaty might create in Indigenous groups. The *Native Title Act* not only enables the Federal Court of Australia to determine the existence of native title, but also authorises the 'right to negotiate' of Indigenous groups in some (though not all) major resource proposals. This right makes possible agreements that provide for the immediate, intermediate and long-term needs of Indigenous peoples, especially in cultural and financial terms.

The *Native Title Act* also provides for the making of broad regional agreements – known as Indigenous Land Use Agreements (ILUAs) – that have the potential to resolve a wide range of native title and non-native title issues between State, Territory and Commonwealth Governments and non-governmental parties, on the one hand, and Indigenous groups, on the other.

Additionally, the *Native Title Act* provides those native title holders whose native title has been confiscated by the 'extinguishing' provisions of the Act, to claim compensation. Whenever native title would exist, but for the extinguishing effect of the *Native Title Act*, the holder of the expropriated native title may claim compensation. Just what should be compensated for in terms of the taken interest remains to be argued in the courts.

Compensation claims under the *Native Title Act* are likely to become the significant 'second wave' of native title proceedings. On their own they may produce significant financial compacts for particular Indigenous groups. They may also provide an impetus for governments to secure a wider regional, State/Territory and Commonwealth financial accord with Indigenous peoples, thereby stimulating the negotiation of a treaty.

The emerging picture then under the *Native Title Act* is of a number of Indigenous peoples having recognition of their traditional rights to land and waters, agreements with governments and other non-native title parties and, increasingly, awards of compensation for their confiscated native title rights. This picture suggests an array of regional compacts that provides outcomes not entirely dissimilar from those contended for by those in the affirmative in the 1980s Treaty debate. At least, that is one view of the prospective outcome of the *Native Title Act* experience.

Another view is that, even if some of these things come to pass (and one should not doubt that they will – indeed they are already), they will not be available generally to Indigenous people. Moreover, the outcomes that native title may deliver to some Indigenous people will not satisfy the deeper demands of many Indigenous people for constitutional recognition of them, of their cultural rights and their desire for a larger degree of sovereignty over their own economic, social, cultural and political development.

The issue of sovereignty, whether written with a little 's' or a big 'S', will never go away in debates that will continue about the Treaty or Reconciliation or the harmonisation of Indigenous relations in Australia. As Dr Lisa Strelein notes:

> Indigenous peoples do not limit their claims against the state to the
> equal distribution of resources and enjoyment of fundamental services,
> although these claims remain an integral part of the 'unfinished
> business' agenda. However, they are only part of the rights claimed.

> The place of collective rights is consistently reinforced, as well as the
> collective enjoyment of distinct cultural rights. Indigenous peoples also
> emphasise that the divide that exists in relation to the equal enjoyment
> of fundamental citizenship rights is a reflection of the much deeper
> issue of their identity as Indigenous peoples.[14]

Native title will produce some small, large and important successes for individual groups of Indigenous peoples. However, it is unlikely that native title will produce the type of constitutional settlement the proponents of a treaty have long had in mind.

As it is, we are already witnessing the politics of native title as larger Indigenous groups splinter into smaller groups, not merely by reason of asserted cultural differences but also because it is well understood by all concerned that significant material benefits may eventually flow to the group that is determined by the Federal Court of Australia to be the 'common law holder' of native title under the Act.

Similarly, many Indigenous persons, fully appreciating that their family's separation from its ancestors' traditional country over the course of many years may prevent them, on their own account, from establishing the 'connection' required by s.223 of the Act to establish native title, seek to incorporate, or re-incorporate, their family or themselves in a larger group that can show the maintenance of 'connection'. This process of attempted integration is not always uncontroversial.

Accordingly, there is a realisation amongst many Indigenous people that not all of them will be able to show they have 'native title' as it is defined by s.223 of the *Native Title Act*. For example, the High Court's controversial decision in Members of the *Yorta Yorta Aboriginal Community v State of Victoria*[15] suggests that Indigenous groups in parts of Australia long-settled by European Australians may find it extremely difficult to show that they enjoy their 'rights and interests' under their 'traditional laws and customs', and that they maintain a 'connection' with lands or waters claimed under those laws and customs.

Such uncertainties may well result in unequal bargains being concluded between different Indigenous groups and governments and other parties. How then are the Indigenous people for whom the *Native Title Act* makes no, or unequal, provision by way of land or compensation to be provided for? A similar question was at the root of the Treaty debate and Indigenous affairs policy developments in the 1980s and is likely to remain relevant in the twenty-first century.

There is, of course, an assumption in this question to the effect that those Indigenous people who do not have access to native title should be provided for in special ways. The historic policies of States such as Western Australia for most of the twentieth century seemed based on the premise that, once 'de-tribalised' and brought into the material 'European' economy, Aboriginal people would, or should, be able to fend for themselves. However, these policies have not proved universally successful, to say the least.

The promise of native title is that some Aboriginal groups will materially and culturally benefit from native title. The promise of a treaty is that all Aboriginal people – especially those without native title – might benefit materially and culturally from the wealth 'European' Australia has

---

[14] Strelein 2000: 259–64.   [15] (2003) 214 CLR 422.

reaped, albeit with the sweat of its collective brow, and not a little luck, from the lands of the forefathers of the Aborigine.

In practical terms, one suspects that the successes – or the lack thereof – of the *Native Title Act* over time will cause some of the planks of the 1980s Treaty proposal, such as statutory land rights, to be put back on the reform agenda in Aboriginal politics. Similarly, the proposal for a defined percentage of GNP or some other measure of the nation's economic performance to be invested in a fund for Indigenous peoples may also re-emerge.

When he raised the treaty issue, Mr Geoff Clark stated that negotiation of a national treaty could settle on:

the roles and responsibilities of the different levels of government: Commonwealth, State, Local and Indigenous communities;

the scope of Indigenous decision-making power: the limits of autonomy and self-rule;

the extent to which Indigenous decision-making is subject to national laws;

Indigenous political representation at a national and state level, including reserved seats in Parliament or other mechanisms designed to ensure representation;

the return of lands, whether specifically identified or to be identified by an agreed process and the relationship between the Indigenous and other land regimes; and

the recognition and protection of cultural practices including copyright protection.[16]

Conclusion

The issues put on the table by talk of a Treaty in the 1980s and now are undoubtedly confronting for many Australians. Not every Australian and not every Indigenous Australian will feel comfortable with a debate about the issues. And not all will agree a treaty is necessary or necessarily the right way forward. However, until the matters that have given rise to the debate over the past 200-plus years are satisfactorily addressed, the demand for a treaty or something that truly looks and sounds like a treaty, and which has a national application, will continue to simmer or boil within the Australian body politic.

While many of these issues could be responded to by individual pieces of Commonwealth or State and Territory legislation, the reality is that they are of concern to Indigenous Australians wherever they may live in our nation: whether they live in Torres Strait, the Centre, the Top End, the West, South or East. A treaty process, undertaken as part of a constitutional amendment process, would have the fundamental advantage of achieving reconciliation at one historic moment for all Australians.

---

[16] Clark 2000.

References

Books, articles and reports

Barker, M 1984, 'Aboriginal Land Rights Law in Australia: Current Issues and Legislative Solutions', *1984 AMPLA Yearbook*: 482–524.

Clark, G 2000, 'From here to a treaty', Address to La Trobe University, 7 September.

Hanks, P 1984, 'Aborigines and government: the developing framework' in P Hanks and B Keon-Cohen (eds) *Aborigines and the Law*, George Allen and Unwin.

Harris, S 1979, 'It's Coming Yet', Aboriginal Treaty Committee.

Keon-Cohen B 1981, 'The Makarrata: A Treaty within Australia between Australians: Some legal issues', *Current Affairs Bulletin* 57: 4–19.

Keon-Cohen, B and B Morse 1984, 'Indigenous land rights in Australia and Canada' in P Hanks and B Keon-Cohen (eds) *Aborigines and the Law*, George Allen and Unwin, St Leonards: 74–102.

Lindell, G 1984, 'The Corporations and Races Powers', *Federal Law Review* 219 at 248.

National Aboriginal Conference 1982, *NAC Newsletter* March 1982, 'Makarrata: Preliminary findings of Makarrata research'.

—— 1983, Submission to Senate Committee on Legal and Constitutional Affairs, 'Two Hundred Years Later…', AGPS, Canberra: 107–83.

Senate Committee on Legal and Constitutional Affairs 1983, 'Two Hundred Years Later…', AGPS, Canberra.

Strelein, L 2000, 'Dealing with "Unfinished Business": A Treaty for Australia', *Public Law Review* 11: 259–64.

Thomson, JA 1983, 'Altering the Constitution: Some Aspects of Section 128', *Federal Law Review* 13: 323–45.

Legislation

Aboriginal Land Fund Act 1974 (Cth).

Aboriginal Land Rights Act 1983 (NSW).

Aboriginal Land Rights (Northern Territory) Act 1976 (Cth).

Native Title Act 1993 (Cth).

Case law

Commonwealth v Tasmania (1983) 158 CLR 1.

Mabo v Queensland (No 2) (1992) 175 CLR 1.

Yorta Yorta Aboriginal Community v State of Victoria (2003) 214 CLR 422.

Customary law and treaty

The Hon Justice Ralph Simmonds

Introduction

This paper, prepared for the conference and this volume, while I was the Chairman of the Law Reform Commission of Western Australia (the Commission), is intended to introduce the Commission and its Aboriginal Customary Law project, and also to indicate the stage that project has now reached, since the conference. I am most grateful to the Commission for its help to me in updating this text.

The Commission is an independent agency charged with providing advice to the Attorney General of WA. This advice takes the form of Final Reports, which the Attorney General (AG) would normally table in Parliament and thus make public. The Commission does this on matters referred to it by the AG. It provides the AG with advice in its Final Reports by way of critical examination of the area or areas of law touching the matter or matters referred to it. In the course of providing such advice the Commission may make any recommendations for reform of the law that it considers desirable.

The Commission has been doing all of this for over 30 years now, and has produced over 92 major reports. Fairly recently, at the AG's request, the Commission produced a review of that 30 year history, the *30th Anniversary Reform Implementation Report*,[1] to indicate what had become of its recommendations and what the government should do with any that remained unimplemented. This Report was well received, and the AG indicated that he would use it as the basis for changes to the law by legislation and otherwise over the coming years. He has in fact been doing just that, and most recently, in December 2004, a package of legislation to reform Western Australian civil and criminal procedure was enacted which implemented some 221 of the recommendations made in the Commission's epochal *Review of the Criminal and Civil Justice System in Western Australia Final Report*.[2]

I mention this history, because the Commission has played and continues to play an important role in public discussion of the law and in law reform in this State. It was thus a significant moment in the State's legal history when, in December 2000, the previous government's Attorney General gave the Commission what is currently its major reference, on 'Aboriginal customary law'. I put the term in quotation marks, because that is how the Commission received it. It is a reference that was adopted subsequently by the current Attorney General when he assumed office.

---

[1] Law Reform Commission of Western Australia 2002.   [2] Law Reform Commission of Western Australia 1999.

The customary law project

The terms of reference that the Commission received and that have been confirmed as I have indicated make it plain that what it was to examine was very broad indeed. It was to consider three principal matters:

1. how Aboriginal customary law is made, altered, recognised and applied;

2. who is bound by such law, and how they cease to be bound; and

3. whether such law should be recognised, and, if so, how it should be recognised, to what extent, and on what basis.

In relation to the third matter, the Commission was particularly asked to consider if certain law reform would be desirable. It was asked to consider whether the rest of the legal system of the State should, in its administration or enforcement, give express recognition to Aboriginal customary law. This was to include the administration and enforcement of state criminal and civil law. And it was also asked whether or not other provisions should be made for the identification and enforcement of Aboriginal customary law.

In relation to all three matters, the Commission was asked to consider the full range of matters of Aboriginal customary law that might fall within state legislative jurisdiction, although two matters were specifically left out. They were matters of native title and those arising under the *Aboriginal Heritage Act* 1972 (WA). This left a huge range, however, covering matters that the rest of the legal system would call matters of criminal law and of civil law. The Commission was also asked to consider Commonwealth legislation and Australia's international obligations, the last a particularly important matter. The Commission was further directed to consider two important matters (here I quote from the reference's Terms of Reference):[3] first, relevant Aboriginal culture, spiritual, sacred and gender concerns and sensitivities; [and] second, the views, aspirations, and welfare of Aboriginal persons in Western Australia.

In undertaking this task, the Commission has drawn on the extraordinary work done by a similar body, at the federal level, in its report, *The Recognition of Aboriginal Customary Law*, published in 1986.[4] This has been revisited in light of the many changes that have occurred since then, at the local, national and international levels. At the same time, the Commission has taken account of the fact that most of the federal body's (now the Australian Law Reform Commission) recommendations remain unimplemented after more than 15 years.

What has occurred since the end of 2000 in working on the project? Here it is appropriate to relate the project to the Conference theme: Treaty: Advancing Reconciliation.

It was evident to the Commission from the outset that it would be unable to produce a report that had the best chance of producing practical and valuable results of the sort the Indigenous community would wish without a form of partnership with them. Such a partnership would promote their input into the project, and assist the Commission in preparing a Final Report that would properly reflect their experience and views. The Commission would of course continue throughout to have responsibility for the production of the final report, in a form that, like the form of its other reports, would have the best chance of making a difference to Western Australians.

---

[3] See Appendix for complete Terms of Reference.   [4] The Law Reform Commission (now the Australian Law Reform Commission) 1986.

The Commission did considerable work on arrangements to make this sort of partnership possible. These arrangements are described in an article in the magazine of the Australian Law Reform Commission, *Reform*, written by three members of the Crime Research Centre at the University of Western Australia.[5]

As the article reports, the Commission, with the advice of representatives of the Indigenous community, appointed Ms Yavu-Kama-Harathuniam, a woman of the Cubbi Cubbi clan (North Queensland), as the full-time Project Manager, and she served the Project over its consultation phase. Dr Neil Morgan and Dr Harry Blagg of the Crime Research Centre were appointed as Research Directors of the Project. The Commission has also seen to it that two Special Commissioners for the project were appointed, in Mick Dodson and Beth Wood. In addition the Commission appointed a twelve-person Aboriginal Research Reference Council, with its membership drawn from across the Aboriginal community in this state, including, as the article explains, 'men and women elders, community representatives and relevant representatives of key Indigenous agencies and peak bodies'.[6] The Special Commissioners and the Council worked throughout the consultation phase of the project with the Project Manager and the Commission on the development and implementation of the strategy for undertaking the research and consultation in the Aboriginal community that the project required.

As the article explains, that research and consultation required the development of protocols and procedures to respect the sensitivities and concerns, while encouraging the participation of, the Aboriginal community. Out of this research and consultation, again as the article explains, was to come a series of background papers and other material on a range of topics within the terms of reference.

At the time of writing, the series of background papers numbered ten. By way of example, one is on court decisions in all Australian states and territories that had drawn on Aboriginal customary law in some way. Another is on the use of interpreters in court proceedings involving Aboriginal parties. Still another is on benchmarking frameworks to reduce Aboriginal disadvantage in the law and justice area. And there were, since the time of writing, five further background papers. All can be accessed from the Commission's website.[7]

The other material produced alongside the research papers principally comprises detailed notes of consultation visits with Aboriginal communities across Western Australia. There were over 20 individual visits, from Wuggubun in the north to Albany in the south. The notes of each such visit were in almost all cases sent back to representatives of the relevant community to permit further consultation to take place with them. This enabled the Commission to refine all of the consultation notes consistently with the protocols for respecting Aboriginal sensitivities and concerns so that the Commission could make the notes available to those interested in the Project. The Commission's website provides a map of Western Australia identifying the areas where consultation visits took place. By clicking on an area it is possible for the visitor to the site to read the consultation notes that were refined in that way.

In addition to the background papers and the other materials I have referred to, the Commission after the time of writing in December 2005, produced a Discussion Paper to bring together its tentative views and recommendations. This Discussion Paper is to stimulate further input

---

[5] Morgan et al 2002.

[6] Morgan et al 2002: 12.

[7] Law Reform Commission of Western Australia at http://www.lrc.justice.wa.gov.au/index.htm

into the Project, particularly from Aboriginal communities. After there has been an opportunity for the Commission to consider that input, the Commission will produce its Final Report that will include the recommendations it will be making to the state government. That Final Report will be published after it has been tabled in the WA Parliament.

Conclusion

It is too early yet to know what recommendations the Final Report of the Commission is likely to contain. But I can at least refer to two ideas for change that one or more background papers addressed, and that the Commission is likely to address in its Final Report. The article in *Reform* to which I referred earlier mentions these ideas also. They are what are called in the article 'community justice mechanisms that assist in actively keeping the peace in Indigenous communities' and forms of 'restorative justice'.[8]

More generally, in this Project, as the Terms of Reference appear to indicate, and as experience in the Project thus far confirms, there is likely throughout to be a particular concern with discussions of the processes of customary law, the processes in the rest of the legal system and the possible forms of accommodation between them, rather than an account in exhaustive detail of particular areas of customary law.

In other words, what the Commission's project on Aboriginal customary law is about is ways our legal system might better accommodate Aboriginal customary law. Such ways of accommodation I see to fall within the much broader forms of social accommodation and mutual exchange that the Conference for which these notes were prepared permitted all of us privileged to be at it to discuss and advance.

References

Law Reform Commission of Western Australia 1999, *Review of the criminal and civil justice system in Western Australia Final Report* (Project 92), The Commission, Perth, September.

—— 2002, *30th Anniversary Reform Implementation Report: Law Reform Commission of Western Australia 1972–2002*, The Commission, Perth.

Morgan, N, H Blagg and C Yavu-Kama-Harathuniam 2002, 'Aboriginal customary law in Western Australia', *Reform* 80: 11.

The Law Reform Commission (now the Australian Law Reform Commission) 1986, Report No 31, *The recognition of Aboriginal customary laws*, AGPS, Canberra.

Legislation

Aboriginal Heritage Act 1972 (WA).

---

[8] Morgan et al 2002: 14.

APPENDIX

Terms of Reference

Project 93 of the Law Reform Commission of Western Australia

'Aboriginal Customary Law'

(December 2000)

Recognising that all persons in Western Australia are subject to and protected by this State's legal system; and there may be a need to recognise the existence of, and take into account within this legal system, Aboriginal customary laws:

The Law Reform Commission of Western Australia is to enquire into and report upon Aboriginal customary laws in Western Australia other than in relation to Native Title and matters addressed under the Aboriginal Heritage Act 1972 (WA).

Particular reference will be given to:

1. *how those laws are ascertained, recognised, made, applied and altered in Western Australia;*

2. *who is bound by those laws and how they cease to be bound; and*

3. *whether those laws should be recognised and given effect to; and, if so, to what extent, in what manner and on what basis, and in particular whether:*

   a) *the laws of Western Australia should give express recognition to Aboriginal customary laws, cultures and practices in the administration or enforcement of Western Australian law;*

   b) *the practices and procedures of the Western Australian courts should be modified to recognise Aboriginal customary laws;*

   c) *the laws of Western Australia relating to the enforcement of criminal or civil law should be amended to recognise Aboriginal customary laws; and*

   d) *whether other provisions should be made for the identification and application of Aboriginal customary laws.*

For the purposes of carrying out this inquiry, the Commission is to have regard to:

- *matters of Aboriginal customary law falling within state legislative jurisdiction including*

- *matters performing the function of or corresponding to criminal law (including domestic violence);*

- *civil law (including personal property law, contractual arrangements and torts);*

- *local government law;*

- *the law of domestic relations;*

- *inheritance law;*

- *law relating to spiritual matters; and*

- *the laws of evidence and procedure;*

- *relevant Commonwealth legislation and international obligations;*

- *relevant Aboriginal culture, spiritual, sacred and gender concerns and sensitivities; [and]*

- *the views, aspirations and welfare of Aboriginal persons in Western Australia.*

Missed meanings: The language of sovereignty in the treaty debate

Lisa Strelein

Introduction

In the 13 years since the High Court's recognition of native title in the *Mabo* case, there has been intense scrutiny of the outcomes achieved through that recognition. For the most part this has focused on the number of successful determinations and the content of the rights reflected in those determinations.

For those of us who look further afield at the changes in the political and legal environment occasioned by the recognition of native title, there is a stark contrast between the potential limits of native title threatened by the adverse outcome in the appeal of the Yorta Yorta Nations on the one hand and the possibilities provided for the emergence of Indigenous rights to self-government on the other.

The then ATSIC chairman, Geoff Clark, repeatedly suggested that the native title process had failed and has called for greater energy to be devoted to a treaty process.[1] It has therefore been assumed that there is necessarily a disjunction between native title and the treaty process.

I have argued elsewhere that native title as a property right cannot be separated from native title as a self-government right.[2] The process of determination and negotiation of Indigenous Land Use Agreements (ILUAs) sets Indigenous peoples as one of hundreds of interest holders and, in its current form, does not adequately recognise the status of native title holding groups as political, legal and social entities. This is despite the fact that the establishment of these elements is part of the proof of native title. Indigenous law and social systems are dealt with as matters of fact.

Collective ownership of land based on Indigenous peoples' status as law-makers necessitates the recognition of a sphere of authority and autonomy in its administration. I will argue that native title in this sense is a recognition of an inherent sovereignty, as I understand that term, residing in Indigenous peoples. This is not a completely outlandish leap to make. Indeed, this necessary connection has been made recently in Canada, both in Federal policy and by the courts.[3]

---

[1] Clark 2001, in which the author spoke specifically about the litigious nature of native title and the gruelling standards of proof being applied to native title claimants, who are being forced 'to prove who they are and where they came from', thereby creating an unworkable and discriminatory regime for the recognition of Indigenous rights.

[2] Strelein 2001: 123–4.

[3] An inherent right to self government has been recognised through both Canada's Federal Aboriginal Self-government policy and more recently, through the courts in *Campbell v AG (BC) and the Nisga'a Nation* (24 August 2000), 2000 BCSC 1123.

I do not subscribe to the view that Indigenous rights to self-government and the recognition of Indigenous sovereignty under common law are precluded. It is my understanding of the jurisprudence that while the international status of Australian state sovereignty is non-justiciable, the internal ordering of authority and jurisdiction and the consequences of settlement as a matter of domestic law are within the purview of the High Court.[4] The question is, would the Court recognise it? It would take a much longer treatise to comprehensively answer that question, but a large part of the answer lies in how the courts understand the concept of sovereignty.

In Australia we are seeing a gradual recognition that native title claims cannot be successfully separated from the claims that Indigenous peoples make, as peoples, directly against the state. This has been recognised in part through the emergence of state framework agreements and more recently in Western Australia to proposed comprehensive agreement pilots for Tjurabalan, Martu and Northbridge. There is a recognised need on both sides that Indigenous peoples and state governments must engage in direct dialogue with each other, without the multitude of parties involved in a native title process.

The recognition of native title and the process of engagement between Indigenous peoples and the state have fostered the environment for the current treaty debate and refocused discussion on concepts of Indigenous sovereignty and self-government. This debate requires a dialogue in which each side seeks to understand the claims of the other and the language they use to express their claims. To move beyond the simplistic assertion that the question of sovereignty is not open the debate must go beyond rhetoric and delve deeper into the concepts at issue.

The idea of competing claims of sovereignty is one of the most difficult conceptual issues in the debate, as well as one of the most problematic political and rhetorical issues. The state claims that Australian sovereignty is indivisible. Indigenous peoples worry that in entering into a treaty they give up their sovereignty as Indigenous peoples.

Each side of the debate relies on the concept of sovereignty, yet their perspectives are so far apart. This raises the question, what concept of sovereignty is it that each party relies on and can they be accommodated through political negotiation?

Indigenous peoples' claims and the language of sovereignty

First, I want to examine the idea of Indigenous sovereignty and the language that Indigenous peoples use to assert their claims against the state. The assertion of identity, autonomy and authority and demands for recognition and respect from the colonial state have led Indigenous peoples to embrace the language of self-determination and sovereignty. The attraction of this language is, perhaps, foremost in the force of its imagery, as much as in its meaning, and also in its application in international law and politics.

The choice of language is by no means arbitrary. It is not simply a matter of suggesting that a debate in these terms will 'scare the horses' and should therefore be jettisoned. These terms are chosen because the implications that are conveyed through their use are intended to draw on other struggles for independence and recognition.

---

[4] *Mabo v Queensland (No 2)* (1992) 175 CLR 1: 32 and 81–2. In contrast Mason CJ rejected leave to appeal in two cases on the basis of a perception of the assertions of competing international sovereignty: *Isabel Coe v Commonwealth* (1994) 118 ALR 193, and *Walker v New South Wales* (1994) 126 ALR 321.

Robert Williams Jr has suggested that the language that Indigenous peoples adopt is often 'an act of self defence' because it 'enables indigenous peoples to understand and express their oppression in terms that are meaningful to them and to their oppressors'.[5] But I sometimes wonder if we as non-indigenous people – especially in legal and public policy debates are sufficiently reflective of the conceptions of sovereignty that are readily employed to deny Indigenous claims.

In our recent history Australia has been much more comfortable with the concept of 'self-determination' than with the concept of Indigenous sovereignty. This is an odd dichotomy because the two concepts are linked in Indigenous claims.

Self-determination has been used by Indigenous peoples to describe the broad array of claims made against the state *as peoples* – from claims to equality and freedom from discrimination asserted collectively, to claims to self-government, land title and the recognition of Indigenous laws and institutions. These are not claims for special rights or privileges. Rather, they are claims for recognition of the prior and continuing authority of Indigenous peoples, respect for their autonomy and distinct identity and status as the first peoples of the land that was colonised as Australia.

This issue of respect is fundamental to Indigenous peoples' claims against the state and is an essential part of the language that is used. Self-determination, for example, has been expressed in international law as the freedom of a people to determine their own political status, and the freedom to pursue their economic, social and cultural development.[6] The idea of 'self' and identity, and the power to 'determine' seems to provide recognition of the many aspirations implicit in Indigenous peoples' claims. But it is the emphasis on process that is imperative.

The possibility of territorial and non-territorial autonomy remains central to the self-determination process.[7] However, self-determination is not, in itself, secession or self-government or the right to vote. Rather, it is seen as a statement of principle, that whatever the nature of the institutions of government, they be chosen by the freely expressed will of the people.[8] Understanding self-determination as a process, it has been argued, means that self-determination should be viewed as a continuum of outcomes up to and including secession.[9]

Many Indigenous peoples also voice their claims in the language of sovereignty. Although the understanding of sovereignty may be different to that put forward by the state, the appeal of sovereignty, similar to that of self-determination, is that it allows a people to 'project onto it a promise of most of their political, socio-cultural, and economic aspirations'.[10] The characteristic of self-rule is implicit in these claims.

In non-Indigenous legal and political theory, self-determination has been associated with the conventions of modern theories of sovereignty and statehood. The impact of this association is significant because states, governments and many theorists use the rhetoric of state-sovereignty to preclude recognition of Indigenous peoples' claims.

179

---

[5] Williams 1990a: 662. Though note Russell 1996 on the influence of framing claims in these terms.

[6] This is the language used in international instruments including Article 1 of both the *International Covenant on Civil and Political Rights* and *International Covenant on Economic, Social and Cultural Rights*.

[7] Anaya (1991: 409) argued that the self-determination principle is capable of embracing 'more nuanced interpretations and applications, particularly in an increasingly interdependent world in which the formal attributes of statehood mean less and less'. As a result, self-determination should be seen as 'a right of cultural groupings to the political institutions necessary to allow them to exist and develop according to their distinctive characteristics'.

[8] Pomerance 1982: 26–34.

[9] Pomerance 1982: 75.

[10] Boldt and Long 1985: 334.

The difficulty for Indigenous peoples, then, is that the legitimacy of demands for the recognition of sovereignty, nationhood, self-determination or self-government are all assessed by non-Indigenous participants in the debate in terms that presume the very universals under challenge.[11] When Indigenous peoples voice their claims in the language of self-determination and sovereignty, there are a number of assumptions within those terms that are not necessarily shared between Indigenous and non-Indigenous peoples. Moreover, those assumptions, while rarely examined, inform the institutions within which Indigenous peoples make their claims. Therefore, they form the context within which those claims will be understood by decision-makers.

It is not simply the assertion of statehood, there are core assumptions in the theories of sovereignty that limit the ways in which *non*-Indigenous people understand the language of self-determination. These theories are based on certain conventions of thought so that a narrow range of familiar terms has come to be accepted as the authoritative traditions of interpretation.[12]

As I mentioned earlier, some may suggest that we should perhaps accept these habits of thought and find a new language to debate these issues. But one of the primary problems, as a number of theorists such as Jeremy Webber and Jim Tully have suggested, remains the limitations of the language of the non-Indigenous participants in this debate.[13] Here, Tully notes, 'the injustice … occurs at the beginning, in the authoritative language used to discuss the claims in question'. He argues that to respond justly to the claims of Indigenous peoples requires the questioning of often unexamined conventions, 'inherited from the imperial age'.[14] Similarly, Irene Watson argues that movement away from colonialism can only occur where the state and non-Indigenous participants in the debate are prepared to question their own institutions and ways of thinking in order to listen to Indigenous peoples' claims.[15]

Indigenous peoples' claims may be difficult to capture in any alternative terms that we may suggest, or they may be distorted by the limits of language they are forced to use. Simply moving from a discussion of a treaty process to discuss Agreements does violence to the nature of Indigenous peoples' claims. This brings me back to my original point – non-Indigenous participants in the debate, particularly legal and political decision-makers need to complicate our understanding of sovereignty to understand what it is that is being protected and where the perceived threat really lies.

Nation-building and the legitimacy of government

The prior discussion leads to a second immense difficulty that Indigenous peoples face when trying to find a place within the theories of sovereignty and self-determination and an accommodation within the state. That is, while not necessarily seeking secession or independent statehood, the claims do challenge the legitimacy of the authority of the state. There is continued resistance to the claims of Indigenous peoples because these claims are perceived as a threat to the sense of Australia's national identity.

---

[11] Boldt and Long 1985: 335–7, and Tully 1995: 9, 36.

[12] Tully 1995: 36.

[13] Webber, 1993: 136, echoes the philosopher Ludwig Wittgenstein, 1974, whose own struggles, particularly with his class, led him to theorise that 'the limits of my language are the limits of my world'. For an explanation of Wittgenstein on culture and constitutionalism, see Tully 1995: 103–13.

[14] Tully 1995: 34, 39, 47–8 and 53.

[15] Watson 1997: 58.

Australia's national identity and the fragility of our shared mythology is an important factor in the ability of non-Indigenous people to engage in a treaty debate. Here, however, I want to make the link between the idea of nation-building and the concept of 'sovereignty'. The concern over a competing sovereignty lies at the base of arguments against the right of Indigenous peoples to self-determination, particularly where they express demands for self-rule. While Indigenous peoples' claims may reflect the same principles of consent and self-rule that colonial states relied upon to assert their own independence, they challenge the legitimacy of that nation-building both from an internal and external perspective.[16]

Understanding the theoretical debates in these spheres is important because the ways that Indigenous peoples' claims are represented are affected by the language they adopt. 'Self-determination' and 'sovereignty' are inextricably linked in political theories of governance and in international law theory, just as they are in Indigenous claims.

Social contract theories and theories of individual rights are often considered to be the most influential philosophies in the process of nation-building through which elaborate mythologies have been created.[17]

The story of sovereignty in modern political theory places authority with the people, in name at least, providing legitimacy to the democratic state. Authority, it was argued, derived from agreement among the people and vested in, or was delegated to, a representative government. Unable to disengage from the idea of a supreme authority, the revolutionary, rhetorical quality of popular sovereignty is coupled with companion theories of governance that legitimise the exercise of sovereign power by governments.[18]

Social contract theories are premised on the notion that individuals freely enter into civil society through a compact to better protect their natural freedom.[19] The constitution of a society is seen as a deliberate self-determining act.[20] The social contract theories rely on the fiction of the 'founding moment' that reinforces the idea of consent.[21] Remembered events in the history of a state, such as Australia's federation in 1901, or the republican revolutions of France and the United States, provide a reinforcing moment. Through this mythical agreement between the people, the authority of government is a delegation of powers from the people.[22] This provides legitimacy for the powers exercised by government and provides a basis for defining the limits of that power.

---

[16] Russell 1996: 3.

[17] Boldt and Long 1985: 342; also Hindess 1996: 14.

[18] Boldt and Long, 1985: 335. Tully, 1995: 52, used the phrase 'unmonarched'. Compare the thoughts of Foucault, 1980: 121, 'we need to cut off the Kings head: in political theory that has still to be done'.

[19] Locke, *[1690]* 1956: 49, and Rousseau *[1762]* 1968: 60. Kant, *[1887]* 1974: 161 [ss.43, 44], explained this as the need to regulate mutual influence when people come into reciprocal contact.

[20] For Locke, *[1690]* 1956: 50–1, there was a presumption that individuals have the capacity to govern themselves and therefore give up only so much of their freedom as is necessary for their better protection in society. This presumption relies on a view of the pre-civic state of nature as one of natural equality and freedom. Compare Hobbes, *[1651]* 1996: 89 chapter 13, whose argument for strong government assumed a state of nature in which life was 'solitary, poor, nasty, brutish and short'. See also Machiavelli *[1640]* 1969. Other theorists saw the purpose of government to provide for a common conception of Right or a common will, for example, Kant, *[1887]* 1974: 163, [s.44]. For Hegel, *[1821]* 1967: 155, the state is committed to the promotion of higher ideals, in direct contrast to the minimalist view of the state adopted by liberal thinkers.

[21] Tully, 1995: 69, pointed to the imposition of a constitution on current generations as premised on the idea that any 'rational' person would agree today, reflecting Locke's own conception of the modern constitution as the pinnacle of human progress. It appears that despite disagreeing with Hobbes's view of irrevocable accession to a ruler, Locke's theory too has a sense of permanence.

[22] Locke, *[1690]* 1956: 122, thought this power could be revoked if misused. Contrast Hobbes, *[1651]* 1993: 88–93, 97, 102–5, who retained elements of absolutism, prioritising the need for order over liberty. Rousseau, *[1762]* 1968: 139, agreed that the powers of government were a mere delegation, while taking a more extreme view of the power of the general assembly.

Indigenous peoples in Australia were excluded from the self-governing communities that came together to federate under a Constitution. The homogenous view of the nation-state created the imperative of assimilation. Diversity was obscured by construing the 'people' as homogenous. Consistent with the political theories that informed these events, the nation was built on institutional foundations where culture was perceived as either 'irrelevant, transcended or uniform'.[23]

The modern political theories of sovereignty that underpin our institutions of governance, beginning with Locke and Rousseau, have generally focused on democratic government as the basis for assessing legitimacy. The colonial states with their assertion of an homogenous polity saw minority interests as being secured by the protection of individual rights.[24]

This universal understanding of legitimacy focusing on citizenship has proved a difficult obstacle for Indigenous peoples, for whom self-determination means more than merely political rights of participation. Michael Dodson argued that self-determination is to peoples what freedom is to individuals, moreover, the enjoyment of all other rights depends on its observance.[25]

Self-determination claims based on distinct, collective rights that are inherent in demands for a negotiated settlement are seen as a profound challenge to the established mythology of Australian nationhood because they appear to fragment the foundations of common citizenship.[26] There is a denial of the depth of the exclusion of Indigenous peoples from the construction of that common identity. Instead we continue to construct a sense of national identity and unity, but do so through exclusion and coercive universalism.[27]

Justifying colonialism: the imperial roots of liberalism

At the same time as democratic states like Australia and the United States were being established from the colonial territories of the British Empire, these new 'nations' were imposing their own empires over Indigenous peoples. The respect for equality of nations that ordered the relations between the states at an international level was not extended to Indigenous peoples either in theory or in practice.[28]

Non-indigenous societies sought moral and theoretical justification for the violence of colonisation from the outset. The political and legal theories of the time were not ignorant of Indigenous peoples. Quite to the contrary, they were often construed to deliberately exclude Indigenous peoples from the community of nations and justify colonial practice.[29]

---

[23] Tully 1995: 63.

[24] Jefferson's inaugural address as President, 1975: 291, which articulated 'the creed of our political faith', exemplified this concern: 'Though the will of the majority is in all cases to prevail, that will to be right must be reasonable; that the minority possesses their equal rights, which equal law must protect.'

[25] Dodson, 1994: 68, referred to Ghazali 1984.

[26] Ivison, 1994: 25, and for an example of this argument, see Glazer, 1975: 197–8, 200, who argues that special treatment of one group will cause instability because others will also demand special rights. Kymlicka, 1995: 66–9, argues that such an approach is concerned more with instability than with justice.

[27] For a critique of objections to Indigenous claims that assert equality as their foundation, see Webber 1993: 149–50 and Dodson 1996: 7.

[28] Pufendorf, 1964, vol II: 367, argued that the equality of all peoples meant that peoples were entitled to prevent the thrusting of foreigners into their territories. For Vattel, 1964 vol III: 3, 5–6, 113, the state possesses the same rights as man. From equality of man Vattel deduced the equality of states. In the same way, states have duties to each other to promote society. These ideas persist in contemporary international law as the principles of respect for the equality of states, territorial integrity and exclusive jurisdiction. However, as Slattery, 1983: 37, points out, the law of nations was not certain because the powerful states did not have a settled practice consistent with it.

[29] For example, see Tully 1993: 137–78. Hendersen, 1985: 189, argues that theorists such as Pufendorf, Grotius and Gentilis and the concept of natural law were essential in this process.

The 'scientific' development view of human history in which the cultures of the world could be ranked according to their progressive stage of socio-economic development was devastating for Indigenous peoples. 'Modern' constitutions had been developed, it was said, in contrast to 'ancient' constitutions based on ad hoc custom.[30] These political and economic systems by which Indigenous peoples lived were equated with the ancient inferior constitutions of the social contract theory, who were therefore incapable of governing themselves, or of managing their own affairs.[31]

It was thought that as societies developed and converged, modern constitutions would establish uniform legal and political institutions, based on liberal democracy and the market economy.[32] On this view, lower or backward cultures would benefit and improve from the implantation of European institutions.[33] Edward Said notes the importance of this view to the legitimacy of colonisation because it provided a justification apart from a purely profit motivation, which would allow settlers to accept that the Indigenous peoples '*should* be subjugated'.[34] The impression was of the benevolent and benign inevitability of colonisation and, moreover, an obligation on Indigenous peoples to accept it graciously.

Therefore, while the ideas of equality and respect among nations formed the basis of modern international law, the influential principles for the government of subject peoples that served to justify colonialism were carried through to the legal and political structures of the new colonial states.[35] The continued assertion or assumption of the benign universality of existing institutions in contemporary debates about sovereignty, whether because they are assumed to be superior or to somehow transcend culture, make challenge difficult and obfuscate the imperial culture embedded in them.

Self determination and statehood: competing sovereignty

From these early roots in colonial practice, the conventions of modern political theory and international law have both developed in ways that assert the primacy of statehood and have excluded the collective claims of Indigenous peoples.

Barry Hindess argues that, in early theories of sovereignty, the fact of power was intimately tied to the conception of power as a function of consent. Hindess suggests that, although this understanding of power has fallen out of fashion since the Second World War, modern conceptions of statehood and sovereignty remain rooted in these same values.[36]

The strong nexus between the legitimacy of government and the international system has led Indigenous peoples, frustrated by the exclusion and denial of Indigenous sovereignty within the state, to challenge the authority of the state through the system of international law. Many Indigenous peoples remain hopeful that the international system will provide the tools for the recognition of Indigenous rights to self-determination and, indeed, self-rule.

183

---

[30] 'Modern' societies in constituting the state were seen to go through a process of critical reflection on their customs to create a uniform system of institutions with a central locus of sovereignty: see Tully 1995: 59.

[31] Locke *[1690]* 1956: 9.

[32] Tully 1995: 67. The debate then centred around whose model was the most superior. For example, Kant's 'republican constitution' was put forward as the method of achieving moral progress.

[33] Mill *[1874]* 1975: 382, 384–5. For a comment on Mill, see Thornberry 1989: 869.

[34] Said 1993: 10 (original emphasis). See also Russell 1996: 5 in agreement.

[35] Williams 1990b: 13, 92–3, 96–107. He argues, 1990b: 98, that one of Vitoria's primary motivations in the lectures 'on the Indians Lately Discovered', in 1532, was to find a justification for the Spanish aggression against the South American peoples that was not wholly based on ecclesiastical assertions of jurisdiction.

[36] See Hindess 1996: 12.

In the face of competing claims from states to their territory and their resources, it would be significant for Indigenous peoples to have an internationally recognised right to self-determination and all that that may entail, with its roots in concepts of sovereignty and consensual government.[37]

International law debates, not surprisingly, however, reflect the same two conceptions of power identified by Hindess in relation to political theory. One, the statist view, is concerned with the fact of power and the preservation of existing states' territory; the other is concerned with the legitimacy of government. As Paul Coe once argued, 'while one group has dominant power and the means to implement it, that does not necessarily give that group the *right* to sovereignty and the exercise of power'.[38] Michael Dodson also criticises international law for giving greatest weight to the 'power to have power'.[39] Dodson suggests that Indigenous peoples seek a recognised 'right' to have power, with support at a 'moral, legal and political level'.[40] Power construed in this way is a question of legitimacy.[41]

The core concepts of self-determination apply to all independent states, in their right freely to choose and develop their political, social, economic and cultural systems, just as these elements should be enjoyed by all peoples. Thus it has been suggested that self-determination is a claim against the self-determination of another socially, politically and legally constituted 'people'. The opposition from the state is not a statement of anti-self-determination or non-self-determination, rather, it is an assertion of the legitimacy of the authority of the state to represent an homogenous and indissoluble whole.[42] The principle that Indigenous peoples rely upon to support their claims to autonomy and independence and the right to enter into a treaty, for example, is one of the central tenets underlying state sovereignty. As a result, the demands of Indigenous peoples are confronted with the ideas of territorial integrity and autonomy that dominate the international, statist sphere and give legitimacy to the states to order their own affairs.

Part of the difficulty for the claims of Indigenous peoples seeking to question this legitimacy and reassert a place within the constitution of the state through concepts of self-rule such as self-determination and sovereignty is that the incorporation of these ideas into international law through the process of state building assumed an indissoluble connection to statehood, even assuming these concepts to be synonymous with the expression of statehood.

Since the Law of Nations of Vitoria and Vattel, international law has been concerned predominantly with external sovereignty, independence and relations between states. In this context, the ideas of sovereign equality and sovereign independence have taken on an exclusively statist character.[43] Sovereignty is often considered in the context of the requirements for recognition of new states.

The barriers to renegotiating the colonial relationship between Indigenous peoples and the states have moved from overt racism and the legitimacy of colonisation, to rest on a conception of the supremacy of the state. Russell describes this as the 'sovereign idea of sovereignty', that is, a notion of absolute and incontrovertible power of the state.[44]

---

[37] Williams 1990a: 668–9.

[38] Coe 1988: 141.

[39] Dodson 1994: 70.

[40] Dodson 1994: 71.

[41] Dodson 1994: 73.

[42] Thornberry, 1989: 375, construed the right of peoples entitled to self-determination as the right to independent statehood itself, to which all the principles of territorial integrity and non-interference apply equally. For this reason, Pomerance, 1982: 73, stated that the determination of 'which self is entitled to determine what, when and how, remains the central question'.

[43] See Hannum 1990: 14–15.

[44] Russell 1996: 17. Watson, 1997: 54, argues that 'we have devolved from racism, to a fear of states disintegrating and collapsing. As though the basis upon which colonial states exist is an honourable and justifiable one that should be preserved.'

The international community may well be increasingly concerned with the internal aspects of self-determination, that is, to ensure that 'the people' freely determine their political structures and are therefore truly represented at the state and, concomitantly, at the international level. In the end, however, the United Nations is constituted by states, although many of them are themselves decolonised nations.[45] The limitation of the international system remains the preference for maintaining the status quo of state sovereignty.

The limitations of the international statist sphere as a forum for renegotiating the legitimacy of British colonisation of Australia should not determine the internal ordering of power and autonomy. It is important to recognise that Indigenous peoples often operate outside the statist conceptions of international law. Michael Dodson argues that:

> When we become disheartened by the apparent monopoly which
> states have on power, it is crucial that we remember that, despite their
> claims to the contrary, states are not sovereign. Peoples are sovereign.
> States do not have rights. Peoples have rights.
>
> And when people are not free they will fight for that freedom. And
> they will continue to fight for that freedom until it is theirs.[46]

The desire for control over decision making in Indigenous communities does begin and end with arguments over statehood.

Conclusion

The response to the claims of Indigenous peoples reveals the realities of power in the current statist world order and the limits of its founding theories. The jealously guarded authority and territory of existing states is supported by the international system. However, Indigenous peoples' claims do not, of necessity, demand concessions in this statist sphere. The conflation of sovereignty and statehood feeds the resistance to Indigenous peoples' claims, as a threat to the ideal of an homogenous national identity.

Theories of sovereignty need not be completely jettisoned in order for a dialogue to occur between Indigenous peoples and the state. The political theory of sovereignty provides useful ideas in the current treaty debate. First, it clearly locates the nature of internal sovereignty as the source of authority within a community. Second, self-determination, as it is currently understood, is a reflection of the notions of popular sovereignty, which posits the ultimate authority of government in the people. Sovereignty also has an external aspect, which respects the autonomy of other sovereign peoples. These are the aspects of sovereignty that Indigenous claims appeal to.

The simplistic view of sovereignty that emerged from modern theory is based on a fiction of homogeneity that cannot be sustained in the context of multi-nation societies. The impact of these assumptions on Indigenous peoples is the lived experiences of coercive assimilation and genocide.

On a more fundamental level, however, the idea that 'the people' are sovereign and entitled to self-rule can accommodate Indigenous peoples' assertions of authority and autonomy. An absence of domination demands recognition of the interests of Indigenous peoples. Internally,

---

[45] Russell 1996: 5.   [46] Dodson 1994: 75.

the ability of a people to determine the political and other structures that will facilitate distinct survival is the measure of self-determination. Freedom from internal domination in the enjoyment of self-determination is an important measure of the legitimacy of the exercise of power within a state.

An understanding of the workings of power in a federal system of shared sovereignty can provide a theoretical and practical basis for a more pluralist approach which recognises the sovereignty of Indigenous peoples. Federalism, or the association of self-governing territories, which exist in Australia, Canada and the United States, for example, provides for mutual recognition and power sharing.[47] The characteristics of sovereignty are more complex in a federal system, where authority is shared between distinct communities.

Self-determination, as a collective right, attaches to a group whose goals 'transcend the ending of discrimination'.[48] The group is not joined simply by external discrimination but by internal cohesiveness. More than equal participation, Indigenous peoples seek distinct group survival and the freedom to determine their relationship with other groups, nations and states.[49]

The notions of meaningful participation and self-rule must be therefore assessed outside the theoretical limitations imposed by the liberal democratic norm. Peter Russell argues that to deny Indigenous peoples' right to exist as enduring political societies is the very essence of imperialism.[50] This distinct identity must find expression in Australia's national identity.

It could be argued that recognition of the right to self-rule through negotiated self-government arrangements may provide a greater sense of stability and thus provide the foundations for a negotiated state structure, that is representative of the cultural and political diversity of Indigenous and non-Indigenous sovereignty.[51]

The call for a treaty process in Australia is not new. It is not a response to the failure of the native title process to deliver native title outcomes or even a response to the failure of 'practical reconciliation' to deliver practical outcomes in health, housing and employment for Indigenous people. It is a recognition that even if these processes had been successful, there would still be an essential element that is missing.

Recognition of Indigenous peoples' claims to self-government will require a fundamental shift in thinking and in the assumptions upon which previous approaches have been based. This would appear to be a difficult task when, as we have seen, the exclusion of Indigenous peoples from recognition has its roots in the earliest principles of international law and political theory.

Dr Mamphele Ramphele, South African academic, suggests that the challenge of the twenty-first century is to find ways to create new social contracts that recognise the competing claims

---

[47] For example, the *Commonwealth of Australia Constitution Act 1901* (Imp) brought together the colonies into a mutually agreed federation. Section 51 reserves certain powers for the Commonwealth and the States to share, the plenary remains for the States. The Canadian Royal Commission, 1996, recognised the ways in which federation can accommodate the same power sharing and mutual recognition of Indigenous peoples. In particular, see vol 1: 67791 which outlines 'the four principles of a renewed relationship': mutual recognition, mutual respect, sharing, and mutual responsibility.

[48] Sanders 1991: 368–9. See also Falk 1988: 585–6.

[49] De Lupis, 1987: 15, argues that there is juridical support for this interpretation of self-determination in the International Court of Justice's advisory opinion: see 1971 *ICJ Reports* 16 at para. 56. De Lupis notes the Court's use of the term 'peoples', referring to the people of the territory as a 'jural' and injured 'entity', who have a right under international law to progress toward independence.

[50] Russell 1996: 17.

[51] For example, United Nations, 1970, general part, para 3, recognised self determination as the basis of friendly relations.

of peoples with separate myths and conflicting historical narratives. She emphasises the responsibility of political leaders, as nation-builders, in this never ending challenge to weave the state together from its fragments.[52]

There is a general imperative to address Indigenous peoples' grievances, apart from all other injustices, with regard to their unique histories.[53] Falk distinguished Indigenous peoples through their deprivation of sovereign rights and a lack of participation or representation in prevailing political arrangements.[54] Michael Dodson expresses a similar view:

> Because the non-indigenous state was founded on the basis of non-recognition of pre-existing indigenous rights and laws, indigenous peoples and the non-indigenous state lack an agreement about the basic principles of nationhood, the structure of government, the source of law, and the shaping and sharing of power, wealth and national resources.[55]

These fundamental grievances result in a variety of encroachments, deficient social services and constant pressure on lands and resources. Essentially, however, Indigenous peoples' claims are centred on their collective identity based upon inherent sovereign rights to government by consent and a history of denial by internal domination.

The change that is required can only come from dialogue between Indigenous peoples and the state, where equality and respect are truly practised and Indigenous voices heard. International law and native title, even with the support of a recognised right of self-government cannot meet the demands from Indigenous peoples for a response to their claims against the state. The implementation of a domestic treaty process may prove the most appropriate mechanism to renegotiate the relationship between Indigenous peoples and the state.

Acknowledgments

This article was first published in *Arena*.

---

[52] Ramphele 2001.

[53] Werther, 1992: 34–6, argued that this historical and moral claim has been the source of their unique advances in the direction of self-determination thus far. See also Crawford 1988: 14.

[54] Falk 1988: 591.

[55] Dodson 1994: 73.

References

Books, articles and reports

Anaya, J 1991, 'The capacity of international law to advance ethnic or nationality rights claims', Symposium: 1990 Moscow Academic Conference, *Human Rights Quarterly*, 13: 403–11.

Boldt, M and JA Long 1985, 'Tribal traditions and European-Western political ideologies: The dilemma of Canada's Native Indians' in M Boldt and JA Long (eds) *The Quest for Justice: Aboriginal Peoples and Aboriginal Rights*, University of Toronto Press, Toronto.

Clark, G 2001, address to the National Native Title Tribunal, 'Native Title Forum 2001: Negotiating Country', Brisbane (August).

Coe, P 1998, 'Laws of the Black People – 1985: Sovereignty' in B Hocking (ed) *International Law and Aboriginal Human Rights*, Law Book Co, Sydney: 141–3.

Crawford, J 1988, 'Outside the colonial context' in WJA Macartney (ed) *Self-determination in the Commonwealth*, Aberdeen University Press, Aberdeen.

De Lupis, ID 1987, *International Law and the Independent State*, 2nd edn, Gower, Hants.

Dodson, M 1994, 'Towards the exercise of Indigenous rights: Policy, power and self-determination', *Race and Class* 25(4): 65–.

—— 1996, Assimilation versus self-determination: no contest, North Australia Research Unit, Australian National University, Discussion Paper No. 1/1996.

Falk, R 1988, 'The rights of peoples (in particular Indigenous peoples)' in L Basso (ed) *Theory and Practice of Liberation at the End of the XXth Century*, International Foundation for the Right and Liberation of All Peoples, Bruylant, Brussels: 585–610.

Foucault, M 1980, *Power/Knowledge: Selected Interviews and Other Writings* [1977], Harvester, New York.

Ghazali, NA 1984, 'Opposition to violations of human rights', in UNESCO, *Violations of Human Rights*, Paris.

Glazer, N 1975, *Affirmative Discrimination and Public Policy*, Basic Books, New York

Hannum, H 1990, *Autonomy, Sovereignty, and Self-Determination: The Accommodation of Conflicting Rights*, University of Pennsylvania Press, Pennsylvania.

Hegel, GWF 1967, *Philosophy of Right* [1821], Oxford University Press, Oxford.

Hendersen, JY 1985, 'The doctrine of Aboriginal rights in Western legal tradition' in M Boldt and JA Long (eds) *The Quest for Justice: Aboriginal Peoples and Aboriginal Rights*, University of Toronto Press, Toronto: 185–220.

Hindess, B 1996, *Discourses of Power: From Hobbes to Foucault*, Blackwell, Oxford.

Hobbes, T 1993, *De Cive: The English Version* [1651], annotated by Howard Warrender, Clarendon, Oxford.

—— 1996, *Leviathan* [1651], (revised student edn), edited by Richard Tuck, Cambridge University Press, Cambridge.

Ivison, D 1994, 'Aboriginal rights and political theory', *Research School of Social Sciences Annual Report*, Australian National University, Canberra.

Jefferson, T 1975, Inaugural Address as President, Washington DC, 4 March 1801, in *The Portable Thomas Jefferson*, Viking Penguin Books.

Kant, I 1974, *The Philosophy of Law* [1887], Augustus M Kelly, New Jersey.

Kymlicka, W 1995, *Multi-cultural Citizenship: A Liberal Theory of Minority Rights*, Clarendon, New York.

Locke, J 1956, *The Second Treatise on Government: An Essay Concerning the True Original Extent and End of Civil Government* [1690], Blackwell, Oxford.

Machiavelli, N 1969, *The Prince* [1640], Scolar, Yorkshire.

Mill, JS 1975, *Three Essays* [1874], Oxford University Press, London.

Pomerance, M 1982, *Self-determination in Law and Practice: The New Doctrine in the United Nations*, Nijhoff, The Hague.

Pufendorf, S 1964, *De Jure Naturae et Gentium Libri Octo [1688]*, vol II, translated by CH and WA Oldfather, Oceania, New York.

Ramphele, M 2001, 'The Glue That Holds Nations Together', in Holding Together: An International Lecture Series, Radio National ABC, http://www.abc.net.au/rn/sunspec/barton/symposium2/ramphele.htm, viewed 11 July 2001.

Rousseau, JJ 1968, *The Social Contract, [1762]*, translated by M Cranston, Penguin, London.

Russell, P 1996, Aboriginal Nationalism: Fourth world decolonisation in English settler societies, Hugo Wolfsohn Memorial Lecture, La Trobe University, Melbourne, 31 October (unpublished).

Said, E 1993, *Culture and Imperialism*, Knopf.

Sanders, D 1991, 'Collective rights', *Human Rights Quarterly* 13: 368–86.

Slattery, B 1983, *Ancestral lands, alien laws: Judicial perspectives on Aboriginal title*, University of Saskatchewan Native Law Centre, Studies on Aboriginal Rights, No 2.

Strelein, L 2001, 'Conceptualising native title', *Sydney Law Review* 23: 95–124.

The Canadian Royal Commission on Aboriginal Peoples 1996, *Report of the Royal Commission*, 6 vols, CRCAP, Ottawa.

Thornbery, P 1989, 'Self-Determination, minorities, human rights: A review of international instruments', *International and Comparative Law Quarterly* 38: 867–89.

Tully, J 1993, *An Approach to Political Philosophy: Locke in Contexts*, Cambridge University Press, New York.

—— 1995, *Strange Multiplicity: Constitutionalism in an age of diversity*, Cambridge University Press, London.

Vattel, E 1964, *The Law of Nations or the Principles of Natural Law Applied to the Conduct of the Affairs of Nations and Sovereigns [1758]*, vol III, translated by CG Fenwick, Oceania, New York.

Vitoria F 1991, 'Des Indis' in A Pagden and J Lawrence (eds) *Francisco Vitoria: Political Writings*, Cambridge University Press, New York:539.

Watson, I 1997, 'Indigenous Peoples' law-ways: Survival against the colonial state', *Australian Feminist Law Journal* 8(58): 39.

Webber, J 1993, 'Individuality, equality and difference: Justifications for a parallel system of justice' in Royal Commission on Aboriginal Peoples, Aboriginal Peoples and the Criminal Justice System: Report of the National Round Table on Aboriginal Justice Issues, Ottawa.

Werther, G 1992, *Self Determination in Western Democracies: Aboriginal Politics in Comparative Perspective*, Greenwood Press, Westport.

Williams Jr, RA 1990a, 'Encounters on the frontiers of international human rights law: Redefining the terms of Indigenous peoples' survival in the world', *Duke Law Journal*: 660–704.

—— 1990b, *The American Indian in Western Legal Thought: The Discourses of Conquest*, Oxford University Press, New York.

Wittgenstein, L 1974, *Philosophical Investigations*, translated by GEM Auscombe, 3rd edn, Blackwell, Oxford.

International covenants, declarations and advisory opinions

Declaration on Principles of International Law Concerning Friendly Relations Co-operation Among States in Accordance with the Charter of the United Nations 1970, GA Resolution 2625 (XXV) 24 October 1970, UNGAOR 25th Sess Supp No 28: 121 (1971).

International Court of Justice 1971, Advisory Opinion on Legal Consequences for States of the Continued Presence of South Africa in Namibia (South West Africa) notwithstanding Security Council Resolution 276 (1970), 1071 ICJ Reports.

International Covenant on Civil and Political Rights 1980 ATS 23.

International Covenant on Economic, Social and Cultural Rights (in force, December 1976), http://www.unhchr.ch/html/menu3/b/a_cescr.htm

Legislation

Commonwealth of Australia Constitution Act 1901 (Imp).

Case law

Campbell v AG (BC) and the Nisga'a Nation
(24 August 2000). 2000 BCSC 1123.

Isabel Coe v Commonwealth (1994) 118 ALR 193.

Mabo and Ors v The State of Queensland (No 2)
(1992) 175 CLR 1.

Walker v New South Wales (1994) 126 ALR 321.

Regional agreements, higher education and representations of Indigenous Australian reality

(Why wasn't I taught that in school?)

Greg McConville

The educational struggles of Indigenous peoples are fundamentally and unequivocally concerned with the right of Indigenous peoples to be indigenous.[1]

Introduction

The rights of Indigenous peoples to self-identify, self-determine and self-represent have been asserted both locally and internationally. The Coolangatta statement, the Kari-Oca declaration entitled 'Indigenous Peoples' Earth Charter'[2] and declarations of the World Indigenous Youth Conference held in Darwin 1993, are recent examples of how Indigenous peoples have stated what to many should be obvious: Indigenous peoples know themselves, their experiences, their land and knowledge systems better than anyone else, and that Indigenous peoples have the right to shape the representation of these realities not only among themselves, but also within colonised nations.

United Nations covenants and declarations have appeared to accept these assertions of the rights of Indigenous peoples to engage with, to shape and to benefit from all levels of education. The record of individual governments, including Australian governments at Commonwealth, state and territory levels, is another matter entirely. Since colonisation, Indigenous Australians have at various times been denied the right to maintain their own knowledge systems, have been re-defined within western scientific and anthropological constructs, and prevented by racism, marginalisation and disadvantage from gaining the economic and social mobility available to non-Indigenous Australians through the education system. While much government policy is based on the assumption that poor educational participation and outcomes stem from a 'deficit' within Indigenous Australians, there is compelling evidence that it is the nature of the education system and the policies surrounding it that entrench Indigenous educational disadvantage.

This paper addresses the rights asserted by Indigenous peoples and recognised by the United Nations to self-identify, self-determine and self-represent. It then examines Australian performance in the area of higher education relating to those asserted rights, and presents some options aimed at enshrining Indigenous education as an enforceable right rather than a matter of administrative and political goodwill.

---

[1] Coolangatta Statement 1999.   [2] Kari Oca Statement 1993.

Indigenous education as a right

In his welcome to country at the start of the Treaty Conference, Mr Mort Hansen, of the Metropolitan Council of Noongar Elders, spoke of his school experiences. Learning the English alphabet, while being told that learning about Aboriginality was bad, were characteristics of Mort's experience shared by many Aboriginal and Torres Strait Islander peoples.

During the years 1971 to 1982, I attended primary school in East Keilor, and attended secondary school in Moonee Ponds and West Essendon. Repeatedly, the matter of the presence of Aboriginal people prior to European contact was discussed among students, but was rarely the subject of any formal teaching. In response to questions about where Aboriginal people went, teachers would sometimes reply that Aboriginals had gone to the desert, because they liked it there.

In about 1974, my parents by chance took me to the office of the Keilor Historical Society, where I learned of the discovery of the Keilor Cranium in 1940. Keilor, as the cranium was known, had been found in a sand bank by the Maribyrnong River, and had been carbon-dated as over 12,000 years old. That Aboriginal people had roamed the plains for at least 40,000 years, along with massive creatures such as Diprotodons,[3] was a revelation to me at that time. I asked myself: 'Why wasn't I taught that at school?'

In fact, in all of my years of schooling in that region, the Keilor Cranium was never mentioned in the classroom.

Mort Hansen's experiences, and my experiences, are to some extent the flip side of the same coin. While the education system denied Mort the right to learn his culture and his peoples' history, the truth of Aboriginal sovereignty was held back from me.

Surely, just as Mort Hansen had a right to learn his own culture and traditions, I had a right to know the truth about sovereignty, colonisation and dispossession. The location of the educational system as an instrument of colonisation, denied us both this right. Both Indigenous and non-Indigenous Australians should have this right today.

Prominent Indigenous Australian educators have, through their experiences as Indigenous Australians and as educators, contributed to the development of a wealth of material which addresses how the educational experience should be informed from Indigenous perspectives, and how in turn the education system must engage with the reality and experiences of Indigenous Australians.

In this paper, I have focused principally on the Coolangatta Statement on Indigenous Peoples Rights in Education,[4] recognised by the United Nations. The work of four Indigenous Australians in contributing to the Statement should be acknowledged: Dr Bob Morgan, Japanangka West, Martin Nakata and Dr Paul Hughes were members of the 1993 task force (drawn from the United States, Canada, Aotearoa and Australia), which was charged with the responsibility of drafting the Statement.

Intended as a dynamic document which can evolve and change, the Statement contains a concise description of how education systems should be transformed to give effect to

---

[3] Keilor Historical Society, 1992, refers to Diprotodon as 'measuring two metres high and three metres in length ... believed to be the largest marsupial ever to have lived'.

[4] Coolangatta Statement 1999.

fundamental human rights as asserted by Indigenous Peoples. Following is an extract from the Preamble to the Coolangatta Statement:

This Statement speaks to the inherent rights of Indigenous peoples as declared in Article 27 of the International Covenant on Civil and Political Rights:

> In those States in which ethnic, religious or linguistic minorities
> exist, persons belonging to such minorities shall not be denied
> the right, in community with the other members of their
> group, to enjoy their own culture, and to profess and practice
> their own religion, and to use their own language.[5]

The Coolangatta Statement[6] also refers to Article 26 of the United Nations Declaration of Human Rights, which addresses the right of all peoples to participate in all levels of education to assist their full development as humans, and to strengthen respect for human rights and fundamental freedoms.

While recognising these instruments are important, the Coolangatta Statement identifies a number of limitations in the extent to which they protect equal access, ensure that Indigenous parents can choose the kind of education available to their children, enable Indigenous peoples to enjoy their own cultures and communities, and facilitate language use and reclamation. In light of these inadequacies, the Statement describes self-determination in Indigenous Education as embodying rights to:

- control/govern Indigenous education systems;
- have learning facilities recognise, respect and promote Indigenous values, philosophies, and ideologies;
- develop and implement culturally inclusive curricula;
- import the wisdom of Indigenous elders to the educational process;
- determine criteria for evaluation and assessment;
- develop standards for the gifted and talented;
- promote use of Indigenous languages;
- establish parameters and ethics for Indigenous education research;
- apply culturally appropriate teacher training;
- participate in teacher accreditation and selection;
- determine criteria for the registration and operation of learning facilities; and
- choose the nature and scope of education without prejudice.[7]

In addition to the articulation of these rights, a number of important observations are made. The importance of land to language and culture, the legitimacy of Indigenous languages and knowledge systems, and the diversity which exists within and between Indigenous peoples are all identified by the Coolangatta Statement as matters to be recognised in the transformation of educational systems based on Indigenous pedagogy. That is not to say that the Indigenous educational experience should occur away from and separate to mainstream or westernised education. Rather, it is about ensuring that mainstream institutions, whether schools, TAFE

---

[5] Coolangatta Statement 1999: 1. [6] Coolangatta Statement 1999: 2. [7] Coolangatta Statement 1999: 6.

colleges or universities, incorporate in all areas of their activity Indigenous terms of reference and values as articulated by Indigenous peoples. The role of non-Indigenous people therefore is to respect and adhere to Indigenous community values and aspirations, while the role of institutions is to accept and uphold the rights of Indigenous peoples as non-negotiable.[8]

For the purposes of this paper, the philosophies embodied in the Coolangatta Statement represent a useful basis on which to assess the nature and performance of the Australian higher education system relating to Indigenous Education. The very term Indigenous Education should therefore be taken as representing the rights, responsibilities and aspirations discussed above.

The performance of higher education in Australia

The role of education for Indigenous Australians, as distinct from Indigenous Education, in colonised Australia has historically been aligned to government priorities and policies. The establishment of institutions of learning at all levels has reflected the various stages of the relationships between Indigenous and non-Indigenous Australians. The inherent privileging of westernised knowledge systems in establishing those institutions, without reference to Indigenous peoples, in the first instance relegated Indigenous Australians to being subjects of the dominant education system, rather than active participants in it. For higher education institutions in particular, serious 'business' exists arising from the nature of their foundation. Universities researched and taught the philosophies which were used to justify policies of separation and assimilation, acquired (stole) many objects of cultural significance thus assisting the cultural dispossession of many Indigenous Australian peoples, while disciplines associated with the pastoral and mining industries contributed to material dispossession. The land on which universities are situated was never ceded, and teaching and research about Indigenous Australian peoples was established from entirely non-Indigenous frameworks.

I will examine four important areas in which our performance can be assessed against the principles enshrined in the Coolangatta Statement. These are governance, Indigenous Education programs, Aboriginal and Torres Strait Islander employment within universities, and research.

Governance

Indigenous involvement in university governance structures as a right should enable the pursuit of many of the principles embodied in the Coolangatta Statement. Controlling and governing Indigenous Education within universities, developing culturally inclusive curricula, and the development of appropriate research ethics and teacher training among other matters cannot occur without direct involvement of Indigenous Australians in the governance structures themselves.

Indigenous Education does not exist as a right; rather universities exist as products of colonial parliamentary and legal systems. The various acts which establish universities create obligations, among other things, to provide for the educational and research needs of the communities and regions in which they are situated, and prescribe categories of membership on governing bodies aimed at ensuring that those needs are articulated and met.[9] That legislators defined those communities within entirely western constructs is evidenced by the fact that of all legislation establishing higher education institutions, the only Act requiring

---

[8] Coolangatta Statement 1999: 7.　[9] See e.g. *Charles Sturt University Act 1989* (New South Wales).

Aboriginal or Torres Strait Islander representation on a governing body is that establishing the Bachelor Institute of Indigenous Tertiary Education (BIITE).[10] While it is positive that the need for this representation has been recognised in establishing BIITE as an institution for educating Indigenous Australians, Indigenous Australians do not have a legislated right to participate in the management and oversight of any Australian university. This is symptomatic of what Dr Bob Morgan describes as the 'guest paradigm' whereby the presence of Indigenous Australians within universities as students, teachers, researchers, and advisors is dependent on the goodwill of those institutions, and of the governments which fund them.

Despite this reliance, there have been some significant advances made in making universities more responsive to Indigenous Australian community needs and aspirations. To many, the importance of education to Aboriginal and Torres Strait Islander peoples was emphasised by Recommendation 202 of the Royal Commission into Aboriginal Deaths in Custody:

> That where such courses are not already available, suitable training
> courses to provide necessary administrative, political and management
> skills should be available for persons elected to regional councils
> of ATSIC, elected to, appointed to, or engaged in Aboriginal
> organisations involved in the delivery of services to Aboriginal people
> and other community organisations. The content of such training
> courses should be negotiated between appropriate education providers
> (including Aboriginal education providers) other appropriate
> Aboriginal organisations and government. Such courses should be
> funded by government and persons undertaking such course should
> be eligible for such financial assistance in the course of studies as
> would be available under ABSTUDY guidelines.[11]

As more and more Aboriginal and Torres Strait Islander students and staff moved into universities, issues of appropriate course content, adequate funding and the accommodation of community and cultural responsibilities have been identified as matters for action. With the advent of the modern reconciliation movement, the role of education as one of the most important areas in which reconciliation can be given some substance is becoming more apparent. Universities are now considering it appropriate to adopt 'Reconciliation Statements', create advisory bodies to advise on 'Indigenous Content', and in some cases make arrangements for the return of objects of cultural significance. At no point, however, have any of these advances been enshrined as non-negotiable rights in the terms of the Coolangatta Statement, which states:

Indigenous Education Programs

> 2.5 Non-Indigenous peoples through the various levels of government
> and bureaucracy have an over-riding responsibility to accept and
> uphold the educational rights of Indigenous peoples and to know
> that these rights and freedoms are non-negotiable.[12]

The events surrounding the Commonwealth Government cuts to the ABSTUDY scheme provide a strong indicator of how politically vulnerable Indigenous Education programs are. The ABSTUDY scheme, an income support scheme for Indigenous Australian students, was

---

[10] *Batchelor Institute of Indigenous Tertiary Education Act 1999* (Northern Territory).

[11] Royal Commission into Aboriginal Deaths in Custody 1991: 76.

[12] Coolangatta Statement 1999: clause 2.5.

introduced in 1969. It aimed to improve the participation and success rates for Indigenous students, and was attributed as the cause of those improvements up to 1998.[13] During the 1996 Federal Election, ABSTUDY was portrayed by extremist political forces as discriminating against non-Indigenous Australians because it provided benefits in excess of those available to non-Indigenous Australian students. Indigenous Australians, it was argued, were on a gravy train of government handouts devised by do-gooders in the 'Aboriginal Industry', and ordinary Australians were missing out.

No amount of research, lobbying or advocacy was enough to convince the Howard Government that criticism of ABSTUDY was unwarranted. Despite the findings of research undertaken by Deakin University that changes proposed to ABSTUDY would significantly disadvantage 94.3% of Aboriginal and Torres Strait Islander students,[14] the Howard Government proceeded to implement those changes on 1 January 2000, thus reducing the income support available to most Indigenous Australian students.

Department of Education, Employment, Training and Youth Affairs (DETYA) student statistics for the year 2000 show that between 1999 and 2000, the number of Indigenous students commencing higher education study had decreased by 15.2%, while overall enrolments had fallen by 8.1%. This was a matter of concern for many in the higher education sector, with the National Tertiary Education Union (NTEU), Australian Vice-Chancellors Committee (AVCC), National Union of Students (NUS) and Council of Australian Postgraduate Associations (CAPA) all pointing to the ABSTUDY changes as underlying the fall in participation.

In response to widespread criticism, DETYA (now the Department of Education, Science and Technology – DEST) Minister Kemp and later Minister Nelson argued that Indigenous Australian students were choosing to enrol in Vocational Education and Training (VET) programs instead of higher education.[15]

In reality, growth in Aboriginal and Torres Strait Islander enrolments and overall participation in higher education slowed to the same extent, around 12.5%, between 1999 and 2000. Against the background of strong growth in participation from the 1970s onwards, the decline in enrolments which corresponded with the timing of the ABSTUDY changes strongly demonstrated the relationship between ABSTUDY and participation in both higher education and VET.[16] More importantly, the fact that a program developed in consultation with Indigenous Australian communities could be abolished in the face of widespread disagreement and criticism, demonstrated the extent to which such a scheme is not only dependant on political goodwill, but also vulnerable to political bad faith.

The net effect of the gutting of ABSTUDY as a scheme for student income support, together with the abolition of Higher Education Merit Equity Scholarships, real reductions in Indigenous Support Funding and other policy changes, is a reversal of sustained improvement:

> Indigenous Australian students now comprise only 1.01% of the non-overseas (university) student cohort: the lowest such figure since 1993 … These figures are now at pre 1991 levels. Ten years of growth in participation of Indigenous Australians in higher education have been reversed in the space of two years.[17]

---

[13] Stanley and Hansen 1998.   [15] DEST 2002: 21.   [17] Bunda and McConville 2002: 13, 18.

[14] Deakin University 1999.   [16] Bunda and McConville 2002: 13, 18.

Aboriginal and Torres Strait Islander employment within universities

> 2.4.3 The teacher is a facilitator of learning, one who promotes
> achievement and success. In this context culturally appropriate
> environments are employed to reinforce knowledge being
> imparted to the learner, reaffirming the learner's significant place
> in the world.[18]

Mentoring and guidance by Indigenous Australian staff is essential to student progress. In the year 2000 Indigenous Australian staff comprised only 0.67% of university staff.[19] To achieve proportionate employment the number of Indigenous Australian staff would need to almost triple. In 2000 there were no Commonwealth-funded schemes aimed at increasing Aboriginal and Torres Strait Islander employment in the public sector and universities, despite the Royal Commission into Aboriginal Deaths in Custody recommendations to implement such schemes.[20]

The status of Indigenous staff in universities is much less secure, on average, than their non-Indigenous counterparts. Limited term employment in Indigenous Units/Centres is much more prevalent than in universities generally. Within Indigenous Units, an estimated 45.4% of staff were in 2000 employed on a limited term basis, compared to 32.7% within the sector. Clearly, staff employed in Indigenous Units/Centres did not enjoy the same security of tenure as staff within the sector generally, and this affects Indigenous staff more than non-Indigenous. Within Indigenous Units/Centres, Indigenous staff were and are more likely to be employed on limited term than their non-Indigenous counterparts.[21] Strong evidence exists of systemic discrimination against Indigenous staff in the area of tenured university employment.

The consequences of this tenuous position for Indigenous Australian university staff, and for the university and its students, are numerous. Contract employment places all staff in a position where they could be subjected to arbitrary action, but for Indigenous Australian staff it may limit their capacity to be free to disagree with senior colleagues, or to challenge university teaching and research from their own Indigenous perspective. The fact that non-Indigenous staff are more secure in positions within centres established for Indigenous Education questions whether opportunities are being created for genuine Indigenous control of Indigenous Education.

The employment status of Aboriginal and Torres Strait Islander people in universities limits involvement of their communities in pedagogical processes, while under-representation of Indigenous staff contributes to a less culturally responsive environment for students.

Research

The particular synergies between teaching and research across various fields of academic endeavour distinguish universities from other educational institutions, and present unique opportunities for Indigenous Australians to shape what is documented, taught and learned. In the processes of determining how Indigenous Australians are represented within academic endeavour, their involvement in managing the process of inquiry and debate about them is essential. This involvement takes place in the form of postgraduate research and research supervision, involving support from DEST, and the Australian Research Council (ARC).

---

[18] Coolangatta Statement 1999: clause 2.4.3.

[19] DETYA 2000a.

[20] Royal Commission into Aboriginal Deaths in Custody 1991.

[21] NTEU 2000, and DETYA 2000a.

Aside from the valuable work undertaken with the assistance of the Australian Institute for Aboriginal and Torres Strait Islander Studies (AIATSIS), there is limited research activity about Indigenous Australians and very little of it is reserved as the specific domain of Indigenous Australian scholars. In all, the ARC funded 2 fellowships, 23 large grants and 11 SPIRT[22] grants of interest to Indigenous Australians in 2000.[23] The total amount of funding allocated to these projects was $1,578,396.[24] This limited funding, was spread across a range of projects which included:

- natural hazard vulnerability, awareness and mitigation strategies for remote and Indigenous communities in Northern Australia;

- GIS (Global Information System) for Natural and Cultural Resource Management by Indigenous People;

- a Research Training Project Examining Leadership in Indigenous Early Childhood Settings in Northern NSW;

- Accountability and Indigenous Service Delivery: Mechanisms, Policy and Process in *Rethinking Indigenous Self-determination: Politics, Land and Law in Australia; A demographic and socio-medical history of the Aboriginal people of Victoria, 1800–2000*: colonisation and epidemiological transitions;

- the impact of premature mortality on Aboriginal men's constructs of risk and health; and

- a study of Aboriginal children removed in Australia, mainly twentieth century.

Of all funding available for research of direct relevance to Indigenous Australians, in 2000 some 9% was specifically allocated to Indigenous Australian scholars in the form of the Indigenous Researchers Development Scheme.[25] The low percentage of Indigenous postgraduate researchers (0.6% of all postgraduate researchers in 1999) meant that the involvement of Indigenous Australian researchers in projects such as those outlined above is seriously limited.

This lack of participation in research by Indigenous Australians is consistent with the overall effects of the past purpose of education for Indigenous peoples, as the Coolangatta Statement succinctly describes:

> 1.3.1 Historically, Indigenous peoples have insisted upon the right of access to education. Invariably the nature, and consequently the outcome, of this education has been constructed through and measured by non-Indigenous standards, values and philosophies. Ultimately the purpose of this education has been to assimilate Indigenous peoples into non-Indigenous cultures and societies.[26]

Aside from direct involvement in the conduct of research, the problems confronting Indigenous Australian peoples in shaping research about them has been well documented. Hart and Whatman describe where Indigenous Australians are placed by western notions of

---

[22] Strategic Partnerships Industry–Research and Training Scheme, now known as Linkage grants.

[23] The definition of 'of Interest to Aboriginal and Torres Strait Islander peoples' is from AIATSIS 1999: 3.

[24] See www.ARC.edu/gov.au The funding includes projects relating to Indigenous peoples' languages, history, culture and art, also projects approved in 1998 and 1999 where funding continued to year 2000.

[25] NTEU 2001: 16.

[26] Coolangatta Statement 1999: clause 3.1.1.

inquiry and research. They argue that while Australia's Indigenous people are excluded from defining the research values of our education sytem through any direct input, non-Indigenous scholars tend to consider that Indigenous people are included (in the acceptance of research values) because research is perceived to benefit the whole community.[27]

Hart and Whatman articulate a number of assumptions identified by James Cook University, in 1995, as contributing to the disempowerment of Indigenous Australian communities in research endeavours. These include the following:

a) the assumed right of researchers to undertake research into the culture of Indigenous Australians;

b) the notion that cultural knowledge recorded in research reports is the only legitimate or lasting medium to protect knowledge and data exposed by such research;

c) that research needs to expose apparent dominant and latent primitivism of Indigenous societies;

d) the assumption that all knowledge, including Aboriginal and Torres Strait Islander knowledge, should be placed in the public domain;

e) that only non-Indigenous researchers do research well;

f) the belief that the privatisation of knowledge is not a social or cultural premise in Indigenous Australian cultures;

g) the assumption that the right of all people to access all knowledge is also an Indigenous cultural absolute;

h) the belief that the apparent absence of sophisticated Indigenous infrastructural mechanisms to maintain cultural continuity requires Western research and techniques to preserve culture; and

i) the apparent right of a conquering nation's intellectuals to both exploit Indigenous Australians and promote their own status and self-esteem by investigative analysis and historical research.[28]

Hart and Whatman conclude that:

> Developing research ethics is just one of the strategies that can
> be employed in reconciling the long history of intrusive study on
> Indigenous peoples. Looking at more enterprising and collaborative
> approaches to learning, studying and researching; where a recognition
> of Indigenous systems of knowledge is given voice and meaning,
> will mean a rediscovery of this country that has endless potential.
> The myth of *terra nullius* implied that this country was uninhabited
> and *terra nullius* social policy supported by research enabled for
> the dispossession of knowledges of Indigenous peoples. It must be
> remembered that university curriculum, teaching methodologies and
> research endeavours have a history of development that contributed
> to this dispossession. Has the time come for change?[29]

199

Re-shaping research within the context of universities inevitably impacts on teaching and learning, and this must be recognised in seeking to enshrine 'Indigenous Education' as a right.

Regional agreements: what are the possibilities?

The performance of the Australian higher education sector in the four areas of governance, student participation, Indigenous employment and research, points to a need to enshrine the rights articulated in the Coolangatta Statement within enforceable instruments, underpinned by acknowledgement of Aboriginal and Torres Strait Islander sovereignty in the Australian Constitution. Here I offer some suggestions on how the four areas of performance already discussed might relate to Constitutional recognition of Aboriginal and Torres Strait Islander peoples, regional agreements, and other instruments.

University Governance

As discussed earlier, the governance arrangements for universities are established by state and territory Acts of Parliament. Amending those Acts provides an opportunity to redress the absence of Aboriginal and Torres Strait Islander representation on governing bodies, but how this should occur, what form this representation takes and how such representation relates to Indigenous communities is a matter for serious consideration.

Can Indigenous communities rely on the goodwill of state governments to effect Indigenous representation on university governing bodies, or should there be constitutional recognition by states of Aboriginal and Torres Strait Islander sovereignty to underpin such representation? What mechanisms exist for Indigenous communities to shape how such representation occurs?

The lattermost question above could in part be answered through memoranda of understanding, and two recent examples are relevant.

In Victoria in 2000, the then ATSIC and the Victorian Government signed a communiqué on Indigenous Economic Development, Tourism, Housing, and Cultural Heritage. A priority area which relates to all of these issues is that of education outcomes. Specifically, the Communiqué commits the parties to:

> Work to improve education outcomes for Indigenous Victorians,
> including increased retention of Aboriginal and Torres Strait Islander
> children in the school system to year 12 and growth in the number
> of Indigenous students at Victorian universities.[30]

This Communiqué raises the prospect of the Victorian Government fully recognising its responsibilities for restorative justice, and raises the question of Indigenous input to university governance arrangements, a matter discussed earlier in this paper.

A different approach was employed in south-east Queensland (SEQ). The Queensland University of Technology (QUT) and ATSIC were finalising a Memorandum of Understanding (MOU), concerning collaborative activity between the two bodies. The MOU was intended as a pilot for future memoranda, and concentrates on two issues: employment, and capacity building partnerships.

---

[30] ATSIC and the Victorian Government 2000.

In employment, the MOU articulates five initiatives:

- Seek to place participants of ATSIC's Graduate Administrative Assistants (GAA) program within suitable areas of QUT, both during the course of their training and after completion.

- QUT will invite trainees in ATSIC's Admin/Clerical Traineeship program (certificate IV) to register their names on QUT's 'expressions of interest' register, for potential employment at QUT.

- Explore the option of using QUT as a work experience area for ATSIC's Admin/Clerical trainees during the course of their traineeship.

- Should QUT develop its own admin/clerical traineeship program, explore areas of collaboration between the two programs such as using ATSIC as a work experience area for QUT trainees, and establishing a trainee network which meets formally and informally.

- Explore partnership possibilities related to growing/developing academic lecturers and researchers from QUT's student body through, for example, post-graduate scholarships; opportunities for employment during their studies ands after graduation; and research/project opportunities during the course of their study.[31]

The premise of the Capacity Building Partnerships set out in the MOU is that the partners are equal in terms of the expertise they bring to bear, and are committed to build the capacity of each organisation to work together and define common interests. With this in mind, the parties have agreed:

> QUT will survey its Faculties and Divisions to map existing partnership activity with Indigenous organisations, and elicit areas of potential interest.
>
> Both organisations will identify and pursue specific opportunities arising from this mapping exercise.[32]

It is foreseeable that in time, both of these documents, in particular the QUT and ATSIC Communiqué, could evolve to address questions of Indigenous Australian involvement in university governance structures. For example, such instruments could provide the opportunity for agreement to be reached between ATSIC and the relevant university (in this case QUT), about how Indigenous representation should be established. This agreement could provide the basis for the parties to approach the State governments seeking amendment of the relevant University Act. Alternatively, the Victorian approach could evolve to a point where such representation is agreed as a matter of principle, (i.e. the Victorian Government will amend University Acts to provide for appropriate Aboriginal representation, and will negotiate with Aboriginal communities to effect such representation) with the details to be determined through negotiation. Additionally, these arrangements could operate in conjunction with, or form a part of, regional agreements within the *Native Title* Act.[33]

University Indigenous Education Programs

It should be apparent that the agreements discussed above, i.e. the Memorandum of Understanding and the Communiqué, are in part intended to address Aboriginal and Torres Strait

---

[31] QUT and ATSIC 2002 (verbatim extract).   [32] QUT and ATSIC 2002: 1.   [33] *Native Title Act 1993* (Cth).

Islander participation in university study. Specific programs funded by the Commonwealth such as ABSTUDY have the same objective, but as discussed earlier they are reliant on political goodwill and vulnerable to political bad faith.

Perhaps a constitutional recognition of sovereignty could elaborate other 'Indigenous Rights' such as those set out in the Coolangatta Statement. For example, as the National Aboriginal Conference (NAC) in its interim report on Makarrata proposed 'compulsory teaching of Aboriginal culture in schools',[34] perhaps there ought to be some recognition of the right of Indigenous people to control Indigenous educational programs. This would be similar to the rights asserted in the Kalkaringi Statement[35] relating to access to education and control of educational programs, but would extend to the funding schemes which underpin Aboriginal and Torres Strait Islander participation.

University employment of Aboriginal and Torres Strait Islanders

As the union representing staff in higher education, the NTEU, as a part of its partnership with Indigenous Australians, is committed to the negotiation of legally binding instruments to enshrine the rights asserted by Indigenous peoples. In speaking for this, it has accepted the priority that it needs to start in its own backyard with its own structures and practices.

While the NTEU is not an organisation controlled by Indigenous Australians, its work in pursuing restorative and social justice is informed by respectful dialogue, which seeks to transform the organisation into one which is culturally responsive and responsible. This dialogue has led to a number of changes to the NTEU structure itself, including:

- changes to union rules to provide for Indigenous representation at all levels of the union;

- annual meetings of an Indigenous Members' Forum which determines the directions to be pursued by the union nationally;

- an Indigenous Tertiary Education Policy Committee (ITEPC), which works with union staff to give effect to the objectives stated by Indigenous members; and

- employment of an Indigenous officer, who works in conjunction with the union's policy, industrial and recruitment staff.

A significant initiative identified at the first meeting of the NTEU Indigenous Members' Forum in 1999 was the pursuit of increased levels of employment in universities. This was based on a number of factors, including:

- the Recommendations of the Royal Commission into Aboriginal Deaths in Custody to increase Indigenous employment in the private and public sectors;

- the discontinuation of commonwealth funding for Indigenous employment programs within universities;

- the severe under-representation of Indigenous Australians within the staff profiles of universities, and the implications of this for teaching, research and scholarly activity of relevance to Indigenous Australians;

---

[34] See ATSIC 2001. 'Makarrata' is a *Yolngu* word meaning 'the end of a dispute and the resumption of normal relations'.

[35] Kalkaringi Statement 1998.

- the perception that Indigenous Australian staff were in less secure employment than their non-Indigenous counterparts;[36]

- the need for unions generally to work to redress within the working environment past social injustice, exploitation and Indigenous employment inequality; and

- the need to recognise the diversity that exists within and between Indigenous Australian communities, and in turn the variety of relationships those communities have with universities.

Through the work of the NTEU Indigenous Members' Forum, the ITEPC, and a working party of Indigenous Australian members convened for the purpose, a draft clause was developed for negotiation. The clause sought the agreement of universities to do a number of things, including:

- increase Indigenous Australian employment at all levels of the university;

- commit to the 'Indigenisation' of Indigenous Units/Centres within universities;

- monitor the performance of the university against agreed criteria; and

- ensure that staff selection panels include Indigenous Australian representation;

Importantly, a guiding principle of the enterprise bargaining claim is:

> The parties give respect and consideration to the cultural, social and religious systems practiced by Indigenous Australians, recognise Indigenous Australian knowledge as a significant contribution to all other bodies of knowledge, and acknowledge the scholarship that Indigenous Australian employees bring to the University. As far as possible, the parties will actively promote and recognise Indigenous Australian cultural practices and identity. The application of this principle needs to recognise the diversity of Indigenous Australian culture.[37]

It follows therefore, that the implementation of the claim within each university requires appropriate Indigenous Australian oversight. This occurs firstly through the right to direct representation on the negotiation team. The clause itself requires the establishment of a Development and Implementation Committee, with majority Indigenous Australian representation drawn from university staff and within the community. In this respect, the bargaining clause can be articulated to other legally binding instruments, such as those described above.

University Research

Clearly, all three of the mechanisms discussed above have some capacity to affect the way in which research is conducted on matters of importance to Indigenous Australians. A step toward shaping such research so that it more closely reflects Indigenous Australian community priorities might include the notion of co-supervision of postgraduate research, which has been advocated by the NTEU in its submission to the recent Senate Inquiry into Higher Education.[38]

---

[36] This perception was borne out by the results of the NTEU research discussed above.

[37] NTEU 1999a: para 1.

[38] NTEU 2001.

Co-supervision would involve appropriately informed and recognised (from Indigenous community perspectives) Aboriginal and Torres Strait Islander people to work in conjunction with the designated supervisor, usually although not always, a non-Indigenous academic.

How such supervision could be arranged can be informed by dialogue occurring in the administration of agreements such as those addressed above. It may be necessary to include the matter of postgraduate supervision within instruments like the Communiqué (Victoria) or the Memorandum of Understanding (Queensland).

Conclusion

Agreements such as those discussed here represent a step forward in transforming educational institutions so that they are more culturally responsive and responsible to the rights of Indigenous Australians in higher education. Such agreements can refer to more formal regional agreements, such as those contemplated by the *Native Title Act*, and provide a degree of flexibility that allows adaptation to local circumstances. How these agreements can relate to a formal constitutional recognition of Aboriginal and Torres Strait Islander sovereignty must be discussed within the broader conversation about a treaty.

The process of making Indigenous Education an enshrined right, rather than a matter of administrative or political goodwill, must continue so that the benefits of the education system are available to all Aboriginal and Torres Strait Islander peoples. It must also continue in order to transform teaching and learning for all Australians so that it truly depicts Indigenous Australian reality: not only at university, but also in turn through the school system.

Acknowledgments

This paper has been informed by many discussions, observations and experiences. I would firstly like to thank the many Aboriginal and Torres Strait Islander people who have had the time and patience to impart their understanding during my work with them. I also thank the members of the National Tertiary Education Union Indigenous Members' Forum, who have contributed their wisdom and commitment to the important work of redressing Indigenous educational disadvantage. Of these members, I would particularly like to thank Dr Bob Morgan, Associate Professor Tracey Bunda, and Victor Hart, for their ongoing contributions to this area. My sincere thanks also go to my *djaambi* Joel Wright, NTEU Indigenous Officer.

References

Books, articles and reports

AIATSIS 1999, *Research of Interest to Aboriginal and Torres Strait Islander peoples*, National Board of Employment, Education and Training, Australian Research Council, Canberra.

ATSIC and the Victorian Government 2000, Communiqué, 22 June, 2pp.

ATSIC 2001, 'Treaty Now', Treaty Secretariat, National Policy Office, ATSIC, Woden, ACT.

Brah, A 1992, 'Difference, Diversity and Differentiation' in J McDonald, J Rattansi and A Rattansi (eds) *Race, culture and difference*, Open University Press, Milton Keynes: 126–45.

Bunda, T and G McConville 2002, 'Indigenous higher education, myths, cuts and obvious decline', *Campus Review*, 29 May–2 June: 3–18.

Coolangatta Statement on Indigenous peoples' Rights in Education 1999, World Indigenous Peoples' Conference on Education, Hilo, Hawaii.

Cordell, J 1995, Indigenous management of land and sea and traditional activities in Cape York Peninsula, Cape York Peninsula Land Use Strategy, Brisbane.

Council of Australian Postgraduate Associations (CAPA) 1997, *Barriers facing Indigenous postgraduate students*, CAPA, Melbourne.

Deakin University 1999, *Analysis of the Proposed Changes to ABSTUDY on Indigenous Students, Final Report*, May, Deakin University, Melbourne.

DEET 1993, *National Aboriginal and Torres Strait Islander Education Policy – Second Triennium 1993–1995*, AGPS, Canberra.

DEST 2002, *Higher Education Report for the 2002 to 2004 Triennium*, AGPS, Canberra.

DETYA 1999a, *Staff 1999, Selected Higher Education Statistics*, DETYA, Canberra.

—— 1999b, *Students 1999, Selected Higher Education Statistics*, DETYA, Canberra.

—— 2000a, *Higher Education Staff Statistics*, AGPS, Canberra.

—— 2000b, *Indigenous Participation in Higher education*, Higher Education Division Occasional Papers, DETYA, Canberra.

—— 2000c, *Staff 2000, Selected Higher Education Statistics*, DETYA, Canberra.

—— 2000d, *Students 2000, Selected Higher Education Statistics*, DETYA, Canberra.

Donovan, RJ and R Spark 1997, 'Towards guidelines for survey research in remote Aboriginal communities', *Australian and New Zealand Journal of Public Health* 21 (1): 89–95.

Durnan, D and J Boughton 1999, *Succeeding against the odds: The outcomes attained by Indigenous students in Aboriginal community-controlled adult education colleges*, NCVER (National Centre for Vocational Education Research), Kensington Park, SA.

Eisenhart, MA and KR Howe 1992, 'Validity in Educational Research' in MP Le Compte, WL Millroy and J Geissle (eds) *The Handbook of Qualitative Research in Education*, Academic Press, London: 643–80.

Fannon, F 1967, *The wretched of the earth*, Penguin, Harmondsworth.

Flick, B 1995, 'Spiritual Healing, Land and Health', *Aboriginal and Islander Health Worker Journal* 19(1): 3–5.

Fredericks, B 1996, 'CAPA Indigenous Postgraduate Project – Progress Report', seminar paper presented at the 1996 QUT Oodgeroo Unit Indigenous Postgraduate Forum, 31 October, Queensland University of Technology, Brisbane.

Harri, A 1994, A good idea waiting to happen: regional agreements in Australia, *Proceedings from the Cairns workshop*, Cape York Land Council, Cairns, Nth Qld, July.

Hart, V and S Whatman 1998, 'Decolonising the concept of knowledge', paper presented at HERDSA98 Conference in Auckland, Queensland University of Technology, Brisbane, available at http://www.qut.edu.au/chan/oodgeroo/hart.htm

James Cook University 1995, Indigenous Research Ethics, *Proceedings of the 1995 Indigenous Research Ethics Conference*, James Cook University, Townsville.

Jull, P 1994, *Australian nationhood and outback Indigenous peoples*, North Australia Research Unit, Australian National University, Casuarina.

Kalkaringi Statement 1998, Constitutional Convention of the Combined Nations of Central Australia, Kalkaringi, August 17–20.

Kari Oca Statement 1993, Indigenous Peoples' Earth Charter, Brazil.

Keilor Historical Society 1992, *Newsletter,* September/October 1992.

Lincoln, Y and E Guba 1985, *Naturalistic Inquiry*, Sage, Beverley Hills, CA.

Lui Jnr, G 1994, 'Torres Strait: Towards 2000', *Race and Class* 35(4): 11–20.

Manne, R 2001, 'In Denial: The Stolen Generations and The Right', *The Australian Quarterly Essay,* 1/2001, Schwartz, Melbourne.

Middleton, S 1996, 'Doing Qualitative Research in the Mid-1990s: Issues, Contexts and Practicalities', *Waikato Journal of Education* 2: 3–23.

Miles, M and A Huberman1994, *Qualitative Data Analysis : An Expanded Sourcebook*, Sage, Thousand Oaks, California.

Nakata, M 1995, 'Cutting a Better Deal for Torres Strait Islanders', *The Aboriginal Child at School* 23(3): 20–7.

—— 1997, 'Who's reading "Misplaced Hopes"?', *Qualitative Studies in Education* 10(4): 425–31.

NTEU 1999 (unpublished), Indigenous Employment Strategy Clause.

—— 2000 (unpublished), Survey of Indigenous Centres in Universities.

—— 2001, NTEU Indigenous Tertiary Education Policy Committee Submission to the Senate Employment, Workplace Relations, Small Business and Education References Committee Inquiry into the capacity of public universities to meet Australia's higher education needs, May.

Queensland University of Technology (QUT) and Aboriginal & Torres Strait Islander Commission (ATSIC) 2002, Draft Memorandum of Understanding, ATSIC, Canberra.

Royal Commission into Aboriginal Deaths In Custody 1991, *National Report Overview and Recommendations* (by Commissioner Elliott Johnson), AGPS, Canberra.

Runciman, C 1994, *Elevating Choice : A study of Aboriginal women's labour market participation in South East Queensland*, AGPS, Canberra.

Scheurich, J 1997, 'From the Editors: Postcolonialism, feminism, critiques, history, caring and fidelity, and telephone talks with mom – we've got it all', *Qualitative Studies in Education* 10(4): 403–6.

Stake, R 1994, 'Case Studies' in NK Denzin and YS Lincoln (eds) *Handbook of Qualitative Research*, Sage, Thousand Oaks: 236–47.

Stanley, O and G Hansen 1998, *ABSTUDY: An investment for tomorrow's employment. A review of ABSTUDY for the Aboriginal and Torres Strait Islander Commission*, Commonwealth of Australia, Canberra.

Taylor, J 1991, *Spatial mobility of working age Aborigines in settled and remote Australia: a preliminary analysis*, Centre for Aboriginal Economic Policy & Research, Australian National University, Canberra.

Taylor, J and B Hunter 1998, *The job still ahead: Economic costs of continuing Indigenous employment disparity*, ATSIC, Canberra.

University of Tasmania 1997, *Ethical guidelines for research projects and teaching exercises using human subjects*, University of Tasmania, Hobart.

Legislation

Batchelor Institute of Indigenous Tertiary Education Act 1999 (Northern Territory).

Charles Sturt University Act 1989 (New South Wales).

Native Title Act 1993 (Cth).

Case Law

Mabo v Queensland (No 2) 175 CLR 1.

Native title holding communities as treaty parties

Greg McIntyre

Introduction

This paper starts from the proposition that a treaty is no more or less than an agreement which may be reached between two or more parties. The particular type of treaty which is under discussion in this paper is a treaty which may contribute to the mutual respect with which Indigenous and non-Indigenous peoples may treat each other within the Australian nation. Such treaties may take many forms, be engaged in between a variety of parties, cover a range of geographical areas and touch upon subject matter of infinite variety. The most important of such treaties are likely to be with governments and government agencies, because governments represent significant portions of the citizens of the nation.

There are many levels at which governments, corporations and non-Indigenous citizens could, and do, engage with Indigenous people, and Indigenous peoples can define themselves in various ways. Governments, corporations and citizens can treat with individuals, with local groups, extended families or clans, with regional aggregates of local groups, with dialect or language groups (sometimes called 'tribes'), with communities or peoples, with groups located within regional areas of States or Territories or with those found in a particular State or Territory, or with all those within the Australian nation.

This paper discusses the form of group which it may be most appropriate for non-Indigenous parties to seek to engage in treaties with, relying upon recent experience as to how Indigenous groups can be defined, in the context of determining native title holding groups. Consideration is given to Common Law, International law and anthropological definitions of indigenous groups.

What is a communal Native title?

In order to approach an understanding of how native title may contribute to identifying the parties to a treaty, one needs to start with an understanding of what a communal Native title is.

A communal Native title is the right to the land itself: Lee J in *Ward on behalf of the Miriuwung and Gajerrong Peoples v State of Western Australia* (1998) 159 ALR 483. It is not limited to the activities engaged in by the holders of such title: *Delgamuukw v The Queen in Right of British Columbia* (Supreme Court of Canada, 11 December 1997) (1998) 1 CNLR 14.

Communal Native title is established by occupancy of the land at the time the Crown asserted sovereignty over the land. Where an Indigenous community is in occupation of an area, its title arises from that occupation, to define the community's title as against the Crown or third parties: Kent McNeil, *The Relevance of Traditional Laws and Customs to the Existence and Content of Native Title at Common Law,* www.usask.ca/native law, 1996: 10; Noel Pearson, Concept of Native Title at Common Law, paper presented at Conference on Land Rights – Past, Present and Future, Canberra, 16–17 August 1996: 118; Gary Meyers, 'The Content of Native Title: Questions for the Miriuwung Gajerrong Appeal', at 6. Native title does not require proof of distinctive aboriginal practices, customs and traditions: *Mabo v Queensland (No 2)* (1992) 175 CLR 1 per Brennan J at 51–2, Deane and Gaudron JJ at 86, Toohey J at 184–92, 194–5, 207–14; McNeil at pp 6–17.

Occupation is established by regular use of definite tracts of the land and exploitation of its resources: *Delgamuukw v The Queen in Right of British Columbia* (Supreme Court of Canada, 11 December 1997) (1998) 1 CNLR 14; Toohey J in *Mabo v Queensland (No 2)* (1992) 175 CLR 1 at 187.

Pre-sovereignty occupation is proved by present occupation where there is no evidence to rebut the presumption that such occupation has continued since sovereignty was asserted: *Delgamuukw* (supra).

Provided a substantial connection between the people and the land is maintained, a change in the nature of the occupation will not preclude a finding of native title: *Delgamuukw*, per Lamer CJ at p 154; *Mabo (No 2)*, per Brennan J at p 61, Deane and Gaudron JJ at 110 and Toohey J at p 192; Beaumont and von Doussa JJ in *Western Australia v Ward* (2000) 170 ALR 159 at 212 and 213 (*Ward* FFC)[1] (majority judges FFC); McNeil 1996: 29–30.

A communal Native title, by definition, includes the right of the community to exclusively use and occupy the land: *Delgamuukw*. Joint title can arise, however, within Aboriginal society from shared exclusivity: *Delgamuukw* per Lamer CJ at para 158, 196; *United States v Santa Fe Railroad Co* (1941) 314 US, 339. Exclusivity, in that context, means that an Aboriginal group must show that a territory is its ancestral territory and not the territory of an unconnected Aboriginal society. Two or more groups may have occupied the same territory and therefore a finding of joint occupancy is not precluded: *Delgamuukw* (supra).

Communal Native Title rights and interests

The *Native Title Act 1993* (Cth) (NTA) s.223 (1) defines both 'native title' and 'native title rights and interests' to mean communal, group or individual rights and interests of Aboriginal peoples under traditional laws and customs which connect them to land or waters.

NTA s.225 (e) provides that a determination of native title includes a determination of 'whether the native title rights and interests confer possession, occupation use and enjoyment of … land and waters on the native title holders to the exclusion of all others'. It reflects the order of the Court in *Mabo v Queensland (No 2)* (supra) that 'the Meriam people are entitled as against the whole world to possession, occupation, use and enjoyment of the land of Mer' (per Brennan J at p 76).

---

[1] Full Federal Court.

Communal Native Title Holding Group

The Courts (e.g., Lee J in *Ward*, FC[2] 1998)) have sought to come to grips with the definition of a native title holding group by posing questions to be determined of the following kind:

(a) whether there is an identifiable group which holds the native title;

(b) what kind of group the land owning group is (local descent group, clan, language group, tribe or some other entity);

(c) what social, cultural and political elements constitute that group;

(d) whether the group comprises one or more traditional societies; and

(e) whether the present claimant group (or groups) held native title to the land claimed.

The conclusion of Lee J in *Ward* (FC 1998), at p 541–2, was that:

> there is an organised community of Aboriginal people described as Miriuwung and Gajerrong, which possesses the languages and the Ngarranggarni [Dreamings] that are part of, or run through, the claim area, being a community which observes traditional laws and customs …
>
> Being satisfied that there is a Miriuwung and Gajerrong community that has an ancestral connection with the Aboriginal community or communities, which occupied the claim area at the time of the assertion of sovereignty in the State or the Territory, it follows that the communal title is the title of the Miriuwung and Gajerrong people … The inter-relation, and allocation of rights between the community and its subgroups is governed by the traditional laws and customs of the community.

The conclusions of Lee J can be related to dicta of the members of the High Court in *Mabo v Queensland (No 2)* (supra) where they use terms such as 'clan', 'community', 'inhabitants', 'people' and 'society', apparently interchangeably, to describe a native title holding group. Justice Brennan, for instance, said (in *Mabo* supra):[3]

(a) 'since European settlement of Australia, many *clans or groups of indigenous people* have been physically separated from their traditional land and have lost their connexion with it. But that is not the universal position. It is clearly not the position of the Meriam *people*. Where a clan or group has continued to acknowledge the laws and (so far as practicable) to observe the customs based on the traditions of that clan or group, whereby the traditional connexion with that land has been substantially maintained, the traditional community title of that clan or group can be said to remain in existence' (pp 59–60).

(b) 'Australian law can protect the interests of members of an indigenous clan or group whether communally or individually, only in conformity with the traditional laws and customs of *the people* to whom the clan or group belongs' (p 60).

---

[2] Federal Court.   [3] emphasis added.

(c) 'native title … may be protected … whether possessed by a
community, a group or an individual' (p 61).

(d) 'the groupings of persons to possess rights and interests in land
are to be determined by the laws and customs of the indigenous
inhabitants' (p 61).

(e) 'Of course in time the laws and customs of any people will change
and rights and interest of the members of *the people* among
themselves will change too. But so long as *the people* remain as an
identifiable community, the members of whom are identified by one
another as members of that community living under its laws and
customs, the communal native title survives to be enjoyed by the
members according to the rights and interests to which they are
respectively entitled under the traditionally based laws and customs
as *currently* acknowledged and observed' (p 61).

(f) '*where an indigenous people (including a clan or group) as a community*,
are in possession or are entitled to possession of land under a
proprietary native title, their possession may be protected or their
entitlement to possession may be enforced by a representative action
brought on behalf of the people or by a sub-group or individual who
sues to protect or enforce rights or interests which are dependent
on the *communal* native title … A communal native title enures for
the benefit of the community as a whole and for the sub-groups and
individuals within it who have particular rights and interests in the
community's land' (pp 61–2).

(g) 'The recognition of the rights and interests of a *sub-group* or
individual dependent on a *community title* is not precluded by an
absence of a *communal law* to determine a point in contest between
rival claimants. By custom, such a point may have to be settled
by community consensus or in some other manner prescribed by
custom. A court may have to act on evidence which lacks specificity
in determining a question of that kind' (p 62).

Justice Brennan drew from the factual findings of Moynihan J (made on remitter from the
High Court) in *Mabo v Queensland (No 2)*, the following conclusions:[4]

(a) 'The *people* who were in occupation of these Islands [the Murray
Islands] before European contact and who have continued to occupy
those Islands to the present are known as the Meriam people' (p 16).[5]

(b) 'The Meriam people of today retain a strong sense of affiliation with
their forebears and with the society and culture of earlier times'
(p 17).

---

[4] emphasis added.   [5] The Plaintiffs in their Statement of Claim para 1 referred to 'the Meriam people' as 'people called the Miriam people, who
speak a distinct language of their own (the Miriam language), who are known as Murray Islanders and who are included
in that group of people generally known as Torres Strait Islanders'. There was no contest raised in the proceedings as to
that claim. The evidentiary proceedings focused on the claims of individual plaintiffs to particular blocks of land.

(c) 'The Meriam people … are *a Melanesian people* (perhaps an integration of differing groups) who probably came to the Murray Islands from Papua New Guinea' (p 17).[6]

(d) 'Some of the features of life in the Murray Islands at the time of first European contact, at the end of the eighteenth century, are described by Moynihan J in his findings in the present case:

> *Communal* life based on *group* membership seems to have been the predominant feature of life. Many of the activities of daily life were *social* activities which took place in the context of *group* activities of a ceremonial or ritualistic nature. Behaviour was regulated in the interest of the community by social pressures … The people lived in *groups* of huts … organized in named villages … Garden land is identified by reference to a named locality coupled with the name of the relevant individuals …

> Gardening was important not only from the point of view of subsistence but to provide produce for consumption or exchange during the various rituals associated with different aspects of *community* life … [or] *social* purposes … and by observations and imitations reinforced by the rituals and other aspects of the *social* fabric gardening practices were passed on …

> … before European contact social cohesion was sought by the combined operation of a number of factors. Children were inculcated from a very early age with knowledge of their relationships in terms of social groupings and what was expected of them by a constant pattern of example, imitation and repetition with reinforcing behaviour. It was part of their environment – the way in which they lived … Initiation and other group activities reinforced these patterns.

> A sense of shame was the outcome of a failure to observe. It could be reinforced by group pressures leading to retribution. Ultimately force might be resorted to by those who had access to the means of exerting it.

> Sorcery, magic and taboo were obviously important cohesive factors and a source of sanction' (p 18).

'The findings show that Meriam *society* was regulated more by custom than by laws' (at p 8).

(e) 'Moynihan J found that there was apparently no concept of public or general *community ownership* among the people of Murray Island, all the land of Murray Island being regarded as belonging to individuals or groups' (at p 22).

(f) '[T]he Meriam people have maintained their own identity and their own customs'(at p 61).

---

[6] See Determination of Moynihan J delivered 16 November 1990, p 91. Justice Moynihan also found, at p 90, that there was 'a close relationship with the other inhabitants of the Eastern Island group with whom the Murray Islanders shared a common language and, in general terms, common Papua New Guinea origins … It seems likely that there was intermarriage between Murray Islanders and the inhabitants of at least the other of the Eastern Islands.'

(g) 'Whatever be the precision of Meriam laws and customs with
    respect to land there is abundant evidence that land was traditionally
    occupied by individuals or family groups and that contemporary
    rights and interests are capable of being established with sufficient
    precision to attract declaratory or other relief' (p 62).

(h) 'Although the findings by Moynihan J do not permit a confident
    conclusion that, in 1879 [the date of annexation of the Islands]
    there were parcels of land in the Murray Islands owned allodially by
    individuals or groups, the absence of such a finding is not critical to
    the final resolution of this case' (p 63).

(i) 'The plaintiffs … claim rights and interests dependent on the native
    title of the Meriam people … In the absence of any party seeking to
    challenge their respective claims under the laws and customs of the
    Meriam people, the action is not constituted in a way that permits
    the granting of declaratory relief with respect to claims based on those
    laws and customs … Declaratory relief must therefore be restricted to
    the native communal title of the Meriam people' (p 75).

(j) 'the Meriam people are entitled as against the whole world to
    possession, occupation, use and enjoyment of the island of Mer'
    (p 76).

Two other judges in *Mabo (No 2)*, Deane and Gaudron JJ, concluded from the findings
of Moynihan J that:

(a) 'the Meriam people lived in an organised community which
    recognized individual and family rights of possession, occupation
    and exploitation of identified areas of land … [U]nder the traditional
    law or custom of the Murray Islanders, there was a consistent focus
    upon the entitlement of the individual or the family as distinct from
    the community as a whole or some larger section of it … [which]
    extended to all the land of the Islands' (p 115).

(b) 'it is impossible to identify any precise system of title, any
    precise rules of inheritance or any precise methods of alienation.
    Nonetheless, there was undoubtedly a local native system under
    which the established familial or individual rights of occupation and
    use were of a kind which far exceeded the minimum requirements
    necessary to found a presumptive common law native title' (pp
    115–16).

(c) 'the Crown ownership of lands in the Murray Islands after their
    annexation to Queensland was qualified and reduced by a *communal*
    native title of the Murray Islanders to the land of the Islands …
    the entitlement of particular families or individuals with respect to
    particular land under that common law communal title falls to be
    determined by reference to traditional laws and customs' (p 119).

Justice Toohey, in *Mabo (No 2)*, said:[7]

(a) 'a distinction should be noted between the existence of native title and the nature of the title. These two questions dictate different lines of inquiry' (p 184).

(b) 'Proof of existence [of traditional title] … is a threshold question. The content of the interests … is that which already exists traditionally; the substance of the interests is irrelevant to the threshold question' (p 187).

(c) 'the problem which arises where … the evidence of the claimed traditional right is so vague that there is doubt that it existed, or exists … is an evidentiary problem and the criterion for dealing with it is not the claimed right's similarity to, difference from, or even incomprehensibility at, common law. Therefore, inquiries into the nature of traditional title are essentially irrelevant' (p 187).

(d) 'an inquiry into the kind of *society* from which rights and duties emanate is irrelevant to the existence of title, because it is inconceivable that indigenous inhabitants in occupation of land did *not* have a system by which land was utilized in a way determined by that society. There must, of course, be a *society* sufficiently organized to create and sustain rights and duties, but there is no separate requirement to prove the kind of society beyond proof that presence on the land was part of a functioning system' (p 187).

(e) 'The requirements of proof of traditional title are a function of the protection the title provides (Bartlett 1983, 'Aboriginal Land Claims at Common Law', *University of Western Australia Law Review*, vol 15 293 at p 310). It is the fact of the presence of indigenous *inhabitants* on acquired land which precludes proprietary title in the Crown and which excites the need for protection of rights. Presence would be insufficient to establish title if it was coincidental only or truly random, having no connexion with or meaning in relation to a society's economic, cultural or religious life. It is presence amounting to occupancy which is the foundation of the title and which attracts protections, and it is that which must be proved to establish title (Bartlett 1983, vol 15 at pp 311, 319–20, See now *Ontario (Attorney-General) v Bear Island Foundation* (1991), 83 DLR (4th) 381; *Hamlet of Baker Lake* [1980] FC at pp 557–8; (1979) 107 DLR (3d) at p 542; *Regina v Sparrow* (1990) 1 SCR 1075; (1990) 70 DLR (4th) 385). Thus traditional title is rooted in physical presence. That the use of land was meaningful must be proved but it is to be understood from the point of view of the members of the society' (p 188).

(f) 'Presence on the land need not amount to possession at common law in order to amount to occupancy' (p 188).

---

[7] emphasis added.

(g) 'proof of occupancy [may be] by reference to the demands of the land and society in question 'in accordance with the way of life, habits, customs and usages of the [indigenous people] who are its users and occupiers' (p 188).

(h) A 'principle of *exclusive occupancy* [of definable territory] is justified in so far as it precludes indiscriminate ranging over land but it is difficult to see the basis of the rule if it precludes title merely on the ground that more than one group utilizes land. Either each smaller group could be said to have title, comprising the right to shared use of and in accordance with traditional use; or traditional title vests in the larger '*society*' comprising all the rightful occupiers. Moreover, since occupancy is a question of fact, the 'society' in occupation need not correspond to the most significant cultural group among the indigenous people' (pp 189–90).

(i) 'It is true that the findings of Moynihan J do not allow the articulation of a precise set of rules and that they are inconclusive as to how consistently a principle was applied in local law, for example, with respect to inheritance of land, but, as has been said earlier in this judgment, the particular nature of the rules which govern a society or which describe its members' relationship with land does not determine the question of traditional land rights. Because rights and duties *inter se* cannot be determined precisely, it does not follow that traditional rights are not to be recognized by the common law.

The only relevance of an argument of uncertainty is if it can be said that the rules or practices governing Meriam society were so capricious and their application so inconsistent as to indicate that the Meriam people's presence on the Islands was coincidental and random. On the findings of Moynihan J that is impossible to conclude' (pp 191–2).

(j) 'There is no question that indigenous society can and will change on contact with European culture … But modification of traditional society in itself does not mean traditional title no longer exists. Traditional title arises from the fact of occupation, not the occupation of a particular kind of society' (p 192).

Given the use in these judgments of this variety of terms to describe the manner in which a native title claim group may be identified, it is desirable to attempt to come to some understanding of the meanings which may be attributed to some of those terms, in order to understand how they may be used in the analysis of how one defines a group for the purposes of contemplating treaty negotiations within a nation.

'Peoples' as Native Title holding communities

The term 'peoples' is a term of International law rather than Anthropology (See expert anthropological evidence of Professor Ken Maddock in *Ward* (FC 1998), Ts pp 8044–5). The term 'peoples' is used in Articles 1 (2) and 55 of the *Charter of the United Nations*.

In a Memorandum prepared by the United Nations Secretariat (United Nations Conference on International Organisation Docs (1945), vol 18, 657), it is said that:

> The word 'nations' is broad and general enough to include colonies,
> mandates, protectorates and quasi-states as well as states … 'nations' is
> used in the sense of all political entities, states and non-states, whereas
> 'peoples' refers to groups of human beings who may, or may not,
> comprise states or nations.

The concept of 'peoples' in International Law has evaded precise definition. It is regarded as neither co-extensive with or mutually exclusive of the categories known as 'minorities': Crawford J, 'The rights of "peoples": "peoples" or "governments"?' in Crawford (ed) *The Rights of Peoples* (Clarendon Press, Oxford, 1988), 55 at 60–61; see also Barsh R L, 'Indigenous peoples: an emerging object of international law (1986) 80 AJILO, 369 at 376.

Nevertheless, in *Cherokee Nation v State of Georgia* (1831) 5 Peters 1, the Court did not have any difficulty with the concept of recognising the Plaintiffs, an indigenous group within the United States of America, who styled themselves the 'Cherokee Nation', as 'a nation within a nation'.

In *Worcester v Georgia* (1832), 31 US (6 Pet) 616, the United States Supreme Court said:

> The Indian nations had always been considered as distinct,
> independent political communities, retaining their original natural
> rights as the undisputed possessors of the soil, from time immemorial,
> with the single exception of that imposed by irresistible power, which
> excluded them from intercourse with any other European potentate
> than the first discoverer of the coast of the particular region claimed.

The United States Supreme Court is in those cases recognising the indigenous title holding groups within US national borders as having the status of a political entity. A similar understanding is manifested in the order of the Court in *Mabo v Queensland (No 2)* (supra), and the findings of Lee J in *Ward* (FC 1998), that a communal native title is one held by an indigenous political entity, defined by its shared customs and traditions, rather than by particular groups or individuals who hold interests within the system of law or customs of the indigenous political entity.

In the Murray Island context, the Indigenous political entity was the Meriam people and interests were held by individuals and families within a system of laws and customs recognised by the Meriam people. In the case of the Miriuwung and Gajerrong people(s) intra-community interests may be described as estate areas or local descent group areas in respect of a larger community of people who share customs and traditions.

In the circumstances of the Miriuwung and Gajerrong peoples' case, the Court recognised the Indigenous groups as comprising 'peoples' who do not comprise states or nations recognised as such in the International community. Likewise, the term 'people', as used in *Mabo (No 2)* (supra) is clearly something less than a nation or state recognised by other nations at an International level.

215

A 'people' is clearly larger than an individual or a family, which may hold an interest in particular land on Murray Island. It was also held, in the *Ward* (FC 1998) case (at p 542), to be larger than an estate group or local group holding an interest in a locally defined tract of land.

In *Mabo (No 2)* (supra) the Court was using 'people' to refer to a group of Melanesian origin or of Torres Strait Islander origin. The 'people' thus referred to were a group greater than those (defined by the pleadings as 'the Meriam people'), who held a communal native title to the Murray Islands.

'People', as used by Brennan and Toohey JJ in *Mabo (No 2)*, is a broader term than 'society', as used by Toohey J in *Mabo (No 2)* (supra) and 'community', as used by Brennan J.

The appropriate analysis, I would suggest, for international and domestic law purposes, is to find a 'people' from those Indigenous groups who share customs and traditions amongst themselves. That is the most appropriate group to be seeking to identify in Australia for the purpose of entering into treaties of the kind which in North America have been entered into with 'indigenous political communities'(who describe themselves as 'nations').

Communities as Native Title Holders

What is comprised by a community, for the purposes of identifying those who are associated with a communal native title may be difficult. It is a commonly held view that a 'community definition is bound to be arbitrary and imposed' (see the expert aaaanthropological evidence of Associate Professor Christensen in *Ward* (FC 1998), Ts p 7247). Different communities are developed depending on the context.

A communal native title may be held by a community located in a particular area who form part of a 'people' or 'society' (such as the 'Meriam people' who were a community located in the Murray Islands).

Within that community particular individuals, local groups or estate groups may hold particular interests in accordance with the laws and customs recognised by the larger 'community', 'society' or 'people'.

'Tribe' or language group

The concepts of 'tribe' and 'language group', also overlap in meaning and content with the concepts of 'community', 'society' and 'people'. They, therefore, merit some discussion.

Australian anthropologists, Peter Sutton and Bruce Rigsby have referred to the 'new tribes' or language groups. Sutton suggests that:

> one of the consequences of the impact of the colonial period in
> Aboriginal Australia has been the rapid rise in the political importance
> of the language group. In some areas, this has become the main
> collective label under which people maintain a local Aboriginal
> identity and a communal land-owning group identity: Sutton,
> *Country: Aboriginal boundaries and land ownership in Australia*:
> Aboriginal History Inc, Monograph 3, 1995, p 47; Sutton, *Native
> Title and the Descent of Rights*: National Native Title Tribunal 1998.

Sutton points out, however, in *Native Title and the Descent of Rights*, at p 55, that language groups or 'regional groups' have an internal structure, typically comprising a set of units usually referred to as 'families'. He notes (at p 56) that a human family is 'always a jural construct and never merely a biological or demographic datum. This is because it belongs to the realm of kinship, or recognised genealogical relationships, rather than merely to the reproductive history of some randomly selected set of individuals.'

Sutton puts the view (at p 60) that the cognatic descent group is central to a post-colonial Aboriginal social system. He explains that a cognatic descent group is 'one formed by those who share recognised descent from a particular ancestor or set of blood-related ancestors, and who trace their links to such ancestors through either parent'. He describes them as 'families of polity in the sense that they form structural elements of public life in Aboriginal society'.

Sutton goes on (at p 63) to refer to 'Tribal units [which] are usually much larger than cognatic descent groups and are based on language affiliation, or occasionally another type of regional affiliation such as a nation (descendents of members of several language groups combined)'.

Sutton's analysis is consistent with the conclusions reached by the High Court in *Mabo* and the Federal Court in *Ward* (FC, 1998 and FFC, 2000) as to the nature of the groups comprising the Meriam people and the Miriuwung and Gajerrong peoples. Sutton would describe those native title holding groups as 'tribal units' and is adopting a use of the word 'nation' which is distinguishable from its use in International law or its application by the US Supreme Court to Native American groups. Sutton is also assigning language groups to the status of a category of tribal unit.

'Tribe' is a classification sourced in anthropological study, generally regarded as describing Indigenous peoples who share a common purpose, language and culture. It is a category which is not popular with Indigenous peoples or in modern anthropological discourse, because it does not have a consistent meaning and has a tendency to promote misleading stereotypes.

Chris Lowe of the Africa Policy Information Center in 'Talking about "Tribe"', Background Paper, at www.africaaction.org/bp/ethall.htm, wrote:

> If by tribe we mean a social group that shares a single territory,
> a single language, a single political unit, a shared religious tradition,
> a similar economic system, and common cultural practices, such a
> group is rarely found in the real world. These characteristics almost
> always never correspond precisely with each other today, nor did they
> at any time in the past.

Lowe argues that the use of the word 'tribe' tends to promote a destructive generalised illusion, myth or stereotype of primitiveness, conservative backwardness and images of irrationality and superstition which avoids any detailed analysis of ethnic groups. This idea that a 'tribal' group was a primitive group or of a lower order of humanity justified Europeans in adopting a position of domination. It also justified the taking of the land and resources of so called 'tribal' groups in return for providing them with European civilisation.

It is for those reasons that there is a general aversion to the use of that term today, in favour of terms with less negative connotations.

In the United States there is a continued use of the term because it is an historical term ensconced in treaties and laws which accord rights to Native Americans. Also, Indigenous people will sometimes refer to themselves by that term because they are of the view that it is one which will be recognised by English speaking Europeans, but it is regarded as offensive by many Australian Aboriginal groups: see *Glossary for Aboriginal Studies*, Charles Sturt University, hsc.csu.edu.au/ab_studies/glossary2.htm

Negotiating a treaty

In the current debate concerning the concept of 'treaty' much energy has been focused upon negotiation by the Australian Nation with the Indigenous or the Aboriginal and Torres Strait Islander peoples of Australia.

In my view the most appropriate group for Indigenous and non-Indigenous stakeholders to commence negotiation of a treaty is with each Indigenous or Aboriginal or Torres Strait Islander group, whether styling itself a 'community', 'people', 'society' or 'nation', which adheres to a common set of laws and customs which control its behaviour. That group will ordinarily be co-extensive with the group who, at least at the time of colonisation, held the communal native title for an area. That form of group will ordinarily be found to be in the nature of a polity which governs itself in accordance with its laws and customs.

If a treaty can be agreed with such a group then it provides a building block upon which treaties within the Australian nation can be recognised at regional, State, national and international levels.

The advantage for Aboriginal and Torres Strait Islander leaders, throughout the nation, of commencing at that level is that it focuses them where they know they need to be focused, within the groups who provide them with their traditional base of law and custom. Aboriginal and Torres Strait Islander people who operate in a regional, national and international context for the benefit of their people recognise that their legitimacy as representatives of their people at those levels must always be grounded in the traditions of the families and local communities from which they come.

The advantage for the broader Australian community of commencing negotiation of a treaty at a local communal level is that it has the potential to engage local urban and rural communities in identifying and understanding the aspirations of local Indigenous and non-Indigenous groups through communication at a personal level. Experience suggests that when individuals communicate at a personal level there is more chance of them understanding and sympathising with one another's aspirations. It provides an opportunity to strip away misunderstanding, pre-judgments and fears about positions being taken which will advantage one group to the disadvantage of a competing group. Ultimately, when individuals confront each other, as individuals, there is a reasonable chance that they will come to understand that their aspirations for a just outcome for themselves and their families are similar. It is from that base that an accommodation may be able to be negotiated. That is the most likely base from which a true reconciliation between Indigenous and non-Indigenous peoples may emerge in Australia.

If Indigenous and non-Indigenous people understand each other and come to agreements about how they can live together in an atmosphere of mutual respect at a local level, in the many urban and rural regions of the nation, then they will be more confident about expressing their accommodation of one another in the form of uniform or similarly drafted documents which apply across regions, States and the nation.

That confidence, based upon a nationally pervasive mutual understanding, may in the fullness of time eventually mature into a degree of acceptance of the existence and rights of Aboriginal and Torres Strait Islander Peoples in Australia which:

> (a) will carry with it a groundswell of public opinion sufficient to assure an amendment to the Australian Constitution which recognises the rights of Indigenous peoples as polities operating within Australian society; and

> (b) allows our nation to feel free to proclaim its recognition at an international level of the agreements it is able to reach with the self determining polities of Aboriginal and Torres Strait Islander peoples in the Australian Nation.

Conclusion

The Aboriginal and Torres Strait Islander Commission, National Treaty Support Group, in its publications under the title: 'Treaty: let's get it right! Frequently Asked Questions', suggests that the discussion it is promoting about a treaty will allow Aboriginal and Torres Strait Islander peoples to look at the different forms a treaty might take. It suggests that there might be:

> – one national treaty;
> – a national agreement of principles that allows for treaties to be signed at the regional level; or
> – a network of regional or local treaties.

The approach this paper recommends is that, provided the negotiations commence at the local level, it may be possible that all of the above alternatives can be achieved, and that, indeed, that may be the most appropriate result.

It is more likely if agreement is reached at a local level in relation to locally significant issues that the necessary goodwill will be engendered to reach agreement at regional levels. It may then be possible to identify from local and regional agreements universal principles which can be nationally agreed, resulting in the possibility of a national treaty of international significance.

References

Books, articles and reports

Aboriginal and Torres Strait Islander Commission, National Treaty Support Group, 'Treaty: let's get it right! Frequently Asked Questions', ATSIC, Canberra.

Barsh, RL 1986, 'Indigenous peoples: an emerging object of international law', 80 *AJILO*.

Bartlett, RH 1983, 'Aboriginal Land Claims at Common Law', 15 *University of Western Australia Law Review*.

Crawford, J 1988, 'The rights of "peoples": "peoples" or "governments"?' in J Crawford (ed) *The Rights of Peoples*, Clarendon Press, Oxford.

Glossary for Aboriginal Studies, Charles Sturt University, available at hsc.csu.edu.au/ab_studies/glossary2.htm

Lowe, Chris, (Africa Policy Information Center) 1997, 'Talking about "Tribe"', Background Paper, available at www.africaaction.org/bp/ethall.htm, viewed 1 December 2006.

McNeil, Kent 2001, *The Relevance of Traditional Laws and Customs to the Existence and Content of Native Title at Common Law*, available at www.usask.ca/native law, viewed 19 September 2001.

Meyers, Gary 2000, 'The Content of Native Title: Questions for the Miriuwung Gajerrong Appeal' in *Land, Rights, Laws: Issues of Native Title*, Native Title Research Unit, Australian Institute of Aboriginal and Torres Strait Islander Studies, vol 2, November, Issues paper no 7.

Pearson, Noel 1996, Concept of Native Title at Common Law, paper presented at Conference on Land Rights – Past, Present and Future, Canberra, 16–17 August.

Sutton, P 1995, *Country: Aboriginal boundaries and land ownership in Australia*, Aboriginal History Inc Monograph 3, Canberra.

—— 1998, *Native Title and the Descent of Rights*, National Native Title Tribunal, Perth.

International charter and memorandum

Charter of the United Nations 1945, UN, San Francisco.

Memorandum prepared by the United Nations Secretariat, United Nations Conference on International Organisation Docs (1945), vol 18.

Case law

Cherokee Nation v State of Georgia (1831) 5 Peters 1.

Delgamuukw v The Queen in Right of British Columbia (Supreme Court of Canada, 11 December 1997) (1998) 1 CNLR 14.

Hamlet of Baker Lake [1980] FC at pp 557–8; (1979) 107 DLR (3d) at p 542.

Mabo and Ors v The State of Queensland (No 2) (1992) 175 CLR 1.

Ontario (Attorney-General) v Bear Island Foundation (1991), 83 DLR (4th) 381.

Regina v Sparrow (1990) 1 SCR 1075; (1990) 70 DLR (4th) 385.

Ward on behalf of the Miriuwung and Gajerrong Peoples v State of Western Australia (1998) 159 ALR 483.

United States v Santa Fe Railroad Co (1941) 314 US, 339.

Western Australia v Ward (2000) 170 ALR 159.

Worcester v Georgia (1832), 31 US (6 Pet) 616.

The Cape York view

Richard Ah Mat

We have to get real about the Holy Grail

Who reading this knows what is a Holy Grail or what is the Holy Grail? We've all probably used the phrase 'we're searching for the Holy Grail', 'I found the Holy Grail', but how many of us have ever understood what in the hell it is? Many of us have probably used the phrase to express the search for or achievement of goals a lot less lofty, a lot less chivalrous, a lot less spiritual – than was intended by the saintly people of medieval times.

Until two days ago I too had no clue what the hell the Holy Grail was. And I've seen as many movies about knights in armour galloping around on horses as anyone. I've even seen the movie with the knights who gallop around on their own two legs, clapping coconuts together.

To this day I've never known what the Holy Grail was. I just had some vague thought that it was some kind of cloak or robe … or was it King Arthur's sword … or what the hell was it? Anyway this is the definition that the dictionary on Microsoft Word gives of the Holy Grail:

> … according to medieval legend, the cup said to be used by Jesus
> Christ at the Last Supper, and by Joseph of Arimathea to collect his
> blood and sweat at the Crucifixion.

The notion of a treaty between the Indigenous people of Australia and the Commonwealth Government on behalf of the non-Indigenous people of Australia – has become something of a Holy Grail to progressive politics in our country.

The Treaty has become a Holy Grail for a number of reasons.

One reason is that the Treaty is seen as the ultimate political destination for the Aboriginal rights movement. It is political heaven. It is that point over the horizon where reconciliation prevails and everything is sweetness and light. It is the place where the meek inherit the earth and all social and economic ills are a thing of the past. Wounds will be healed, the blind will see, the lame shall walk again. If not Heaven on Earth, then it may be the kind of utopia that the socialists had in mind when they dreamed of a better future for the workers of the world.

I am of course slightly exaggerating the hopes that people have for a treaty – but probably not as much as I think. The Treaty is seen as some kind of Nirvana.

Another reason is that the Treaty represents the legal and political instrument that will put paid to all ambiguity and argument. It will be a final settlement of all political and legal disputation about the place of Aboriginal people in the Australian nation. It will be the mother of all comprehensive settlements, and it will contain every solution to every conceivable problem – including those things that we cannot now conceive of as issues to resolve.

Like the Holy Grail, we are all agreed on its fundamental importance and that it is the crusade that we must all embark upon – and yet we are unclear what we mean by it. We are very vague about what the destination is that we are seeking. To what new land over the horizon are we seeking to travel? And how will we know when we have arrived? What will the Holy Grail look like if we don't have a detailed picture of it? Do we have anything more detailed than some generally misty, cloudy place behind which lies a place called Heaven?

And how come we have been talking about a treaty for nearly three decades now and yet our general understanding of it is not a great deal advanced beyond the concept of some kind of profound agreement between black and white? We are still unclear on basic questions like:

- who will be the parties to the Treaty?

- who will represent the Aboriginal parties?

- what authority will the Aboriginal parties have to negotiate the Treaty?

- what authority will they have to sign the Treaty?

- is there a treaty or treaties?

Or has the quest for the Holy Grail become more important than actually finding it? Will we be psychologically capable of seizing the Grail when we come upon it? Will we be prepared to pull the sword from the stone? Or is our hesitation about reaching such a moment of historical decisiveness – where we have to make a settlement with those who have colonised our people and our country – the thing that makes it more comfortable for us to float around in a fog of vagueness, rhetoric and mournful hope?

The message from the leaders from my region is this: we have to get real about the Holy Grail. We can't continue to stumble around – in full metal armour – on poor, bony and starving horses – charging at windmills on the horizon. We need first:

- to know what we are looking for;

- to work out a plan to get there; and

- to ride forward deliberately and carefully, and in accordance with the plan.

Those of us with our heads in the clouds must think about descending to planet Earth, or at least somewhere approximately within orbit of it. ATSIC must stop authorising any travel request forms for those who wish to continue their travels to Outer Space. Those of us who are plunging swords into the backs of our troops and who are using our leaders for archery target practice – must attend re-training classes so that we can properly recognise who the real enemies are. Those of us who are devouring our own horses must reconsider the wisdom of doing this and realise that we will have need for them in the long march ahead of us.

The point is: we have to get real. If we're gonna talk about a treaty, let's talk in the here and now. Let's be ambitious, but let us also be realistic. Let's be hopeful, but let's not be naive. Above all, let us realise that we are not seeking to recreate heaven on earth. We are instead seeking a political and moral reconciliation between the old and new Australians in relation to matters of great significance and importance to human beings who live in a real world, whose futures must necessarily be founded upon coexistence.

The lessons from '67

The first reality check that we have to face up to is this: what lessons do we take from the 1967 Referendum which finally recogniseded Aboriginal people as Australians citizens?

Before I talk about what we from Cape York think are the lessons from '67, let me first clarify that I am talking about the concept of a treaty which is founded upon amendment of the Australian Constitution. I am not talking about treaty in the sense of an agreement between two international nations, and I am not talking about an agreement that is set out in legislation enacted by the Commonwealth Parliament. I am talking about what I think we should be talking about – that is, a treaty that is backed by amendment to the Australian Constitution.

Now the lessons that we should take from 1967 are pretty obvious. They are as follows:

1 The '67 Referendum was passed by 90 something per cent of the Australian electorate. We are constantly told that the Australian Constitution is one of the hardest constitutions in the world to change, because you need 'a majority of voters in a majority of the States'. So you need 80–90% of the country to support the change.

2 To get 80–90% of the country to support a Referendum, you need bipartisan political support. And you need support from the States and Territories as well, so that they're not running a 'NO' case against you.

3 In order to get bipartisan support, you will need a conservative government to propose the amendment and you need Labor to offer bipartisan support. It is unlikely that you will get bipartisan support the other way around. In 1967 the conservative government of Harold Holt proposed the amendment and it was supported by the Whitlam Labor Opposition.

4 To get 80–90% of the country you need to convince rural, conservative and regional Australia of the need for change. In other words you need to convince those people who usually vote for the National Party.

5 It took 10 years of outstanding and dignified advocacy by Indigenous leaders like Faith Bandler and the late Pastor Doug Nichols and many others, to build the groundswell of support across the political spectrum. The Indigenous leadership of this period was smart, dignified, very capable and very united. This is in sharp contrast to our leadership today.

Those who think that the Treaty is somehow a 'radical' cause or a 'radical' option, need to think again. If you want a treaty to turn into reality you need to have a strategy of convincing conservative and regional Australia in favour of your cause. Do you really think that conservative and regional Australia are going to simply put their hands up and say 'YES' to something that is sold to them as a radical cause?

We have to get real. If we talk treaty, we need to talk about how we're going to get 80–90% of the country to back us in a referendum. Otherwise we are just kidding ourselves.

One last lesson that we should take from '67. The question of recognising Aboriginal people as citizens of Australia was a pretty easy question in the whole scheme of things. It would have been ridiculous for Australia to have gone on much further in its history without addressing this racist exclusion of its Indigenous peoples from the Constitution. White Australia was not being asked to give anything substantial to black fellas in 1967.

When we talk about a treaty that is aimed at settling questions to do with the rights of our people and dealing with contentious questions of land rights, economic development and governance – then you really are asking the hard questions. The constitutional change needed to underpin a treaty is a much harder and a much more complicated question than the question of whether Aboriginal people should be counted as citizens of their own country.

We must show that self-determination can work in practice – and we must get ourselves organised at the regional level

The question of self-determination and governance will be central questions for a treaty. It is sure to be one of the most contentious issues.

Our view from Cape York is that we must show that self-determination can work in practice – on the ground, in our regions, in our communities, in our traditional owner groups. The problem with our talk about self-determination, is that in practice we are severely disorganised and disunited. So whilst self-determination is easy to talk about in theory, we are not translating it into reality – and doing the hard yards to make Indigenous governance work amongst our people.

The levels of disputation, division, jealousy, infighting, power-plays, backstabbing, mistrust are very, very high amongst our people. Our organisations don't work together. Leaders won't cooperate with one another, whether at the community or the regional or the national levels. There is a breakdown of Aboriginal Law and authority, and as a result our families and communities are falling apart with no law and order. Our social problems are in no small part due to the breakdown of governance within our own communities.

If we won all of the necessary legal and political victories tomorrow to give us the fullest right to self-determination within this country – what would it mean in reality? I don't think it would mean much. It would not mean much because self-determination is about practice, it is about actions, it is about what we do from day to day to make changes, it is about governance. It is about taking responsibility for our problems and for our opportunities: because nobody else will take responsibility for our families, our children, our people. We have to do it ourselves.

Our view from Cape York is that we must get organised around the regions. There are, and there always will be, three main levels of Aboriginal community – national, regional and local. We believe that the regional level of governance needs to be developed. We need Aboriginal organisations to be united and working together at the regional level. It is at this level that our people can have the necessary scale and political organisation and capacity – to deal with governments and the outside world. It is also the level that our people need to develop economically and to carve out a place in the wider regional economies in which Aboriginal people are located.

Regional organisation is still under-developed. We have been working in Cape York for the past 10 years, putting together the foundations of regional governance and self-determination. We now have:

- The Peninsula ATSIC Regional Council
- Tharpuntoo Aboriginal Legal Service
- Cape York Land Council
- Apunipima Cape York Health Council, and
- Balkanu Cape York Development Corporation

We also now have Cape York Partnerships as an interface for partnerships with government and external non-government sectors. We have endeavoured to develop unity, common purpose and vision for the future of Cape York. To develop plans and strategies, and to work together towards their achievement. It has been – and it is still – hard work. But we believe that getting organised regionally is a necessary part of development of our people at the local level. If we don't get organised regionally, we can't represent the local level in the ways that are needed in order to deal with governments and the outside world. In developing ourselves at the regional level in Cape York, we are also conscious that if a national agreement in the form of a treaty is to be reached agreements at the regional level will be necessary.

In fact any future treaty is likely to set a framework and general principles whilst the agreements of substance are negotiated and settled at the regional level. The concept of regional agreements – which has disappeared from discussion in this country in recent years – are probably going to be the only way treaties can be implemented in practice.

How do we get 80–90% of the country to support a treaty?

My Cape York colleague, Noel Pearson, explains the difference between what he calls 51% and 80–90% strategies.

> 51% strategies are strategies that we use when we need:
>
> the Government of the day to make some policy or administrative decision that we want, or
>
> we need the Government of the day to get legislation passed by the Commonwealth Parliament

It means we only need to convince one side of politics (usually the Left side of politics) to champion a particular issue – and as long as they carry 51% of the country behind them, we can get executive or legislative victories.

When we pursue 51% strategies, our main challenge is to convince those who are in power to do the right thing. It doesn't matter if the other Right side of politics goes against us – as long as the Left have 51%, we can get a result.

But of course convincing the Left, when it is in power, is not an easy thing. They are always afraid that if they agree to what we want, they will go from 51% to 49% at the next election.

But, 51% strategies won't work if we are talking about a treaty and constitutional change. As we have already discussed, if we want to change the Australian Constitution we need 'a majority of voters in a majority of the states'. That is, we need an 80–90% strategy.

We in Cape York are of the view that 80–90% strategies are fundamentally different from 51% strategies. Let me make four points about the differences:

1 Firstly, if you want 80–90% of the electorate to support our cause, we have to work counter clockwise – from the Right to the Left. We have to convince the people on the furthest Right. In other words, we have to convince the National Party's regional and conservative constituency. If we can convince these people to treat with us, then everybody else to the Left of them should fall into position.

2 Secondly, the people on the furthest Right must be made the primary owners and the primary advocates of a treaty deal with our people. It is only by them making the deal, and playing the leading role in such a reconciliation, that they will then champion the treaty. If the treaty is owned as an issue and championed by the Left, we will get nowhere with the Right.

3 Thirdly, the more we push the treaty through 51% strategies – that is, as a movement starting from the Left and moving rightwards – the greater the likelihood that the Right will oppose it, and we will never build the 80–90% constituency we need to get constitutional change. The Bridge Walkers, the Reconciliation Movement and so on – these are 51% strategies.

4 Fourthly, we get nowhere if we spend all of our energy and time preaching to the converted (or to the people who are easy to convert). Never mind this mob – they're the easy ones. Let's now think hard about how we're gonna swing the hard nuts.

So the big political questions facing those who advocate a treaty are these: is it at all imaginable that we could find common ground with conservative and regional Australia such that they would support a treaty? In what conditions could this scenario come about? What would we need to do to locate this common ground?

These are not easy questions to answer. But we must turn our minds to them. Because the reality is this: if we can't find common ground with the National Party and its conservative and regional constituency – then we can't get a treaty in the form of constitutional change.

The treaty must start in the bush and then move to the cities. If we develop the treaty in the cities and try to take it out into the bush – the bush will kill it.

What is involved in moving towards a treaty?

Let me very briefly summarise the ingredients necessary to bring a treaty into existence.

- 5% involves legal and political theory. This is what we are doing at this Conference. This is what we have been doing at all of the other conferences and seminars on the subject of the treaty. We have not made much progress with the theory, because our thinking about the details is still largely stunted.

  The point that we from Cape York want to make about the theory is this: theory is important, but let's understand that it is only a small part of what is needed to get a treaty.

- 5% involves developing and deciding on the constitutional mechanism. This is very, very important. But it is also the easy part and is only 5% of our challenge.

- 90% of the challenge involves political strategy and prosecution of the strategy. This is the hard work. This is about lining all of the planets up. This is about herding a million feral cats dispersed throughout bushlands all over the continent. This about lining up all of the thousands of ducks in the Kakadu wetlands into one orderly line. This is the truly hard business.

Conclusion: leadership and unity

It is our belief from Cape York Peninsula that the achievement of a treaty between the Indigenous peoples of Australia and the Commonwealth on behalf of the non-Indigenous peoples of Australia – is a conceivable reality. It is within the realms of possibility.

But if a treaty is to be reached, then there will need to be leadership and unity amongst the Indigenous peoples of Australia. If we are united and we recognise and support our leadership – then I have no doubt we could get there. We have the people. We have the opportunities. In fact, it is probably true that there has never been a better time for us to move to a treaty, than now. Will we have the unity and will we be clever enough to recognise the opportunity and make the plans and strategies so that we can reach the Holy Grail?

The Coolangatta Statement on Indigenous Peoples' Rights in Education[1]

Preamble

The Coolangatta Statement represents a collective voice of Indigenous peoples from around the world who support fundamental principles considered vital to achieving reform and transformation of education for Indigenous peoples.

The need for such an instrument is self-evident. Over the last 30 years, Indigenous peoples throughout the world have argued that they have been denied equity in non-Indigenous education systems which has failed to provide educational services that nurture the whole Indigenous person inclusive of scholarship, culture and spirituality.

Almost all Indigenous peoples, and in particular, those who have suffered the impact and effects of colonization, have struggled to access education that acknowledges, respects and promotes the right of Indigenous peoples to be indigenous – a right that embraces Indigenous peoples' language, culture, traditions, and spirituality. This includes the right to self-determination.

This Statement speaks to the inherent rights of Indigenous peoples as declared in Article 27 of the International Covenant on Civil and Political Rights:

> In those States in which ethnic, religious or linguistic minorities
> exist, persons belonging to such minorities shall not be denied
> the right, in community with the other members of their group,
> to enjoy their own culture, and to profess and practice their own
> religion, and to use their own language.

As an instrument which derives its vision and strength from Indigenous Nations and peoples, the Coolangatta Statement on Indigenous Peoples' Rights in Education is and will remain a living document which addresses the educational rights of Indigenous peoples now and into the future. It is reproduced below.

I. Indigenous Education: a global overview

1.1 There exists a proliferation of international charters, conventions and other instruments that recognize the basic human rights of all peoples, amongst which is the right to education. Some of these instruments have been analyzed in the preparation of this statement. These include:

• Universal Declaration of Human Rights

---

[1] Presented at the World Indigenous Peoples' Conference on Education (WIPCE), Hilo, Hawai'i, 6 August 1999.

- International Covenant on Economic, Social and Cultural Rights;

- International Covenant on Civil and Political Rights;

- Declaration on the Elimination of all Forms of Racial Discrimination;

- Discrimination (Employment & Occupation) Convention;

- Convention Against Discrimination in Education;

- Working Group on Indigenous Populations – Draft Declaration on Indigenous Rights; and

- Kari-Oca Indigenous Peoples Earth Charter.

1.2   Indigenous peoples acknowledge that select principles and articles from international human rights instruments provide some basis for recognizing the rights of Indigenous peoples to education.

1.2.1   For example, Article 26 of the United Nations Declaration of Human Rights states:

> i.   *Everyone has the right to education. Education shall be free, at least in the elementary and fundamental stages. Elementary education shall be compulsory. Technical and professional education shall be made generally available and higher education shall be equally accessible to all on the basis of merit.*

> ii. *Education shall be directed to the full development of the human personality and to the strengthening of respect for human rights and fundamental freedoms. It shall promote understanding, tolerance and friendship among all nations, racial or religious groups, and shall further the activities of the United Nation for the maintenance of peace.*

> iii. *Parents have a prior right to choose the kind of education that shall be given to their children.*

1.2.2   Article 27 of the International Covenant on Civil and Political Rights further states:
> *In those States in which ethnic, religious or linguistic minorities exist, persons belonging to such minorities shall not be denied the right, in community with the other members of their group, to enjoy their own culture, and to profess and practice their own religion, and to use their own language.*

1.3   Although the capacity for such instruments provides some basis for recognizing rights of Indigenous peoples, the 1999 WIPCE asserts that such instruments are limited in their capacity to recognize and protect the rights of Indigenous peoples.

Human rights, by definition, are inalienable, inviolable and innate. The freedom to enjoy and indeed celebrate these rights has been, and continues to be, denied and obstructed for Indigenous peoples throughout the world.

Specific limitations include the extent to which these instruments:

- Protect the right of Indigenous peoples to equal access to education systems;

- Ensure that Indigenous parents have a prior right to choose the kind of education that shall be given to their children;

- Promote the right of Indigenous peoples to enjoy their own cultures in community with other members of their group;

- Provide conditions that are conducive to the use and maintenance of Indigenous languages.

1.3.1 Historically, Indigenous peoples have insisted upon the right of access to education. Invariably the nature, and consequently the outcome, of this education has been constructed through and measured by non-Indigenous standards, values and philosophies. Ultimately the purpose of this education has been to assimilate Indigenous peoples into non-Indigenous cultures and societies.

Volumes of studies, research and reports dealing with Indigenous peoples in non-Indigenous educational systems paint a familiar picture of failure and despair. When measured in non-Indigenous terms, the educational outcomes of Indigenous peoples are still far below that of non-Indigenous peoples. This fact exists not because Indigenous peoples are less intelligent, but because educational theories and practices are developed and controlled by non-Indigenous peoples. Thus, in more recent times, due to the involvement of Indigenous peoples, research shows that failure is indeed present, but that this failure is that of the system, not of Indigenous peoples.

In this context the so-called 'dropout rates and failures' of Indigenous peoples within non-Indigenous educational systems must be viewed for what they really are – rejection rates.

1.3.2 The rights of Indigenous peoples to access education – even when these rights are recognized in treaties and other instruments – are often interpreted to read that Indigenous peoples only want access to non-Indigenous education. Presumably it is considered that the core of Indigenous cultural values, standards and wisdom is abandoned or withering in the wilderness of Indigenous societies.

Yet, Indigenous peoples across the world are demanding and, in some cases, achieving the establishment of systems of education which reflect, respect and embrace Indigenous cultural values, philosophies and ideologies – the same values, philosophies and ideologies which shaped, nurtured and sustained Indigenous peoples for tens of thousands of years.

One of the greatest challenges confronting Indigenous peoples in the final year of the twentieth century is how to promote, protect and nurture Indigenous cultures in an ever-changing modern society. This is of particular concern for Indigenous peoples who are forced into cities and away from their homelands.

1.4 It is of concern to the 1999 WIPCE that many international instruments have a limited capacity to recognize the most fundamental human right of Indigenous peoples – the right to be Indigenous. The right to be Indigenous involves the freedom of Indigenous peoples themselves to determine who is Indigenous; what it means to be Indigenous; and, how education relates to Indigenous cultures.

1.4.1 Recently a number of international documents prepared in response to the limited capacity of international human rights instruments recognize and protect the right of Indigenous peoples to be Indigenous. The 1999 WIPCE acknowledges and supports such documents, which include the Draft Declaration on the Rights of Indigenous Peoples and the Kari-Oca Indigenous Peoples' Earth Charter.

1.4.2 The Draft Declaration on the Rights of Indigenous Peoples, as revised by the members of the Working Group on Indigenous Populations in July 1993, asserts:

> *Indigenous peoples have the right of self-determination. By virtue of that right they freely determine their political statutes and freely pursue their economic, social and cultural development.* (Article 3)
> *Indigenous peoples have the right to participate fully, if they so wish, in the political, economic, social and cultural life of the state, while maintaining their distinct political, economical, social and cultural characteristics, as well as their legal systems.* (Article 4)

The draft declaration goes on to add:

> *Indigenous peoples have the right to all levels and forms of education. They also have the right to establish and control their educational systems and institutions providing education in their own language.* (Article 14)
> *Indigenous peoples have the right to have the dignity and diversity of their cultures, traditions, histories and aspirations appropriately reflected in all forms of education and public information. States shall take effective measures, in consultation with Indigenous peoples, in eliminating prejudice and to promote tolerance, understanding and good relations.* (Article 15)

1.4.3 The Kari-Oca Declaration entitled 'Indigenous Peoples' Earth Charter' (formulated in Brazil in May 1993) includes the following statements on Indigenous education:

Indigenous peoples should have the right to their own knowledge, languages and culturally appropriate education, including bicultural and bilingual education. Through recognizing both formal and informal ways the participation of family and community is guaranteed.

Indigenous peoples must have the necessary resources and control over their own education systems. Elders must be recognized and respected as teachers of the young people. Indigenous wisdom must be recognized and encouraged.

The use of existing Indigenous languages is our right. These languages must be protected. At local, national, and international levels, governments must commit funds to new and existing resources to education and training for Indigenous peoples to achieve their sustainable development, to contribute and to participate in sustainable and equitable development at all levels. Particular attention should be given to Indigenous women, children and youth.

The United Nations should promote research into Indigenous knowledge and develop a network of Indigenous sciences. As creators and carriers of civilizations which have given and continue to share knowledge, experience and values with humanity, we require that our right to intellectual and cultural properties be guaranteed and that the mechanism for each implementation be in favor of our people and studies in depth be implemented.

1.5 Evident from recent international documents on the Rights of Indigenous peoples, the right to be indigenous is an essential prerequisite to developing and maintaining culturally appropriate and sustainable education for Indigenous peoples.

Also evident, the educational struggles of Indigenous peoples of the world involve more than the struggle for access to and participation in both non-Indigenous education systems and culturally appropriate education. The educational struggles of Indigenous peoples are fundamentally and unequivocally concerned with the right of Indigenous peoples to be indigenous.

1.6 Youth and the young have a special place and responsibility in the struggle to nurture and protect Indigenous cultures. It is to them that truth and wisdom is bequeathed. When Indigenous youth and the young are separated from their cultural base and communities, Indigenous cultures and peoples are threatened with cultural extinction.

1.6.1 The forced removal of Indigenous children from their families and communities was a favored policy and practice of colonial powers throughout the world. The pain and emotional scars that are the legacy of this insidious form of cultural genocide continues to torment many of today's Indigenous peoples.

1.6.2 Acknowledging and respecting their role and responsibilities, delegates from the World Indigenous Youth Conference held in Darwin, Australia in July 1993, declared:

- We, Indigenous youth, believe we must maintain our right to self-determination. Our people have the right to decide our own forms of government, the use of our lands, to one day raise and educate our children in our own cultural identities without interference.

- We, Indigenous youth must have the freedom to learn our true histories. We make a call to our elders to open the way for us to learn about our heritages – to help us reclaim our past, so that we may claim our future.

- We, Indigenous youth, recognize our languages as an important link to maintaining our cultures. Indigenous languages must be maintained at a local level.

1.7 The 1999 WIPCE recognizes an existence of a commonality of purpose and desire amongst the Indigenous peoples of the world for education. It further recognizes that this commonality involves a shared belief that education must be scholarly and empowering whilst at the same time the processes of education must be embedded in Indigenous culture and wisdom.

1.7.1 Meaningful, empowering and culturally sustainable education for Indigenous peoples will be possible only when Indigenous peoples have the control (a fundamental right) and the resources (an inarguable responsibility of States/governments) to develop educational theories, curriculum and practices that are indigenous and are able to determine the environment within which this education can best occur.

1.7.2 Indigenous self-determination involves choice and diversity. If an Indigenous person chooses to access an Indigenous education system, then this is a choice, which must be respected. If an Indigenous person chooses to access non-Indigenous education, then this choice must also be respected. If an Indigenous person chooses to access both non-Indigenous and Indigenous systems of education, then this choice too must be respected. Not to do so is in itself a violation of a basic human right.

II. Rights in Indigenous Education

2.1 The right to be Indigenous is the most fundamental and important of all Human Rights.

234

2.2 The right to be Indigenous is a precursor to self-determination. The right to self-determination and the achievement of other inherent rights and freedoms for Indigenous peoples is inextricably connected to the physical and spiritual phenomenon of what most call 'the earth'. The sense of connectedness and belonging to Mother Earth is similar to the special bonds that unite parent and child. As a child's hopes and securities, aspirations and comforts are fundamental to its relationships with its parents, so too are Indigenous peoples' hopes and securities, aspirations and comforts fundamental in their relationship to Mother Earth.

2.2.1 Non-Indigenous peoples and their representative governments must accept this parent relationship with Mother Earth that characterizes Indigenous cultures. This relationship enables Indigenous peoples to negotiate, use and maintain the land, and to build and rebuild the social structures needed for cultural survival.

2.2.2 There are no single, simple or common answers to the question of Indigenous self-determination. Only Indigenous peoples who are spiritually focused and land-based.

2.2.3 The provision and application of material and political responses by Nation States to the right of Indigenous peoples to self-determination, governance and control over Indigenous life and futures must cease.

2.2.4 Self-determination in Indigenous education embodies the right of Indigenous people:

- To control/govern Indigenous education systems;
- To establish schools and other learning facilities that recognize, respect and promote Indigenous values, philosophies and ideologies;
- To develop and implement culturally inclusive curricula;
- To utilize the essential wisdom of Indigenous elders in the education process;
- To establish the criterion for educational evaluation and assessment;
- To define and identify standards for the gifted and talented;
- To promote the use of Indigenous languages in education;
- To establish the parameters and ethics within which Indigenous education research should be conducted;
- To design and deliver culturally appropriate and sensitive teacher training programs;

- To participate in teacher certification and selection;

- To develop criterion for the registration and operation of schools and other learning facilities; and,

- To choose the nature and scope of education without prejudice.

2.3 Indigenous peoples have strong feelings and thoughts about landforms, the very basis of their cultural identity. Land gives life to language and culture.

2.3.1 Indigenous languages in all forms are legitimate and valid means of communication for Indigenous peoples.

2.3.2 Language is a social construct; it is a blueprint for thought, behavior, social and cultural interaction and self-expression.

2.3.3 Language is the medium for transmitting culture from the past to the present and into the future. Acknowledging that many Indigenous languages have been destroyed, the 1999 WIPCE asserts that Indigenous languages are the best way to teach Indigenous knowledge and values.

2.3.4 Languages are the foundations for the liberation of thoughts that provide direction for social, political and economic change and development.

2.3.5 The survival and revival of Indigenous languages is imperative for the protection, transmission, maintenance and preservation of Indigenous knowledge, cultural values, and wisdom.

2.4 Pedagogy is the interrelationship between learning styles and teaching methods. There are pedagogical principles shared by all Indigenous peoples, but there are also those that are characteristic to the specific cultures, languages, environment and circumstances of Indigenous peoples across the world. Indigenous peoples and cultures are not homogenous.

2.4.1 Indigenous pedagogical principles are holistic, connected, valid, cultural, value-based, thematic and experiential. They promote and reward cooperative learning and the unified co-operation of learner and teacher in a single educational enterprise. They describe who teaches, as well as, how and when teaching occurs. Indigenous pedagogical principles, unlike western paradigms, recognize the important role of non-verbal communication in the learning–teaching process.

2.4.2 Indigenous learning is clothed in the medium of spirituality. Notions of well being/ wellness and ethos are important in the process of learning.

2.4.3 The teacher is a facilitator of learning, one who promotes achievement and success. In this context culturally appropriate environments are employed to reinforce knowledge being imparted to the learner, reaffirming the learner's significant place in the world.

2.4.4 The involvement of community in all pedagogical processes is valued.

2.5 Indigenous peoples at the local level must determine how and to what degree non-Indigenous peoples are involved in Indigenous education. Once this role is determined it is the responsibility of non-Indigenous peoples to respect and adhere to the wishes of the local community.

2.5.1 Non-Indigenous peoples come from a different cultural background. Since Indigenous education is centered in Indigenous culture, non-Indigenous people must only be involved in the process of achieving educational objectives as determined by Indigenous peoples. Non-Indigenous peoples should not involve themselves in the processes of Indigenous decision-making.

2.5.2 Non-Indigenous peoples through the various levels of government and bureaucracy have an over-riding responsibility to accept and uphold the educational rights of Indigenous peoples and to know that these rights and freedoms are non-negotiable.

III. Conclusions

3.1 Indigenous peoples throughout the world survive policies and practices ranging from extermination and genocide to protection and assimilation. Perhaps more than any other feat, survival is the greatest of all Indigenous peoples' achievements.

3.2 Indigenous peoples have the right to be Indigenous. They cannot exist as images and reflections of a non-Indigenous society.

3.3 Indigenous education, as a medium for both personal development and intellectual empowerment, is critical for the continuance and celebration of Indigenous cultures.

3.4 To be Indigenous is both a privilege and a birthright. It is therefore the responsibility of all Indigenous peoples to ensure that their respective cultures, philosophies and ideologies remain strong and continue to grow.

3.5 We, the Indigenous peoples of the world, assert our inherent right to self-determination in all matters. Self-determination is about making informed choices and decisions and creating appropriate structures for the transmission of culture, knowledge and wisdom for the benefit of each of our respective cultures. Education for our communities and each individual is central to the preservation of our cultures and for the development of the skills and expertise we need in order to be a vital part of the twenty-first century.

Biographical notes

Richard Ah Mat was Executive Director of the Cape York Land Council at the time of writing.

Professor Larissa Behrendt is Professor of Law and Director of Research at the Jumbunna Indigenous House of Learning at the University of Technology, Sydney.

Steven Churches is a senior lecturer at the University of Adelaide Law School, and has a national public law Bar practice based in that city. His clients in the High Court have included Robert Bropho, the Bakhtiyari children, Ah Hin Teoh, Snowy Judamia and Crow Yougarla.

Ravi de Costa is a Research Fellow in the Institute on Globalization and the Human Condition, at McMaster University in Canada. For the last three years he has been co-ordinating an interdisciplinary project on 'Globalization, autonomy and Indigenous peoples'. In 2006, his book *A higher authority: Indigenous transnationalism and Australia,* was published by UNSW Press.

Mick Dodson is a Yawuru man from Broome in Western Australia. He is presently the director of the National Centre for Indigenous Studies at the Australian National University. He is a long time advocate for the rights of Indigenous Peoples.

Dr William Jonas AM is a Worimi man from the Karuah River area of New South Wales. He was the Aboriginal and Torres Strait Islander Social Justice Commissioner with the Human Rights and Equal Opportunity Commission from 1999 to 2004. He was previously Director of the National Museum of Australia and Principal of the Australian Institute of Aboriginal and Torres Strait Islander Studies. He has held academic positions in Australia and overseas. In 1993 he was made a Member of the Order of Australia for his contribution to preserving Aboriginal culture and heritage.

Edde Mabo Jnr is the son of Edward Koiki Mabo

Greg McConville has worked in a range of policy, advocacy and consulting roles for government, community and union organisations. At the time of writing, Greg was Policy and Research Officer with the National Tertiary Education Union. Greg is now Industrial Officer for the United Firefighters Union of Australia (Victoria Branch).

Greg McIntyre SC is a Barrister based in Perth and Adjunct Professor of Law at the University of Notre Dame, Fremantle, where he teaches Constitutional Law and Indigenous Law. He was involved with the establishment of the Aboriginal Legal Service of WA in 1973-74 and the Njiku Jowan Legal Service in Cairns in 1983. He had the conduct of the Mabo case from 1982-1992 and *Koowarta v Bjelke Petersen* from 1981-88 and has had a substantial practice in native title and human rights cases in the years since.

Hon David Malcolm AC QC retired as Chief Justice of Western Australia on 7 February 2006. He is now Professor at the School of Law, University of Notre Dame, Western Australia.

Dr Gary D. Meyers is Professor of Law at Murdoch University School of Law, where he has held the positions of Associate Dean/Research and Chair of the LLM and Post-Graduate Studies Programs. He has a long background in Indigenous Land Rights issues. He is currently the Director of the Law School's Indigenous Lands: Rights, Governance and Environmental Management Project. From 1995-97 he was the inaugural Director of the National Native Title Tribunal Legal Research Unit and in 1996 was Director of the Tribunal's Research Division.

Garth Nettheim is Emeritus Professor of Law at the University of NSW. Much of his teaching and research has been in the areas of Indigenous legal issues and also human rights law. He helped to establish the Indigenous Law Centre, the Australian Human Rights Centre, and the Diplomacy Training Program.

Dr Roderic Pitty is a Lecturer in Political Science and International Relations at UWA with extensive experience assisting barristers in the investigation of Aboriginal deaths in custody, particularly in NSW. Together with Robert Cavanagh, he wrote *Too Much Wrong: A report on the death of Edward James Murray*, which led to new evidence of Eddie Murray's broken sternum being discovered following an exhumation. Dr Pitty has also conducted research in Aotearoa New Zealand on the Waitangi Tribunal and its relevance for Australia.

Professor Peter Read is Deputy Director of the National Centre for Indigenous Studies, Australian National University, and the Chairperson of *Aboriginal History*.

Professor Bob Reece is Professor in History at Murdoch University, Western Australia. He established himself as an authority on Aboriginal history with the publication in 1974 of *Aborigines and Colonists* and was a co-founder of the journal *Aboriginal History* in 1977 with the late Diane Barwick. He subsequently published a number of articles on early Aboriginal-European relations in the Perth area, notably the seminal 'Inventing Aborigines', and was a major contributor to the Encyclopedia of Aboriginal Australia. In 2002 he was a member of the organising committee for the Treaty - Advancing Reconciliation Conference at Murdoch University in October 2002. Most recently he has been working on a book based on the letters of Daisy Bates.

Tim Rowse is Head of the History Program in the Research School of Social Sciences, ANU. He is interested in the history of Australian public policy and particularly in the political history of Australia's colonial processes. His contribution to this book arises from his work on the life of HC Coombs, research that produced his *Obliged to be difficult* (2000) and *Nugget: a reforming life* (2002).

The Hon Justice Simmonds has been a member of the Supreme Court of Western Australia since February 2004. Prior to that time, most of his professional career had been spent as a legal academic, in both Australia and Canada. In recent times his interest in indigenous issues stemmed from his involvement, prior to his appointment to the bench, in the Law Reform Commission of Western Australia's project on Aboriginal Customary Law.

Sue Stanton is a Kungarakan-Gurindji woman from the Northern Territory. She is Associate Professor, School of Politics and History, Faculty of Arts, University of Wollongong.

Dr Lisa Strelein is a Research Fellow and Manager of the Native Title Research Unit at the Australian Institute for Aboriginal and Torres Strait Islander Studies. Lisa's research and publications have focussed on conceptualising the relationships between Indigenous peoples and the state, Indigenous sovereignty and self determination and the role of the courts in defining indigenous rights. Her most recent book – *Compromised Jurisprudence: Native Title Cases Since Mabo* – reflects her expertise in the native title field.

239

www.ingramcontent.com/pod-product-compliance
Lightning Source LLC
Chambersburg PA
CBHW041839260726
48664CB00037BB/1683

* 9 7 8 1 9 2 0 9 4 2 9 0 8 *